The Consumer Federation of America

THE PRODUCT SAFETY BOOK

The Ultimate Consumer Guide to Product Hazards

Stephen Brobeck & Anne C. Averyt

Edited by Jack Gillis

E. P. DUTTON, INC. • NEW YORK

To Susan and Bill

Copyright © 1983 by Consumer Federation of America
All rights reserved. Printed in the U.S.A.
No part of this publication may be reproduced or transmitted
in any form or by any means, electronic or mechanical,
including photocopy, recording or any information storage and
retrieval system now known or to be invented, without permission
in writing from the publisher, except by a reviewer who wishes
to quote brief passages in connection with a review
written for inclusion in a magazine, newspaper or broadcast.

Published in the United States by E. P. Dutton, Inc.,
2 Park Avenue, New York, N.Y. 10016

Library of Congress Catalog Card Number: 83-71915

ISBN: 0-525-48087-0

Published simultaneously in Canada by
Fitzhenry & Whiteside Limited,
Toronto

W

10 9 8 7 6 5 4 3 2 1

First Edition

PREFACE

Never have American citizens been more concerned about product safety. Recent Harris surveys on consumerism reveal a greater increase in concern about "dangerous products" than about any of the other eight major consumer problems listed. In part, this heightened public apprehension reflects is a growing awareness of the enormous (and escalating) costs of unsafe products: Last year, more than 70,000 Americans died in product-related accidents while millions more suffered disabling injuries. The economic costs of these accidents were also staggering—over $100 billion in property damage, lost wages, insurance, litigation, and medical expenses.

As the first publication to identify all known dangers associated with consumer products, *The Product Safety Book* provides information about hazardous products that can help consumers avoid related injuries and expenses. Its 700 entries specify the risks of using different types of products and the potential hazards posed by some 2000 separate product models.

But beyond this obvious purpose, this comprehensive encyclopedia of product safety is intended as a stimulus to manufacturers and retailers to produce and sell safer consumer products. No business wants to be identified with products that contain safety-related design or manufacturing defects. By making available information about these problems to sellers, as well as to consumers, this book will increase concern about hazardous products within the business community.

As the nation's largest consumer advocacy organization, the Consumer Federation of America concentrates on defending and strengthening federal regulations and programs. Yet while doing so, we recognize that government regulation is not enough. Because government regulators cannot prevent the introduction of all dangerous products or insure that all unsafe units are recalled, the public must be informed about hazardous products *and* about the hazards of essentially safe products. The information in this encyclopedia complements the necessary work of government safety regulators.

Both of us are deeply grateful to several people for their assistance in the preparation of this book: Jack Gillis, author of *The Car Book*, contributed the entries on recreational vehicles, motorcycles, and tires as well as reviewing the entire manuscript. Dr. John Brobeck, distinguished editor and physiologist, considerably improved the legibility and accuracy of the text. Attorney Michael Pollet and CFA volunteers Susan Brobeck, Shirley Gregory, and Donna Arquilla and CFA interns Joe Hanzlick, Blair Tily, Robyn Shepherd, and Carolyn Carter provided invaluable assistance researching and checking facts. Staff members at the Consumer Product Safety Commission, Food and Drug Administration, and National Highway Traffic Safety Administration were extremely helpful in making available government sources. Finally, we are indebted to Consumers Union and its Executive Director, Rhoda Karpatkin, for permitting us to use material from *Consumer Reports* and for arranging a review of this information by former Technical Director Monte Florman.

STEPHEN BROBECK
ANNE C. AVERYT
May 11, 1983

HOW TO USE THIS BOOK

The Product Safety Book alphabetically lists over 1200 consumer products which have been judged to create possible hazards under various circumstances. These include household products; sports equipment; shop and garden equipment; over-the-counter and prescription drugs; cosmetics; foods; toxic substances found in the home such as fertilizers, paints, and insecticides; as well as cars; recreational vehicles; and motorcycles.

These entries contain the following types of information:

- Product Hazards
- Number of Related Injuries and Deaths
- Government or Voluntary Standards
- Precautions and Warnings
- Identification of Hazardous Models

To make the vital information in *The Product Safety Book* readily accessible and easy to understand, our entries summarize, rather than exhaustively report, safety-related information about products. Additional information on any entry can be obtained by consulting the sources given in the entry and in this chapter and also by calling the government hotlines we list in this section.

Most of the material in *The Product Safety Book* was drawn from documents at three Federal agencies: the Consumer Product Safety Commission, the National Highway Traffic Safety Administration, and the Food and Drug Administration. Another source of information was *Consumer Reports*, the monthly magazine published by Consumers Union, which, for decades, has represented the most exhaustive and authoritative source of consumer product information.

In the interests of economy, the seven organizations most often referred to in the entries are listed by their acronyms:

CU   = Consumers Union
CPSC   = U.S. Consumer Protection Safety Commission
EPA   = U.S. Environmental Protection Agency
FDA   = U.S. Food and Drug Administration
NRC   = National Research Council
USDA   = U.S. Department of Agriculture
USPHS = U.S. Public Health Services

The dozens of other sources we have used for this book range from newspaper articles to specialized consumer publications and technical monographs.

All the products listed in *The Product Safety Book* can be grouped into one of seven product categories: motor vehicles; household products; drugs; medical devices; foods; toxics; or cosmetics. The sections which follow describe for each category: types of products, kinds of information listed for each product, key information sources, and suggestions for additional consumer information including those government hotlines.

MOTOR VEHICLES

Nearly all Motor Vehicle entries list individual models: cars; recreational vehicles; motorcycles; tires. Vehicles used primarily in work, such as pick-up trucks, have not been included.

Most of the Motor Vehicle information was drawn from reports of car models tested by Consumers Union and published in *Consumer Reports*, or from National Highway Traffic Safety Administration reports on safety-related recalls. The latter can be found in annual volumes through 1981 and in individual sheets for 1982 and 1983 collected in a three-ring binder available at NHTSA's Washington, DC, library.

For each model, potential hazards are listed by model year. Most information on design defects was taken from *Consumer Reports* and applies to all vehicles of that model produced. Most manufacturing defects were reported by NHTSA and exist in only a portion of all cars in each model year, but in no fewer than 500. Descriptions of these manufacturing defects identify the mechanical problem and its related hazard.

For additional information about individual models, refer to *Consumer Reports* and to *The Car Book* (published yearly by E. P. Dutton, New York). For information on the recalls, call NHTSA's toll-free Auto Safety hotline: (800) 424-9393 (426-0123 in Washington, DC).

HOUSEHOLD PRODUCTS

These entries, by contrast, list products rather than models. They include appliances, features of the house and its electrical system, bathroom- and kitchen-related items, household chemicals, yard equipment, and sports equipment. Most of the information gathered here was found in one of three sources: *Consumer Reports* articles; Consumer Product Safety Commission fact sheets on individual products; or CPSC releases announcing recalls of hazardous models.

Entries include a wide range of information including: product hazards, related government or voluntary standards, precautions and warnings, and potentially hazardous models. For more information on the safety of a particular household product, refer to *Consumer Reports* and to Consumer Product Safety Commission fact sheets, or call the CPSC's toll-free hotline: (800) 638-8326, (800) 492-8363 in Maryland, and 492-6800 in Washington, DC. The hotline is particularly helpful in explaining what to do about recalled products.

DRUGS

Most of these entries list individual prescription drugs or types of over-the-counter (nonprescription) drugs such as cold or diarrhea medicines, although there are general entries on topics such as Pregnancy and Drugs and Drug and Food Interactions.

Most information was drawn from three types of sources: Food and Drug Administration releases and publications; publications of public-interest groups like the Center for Science in the Public Interest; and drug package inserts.

The only prescription drugs listed are those we view as representing a substantial risk to users; they should be used with caution. These include drugs whose risks may outweigh potential benefits, such as minor tranquilizers. Effective drugs with only routine or minor side-effects were excluded.

There are several books available that evaluate the safety of both the prescription and over-the-counter drugs products, but among the most helpful are: *Wigder's Guide to Over-the-Counter Drugs*, by H. Neal Wigder, M.D. (Los Angeles: J. P. Tarcher, Inc., 1979) and Consumers Union's *The Medicine Show* (Mt. Vernon, NY: Consumers Union, 1980). Additional information is available by calling the FDA hotline: (301) 443-3170. If you have a drug-related consumer complaint, you should call (301) 443-1240. Although these are not toll-free hotlines, the FDA will return long-distance calls.

MEDICAL DEVICES

Entries in this category list common medical devices including contact lenses, IUDs, pacemakers, protein kits, and muscle stimulators. Information on related hazards was obtained from the Food and Drug Administration and from public-interest health groups. For information, call the FDA hotline: (301) 443-3170.

FOODS

These entries contain information on potential hazards related to foods and food additives. They list individual foods (e.g., hot dogs), substances (e.g., caffeine), or nutrients (e.g., vitamins). Information was obtained from the FDA, the U.S. Department of Agriculture, and public-interest organizations. More information can be obtained by calling the FDA hotline (301) 443-3170 or the USDA hotline (202) 472-4485. Personnel maintaining both will return long-distance calls.

TOXICS

These entries list toxic substances such as formaldehyde or asbestos, or products containing toxic substances such as insecticides or household cleaners. Information on industrial pollutants and agricultural pesticides was not included. Some of the information was drawn from Consumer Product Safety Commission data or *The Household Pollutants Guide* (Garden City, New York: Anchor Press, 1978) prepared by the Center for Science in the Public Interest.

For more information on related product hazards, call the CPSC's toll-free hotline: (800) 638-8326. The Environmental Protection Agency hotline may also be helpful: (202) 755-0707. For poison-prevention hotline numbers, see the entry POISONS, HOUSEHOLD.

COSMETICS

Potentially hazardous cosmetics are listed with information on questionable or dangerous ingredients. Most information was drawn from FDA sources though Tom Conry's *Consumer's Guide To Cosmetics* (Garden City, New York: Anchor Books, 1980) was also helpful, as were the reports of the Cosmetic Ingredient Review, an industry-sponsored panel of scientific and medical experts that reviews the safety of individual cosmetic ingredients. Consumers can obtain further information or file complaints by calling FDA hotlines: (301) 443-3170 or (301) 443-1240.

HOW TO ENSURE SAFER PRODUCTS

Undoubtedly products could be made much safer if we all took the time to report safety-related hazards to appropriate Federal agencies (see hotline numbers listed above). Only these agencies or Congress can require manufacturers to alter the design of products or recall defective items.

If you wish to take an even more active role, join the Consumer Federation of America's Consumer Product Safety Network. Just send us a note with your name, address, and phone number at the following address: Consumer Product Safety Network, 1314 14th Street, NW, Washington, DC 20005. The only qualification for membership is a willingness to support the work of product safety agencies.

A-200 PYRINATE. *See Kwell Shampoo and Cream.*

ACCUTANE. *See Isotretinoin.*

ACETAMINOPHEN (TYLENOL)

This pain reliever, commonly known by its brand name Tylenol, reduces fever but does not reduce inflammation like aspirin. It is the most popular non-aspirin pain killer available without a prescription. Many people prefer it to aspirin because it does not cause stomach upset or gastrointestinal bleeding. However, it provides little help for arthritis sufferers.

HAZARDS
Liver damage may result if acetaminophen is taken in much larger than recommended doses. Chronic alcoholics with liver disease should be especially careful to avoid acetaminophen.

> WARNING
>
> Do not use if you have liver disease or liver damage.

BRAND NAMES: Amphenol, Anacin-3, Bayer Non-Aspirin, Febrinol, Fendon, SK-APAP, Tempra, Tylenol liquid or tablets, Valadol.

ACNE MEDICATIONS, NONPRESCRIPTION *(See also Isotretinoin)*

The best medication for treating acne is benzoyl peroxide, in strengths up to 10 percent. Products with 10 percent benzoyl peroxide, however, are not necessarily the most effective, and they may cause more irritation to the skin. Also, use caution with acne scrubs, as cleansers with abrasives or rough surfaced sponges can irritate the skin and make acne worse.

ADHESIVES

INJURIES
In 1980, 13,000 cases involved household chemicals, including adhesives.

HAZARDS
Most injuries are caused by the adhesive squirting in the eyes, causing irritation, chemical burn, conjunctivitis, or a similar malady.

AEROSOL CONTAINERS

INJURIES
In 1973, 5,000 injuries involved aerosols used by consumers to dispense pesticide, paint, hairspray, medication, and other household products.

HAZARDS
Aerosol sprays release their active ingredient by the force of pressurized liquid or gaseous propellants. The pressure expels the moisture in the form of a fine mist. These aerosols can become powerful bombs when exposed to heat, external pressure, or puncture. They also pose dangers to people's health and the environment. Aerosol sprays are a major source of air pollution in the home, particularly when used in small closed rooms, such as the bathroom.
Aerosolized particles are so small that chemicals can be inhaled deeply into the lungs and quickly absorbed into the bloodstream. Al-

though some of these chemicals are relatively harmless externally, they can be extremely dangerous to internal tissues and organs. Potential dangers from the use of these products include the induction of cardiac arrhythmias—known as "sudden death"—birth defects, and lung cancer. Acute symptoms include headaches, nausea, dizziness, shortness of breath, eye and throat irritation, skin rashes, burns, lung inflammation, and liver damage. Aerosol sprays can also cause chemical burns or eye injury if the spray is misdirected.

Freon can cause corneal irritation, freeze burns to body surfaces, and even frostbite. Nitrous oxide, found in food sprays and shaving creams, and methylene chloride, used in some hairsprays, can simulate anesthesia. Propane, also used in hairspray, is extremely flammable.

Fluorocarbons, found in aerosol sprays, can cause heart attack and death. The use of fluorocarbons in aerosols caused considerable controversy in the late 1970s because fluorocarbons depleted the ozone layer in the upper atmosphere. Fluorocarbons were banned in early 1979 and replaced by pressurized petroleum, a less ecologically dangerous chemical.

Flammability, health hazards, and waste disposal still remain serious issues with the use of aerosol spray products.

PRECAUTIONS

It is better not to use aerosol products. But if they are used, do so cautiously. Keep them out of reach of children.

AFLATOXIN, IN PEANUT PRODUCTS *(See also Health Foods)*

HAZARDS

Aflatoxin is a poison produced by a natural mold that grows on peanuts and other agricultural products, such as rice and corn. The danger of aflatoxin in food lies in its ability to cause cancer. Controlled tests of aflatoxin exposure to laboratory animals has produced liver cancer in the majority of these animals. It is not certain whether people get cancer from aflatoxin; however, most substances known to cause cancer in experimental animals also cause cancer in humans.

PRECAUTIONS

Aflatoxin contamination can be prevented by immediately drying the crop after harvest and by using proper moisture-free storage. Moisture on improperly stored crops allows mold to grow and aflatoxin poisoning to occur. If rice and corn are immediately dried after harvest, aflatoxin is not produced.

The FDA allows 15 ppb (parts per billion) of aflatoxin in peanuts and peanut products. However, since aflatoxin can be stopped from contaminating crops by preventive measures, many health groups claim the FDA standard is far too lenient. Health standards should be raised to protect peanuts and peanut products because they are such a good source of low-cost protein.

AFP. *See Alpha-Fetoprotein Test Kits.*

AFRIN. *See Nasal Sprays and Decongestants.*

AIR CONDITIONERS

INJURIES

There were 6,000 cases in 1980.

HAZARDS

Poisoning can result from the emission of freon refrigerants used in thermal systems. The refrigerants most commonly used are the same as the fluorocarbons used in aerosol sprays and, therefore, add to the atmospheric ozone-layer depletion problem. Fluorocarbons are invisible and odorless, and normally leak at a very slow rate. Severe leakage from damaged systems can cause fluorocarbon inhalation or decompose into highly toxic chemicals (hydrochloric acid, hydrofluoric acid, and phosgene) when it contacts heated surfaces, sparks, or flames of a furnace or fireplace.

HAZARDOUS MODELS

Between 1962 and 1964, the Carrier Corporation recalled two models of room air conditioners. Engineering tests revealed deterioration of a terminal board insulator that could cause an electrical short that might ignite adjacent combustible material. The product is a 6000 BTU air conditioner sold under the Carrier Weathermaker brand name and bearing model number 51GA0661 or 51GB0661.

In July 1982, Consumers Union reported that Emerson Quiet

Kool 8JS7E and Whirlpool AHFP802 may be insecure because they have no sill bracket or leveling provision. Also in the Amana ES92MS model, the fan blade is exposed when the filter is being removed.

AIR FRESHENERS. *See Germicides and Disinfectants.*

AIR POLLUTION, INDOOR *(See also Asbestos; Carbon Monoxide; Formaldehyde; Kerosene Heaters; Mobile Homes; Smoking; Space Heaters)*

As energy-conscious Americans seal their homes to keep out the cold, they inadvertently keep in a number of toxic chemical pollutants. Because they spend up to 70 percent of their day indoors, the risk from inhaling these chemicals is significant. In mobile homes and trailers, increased energy efficiency, lack of ventilation and the possible presence of harmful gasses in a confined area, increase the danger of inhaling harmful chemicals. The following are the most common indoor air pollutants.

• Nitrogen dioxide is a combustion product found in cigarette smoke, car exhaust fumes, and emissions from kerosene heaters, gas stoves, furnaces, and space heaters. Nitrogen dioxide has been linked both in animal studies and human epidemiologic studies to an increased risk of infectious airway disease and respiratory disorders. Higher levels of exposure also increase airway resistance, and over time produce emphysematous lesions in the lungs. Individuals with existing respiratory disease, such as asthma, are affected more seriously by exposure to nitrogen dioxide.

Animal studies also show that concentration of nitrogen dioxide is a greater health risk than the length of time exposure. Thus, even short exposure to a high-emitting source of nitrogen dioxide, such as some kerosene heaters, may significantly increase susceptibility to nose and throat as well as breathing irritation and disease.

• Carbon monoxide is a colorless, odorless, and tasteless gas released from combustion sources such as cigarette smoke, automobile exhaust, kerosene heaters, gas stoves, furnaces, and space heaters. Even low levels of carbon monoxide in the air lowers the level of oxygen in the blood. As room levels of carbon monoxide increase and blood levels of oxygen decrease, shortness of breath, a slight increase in pulse, tightness across the forehead, headaches, and flushed skin can occur. As the levels of the chemical further increase, breathing difficulty, coma, convulsions, and death can occur. Because the heart has to pump harder when even low levels of carbon monoxide are in the air, the pollution represents a significant threat to heart patients and infants. People with anemia also run a greater risk of adverse reactions if exposed to low levels of carbon monoxide.

- Sulfur dioxide and suspended particulate matter are often found together as by-products of combustion from cigarette smoke, car exhaust, kerosene heaters, gas stoves, furnaces, and space heaters. As the concentration of sulfur dioxide and suspended particulates increases, so does vision difficulty and irritability (0.03 parts per million); diminished breathing capacity (0.04 ppm); worsening of pulmonary disease (0.08 to 0.17 ppm), and increased hospital admission and death of persons with cardiac or respiratory disease (0.17 ppm).

- Radon gas is emitted by radium-containing substances such as soil, stone and concrete, building materials, and ground water. When radon leaks into indoor air, it substantially increases the incidence of lung cancer if it reaches high concentrations, as in uranium mines. The significance of low-level exposure is not known, but adverse reactions to radon have been reported by occupants of underground homes. The levels of radon encountered in homes varies greatly, depending upon geographic location. Some areas have higher levels of radium in the soil and ground water. Other factors are building materials in the home (stone or concrete are the highest emitters of radon, wood the lowest), and the amount of ventilation to outdoor air.

- Asbestos is a fire-resistant mineral fiber that is not easily destroyed or decomposed by natural processes. It was used extensively in the past as a material strengthener, a flame retardant, and insulation. When asbestos fibers become airborne, however, they present an increased risk of stomach and lung cancer as well as other respiratory diseases. Asbestos is commonly found in older homes, in vinyl flooring or tiles, patching compounds and textured paint, stoves and furnaces, and wall and pipe insulation. Most asbestos-containing products have now been banned, but the problem of dislodging asbestos fibers into the air when repairing or renovating older homes is a significant hazard. (See general guidelines for removing asbestos products under ASBESTOS.)

- Formaldehyde is the most common aldehyde used in consumer products. It is found in thousands of consumer products ranging from urea–formaldehyde foam insulation to cosmetics; pressed-wood products such as furniture, paneling, and countertops; cigarette smoke; paper bags; and kerosene heater emissions. Exposure to formaldehyde gas can cause eye, nose, and throat irritations; nausea; headache; dizziness, memory loss, and many asthmalike symptoms.

People with respiratory illness such as asthma and emphysema or allergies often have more serious reactions to formaldehyde. A small percentage of people can become sensitized to formaldehyde; they experience a severe reaction when they come in contact with products containing even a minuscule amount of the chemical, like felt-tip pens or newspapers. Laboratory studies have also linked formaldehyde to cancer, although the effect of long-term exposure to low levels of the chemical is unknown.

AIRSTREAM TRAILER

1969 MODEL
Electrical short circuits may result from improperly designed battery covers.

AIRSTREAM TRAVEL TRAILER

1977, 1978 MODELS
The assembly holding the LP gas bottles may not have been installed properly. As a result the bottles may fall o} the trailer while in transit.

1978 J-1011 MODEL
A poorly designed main door latch has resulted in the door flying open during transit.

1978 EXCELLA MODEL
Front shock absorbers have a tendency to damage main brake lines during rough rides. The result of rupturing the brake lines is complete loss of brakes.

1974–1979 MODELS (with refrigerator service compartments)
The louvered openings in the service door may not be adequate to provide enough ventilation in the event of an LP gas leak in the compartment. Gas pockets that result could easily explode.

ALARMS. *See Burglar Alarms.*

ALCOHOL *(See also Alcohol and Pregnancy; Beer Additives; Drugs and Alcohol; Sulfites)*

HAZARDS

Thirteen million Americans abuse or are addicted to alcohol. According to a 1982 Gallup Poll, 81 percent of Americans think alcohol is a major national health problem. Alcohol abuse can cause heart disease, alcohol hepatitis, cirrhosis, and malnutrition. Associated with cigarette smoking, alcohol can cause cancer of the mouth, esophagus, larynx, liver, or other organs. Even small amounts of alcohol can be detrimental during pregnancy and can cause both physical and mental birth defects in the developing fetus.

The economic costs of alcohol abuse are also significant. Medical bills, time missed from work, property damage, and other costs of alcohol abuse totaled an estimated 100 billion dollars in 1982 in the U.S. Only heart and vascular diseases exceeded alcoholism and alcohol abuse in the total economic cost to the nation. Alcohol is also a major factor in crime: 86 percent of homicide cases involve alcohol, 79 percent of assaults, 72 percent of robberies, 50 percent of rapes, and 50 percent of automobile accidents.

ALCOHOL AND PREGNANCY

HAZARDS

A recent report by the Surgeon General concludes that alcohol consumption during pregnancy, especially in the early months, can harm the fetus. The report found significantly decreased birth weight among the children of women who drank only one ounce of alcohol (two standard drinks) per day during pregnancy. It also found sizeable and significant increases in spontaneous abortions when alcohol consumption by the drinker was as low as one ounce of alcohol twice a week.

Women consuming alcohol in amounts consistent with a diagnosis of alcoholism are at risk of bearing a child with a specific cluster of severe physical and mental defects known as fetal alcohol syndrome (FAS). This syndrome often produces mental retardation, central nervous system disorders, growth deficiencies, facial abnormalities, and other malformations, particularly relating to skeletal, urogenital, and cardiac functions.

In addition, the Surgeon General's report found that alcohol readily enters breast milk and is transmitted to the nursing infant. Heavy alcohol consumption is also known to decrease mother's milk.

PRECAUTIONS

The Surgeon General advises women who are pregnant or considering pregnancy to avoid alcoholic beverages and be aware of the alcoholic content of foods and drugs.

ALCONEFRIN. *See Nasal Sprays and Decongestants.*

ALDACTONE. *See Spironolactone.*

ALFA ROMEO ALFETTA

1977 MODEL
Rear driveshaft coupling may crack, causing transmission vibrations.

ALFA ROMEO SPIDER VELOCE

1977–1979 MODELS
Fuel pumps may be defective, causing stalling.

ALFA ROMEO SPORT SEDAN

1978 MODEL
Rear seat-belt mounting brackets may fracture in collision.

ALGICIDES, SWIMMING POOLS. *See Water Contaminants.*

ALKA-SELTZER. *See Antacid Medications.*

ALKA-SELTZER PLUS COLD MEDICINE. *See Decongestants, Oral.*

ALLEREST. *See Allergy Medications.*

ALLERGY MEDICATIONS *(See also Caffeine; Decongestants, Oral; Nasal Sprays and Decongestants)*

Although there are many kinds of allergies, over-the-counter medications are effective only in treating hay fever or allergic sinusitis. Antihistamines in combination with oral decongestants are the ingredients most helpful. Topical decongestants (nasal sprays) are not as helpful in allergy treatment as in cold treatment because of the likelihood of rebound congestion with long-term use.

HAZARDS

Although time-release brands are convenient to use, they should be avoided because they dissolve erratically and do not maintain an even level of medication in the body. Products containing phenylephrine should also be avoided because the drug is destroyed rapidly in the stomach and intestine, and unpredictable amounts of medication actually get into the bloodstream. Also avoid products containing caffeine, aspirin, or acetaminophen. Allergies do not require fever or pain medication, and caffeine has no effectiveness in treating allergy symptoms. In addition, caffeine stimulates the heart and compounds the stimulation effect caused by decongestants.

PRECAUTIONS

Methapyrilene has often been an ingredient in allergy medications, but it is now considered a possible carcinogen. Throw out any old medications containing methapyrilene.

If you are sensitive to aspirin, you may also be sensitive to tartrazine (yellow dye number 5), which is present in most colored drug tablets.

ALPHA-FETOPROTEIN (AFP) TEST KITS

Commercial AFP test kits help detect neural tube defects in unborn babies. Neural tube defects are crippling and often fatal deformities due to the brain being malformed or missing, or the spinal column being open or failing to develop properly. These defects affect about 5,000 of the three million babies born in the United States each year.

The AFP kits used by testing laboratories measure the amount of alpha-fetoprotein in the blood of a pregnant woman. AFP is a substance produced by all developing fetuses and is found in the amniotic fluid surrounding the fetus. Some AFP also passes normally into the mother's blood. A high level of AFP in the mother's blood can indicate the child will be born with a neural tube defect, but it can also indicate twins, triplets, the death of a fetus, a threatened miscarriage, or an incorrect estimate of the age of the fetus.

The test, therefore, is not conclusive but must be followed by further tests before a physician can confirm that the high AFP level indicates neural tube defects and order an abortion.

The Health Research Group petitioned the FDA in 1979 to restrict the sale, distribution, and use of the test kits to pilot FDA-approved screening programs. In response to the petition as well as to growing concern from other public-interest and medical groups, the FDA proposed regulations in 1980 to restrict the use of the test to FDA-approved testing programs to ensure the screening tests are done properly and that necessary follow-up procedures are carried out. The original regulations were never implemented, but in June 1983, the FDA issued new guidelines to physicians and laboratories using the test.

PRECAUTIONS

Considerable care should be taken by women using the test. Always do so under a physician's supervision and complete all necessary follow-up testing before assuming that a positive test result indicates neural tube defects.

ALUMINUM WIRING *(See also Home Electrical System)*

HAZARDS

Because of escalating prices of copper wire, between 1965 and 1973 aluminum wiring was attached to switches, wall outlets, and lighting fixtures in about 1.5 million houses. Aluminum wiring is much more likely to work loose from these fixtures than copper wiring, thereby creating a fire hazard, according to the CPSC. In 1979, the CPSC commissioned a study by the Franklin Research Center, which found a "fire hazard condition"—sparks, arcing, or 300°F at the outlet cover plate—to be 55 times greater in homes with aluminum wiring than in those with copper wiring.

PRECAUTIONS

To reduce the risk of fire, the CPSC recommends "pigtailing"— that is, attaching the aluminum wire to short lengths of copper wire that are then connected to the receptacle—with the use of a special tool, an AMP crimp connector. This repair should be made by an electrician if one or more of the following trouble signs appear:

- If plates, switches, or outlets are warm to the touch, they should be covered.

- Smoke, sparks, or arcing at switches or outlets.

- Strange odors, such as the smell of burning plastic, near switches or outlets.

- Lights that flicker periodically.

- Receptacles or entire circuits that do not work.

ALUPENT. *See Asthma Inhalers.*

AMC CONCORD

1978 MODEL
  Steering is vague during normal driving. Visibility is mediocre. Safety belts are poorly designed. Fuel filler is vulnerable in crash. Open trunk lid is hazardous to tall persons.

1979 MODEL
  Rear view is partially blocked by wide rear roof pillars and high rear windowsill. Open trunk lid is hazardous to tall persons. Occupant protection of 2-door model was rated poor in the U.S. Department of Transportation's 35 mph crash-test program.

1980 MODEL
  Improper bulb socket may have been installed, possibly causing dim rear signal lights. Fuel filler is vulnerable to rear-end crash. Open trunk lid is hazardous to tall persons.

1981 MODEL
  Safety-belt assembly may have been incorrectly installed. Servo chain design could cause throttle to remain partially open.

1982 MODEL
  Windshield may be improperly installed. Rear brakes may lock prematurely. Manual transmission could be inadequately lubricated, possibly causing transmission to break down.

AMC EAGLE

1980 MODEL
  Improper bulb socket may have been installed, possibly causing

dim rear signal lights. Incorrect universal joint may have been installed.

1981 MODEL
Front-axle spacer may have been omitted. Safety-belt assembly may have been incorrectly installed. Servo chain design could cause throttle to remain partially open.

1982 MODEL
Windshield may be improperly installed. Manual transmission could be inadequately lubricated, possibly causing transmission to break down. Handling is unsteady in emergency maneuvers.

1983 MODEL
Handling is unsteady in emergency maneuvers.

AMC GREMLIN

1977 MODEL
Long accelerator cable sleeve may cause throttle to stick open. Instrument-panel wiring harness may be chafed, possibly causing electrical short and fire. Hard to control in accident avoidance. Brakes are poor to fair. Seat belts ride up. Rear view is restricted; right front view is obstructed for tall drivers. Instruments are hard to read in daytime because of reflections. Open rear window and latch could be hazardous while cargo is being loaded or unloaded.

AMC PACER

1977 MODEL
Emergency handling is fair. Front seat belts ride up. Side view is obstructed by wide center roof pillars. Brakes are poor to fair.

1978 MODEL
Steering may lock up. Seat belts are uncomfortable. Lower control arm ball joint assembly may be defective. Handling is unpredictable in emergency maneuvers.

1979 MODEL
Brakes may suddenly pull to one side. Handling is unpredictable in emergency maneuvers.

AMC SPIRIT

1979 MODEL
Handling is sluggish in hard cornering. Head restraints interfere

with rear view. Rear seat belts are difficult to attach. Front seat belt sometimes "sawed" at neck level and tends to ride up.

1980 MODEL
Braking is uneven. High-speed road vibrations are excessive. Handling is sluggish in emergency maneuvers.

1981 MODEL
Servo chain design could cause throttle to remain partially open.

1982 MODEL
Manual transmission could be inadequately lubricated, possibly causing transmission to break down.

AMERICAN CLIPPER MINIHOMES

1976, 1977, 1978 MODELS
Propane gasline from tank to hot-water heater may rupture under severe road conditions. The leaking gas could cause an explosion.

AMERICAN JAWA MOPED

1975 MODEL
This moped fails to conform to a number of federal motor vehicle safety standards including: incorrect headlight, missing stop light, nonvisible brake linings, missing identification on some controls and missing certification labels.

AMCILL. *See Ampicillin.*

AMMONIA *(See also Chlorine Bleach; Drain Cleaners; Oven Cleaners)*

Ammonia can be found in oven and window cleaners as well as in household cleaners and wax removers. It chemically attacks and dissolves organic material very well, but in strong concentrations it can also attack the skin, eyes, and lungs, and cause irritation and burns.

PRECAUTIONS
Ammonia should only be used in well-ventilated areas.

AMOXICILLIN. *See Ampicillin.*

AMPICILLIN *(See also Drug and Food Interactions)*

Ampicillin is a form of penicillin used to treat bacterial infections in the ear, throat, urinary tract, or lungs (for example, pneumonia). Amoxicillin is a similar antibiotic drug, for which many of the same precautions apply. These drugs should not be taken if you are allergic to any form of penicillin. Serious reactions to the drug are possible, so if you develop a rash, hives, nausea or vomiting, itching or difficulty breathing, call your doctor immediately.

Although ampicillin has not been shown to have a harmful effect on the fetus, it is preferable to avoid any drug use during pregnancy. It is not known if ampicillin, transferred to an infant by breast milk, has any adverse effects. Serious reactions to ampicillin are more common when it is given by injection or when taken by someone with asthma, hay fever, or other allergies. To be effective, all of the prescribed medicine must be taken. Two doses should never be taken together. The drug must be refrigerated if it is in a liquid form.

> WARNING

Ampicillin may cause diarrhea, which is a dangerous condition in young children because of the risk of dehydration. Call your doctor if it continues.

BRAND NAMES: Amcill, Omnipen, Polycillin, Principen.

AMUSEMENT PARK RIDES

INJURIES

There have been 6,000–8,000 injuries from rides at amusement parks and traveling carnivals annually.

HAZARDOUS MODELS

The CPSC has filed complaints against several amusement parks.

- In 1977, against the Chance Manufacturing Company for a ride called the Zipper, which killed four persons in four separate accidents when the locking mechanism on the Zipper's door failed.

- In 1980, against the owner and operator of the Sky Ride at the state fair of Texas.

- In 1980, against the Marriott Corporation, which owns and operates Willard's Whizzer roller coasters at its Great America amusement parks in Santa Clara, California, and Gurnee, Illinois.

The first and third cases were settled, and the second was dismissed after Congress passed legislation removing amusement rides from the CPSC's jurisdiction.

ANACIN. *See Aspirin; Caffeine.*

ANACIN-3. *See Acetaminophen.*

ANTABUSE. *See Warfarin Potassium/Sodium.*

ANTACID MEDICATIONS *(See also Digoxin; Pregnancy and Drugs; Salt)*

Although occasional indigestion is common, three situations call for immediate medical attention: 1) any single episode of severe or persistent discomfort accompanied by sweating, weakness, or pain radiating upward or into the arms, 2) any single episode accompanied by vomiting of blood, or 3) repeated episodes of indigestion, no matter how mild.

HAZARDS

Even the oldest and most trusted antacid, sodium bicarbonate (baking soda), should not be taken for any extended period of time without a physician's supervision. Sodium bicarbonate is the principal ingredient in both Alka-Seltzer and Bromo Seltzer and in such brands as Brioschi, Eno, and Fizrin. Although baking soda is a potent and fast-acting antacid, it is one of the least desirable for regular or frequent use because it may lead to the formation of calcium stones in the kidneys and may also contribute to recurrent urinary tract infections. In addition, the amount of sodium in both Alka-Seltzer and Bromo Seltzer can be harmful to people with hypertension or congestive heart failure, or to anyone who must restrict salt intake. The use of antacids containing baking soda should be limited to healthy individuals on an occasional basis only. (Another disadvantage of Alka-Seltzer is its aspirin content, which can exacerbate the symptoms of an ulcer sufferer.)

For many years, calcium carbonate in powder form was the choice of many physicians to treat stomach upset. Calcium carbonate is still the principal antacid in many over-the-counter preparations such as Tums, Alka-2, Chooz, Titralac, Tempo, Bisodol, and Lo-Sal. In addition to causing constipation, calcium carbonate, if used regularly, may raise calcium levels in the blood to undesirable levels, and cause possible kidney damage and kidney stone formation.

PRECAUTIONS

Good rules to follow in the use of an antacid include limiting use to an occasional basis and checking with a physician if the problem persists. Restrict use of sodium bicarbonate or calcium carbonate antacids and give preference to products with aluminum and magnesium ingredients. If you are on a salt-restricted diet, look for an antacid low in sodium. Low-sodium brands include Bisodol, Tums E-X, Riopan, and Riopan Plus. Antacids high in sodium content include Alka-Seltzer, Brioschi, Bromo Seltzer, Eno, Fizrin, Rolaids, Soda Mint, and Di-Gel tablets.

Antacids should also be avoided if you are taking any tetracycline drugs. Taking antacids concurrently with tetracycline prevents the proper absorption of the tetracycline into the bloodstream.

WARNING

Pregnant women should check with their physician before using an antacid.

ANTENNAS *(See also Home Electrical System)*

INJURIES

The CPSC estimates that over 600 deaths by electrocution occurred between 1975 and 1979 when television or citizen band antennas came in contact with overhead high-voltage power lines. At the time of the accident, the person was holding the metal antenna for installation or removal, and the electric current flowed from the power line through the conductive metal to the victim.

ANTIBIOTICS / 24

HAZARDS

High-voltage power lines or the lines going from the transformer into the house can create a shock even if the person is electrically shielded from the ground. The following conditions increase the chances of electrocution and should be avoided:

- Moisture. Wet or sweaty feet and hands decrease the body's resistance to electric current.

- Metal. Touching a grounded metal ladder or gutter while holding an antenna against a power line turns the body into a route for electrical current.

- Wind. Wind can blow the antenna into a nearby power line.

- Power Lines. All lines strung between poles are potentially dangerous. Most power lines are not insulated, and in those that are, the insulation may have degraded, peeled, or cracked. Moreover, it is easy to mistake high-voltage electric power lines for low-voltage telephone lines. Since it is easy to mistake the two, you should avoid all lines.

ANTIBIOTICS. *See Digoxin; Drug and Food Interactions; Warfarin Potassium/Sodium.*

ANTICOAGULANTS. *See Cimetidine; Food and Drug Interactions; Vitamin C.*

ANTIDIABETIC AGENTS, ORAL *(See also Clofibrate; Spironolactone with Hydrochlorothiazide; Thiazides)*

These drugs are prescribed by physicians to control the blood sugar level in the body and to treat diabetes mellitus. It is important to let your doctor know if you are taking other drugs, such as aspirin, Butazolidin, anticoagulants, blood pressure medication, or diuretics, thyroid medicine, phenytoin, sulfa drugs or other antibiotics, or drugs for depression such as Nardil, Marplan, or Parnate. The effectiveness of your diabetic medication is affected by these drugs, and your physician will have to adjust your dosage if you are taking any of them.

HAZARDS
Side effects associated with these diabetic medications include headache, nausea, loss of appetite, and vomiting.

PRECAUTIONS
Call the doctor if you do not feel as well as normal or if you notice any of these side effects: itching, rash, bruises, jaundice (yellowing of the skin or eyes), dark urine, light-colored stools, fever, or sore throat. But continue your medication until you have contacted your doctor.
You should also avoid excess heat on your feet (hot bath or heating pad), and check for sores and cuts on your feet.

ANTIHISTAMINES. *See Benzodiazepines.*

ANTIPERSPIRANTS. *See Deodorants and Antiperspirants.*

ANTISPASMODIC PHAH. *See Belladonna Alkaloids and Barbiturates.*

ANUSOL SUPPOSITORIES. *See Hemorrhoid Medications.*

APPEDRINE. *See Diet Aids, Nonprescription.*

AQUA-BAN. *See Caffeine, Menstrual Pain Medications.*

ARGOSY MOTOR HOME

1974, 1975 MODELS
Propane gas regulator may be improperly mounted. As a result moisture will not drain out of vent and freeze causing regulator to fail.

ARGOSY TRAILER *(See also Air Pollution, Indoor; Asbestos)*

1976 MODEL
Possibility of furnace exhaust vent not sealing against asbestos gasket on vent tube. This can cause carbon monoxide to be drawn into the duct system and expelled throughout the trailer.

1977, 1978 MODELS
The assembly holding the LP gas tanks may not have been installed properly. As a result, the gas tanks may fall off in transit.

ARMSTRONG TIRES H78-15

These tires were recalled on March 16, 1981 for failure to meet the federal government's high speed safety standards. See TIRES for more information on tire recalls.

ARROW TRAILER, GREAT DANE, AND ARROW

1971, 1972, 1973, 1974 MODELS
Highly concentrated loads or inadvertent dropping of trailer on landing gear may cause the center beams and web plate to fail. This can cause the trailer to dump its load in transit.

ARTHRITIS MEDICATIONS *(See also Acetaminophen; Aspirin; Warfarin Potassium/Sodium)*

Arthritis is a chronic disease that should be carefully monitored by your physician. Drugs prescribed for the treatment of arthritis also need to be carefully monitored. Certain arthritis medications cause the retention of fluids and should not be taken if you are already taking a diuretic.

If you have a history of acute asthma attacks, severe nasal congestion (rhinitis), or skin rash, tell your physician because some arthritis drugs can cause these conditions to recur.

Almost all arthritis medications cause stomach upset, so they should be taken at mealtime or with soda crackers and milk. Never take these drugs on an empty stomach.

ASBESTOS *(See also Water Contaminants; Air Pollution, Indoor)*

Asbestos is a generic term for a number of naturally occurring hydrated mineral silicates. Its high resistance to heat and chemical abrasion made asbestos a popular ingredient, until recently, in home insulation, fireproofing materials, tiles and ceilings, brake linings, cement, and wallboard. Consumer products manufactured with asbestos included ironing board covers, draperies, work gloves, and hair dryers.

HAZARDS

Asbestos poses a threat to humans when tiny particles are inhaled and become embedded in lung tissue. Once they are released, asbestos fibers never break down. If inhaled, they remain in the lungs as a permanent irritant. These fibers have been associated with asbestosis, lung cancer, and mesothelioma. The latter is a form of cancer uncommon in the general population, but often found in asbestos workers. Mesothelioma cancer may affect the membrane lining of the chest cavity or the abdominal cavity.

Although most reports of disease associated with asbestos have been from exposed workers, asbestos is also a consumer problem. The CPSC recalled hair dryers lined with asbestos in the late 1970s, and banned the future use of asbestos in these products. Currently, the CPSC has a task force at work on other asbestos problems in consumer products.

The most common exposure to asbestos is in older homes that contain many building materials and insulation manufactured with the product. When plaster, wallboard, or tiles containing asbestos are disturbed, the fibers are released into the air where they can remain for years. This displacement occurs most often during home renovation or repair. Not only does it pose a hazard to workers doing the remodeling, but to the inhabitants of the home as well.

Once fibers are disturbed they can remain airborne in the home for considerable periods of time. These fibers never break down, and they will remain in the air or resettle as dust only to be displaced again with housecleaning. The amount of asbestos released depends upon the product in which it is found, the asbestos concentration in the product, and the amount of force generated in removing the product.

As with other toxic chemicals, asbestos-related disease may not appear until 20 or 30 years after exposure.

GENERAL GUIDELINES FOR THE REMOVAL OF ASBESTOS

If possible, do not disturb any material you think may contain asbestos. Removal of material is recommended only as a last resort for irreparable situations. If asbestos material must be removed or altered, the following precautions should be taken.

- Seal off the work area from the rest of the residence and take care not to track asbestos dust to other areas of the residence. Plastic sheeting and duct tape may be used to seal off passageways.

- Always wear an approved respirator, protective gloves, hat, and clothing. Dispose of all this equipment immediately after using it. If you cannot, wash these clothes separately from other laundry. Wash these clothes twice. The machine should be thoroughly rinsed before use with other laundry.

- Cutting, breaking, scraping, sanding, and removal of asbestos materials should be kept to a minimum and avoided whenever possible (for example, avoid breaking asbestos material into small pieces simply for ease of handling). All these activities are more likely to release asbestos fibers. Before performing any of these activities, thoroughly dampen the material (do not make dripping wet) with a solution of one teaspoon of low-sudsing dishwashing or laundry detergent per quart of water (the detergent helps penetration of water into the material). Use a hand sprayer with a fine mist as an applicator.

- Do not dust, sweep, or vacuum materials containing asbestos particles. Except for specially designed vacuum cleaner filters, these activities will simply disturb asbestos fibers and possibly send them airborne. Instead, asbestos dust should be wetted and removed by wet-mopping. Wet-mop the entire work area twice when the job is finished, and daily if the job takes more than one day. Throw away all rags, mops, and sponges used in the wet-mopping cleanup, if possible. If not, flush them thoroughly and repeatedly in a basin. The basin should then be thoroughly cleaned before any other use.

- Place all material and debris from the job in plastic bags—be careful not to tear them—and then dispose them in a proper landfill (call your local health department for instructions).

- Have disposal done by a contractor familiar with handling problems of asbestos.

ASPARTAME *(See also Sweeteners, Artificial)*

Aspartame is a natural sweetener made from amino acids. It was approved by the FDA for use 17 years after its discovery. Unlike saccharin and cyclamate, which were on the market before 1958, it has undergone rigorous testing as required by law, and these studies have concluded it is safe.

Aspartame is being marketed in the powder form under the name Equal. It is available for use in breakfast cereals, powdered beverages, dessert toppings, chewing gum, and gelatins. It will be listed as Nutra Sweet on the labels of these foods. Shortly, the major soft drink companies will be using it to replace saccharin in their diet drinks. One teaspoon of aspartame has one-tenth of a calorie with 200 times the sweetness of sugar. Many people claim it tastes as good as sugar because it has no bitter aftertaste.

One drawback of aspartame is cost. It is much more expensive than sugar or saccharin. A box of 100 packets of Equal costs about three times more than Sweet 'N Low. The higher cost will obviously be reflected in the price of the products containing this substance.

HAZARDS

Because aspartame has not been widely used, long-term effects are unknown. Aspartame might cause brain damage in young children suffering from a rare genetic disorder called phenylketonuria. A warning label will appear on packages of products using aspartame.

ASPERGUM. *See Aspirin; Throat Medications.*

ASPIRIN *(See also Cimetidine; Drug and Food Interactions; Food Additives; Pregnancy and Drugs; Spironolactone; Vitamin C; Warfarin Potassium/Sodium.)*

Aspirin is one of the most effective pain relievers available without a prescription. It is also an excellent fever reducer and, unlike other over-the-counter pain relievers, it can help reduce inflammation. It is available in powder, tablet, suppository, and time-release form. The powder form is absorbed most quickly into the bloodstream and reduces the amount of gastrointestinal bleeding common with the tablet form. However, the powdered aspirins contain a significant amount of sodium and should not be used by people with high blood pressure. Aspirin's absorption is also erratic in the suppository form, which should only be used if vomiting precludes oral medications. Time-release forms of the medication are not effective for quick pain relief, because release of the medication into the bloodstream can be erratic.

HAZARDS

The most common, although rare, adverse effect of aspirin therapy is stomach bleeding. Consequently, anyone with ulcers or a bleeding condition should avoid the use of aspirin. Because alcohol increases the amount of bleeding caused by aspirin, the pain reliever should not be used to treat a hangover. Other common side effects of aspirin are heartburn and upset stomach, which occur in about 5 percent of people using the drug. Some people are also allergic to aspirin. The most frequently used substitute for aspirin is acetaminophen (Tylenol).

Buffered aspirin is equally as good a pain reliever as regular aspirin. It includes antacids to relieve stomach distress. However, most people do not need these additional ingredients. Usually, taking aspirin with a glass of water will work just as well as the small amount of antacids found in the buffered products. Any significant stomach distress indicates a need to switch to acetaminophen. Coated aspirin is not an effective alternative and may cause slower, incomplete absorption.

In support of the use of buffered aspirin is the recent finding that one tablet a day helps prevent heart attacks. In a study of over 1,300 men with a condition called unstable angina, the use of aspirin in the form of Alka-Seltzer decreased the number of heart attacks by half.

It should be noted that any generic aspirin works as well as a highly advertised, more expensive product. An "extra strength" or "more potent" product means only that the dosage is higher than ordinary aspirin.

Aspergum contains a small dose of aspirin for an adult, and is no more effective for curing sore throat pain than swallowing the same amount of regular aspirin. In addition, particles of the coating of the gum may cause greater throat irritation.

Children's flavored aspirin is potentially dangerous because the pills taste too much like candy to be safe. Accidental poisoning of a child who eats an entire bottle of flavored aspirin is far too common in the U.S.

Another danger of aspirin given to children is the development of Reye's Syndrome (pronounced "ryes"). Reye's Syndrome (RS) attacks children aged 5 to 16 while they are recovering from chicken pox or other viral infections. The disease is characterized by ambiguous symptoms such as repeated, forceful vomiting, and unusual behavior such as lethargy, confusion, irritability, or aggressiveness. RS can then rapidly progress to convulsions, coma, and death.

RS is diagnosed by a series of tests detecting swelling of the brain, imbalance of blood chemicals, and malfunction of the liver, which loses its ability to detoxify poisons, including ammonia. The only known preventive measure is to avoid giving aspirin and medications containing aspirin to children with viral illness including chicken pox. Some experts feel that the connection of aspirin to Reye's Syndrome is inconclusive; but with children, the use of non-aspirin substitutes is safer than risking death or brain damage.

PRECAUTIONS

Aspirin is the common name for products containing salicylates, and is the most widely used and most widely sold drug in the world. But rarely are the side effects and dangers associated with aspirin use mentioned when the product is purchased.

• Do not give aspirin to children under age 18 with chicken pox or flu. It contains an ingredient associated with Reye's Syndrome, an often fatal disease.

• Stop taking aspirin if ringing of the ears or other symptons occur that indicate an overdose.

HAZARDS
• Aspirin interferes with blood clotting. Persons with a history of coagulant defects or severe anemia should avoid this product.

• Aspirin interferes with the action of some prescription drugs for anticoagulation, diabetes, gout, and arthritis. If you take any of these drugs, do not take aspirin except under the advice and supervision of a physician.

• Aspirin may augment peptic ulcers, cause stomach distress or heartburn; used chronically this drug may cause a persistent iron-deficient anemia; in high doses this drug may produce a reversible hepatatic dysfunction of the liver; in overdoses this drug produces stimulation followed by depression of the central nervous system; and, rarely, this drug may exacerbate existing severe kidney disease.

• Aspirin increases the incidence of stillbirths and neonatal deaths, lengthens the duration of pregnancy and birthing, and interferes with maternal and infant blood clotting. Pregnant patients should seek the advice of a physician before use.

ASTHMA INHALERS

Late in 1982, the FDA changed the status of asthma inhalers

containing the drug metaproterenol sulfate from prescription drug products to over-the-counter products. These inhalers released a metered dose of medicine to unclog air passages to and from the lungs. The FDA thought the inhalers containing metaproterenol sulfate would not be as overused as the other over-the-counter inhalers that contain epinephrine, which is a less effective drug. However, in response to persistent expression of concern regarding potential product abuse, asthma inhaler manufacturers have voluntarily recalled the product from the over-the-counter marketplace. Some brand names include Allupent and Metaprel.

HAZARDS

More than 100 members of the American Academy of Allergy and Immunology have expressed concern that metaproterenol sulfate inhalers will result in overuse or abuse by asthmatics. Physicians warn that if overused, the new inhalers can cause irregular heartbeats, heart failure, or respiratory failure. The lack of data on dosage levels for children is also a problem.

WARNING

Children under 12 should not use metaproterenol sulfate.

ATHROMBIN-K. *See Warfarin Potassium/Sodium.*

ATLAS GOLDENAIRE II TIRES. *See Firestone 500 Tires.*

ATIVAN. *See Benzodiazepines.*

ATROMID-S. *See Clofibrate; Warfarin Potassium/Sodium.*

ATTIC VENTILATORS

HAZARDOUS MODELS

In 1983, in cooperation with the CPSC, Westinghouse Electric

Corporation and Broan Manufacturing Company voluntarily began recalling approximately 16,000 electric motors supplied for Broan Model 346 and Nautilus Model N346 attic ventilators. The ventilator motors that are miswired may, under certain conditions, overheat and cause fires. The motors subject to recall have a Westinghouse sticker with the model number E322P159 and are painted gray.

ATWOOD TENT CAMPERS

1975 MODEL
Stabilizing jack may not hold in locked position, causing the camper to collapse.

AUDI FOX

1978 MODEL
Insufficient tightening of bolts in brakes may cause vibrations when brakes applied.

AUDI 100

1977 MODEL
Brake fluid servicing labels complying with federal standard are missing.

AUDI 4000

1980 MODEL
In a crash, right rear-side panel could damage fuel tank, causing fire hazard. Occupant protection was rated poor in the U.S. Department of Transportation's 35-mph crash test of the 4-door model.

1981 MODEL
Brake calipers may have porous spots that allow brake fluid leakage and eventually complete brake failure. In a crash, right-side panel could damage fuel tank, causing fire hazard.

AUDI 5000

1978 MODEL
Floor mat could prevent throttle from closing fully. Rear head restraints block driver's view.

1979–1982 MODELS
Floor mat could prevent throttle from closing fully.

AUTO BATTERIES. *See Batteries, Wet Cell.*

AUTO BODY KITS

HAZARDS AND PRECAUTIONS
Auto body kits contain several hazards. They can cause skin irritation. Most liquid materials in the kits are flammable and emit toxic fumes. Use a mask to avoid inhaling fiberglass and keep uncured resins and hardeners away from children.

AUTOMATIC TRANSMISSIONS. *See Automobile Transmissions.*

AUTOMOBILE SAFETY DEFECTS *(See also individual models)*

Every year millions of automobiles and trucks are recalled for safety defects. These recalls represent problems that can be corrected at no cost to the consumer.

The effectiveness of a safety recall rests, in part, with the owner. The owner is responsible for bringing the car to a dealer for inspection and repair. To find out if your car has ever been in a recall, call the toll-free auto safety hotline: 800-424-9393 (in Washington, D.C., call 426-0123). Operators are standing by from 7:45 A.M. to 4:15 P.M. (Eastern Time) Monday through Friday. You can use the hotline to report safety defects as well.

You may also contact your dealer to find out if your car has been recalled. In addition, your dealer will be able to tell you if defects in your particular car have been corrected.

Remember, a recalled car can be returned to any authorized dealer and the manufacturer is responsible for fixing the defect no matter how long ago the recall occurred.

AUTOMOBILES. *See Air Pollution, Indoor; Automobile Safety Defects; Automobile Transmissions; Gasoline; Lead; individual models.*

AUTOMOBILE TRANSMISSIONS

HAZARDS

There are 21 million Ford, Lincoln, and Mercury vehicles with automatic transmissions that may inadvertently shift into reverse. This defect has been and continues to be responsible for a large number of deaths and injuries. The defect occurs in transmission models C3, C4, C6, FMX and JATCO.

PRECAUTIONS

Safety experts have spent many years trying to get Ford to correct the problem. Instead, the federal government simply required Ford to send owners of 1970 through 1980 model Fords a stick-on label warning drivers that the car may shift into reverse. The defect also occurs in 1966 through 1969 models; however these were not included in the government's notification system.

If you own or are considering buying one of these cars, use extreme caution when parking the car.

AYDS. *See Diet Aids, Nonprescription.*

AZENE. *See Benzodiazepines.*

BABY BACK CARRIERS

HAZARDOUS MODELS

In October 1982, Gerico, Inc., recalled approximately 238,000 Gerry Carrier and Pak-A-Poose baby back carriers. The fingers of infants may become entrapped in the hinge mechanism on the moveable stand supporting the carrier when it is placed on a surface.

BABY POWDER CONTAINERS

HAZARDS

Poison control specialists claim that baby powder containers are hazardous because they resemble nursing bottles that infants may try to suck. Even though only a small percentage of the infant patients require hospitalization, the talcum is closely related to the carcinogen asbestos and may contain microscopic asbestos particles. Experts have urged the baby powder industry to change the appearance of containers and use a safety device on the cap to control dispensing of the powder.

BABY RATTLES *(See also Toys, General)*

INJURIES
Ten children have been reported having choked to death.

HAZARDS
In the above cases the victims—the oldest of whom was 13 months—either partially swallowed the rattles while sucking on them or fell with the rattles in their mouths, causing the rattles to be jammed down their throats.

FEDERAL STANDARDS
CPSC regulations ban rattles with rigid wires, sharp protrusions, or loose, small objects that could cut or be inhaled or swallowed. Also, rattles must be large enough to prevent choking and must not come apart in small pieces.

PRECAUTIONS
When purchasing a rattle, keep in mind that no part or end should be small enough to fit in your baby's mouth. To date, the largest rattle known to have lodged in a baby's throat had an end $1\frac{3}{8}$ inches in diameter.

HAZARDOUS MODELS
In September 1981, the Montgomery Schoolhouse, Inc., recalled approximately 61,000 baby rattles. In the same month, Schowanek recalled approximately 2,900 baby rattles: model numbers 10875/2, 10875/33, 10876/17, 10876/3, 10876/26, and 10876/19. These wooden rattles could become caught in an infant's throat and cause choking and suffocation.

BABY SHAMPOOS. *See Shampoos, Baby.*

BABY STROLLERS. *See E-Z Roller Baby Stroller.*

BABY WALKERS

INJURIES
Of the 10,000 injuries in 1980, most of the victims were children under two years of age who suffered head injuries.

HAZARDS
- Tipping over. A baby walker tips over easily when a child attempts to move from a floor to a rug, over a door threshold, or onto any uneven surface. It can also tip over when the child leans to one side or attempts to pick up a toy.

- Falling downstairs.

- Finger entrapment, as children are lifted in or out of some of the older x-frame baby walkers. The Federal Hazardous Substances Act regulation bans any baby walker with exposed parts that can amputate, crush, cut, break, or bruise a child's fingers or toes.

PRECAUTIONS
In purchasing a baby walker, look for:

- Protective covers over accessible coil springs, spacers between scissoring components, and locking devices to prevent the x-frame from collapsing.

- A wheel base that is both wider and longer than the frame of the walker itself, ensuring greater stability.

BACON. *See Nitrites and Nitrosamines; Salt.*

BAKED GOODS. *See Food Colors, Artificial; Nitrites and Nitrosamines; Salt.*

BAKING POWDER. *See Salt.*

BAKING SODA. *See Antacid Medications; Salt.*

BAN-BUG RESIN STRIP. *See Insecticides, Household.*

BANTRON. *See Smoking Deterrents.*

BARBITURATES. *See Belladonna Alkaloids and Barbiturates; Sleeping Aids, Nonprescription; Sleep Medications, Prescription.*

BARON BOAT TRAILERS

1976 MODEL
The manufacturer failed to install the proper lighting as required by law. Owners of these trailers should return them to the dealer for correct installation of the lights.

BAR STOOLS. *See Stools.*

BATAVUS MOPED

1973–1976 MODELS
These mopeds fail to meet the federal safety standard which requires that the throttle return to off position when released.

1973–1976 VA, HS-50 MODELS
The fuel control valve was not labeled as required by federal safety laws.

1978, 1979, 1980 STARFLIGHT VA AND HS REGENCY MODELS
Certain models were imported with no tire, rim, and inflation information as required by law. Not knowing the proper tire inflation pressure can be a safety hazard.

BATHTUBS *(See also Hot Tubs)*

INJURIES
In 1980, 72,000 involved bathtubs or showers.

BATTERIES / 40

HAZARDS
Most injuries are caused by the following:

• Falls resulting from the combination of smooth nonporous surfaces and soapy water.

• Burns from hot water, which often are suffered by the very young or very old.

• Electrocution while bathing as a result of contact with electrical equipment such as radios, phonographs, hair dryers, or sunlamps.

• Drowning, mainly of the very young or very old.

PRECAUTIONS
A suction-cup rubber mat or rough-surfaced adhesive strips should be placed on the floor of the tub.
There should be at least two grab bars securely mounted on the wall beside the bathtub—at different heights—and one in every shower stall.
Tub and shower accessories should be free of sharp edges.
Young children and older persons should be accompanied when taking a bath or shower.
Avoid using electrical appliances in the bathroom.

BATTERIES. See *Batteries, Button; Batteries, Dry Cell; Batteries, Wet Cell.*

BATTERIES, BUTTON

HAZARDS
According to the U.S. Consumer Product Safety Commission and the National Capital Poison Center (NCPC) at Georgetown University in Washington, D.C., consumers swallow an estimated 500 to 800 button (miniature or disc) batteries each year. Officials say that the majority of the tiny batteries—which are used to power watches, calculators, cameras, hearing aids, and games—will pass through the swallowers without any problem. However, severe complications, even fatalities, occasionally have been reported. Button batteries may become lodged in the esophagus or intestine, slowly leaking alkaline electrolytes and causing internal chemical burns.

PRECAUTIONS

Battery ingestion is preventable. Of 62 button battery ingestions reported to the NCPC in recent months, 59 percent involved batteries that were left out loose rather than properly discarded or stored; 39 percent of the batteries were removed from the product they were intended for. Half of these batteries were for hearing aids.

Accidental ingestion of button batteries is not restricted to young children. In one study, only 66 percent of patients were under the age of 5, while 10 percent were 18 years or older. A surprising 24 percent were in the 5-to-12-year age range. Many of the major U.S. battery manufacturers have voluntarily placed warnings on the battery packages, which are routinely sold in blister packing that forms an excellent child-resistant closure. The effectiveness of this packaging is supported by a NCPC study that shows fewer than 2 percent of batteries ingested were obtained from the manufacturers' original packaging.

To help prevent button battery ingestion:

- Keep button batteries out of children's reach. Carefully discard batteries.

- Do not allow children to play with button batteries.

- Never put button batteries in your mouth for any reason—they are slippery and easily swallowed.

- Always check medications before swallowing them. Adults have swallowed batteries, mistaking them for tablets.

- Hearing aid users should be careful to keep hearing aids and batteries out of the reach of children.

If a button battery is swallowed, contact the poison control center, your physician, or the National Button Battery Ingestion hotline at (202)625-3333. The majority of batteries ingested will pass through the intestine without any difficulty. In the absence of symptoms, an x-ray and laxative are usually all that are required. If symptoms are present or the battery is lodged in the esophagus, complications are more likely, and medical treatment should be sought.

BATTERIES, DRY CELL *(See also Batteries, Button)*

INJURIES
In 1980, 22,000 involved batteries.

HAZARDS
Dry-cell batteries—such as carbon-zinc, alkaline, or mercury—are used in flashlights, portable radios, and battery-operated toys, as well as for other household uses.

Specific injuries are caused by:

- Exploding batteries. Batteries explode when polarity is inadvertently reversed for one battery in a group. It can also occur if batteries are disposed of in an incinerator or fire. It may occur when an attempt is made to recharge nonrechargeable batteries, causing a buildup of gases to generate enough pressure to explode the battery.

- Leaking batteries. The leakage of a chemical substance in batteries may cause chemical burns or skin irritation. This may occur when children chew on batteries or when they swallow miniature batteries that become lodged in the esophagus or intestine.

PRECAUTIONS
To minimize the risk of chemical burns, keep batteries out of the reach of children; do not allow children to play with them. Always check medications before swallowing them since even adults have swallowed miniature batteries, thinking they were medication.

BATTERIES, WET CELL

INJURIES
In 1980, 22,000 involved batteries.

HAZARDS
The most common use of wet-cell storage batteries is in automobiles. Car batteries contain a solution of sulfuric acid and water that, when activated, produces explosive gases that are easily ignited. Most accidents occur when batteries are jumped, recharged, or otherwise serviced.

Specific injuries are caused by:

- Exploding batteries. When a spark from the cable connection detonates the combustible gases in a battery, the explosion could cause the battery cap to fly off and strike the victim, or could cause the battery acid to splash on the victim, causing chemical burns.

Typically, explosions occur when batteries are being jumped or charged, often when jumper cables are connected. These cables should never be cross-connected between positive and negative poles. Batteries can also explode when a match or other flame is held near battery vent holes when checking the acid level.

- Other contacts with battery acid, including rubbing unwashed hands in the eyes or mouth after cleaning a battery, or being splattered by battery acid when standing by an uncapped battery when the car motor is running.

- Contacts with battery corrosion, which can get into a person's eyes when battery cable connectors are being cleaned or repaired.

FEDERAL STANDARDS
Under the Federal Hazardous Substances Act, the CPSC requires manufacturers of batteries containing sulfuric acid to include precautionary labels on batteries and boxes warning consumers of the dangers from battery acid and accumulated gases.

PRECAUTIONS
The CPSC urges consumers to keep all flame sources, including lighted cigarettes, away from car batteries. When even attempting to "jump start" a car using jumper cables connected to another car's battery it is best to connect the negative (ground) wire to a metal part of the car rather than the negative post on the battery.

BAYER NON-ASPIRIN. *See Acetaminophen.*

BB GUNS. *See Guns, BB.*

BEACH CHAIRS. *See Folding Chairs.*

BEDDING. *See Mattresses.*

BEDS, BUNK

INJURIES
In 1980, 168,000 bunk bed-related injuries were reported to the CPSC. Most injuries were fractures, lacerations, or contusions affecting children who fell off or against a bed. In 1973, an estimated 10,000 persons received hospital emergency-room treatment for injuries associated with these beds.

HAZARDS
Bunk-bed injuries are caused mainly by:

- Inadequate guard rails that, for example, are not fastened securely and can fall off when a child rolls against them.

- Sharp metal or wood edges of the bedframe, which can be more hazardous if mattresses are loose-fitting.

- Unstable or broken ladders that can slip if they are not secured firmly to the bedframe. Ladders can also be hazardous if missing or loose rungs make them difficult to climb.

- Rough playing of children in bed.

PRECAUTIONS
Consumers should choose bunk beds that have:

- Wood or metal frame with rounded edges;

- A mattress that fits tightly to prevent exposure of metal edges;

- A ladder that grips the bedframe firmly and does not slip when a child climbs on it;

- A guard rail that does not provide open spaces through which a child could fall; and

- A guard rail that can be secured into position.

BEER ADDITIVES *(See also Nitrites and Nitrosamines)*

HAZARDS
Beer contains chemical additives that may be hazardous to health. Most of these additives have never been tested in conjunc-

tion with alcohol. Many are known to cause allergic reactions in some consumers. One additive, yellow dye number 5, causes allergic reactions in thousands of aspirin-sensitive people. Certain grains in beer also cause allergic reactions in sensitive individuals. Other additives have been linked to an increase in certain types of cancer, and additives that people try to avoid in processed foods are sometimes found in beer.

Beer manufacturers are not required to list ingredients on their product labels and most of them do not do so; therefore, it is difficult to determine if a particular brand of beer contains a substance one wishes to avoid. The FDA requires labeling on all other food and beverages but, because of a loophole in the law, the FDA has no authority over alcoholic beverages. If you suspect an allergic reaction to beer, write to the brewer directly for the ingredients.

BELLADONNA ALKALOIDS AND BARBITURATES

These combination drug products are prescribed to relieve cramping and spasms in the stomach, intestines, and bladder. They are commonly used for the treatment of intestinal ulcers, irritable or spastic colon, and colitis.

HAZARDS

Possible side effects include disorientation and confusion, drowsiness or dizziness, headaches, blurred vision, constipation, nausea, vomiting, trouble sleeping, or impotence.

Call your doctor at once if you have diarrhea, difficulty urinating, eye pain, hallucinations, sore throat, fever, unusual bleeding or bruising, slurred speech, skin rash, or yellowing of the eyes or skin.

BRAND NAMES: Antispasmodic PHAH, Barbidonna, Belbarb, Butibel, Donnatal

PRECAUTIONS

Since these products interfere with the action of antacids, they should not be taken together. Take the two medicines at least one hour apart. Do not stop taking the medication without consulting your physician. If a dose is missed, take remaining doses as scheduled but do not take the missed dose off-schedule and never take two doses together. Do not use any other drug, including nonprescription drugs, in combination with these drugs unless your physician knows and approves. Do not use this drug product if you are already taking an anticoagulant (blood thinner), monoamine oxidase (MAO) inhibitor (Nardil, Marplan, or Parnate), antidepressant (Elavil, Tofranil, or Sinequan), or cortisone medication, heart medicine, or antihistamine.

Be careful when driving a car, operating machinery, or using household appliances until you see how the drug affects you. Avoid too much heat, sunlight, or saunas, as lengthy exposure may cause heat prostration.

Be sure to tell your physician if you have or ever had eye problems, including glaucoma; kidney, thyroid, liver, or lung disease; difficulty with urination or prostate problems; chronic intestinal problems or diarrhea; rapid heartbeat; hiatal hernia or myasthenia gravis.

BENDECTIN. *See Doxylamine and Pyridoxine; Pregnancy and Drugs.*

BENDIX MOTOR HOMES

1974, 1975 MODELS
Corsair and Aristocraft models have the incorrect axle weight data shown on the certification label. As a result, owners could inadvertently overload the vehicle, causing tire failure.

BENOXYL. *See Acne Medications, Nonprescription.*

BENZODIAZEPINES

HAZARDS

This group of minor tranquilizers is prescribed to relieve incapacitating anxiety, nervousness, or other conditions, such as cerebral palsy, spinal cord damage, or muscle spasm from sprains. It is a short-term treatment and may cause dependency if taken too long or in high doses. Patients often become addicted to minor tranquilizers such as Valium without realizing they are addicted. Overcoming the addiction is very difficult and should be done under a physician's supervision. Do not stop taking a minor tranquilizer you have been taking for more than a month unless you consult your doctor. Abrupt withdrawal can cause anxiety, cramps, tremors, convulsions, hallucinations, and other side effects.

PRECAUTIONS

Never take more than one dose of benzodiazepine at a time. Avoid drinking alcohol or using drugs such as sleeping pills, cough and cold medicines, antihistamines, antidepressants, pain killers, or other tranquilizers in combination with benzodiazepines. *The interaction of such drugs can be fatal.*

When you first take the drug, you may experience clumsiness, drowsiness, especially in the elderly. If this continues more than a few days you may need a smaller dose, so consult your physician. Be careful when driving or operating appliances or machines.

Your doctor needs to know if you have an allergy to benzodiazepines, a history of glaucoma, liver or kidney problems, diabetes, or epilepsy.

Symptoms of an overdose include extreme sleepiness, weakness, staggering, shakiness, or confusion. Get emergency help immediately.

Less common side effects include confusion, excitement, depression, rash, blurred vision, and difficulty urinating. Call your doctor if they continue: You may need a lower dose.

WARNING

Birth defects are more common in babies whose mothers took benzodiazepines in their first three months of pregnancy. During breast-feeding, these drugs get into the mother's milk and may cause drowsiness and addiction in the infant. Avoid minor tranquilizers if you are pregnant, planning pregnancy, or breast-feeding.

BERLINER MOTO GUZI ROBIN MOPED

1974, 1975 MODELS

These mopeds were imported without the proper control identification labels as required by federal law.

BETTY CROCKER HICKORY SMOKE CHEESE FLAVORED POTATOES. *See Sulfites.*

BETTY CROCKER SNACKIN' CAKE CARROT NUT CAKE MIX. See *Sulfites*.

BEVERAGES, FRUIT-FLAVORED. See *Brominated Vegetable Oil (BVO)*.

BEVERAGES, POWDERED. See *Aspartame; Food Colors, Artificial*.

BEVERLY HILLS DIET, THE *(See also Diets)*

Judy Mazel's *Beverly Hills Diet* book combines sound health advice (limited sodium intake) with trendy ideas (use of bran and raw butter). Basically, the regimen is a low-calorie fruit diet based on the theory that protein and carbohydrate digestive enzymes cannot work together. The Beverly Hills Diet involves eating proteins with proteins, eating fats and carbohydrates only with other fats, and eating carbohydrates and fruits alone.

HAZARDS

An article in the *Journal of the American Medical Association* states that there is no scientific evidence to support this diet's claims. Some physicians have cautioned that the Beverly Hills Diet has the potential of causing such side effects as diarrhea, gout, kidney stones, heart problems, and strokes.

B.F.I. POWDER. See *First-Aid Skin Ointments and Antiseptics*.

BHT and BHA

BHT and BHA are man-made substances used as preservatives to prevent or delay fats, oils, and fat-containing foods from becoming rancid and developing objectionable tastes and odors. The shelf life of such foods as vegetable oils, potato chips, baked goods, and breakfast cereals is extended by using these additives.

HAZARDS

Extremely large doses of BHT and BHA have caused considerable enlargement of livers in laboratory animals. This condition was accompanied by marked increases of microsomal enzymes. Evidence suggests that these enzymes can play a part in increasing the vulnerability of tissues to cancer-causing and other toxic substances. BHA and BHT may also stimulate the activity of steroid enzymes that may affect the functioning of steroid hormones, with adverse effects on reproduction. In contrast to these concerns, other data indicate that BHT and BHA reduced the occurrence of certain tumors and that they do not have an adverse effect on reproduction.

PRECAUTIONS

Further investigation is needed to resolve the uncertainties about BHT and BHA. It may be prudent to avoid foods containing these additives until these studies are complete.

BIG O TIRES. *See Uniroyal Tires.*

BICYCLES *(See also Mini-Bikes)*

INJURIES

In 1980, 514,000 were reported.

HAZARDS

The major causes of injuries are:

• Loss of control occurring because of difficulty in braking; riding too large a bike; riding double on banana seats, or on rear fenders, handlebars, or the horizontal top tube of a man's bike; stunting and striking a rut, bump, or obstacle.

• Mechanical and structural problems including brake failure; wobbling or disengagement of the wheel or steering mechanism; difficulty in shifting gears, chain slippage, pedals falling off; and breakage of spokes.

• Entanglement of feet, hands, or clothing in the bicycle.

• Foot slipping from the pedal.

- Collision with a car or another bicycle.

FEDERAL STANDARDS

In 1976, the CPSC set standards for new bicycles to include requirements such as reliable brakes, protective chain guards, pedals with treads, strong forks and frames, reflectors on the front, rear, sides and pedals, and no sharp edges or protrusions, among others. Sidewalk bicycles with a seat height of 22 inches or more must have footbrakes. Those with a lower seat height must carry the label "No Brakes" and cannot have a free-wheeling coasting feature.

PRECAUTIONS

Consumers should not purchase a used bicycle with sharp points and edges, with protruding bolts that could scrape or tear clothing, or with gear controls or other protruding attachments mounted on the top tube of a man's bicycle. Also, buyers should check the headlights and brakes on all bicycles before purchasing.

HAZARDOUS MODELS

In 1981, Yamaha International Corporation began recalling approximately 30,000 Viscount 10-speed bicycles because of potential fatigue fracture of the forks. Fracture of the fork may occur unexpectedly and cause loss of control or separation of the front wheel from the bicycle with a possibility of injury. Models GPM, PRC, and PRT are the only Viscount bicycles involved.

In November 1981, Consumers Union rated the following bikes as having safety-related problems.

- Gold Crest Lenox 3633 and 3634, Columbia Commuter 1633 and 1634, and Ward's Omega catalog numbers 80167 and 81167 handled poorly.

- Sears Free Spirit catalog numbers 47402 and 47401 and Murray Sands 1-6541 had poor brakes.

- AMF Nimble J-1613, Murray Sands 1-6440 and 1-6541 had poor quality bearings, which made for unstable handling.

In November 1982, Consumers Union rated the following motocross bikes as having safety-related problems.

- The Murray X-20 Team Murray 2-5432, Huffy Pro Thunder BMX 20402, Murray Team Murray BMX 2-5646, J.C. Penney Dirt Tracker II 0966, Ward's BMX 34 Open Road catalog number 80691, AMF Avenger Motocross EX221 K9221, Columbia Formula 16 BMX 2316, and Huffy Thunder BMX 36 20362 handled poorly.

- The Raleigh R-10 Tuff BMF, Schwinn B43 Scrambler, Ross 142-25 THX, Sears Free Spirit BMX FS500 catalog number 45987, and Huffy Pro Thunder BMX 20402 had poor wet braking.

BIRTH CONTROL DEVICES. See *Contraceptive Sponge; Dalkon Shield; Oral Contraceptives.*

BLACK FLAG LIQUID ANT AND ROACH KILLER. See *Insecticides, Household.*

BLACK FLAG PROFESSIONAL POWER ANT AND ROACH KILLER. See *Insecticides, Household.*

BLACK FLAG SOLID INSECT KILLER. See *Insecticides, Household.*

BLACK FLAG SPECIAL CITY FORMULA. See *Insecticides, Household.*

BLACK LEAF ANT TRAPS. See *Insecticides, Household.*

BLACK LIGHTS (*See also Fluorescent Lights; Television Sets*)

HAZARDS

Ultraviolet (UV) radiation is emitted by black lights, broken or unshielded mercury vapor lamps, and fluorescent lights. They can cause sunburn, snow blindness, and skin cancer.

Black lights—and to a limited extent fluorescent lights—emit near-ultraviolet (NUV) rays as well. NUV rays cause the lens of the eye to fluoresce, resulting in blurred vision, headaches, and feelings of tiredness and discomfort. Long-term effects can include cataract formation and retarded cell growth.

The FDA has expressed great concern over black-light radiation, but no manufacturers' standards have yet been set. UV radiation should be especially avoided by glaucoma patients. Amber sunglasses best absorb dangerous UV frequencies.

Sunlamps produce little visible radiation, but skin and retinal burns result when users exceed recommended exposure limits or fail to cover their eyes.

There are no absolute guarantees for the safe radiation levels emitted from TV sets, whether black and white or color. Although significant improvements in TV designs in recent years have reduced the likelihood of exposure, sets operating improperly represent a hazard.

BLEACH. *See Bleachers; Chlorine Bleach.*

BLEACHERS *(See also Cleaning Agents)*

INJURIES
In 1980, 13,000.

HAZARDS
Most laundry boosters have eye and skin irritants. Biz, Axion, Amway, Magic, Purex, Dynamo, Era, and Wisk are especially strong.

PRECAUTIONS
Wear rubber gloves when using these laundry boosters, especially if you have open cuts or a rash. Also, keep them away from children since they are harmful if swallowed. Finally, if using an aerosol spray, be careful not to expose the spray to a flame since the bleach is flammable.

BLENDERS

INJURIES
In 1980, 8,000 involved blenders, mixers, or food processors.

HAZARDS
Injuries include lacerations caused by contact of moving parts with hands, and burns or shock caused by overheating.

PRECAUTIONS

In purchasing a blender, look for one in which the jar is screwed to the collar in the same direction that the blades rotate or has the blades contained within the jar.

BLOOD PRESSURE MEDICATIONS. *See Drug and Food Interactions.*

BLUE BIRD WONDERLODGE MOTOR HOMES

1966–1972 MODELS

The seat belts for the driver and passenger were anchored to the floor with incorrect bolts and no reinforcing washer. As a result, the belts may not properly restrain the occupants.

BMW BAVARIA

1977 MODEL

Power-operated windows may contain defect, allowing activation of windows when ignition is off.

BMW MOTORCYCLES

1973 R75-5 MODELS

The bolts used to fasten the flywheel may not have been properly tightened. As a result, these bolts could break under normal usage causing immediate loss of power.

1977 R60-7, R75-7, R100-S, R100-7, R100-RS MODELS

Some of the gears were not hardened properly causing the gear teeth to break under normal usage. This could cause the transmission to seize. Some of the fuel filler cap relief pressure valves may not function properly, allowing pressure to build up in the fuel tank. If this occurs, gas overflow could create a fire hazard.

BMW 320i

1977 MODEL
Wiring-harness bolt may be insufficiently tightened, threatening electrical breakdown. If spring breaks, accelerator system may not return to idle speed. Fuel vapor bubbles may form, causing stalling. Accident-avoidance ability is poor to fair. Poor traction on ice and snow. Fuel plumbing is vulnerable in a crash. Damper sleeves may deform, causing high idle speed.

1978 MODEL
Fuel vapor bubbles may form, causing stalling. Tires may be defective. Wiring-harness bolt may be insufficiently tightened, which could cause failure of the electrical system. Poor traction in ice and snow. Damper sleeves may deform, causing high idle speed.

1979 MODEL
Fuel pump may be defective, possibly causing engine to stall. Poor traction in ice and snow. Damper sleeves may deform, causing high idle speed.

1982 MODEL
Traction and directional stability are poor on slippery surfaces.

1983 MODEL
Traction and directional stability are poor on slippery surfaces.

BMW 528E

1982 MODEL
Ice may build up around throttle plate in cold weather, preventing throttle from closing fully. Bolts supporting rear differential may have been overtorqued, possibly causing bolts to fall out and difficult steering and handling.

1983 MODEL
Bolt supporting rear differential may have been overtorqued, possibly causing bolts to fall out and difficult steering and handling. The four studs and self-locking nuts connecting the upper and lower steering column shaft to a flexible coupling may have been insufficiently torqued, threatening a loss of steering.

BMW 530i

1978 MODEL
Original tires may be defective.

BMW 533i

1983 MODEL
The four studs and self-locking nuts connecting the upper and lower steering column shaft to a flexible coupling may have been insufficiently torqued, threatening a loss of steering.

BMW 633CSi

1983 MODEL
The four studs and self-locking nuts connecting the upper and lower steering column shaft to a flexible coupling may have been insufficiently torqued, threatening a loss of steering.

BOISE CASCADE TRAILER

1971 MODEL
The elector magnets in the electric brakes may be defective, causing one or more of the brakes to fail.

BOISE CASCADE ARISTOCRAT MINILINER

1971, 1972 MODELS
Flame furnace under bed may not have proper ventilation, causing a heat buildup that could set the bed on fire.

BOLOGNA. *See Bone Meal; Food Colors, Artificial; Nitrites and Nitrosamines.*

BONE MEAL *(See also Lead)*

Bone meal is used primarily as a calcium and/or phosphorous supplement. Bone-meal supplements are composed of finely crushed, processed bone, and are packaged in powder, capsule, tablet, or wafer form.

HAZARDS

All bone-meal products contain lead because of the diet of the cattle or horses from which the bone is taken. The animal's bone tissue retains lead, which is then passed on to the person consuming the bone-meal product. Another source of calcium is dolomite, a mineral deposit. Dolomite can also contain lead and should be avoided by the populations at risk. Lead is absorbed more efficiently by children than by adults, and when consumed in excess, can produce central nervous system damage, anemia, and abdominal pains, as well as learning disabilities. In large quantities it can cause death.

PRECAUTIONS

The FDA has warned that infants, young children, and pregnant or nursing mothers should avoid ingesting bone meal in products such as hot dogs and luncheon meat because they often contain substantial amounts of lead.

BONINE. *See Nausea Medications.*

BOOKCASES. *See Pressed-Wood Products.*

BORIC ACID

Boric acid and sodium borate are widely used as preservatives, antiseptics, pH adjusters, water softeners, and stabilizers in cosmetic preparations ranging from talcum powder to hair products and skin creams. Although they are banned as direct food additives, they come in contact with foods as indirect additives because they are used extensively as adhesives and coatings for food packages. Boric acid and sodium borate are also used as insecticides to control cockroaches, ants, and flies, and in the manufacturing of numerous consumer products ranging from carpets, lumber, porcelain, latex paint, starch, fertilizer, to antifreeze.

HAZARD

Boric acid and sodium borate can be toxic if absorbed through the skin. Although there is little or no absorption of these chemicals through normal skin, absorption through damaged skin has been well documented. In the 1950s numerous cases of fatal poisonings were reported when boric acid was used as a talc for infants with moderate-to-severe diaper rash.

PRECAUTIONS

According to the FDA figures, boric acid and sodium borate are used in over 300 cosmetic skin-cleansing and skin-care products. Although the amount of the chemical in these preparations is small, care should be taken not to use them on damaged or irritated skin. Anyone with kidney damage or disease should avoid using products containing boric acid or sodium borate. Even the small doses in cosmetics absorbed through damaged skin can be a problem for small children or persons with kidney disorders. The European Economic Community requires a warning on its cosmetic and talcum labels that products containing these chemicals should not be used on children under three years of age.

BOTTLED WATER. *See Water Contaminants.*

BOTTLES

INJURIES

In 1974, 32,000 involved carbonated beverage bottles.

HAZARDS

- Explosion of bottles, which propel glass fragments at great speeds and distances. Some bottles may explode spontaneously by themselves or after ordinary handling, while others explode after being jostled or dropped.

- Propulsion of bottle caps because of internal pressure while the bottles are being opened.

- Breakage from falling while holding or dropping a bottle.

- Contact with already broken glass.

PRECAUTIONS

There seems to be an increased danger of breakage and injury with nonreturnable bottles, which are usually made with thinner glass than returnable bottles. Also, carbonated-beverage bottles larger than 16 ounces may involve more accidents than smaller bottles.

To reduce the chances of injury, do not buy bottles in wet or damaged cartons; look for bottles with plastic protective covering or coating; and buy commodities in returnable bottles whenever possible.

When using these bottles, point the cap away from your face and body when opening and be careful when opening a bottle that is warm or has been jostled. Wrap the bottle in a towel to help contain flying glass in case the bottle explodes.

BOTULISM *(See also Botulism, Infant; Canning, Home)*

HAZARDS

Food-borne botulism occurs when spores of bacteria are not killed by sufficient heat treatment in canning and the food item becomes toxic. Botulism is easiest to diagnose when an outbreak involves a large number of people, but most often it appears in only one or two persons at a time. This poses a difficult diagnostic task for the physician, but it is essential that the illness be identified quickly so appropriate therapy can be started. Symptoms of food-borne botulism include: nausea vomiting, abdominal cramps and diarrhea, dry mouth, paralysis, constipation, and weakness. Often there is no fever, unless an infection develops. The incubation period of all types of human botulism can vary from a few hours to 8 days, but 18 to 36 hours is usual.

PRECAUTION

In home canning, care should be taken to properly sterilize and heat jars and food.

BOTULISM, INFANT *(See also Botulism)*

Although most infants, older children, and adults regularly consume *Clostridium botulinum* spores found in house dust (especially in and under beds), soil, honey, syrup, and a variety of raw and cooked foods including fresh fruits and vegetables, the intestinal tracts of some young infants are susceptible to infant botulism from these spores. Symptoms include constipation, opthalmoplegia, sucking problems, irritability, lethargy, and "floppy-baby syndrome." Often, however, the symptoms are not recognized by parents, and the babies are not taken to a doctor until the illness is advanced.

PRECAUTIONS

Because of the risk of infant botulism, the FDA warns against the use of such nutritionally nonessential foods as honey and corn syrup in infant feeding. Commercially sterilized low-acid canned foods, including infant formula, do not contain the *C. botulinum* spore or toxin.

BOWS AND ARROWS. See *Toy Projectiles; Toys, General.*

BREVICON. See *Oral Contraceptives.*

BRIM DECAFFEINATED COFFEE. See *Coffee, Decaffeinated.*

BRIOSCHI. See *Antacid Medications.*

BROILERS. See *Cooking Appliances, Small Electric.*

BROMINATED VEGETABLE OIL (BVO)

Brominated vegetable oil is used in citrus soft drinks and fruit-flavored beverages. This additive provides a cloudy appearance, enabling drinks to resemble natural fruit juices. BVO also stabilizes the flavoring oils in these beverages.

HAZARDS

Toxicology studies during the past decade raised questions about the safety of this additive. BVO has been deleted from the

FDA's list of Generally Regarded as Safe Substances. Evidence to date has demonstrated that BVO can cause harm to vital organs when administered to laboratory animals. It is generally thought that the technological benefits of BVO do not justify potential health risks, so it would be prudent to avoid products containing it.

BROMO SELTZER. *See Antacid Medications.*

BRONCHO-TUSSIN. *See Cough Medications.*

BROUGHAM TRAILER MINIHOME

1969–1973 MODELS
Manufacturer failed to install stop, tail, and backup lights that met the requirements of the law. In addition, the head and side marker lights are illegal, resulting in the vehicle being more difficult to see at night.

BROWNLOW BOAT TRAILER

1976 MODEL
The manufacturer failed to install the proper lighting as required by law and failed to attach the certification labels that tell the consumer about load capacity.

BSA MOTORCYCLES

1969, 1970 MODELS
B25 models—The front brake cable may loop and become trapped on the front mudguard causing the brakes to lock.

BUBBLE BATHS

HAZARDS
Bubble baths and sudsy bath oils, particularly when used in hot

water, strip away natural skin oils and increase the chance of rashes in cold weather. These bath products also affect the mucous membrane of the urinary tract, which may lead to infection. A common ingredient in liquid bubble baths is TEA-lauryl sulfate. TEA is an amine that can become contaminated and form a nitrosamine that has been proved to cause cancer in laboratory animals.

In 1980, the FDA proposed a warning label on bath products, but after industry pressure and a change of administration in Washington, the idea was dropped.

PRECAUTIONS

All bathers, especially children, should avoid prolonged exposure to bubble bath products. Products containing TEA or TEA combinations should be avoided.

BUICK CENTURY

1978 MODEL

Front-wheel bearing may fail, possibly causing loss of control. Rear-wheel mounting bolts may be defective, causing wheel to come off. Rear-axle shaft may be defective, causing separation of tire and wheel assembly. Fan blade may separate. Gauges are hard to read; switches confusing.

1979 MODEL

Incorrect lubricant may cause rear-brake stoplights to fail and cruise control to remain engaged. In wagon, defogger backlights may have defect that shatters glass. Lower rear-control arm bolts may fracture, causing loss of control.

1980 MODEL

In wagon, defogger backlights may have defect that shatters glass. Lower rear-control arm bolts may fracture, causing loss of control.

1981 MODEL

Sharp corner and latch of trunk lid are hazardous to tall persons. Lower rear-control arm bolts may fracture, causing loss of control. Gauges are difficult to read during the day.

1982 MODEL

Fuel hose clamps may fracture, causing fuel leakage and possibly fire. Difficult to stop short without locking wheels. Daytime reflections on instrument panel.

1983 MODEL
Gauges are difficult to read because of glare.

BUICK ELECTRA

1978 MODEL
Fan blade may separate.

1979 MODEL
Incorrect lubricant may cause rear-brake stoplights to fail and cruise control to remain engaged. Front seat-belt anchorage could fail.

1981 MODEL
Brake pedal support bracket may be incorrect, possibly causing brake overheating and reduced effectiveness.

1982 MODEL
Injection pump may fail, causing throttle valve to remain open.

BUICK ESTATE WAGON

1977 MODEL
Child could become entrapped in rear side-storage compartment.

1978 MODEL
Rear-wheel mounting bolts may be defective, causing wheel to come off. Child could become entrapped in rear side-storage compartment.

1979 MODEL
Child could become entrapped in rear side-storage compartment. Gauges are hard to read.

BUICK LE SABRE

1978 MODEL
Rear-wheel mounting bolts may be defective, causing wheel to come off. Fan blade may separate.

1979 MODEL
Incorrect lubricant may cause rear-brake stoplights to fail and cruise control to remain engaged. Front seat-belt anchorage could fail.

1980 MODEL
Sun may cause glare on instrument panel.

1981 MODEL
Brake pedal support bracket may be incorrect, possibly causing brake overheating and reduced effectiveness.

1982 MODEL
Injection pump may fail, causing throttle valve to remain open.

BUICK OPEL

1977 MODEL
Driver's rear vision is restricted. Ventilation system expels fragments that could fly into driver's eyes.

1978 MODEL
Rear-wheel mounting bolts may be defective, causing wheel to come off.

BUICK REGAL

1977 MODEL
Rear-axle shaft may be defective, allowing separation of tire and wheel assembly.

1978 MODEL
Lower rear-control arm bolts may fracture, causing loss of control. Front-wheel bearing may fail, possibly causing loss of control. Rear-wheel mounting bolts may be defective, causing wheel to come off. Fan blade may separate. Gauges are hard to read, controls confusing. Open trunk lid is hazardous to tall persons.

1979 MODEL
Incorrect lubricant may cause rear-brake stoplights to fail and cruise control to remain engaged. Lower rear-control arm bolts may fracture, causing loss of control.

1980 MODEL
Lower rear-control arm bolts may fracture, causing loss of control. Understeer is considerable.

1981 MODEL
Lower rear-control arm bolts may fracture, causing loss of control.

1982 MODEL
Injection pump may fail, causing throttle valve to remain open.

1983 MODEL
Gauges are hard to read. Driver's view to right front and right rear is restricted because of the low seat cushion and wide rear roof pillar. Open trunk lid is hazardous to tall persons.

BUICK RIVIERA

1979 MODEL
Incorrect light bulbs may have been installed.

1981 MODEL
Front left upper-control arm nuts may come off, causing loss of control.

1982 MODEL
Injection pump may fail, causing throttle valve to remain open.

BUICK SKYHAWK

1978 MODEL
Rear-wheel mounting bolts may be defective, causing wheel to come off. Steering shaft coupling may be defective, causing loss of steering. Fan blade may separate.

1979 MODEL
Carburetor-fuel feed hose may rupture, causing fuel leak and possibly fire.

1982 MODEL
Fuel-hose clamps may fracture, causing fuel leakage and possibly fire.

1983 MODEL
On cars with two-liter engines, fuel system may leak at the throttle-body injection-fuel-feed connection, creating a fire hazard.

BUICK SKYLARK

1977 MODEL
Rear-axle shaft may be defective, causing loss of control. Front lap belts tend to ride up.

1978 MODEL
Rear-axle shaft may be defective, causing loss of control. Rear wheel-mounting bolts may be defective, causing wheel to come off. Fan blade may separate.

1979 MODEL
Electrical short in engine oil pressure switch may start engine when ignition is in "on" position. Engine stalls during left turns. Gauges are hard to read. Fuel filler is vulnerable to sideswipe. Driver's visibility is restricted.

1980 MODEL
Brake pipe could fail, causing loss of brake fluid and partial loss of braking. Fuel hose may be incorrectly positioned, causing fuel leakage and fire. Front suspension coil spring could be defective, causing damage to brake hose and suspension. Transmission cooler-line hoses may be defective, causing leakage of fluid and possibly fire. Steering-gear mounting plate may develop fatigue cracks, causing partial loss of steering control. Rear brakes may lock up during moderate to heavy breaking, causing the car to spin out of control.

1981 MODEL
Metal coat hooks could be dangerous in a crash. Head restraints and rear roof pillars obstruct rear view. Power-steering hose could deteriorate and leak fluid, possibly causing fire. Engine-to-body ground cable may be defective, causing headlights to dim. Rear brakes may lock up during moderate to heavy breaking, causing the car to spin out of control.

1982 MODEL
Fuel-hose clamps may fracture, causing fuel leakage and possibly fire. Clutch may rub against brake pipe, causing loss of brake fluid and partial braking action.

BULB REFLECTORS *(See also Home Electrical System)*

HAZARDOUS MODEL

In October 1980, Consumers Union reported that Spencer Gifts was recalling a product it distributed, the Amazing Energy-Saving Bulb Reflector, which is capable of delivering a lethal shock.

BURGLAR ALARMS

In August 1981, Consumers Union tested 26 relatively simple security systems that a handyman could install. Although these systems would not protect against professional thieves, they may well scare off the novice burglar.

There are two types of systems: perimeter protectors and motion detectors. Perimeter protectors detect burglars in the act of entering, whereas most motion detectors detect motion only within the house. Perimeter systems can provide protection even if you are home; they do not restrict the movement of people or pets. But they will not stop an intruder who climbs through a broken window. Perimeter protector installation can be difficult; most motion detectors are easy to set up and move around. But they do inhibit your movement, and they are more likely to produce nuisance alarms.

Consumers Union noted the following disadvantages in the perimeter systems.

• Two wired systems—Radio Shack 49474 and Universal BA 330—have antitamper switches that work only when the system is armed and have no provision for a second horn or bell.

• Three wireless systems—Fyrnetics 1719, Nutone S2255, and Sears catalog number 57051—lack provision for simple overall testing.

• One wireless system, the Sears, does not have available a panic-button transmitter.

Consumers Union noted the following disadvantages in motion detectors.

• The Emhart Vectalert 160 alarm sounds for only 12 seconds.

• The Colorado IP.16, General Electric Zonar, Master 2606, and Statitrol 1152A lack sensitivity control.

- The Master 2606 and Sears catalog number 57151 have a poorly designed sensitivity control.

- The General Electric Zonar, Sears, and Universal Ultrar U.101 are more sensitive than most to moving hot air.

- The General Electric, Heathkit GD49, Honeywell Defender II CK200A, Master 2606, and Sears lack test light or sound.

BUTIBEL. *See Belladonna Alkaloids and Barbiturates.*

BUTISERPAZIDE. *See Reserpine.*

BUTTER. *See Casein; Food Colors, Artificial.*

C

CADILLAC BROUGHAM

1977 MODEL
　　Lighted materials could ignite front ashtray.

1978 MODEL
　　Lighted materials could ignite front ashtray. Accelerator pedal could stick.

CADILLAC CIMARRON

1982 MODEL
　　Fuel-hose clamps may fracture, causing fuel leakage and possibly fire. On cars with two-liter engines, fuel system may leak at the throttle-body injection-fuel-feed connection, creating a fire hazard.

CADILLAC DEVILLE

1977 MODEL
　　Lighted materials could ignite front ashtray. Accelerator pedal could stick.

1978 MODEL
Lighted materials could ignite front ashtray. Accelerator pedal could stick. Windshield washer bottle may crack and allow washer fluid to drain out.

1979 MODEL
Front seat-belt anchorage could fail.

1982 MODEL
Injection pump may fail, causing throttle valve to remain open.

CADILLAC ELDORADO

1977 MODEL
Fuel connections may leak because of hose deterioration, possibly causing fire. When transmission level is shifted to park, parking pawl may not engage and car could roll freely.

1978 MODEL
Fuel connections may leak because of hose deterioration, possibly causing fire. Rear-wheel mounting bolts may be defective, causing wheel to come off.

1979 MODEL
Rear view is obstructed by wide rear roof pillars. Sharp corners of open trunk lid are hazardous to tall persons.

1980 MODEL
Transmission selector may indicate neutral or park when transmission is in gear.

1981 MODEL
Front-left upper-control-arm nuts may come off, causing loss of control.

1982 MODEL
Injection pump may fail, causing throttle valve to remain open.

CADILLAC FLEETWOOD

1977 MODEL
Fuel connections may leak because of hose deterioration, possibly

causing fire.

1978 MODEL
Fuel connections may leak because of hose deterioration, possibly causing fire. Rear-wheel mounting bolts may be defective, causing wheels to come off.

1979 MODEL
Front seat-belt anchorage could fail.

CADILLAC SEVILLE

1977 MODEL
Fuel connections may leak because of hose deterioration, possibly causing fire.

1978 MODEL
Fuel connections may leak because of hose deterioration, possibly causing fire. Consoles do not have latching mechanisms to ensure that lids stay closed in collisions. Rear-wheel mounting bolts may be defective, causing wheel to come off. Gas may leak from deteriorated hose connection, possibly causing fire.

1980 MODEL
Transmission selector may be in neutral or park when transmission is in gear.

1981 MODEL
Front-left upper-control-arm nuts may come off, causing loss of control.

1982 MODEL
Injection pump may fail, causing throttle to remain open.

CAFFEINE

Caffeine is a substance found in coffee, tea, cocoa, chocolate, and the kola nut extract used in cola beverages. Sometimes caffeine is added to soft drinks, drugs, and foods.

HAZARDS

The health effects of caffeine are controversial. It has been linked to birth defects, breast disease, and pancreatic cancer, but research studies have thus far been inconclusive and offer conflicting results.

There is no dispute about caffeine's effect as a central nervous system stimulant. For some people, caffeine acts like an amphetamine, pepping them up temporarily. Too much caffeine may cause such symptoms as headache, nervousness, insomnia, irritability, or rapid heart rate. However, the effects of caffeine are extremely variable. Some persons are more sensitive than others: One person may get jumpy and nervous after drinking only one cup of coffee while another may consume several cups without exhibiting any ill effects. Generally, most people can consume up to 200 milligrams of caffeine daily without apparent harm.

A single cup of coffee may contain 75 to 155 milligrams of caffeine, with drip coffee in the higher range and percolated coffee in the lower. Instant or freeze dried coffee has 66 milligrams. The caffeine content of tea also varies, depending on brewing time. A one-minute brew of a bag of black tea has 28 milligrams while a three-minute brew has 44 milligrams. Milk chocolate, the most popular type of chocolate, contains about 6 milligrams per ounce. Nonprescription stimulant drugs such as No Doz or Vivarin contain about 200 milligrams per dose. Some over-the-counter pain relievers that have caffeine are Midol, Anacin, and Excedrin. They contain from 65 to 130 milligrams of caffeine. Plain aspirin and Tylenol contain no caffeine. If you are concerned about the caffeine content of a drug, read the label carefully. Manufacturers are required to list caffeine as an added ingredient if it composes more than 0.2 percent of the product.

It has still not been determined if caffeine causes birth defects, lumps in the breast, or cancer. There have been many studies on the relationship between caffeine and birth defects, but most have been performed on animals. In an FDA study of rats in 1980, high levels of caffeine caused digital deformities in some of the animals. Low levels, the equivalent of just two cups a day for humans, delayed skeletal development. Scientists cannot agree on the relevance of animal studies for humans. Rats metabolize coffee differently than people do, and scientists do not know whether people are more or less sensitive to caffeine than are animals. Recent studies using humans as subjects report no relationship between coffee consumption and birth defects, but FDA investigators believe those studies did not follow a large enough group to detect abnormalities. They believe a more appropriate study would be to identify babies born with birth defects linked to caffeine and evaluate the mothers' exposure to caffeine.

Based on present information, the FDA advises pregnant women to avoid food and drugs containing caffeine. This advice is based on the fact that caffeine is a stimulant and has druglike effects, as well as information gained from animal and human studies. In general, all drugs should be avoided during pregnancy, and since caffeine has druglike effects, it should be avoided as well.

There is less evidence available on the relationship between fibrocystic breast disease and caffeine. A 1979 Ohio State University report stated that symptoms of fibrocystic breast disease were reduced in a significant percentage of patients who eliminated caffeine and all other methylxanthines from their diet. Methylxanthines are compounds that include caffeine, theobromine, and theophylline. Theobromine is found in chocolate, tea, certain soft drinks, some muscle relaxants, and diuretics. Theophylline is found in tea and some bronchial and asthma remedies. A later study at the University of California that attempted to replicate the original study produced less clear-cut results.

The relationship between coffee and pancreatic cancer was first reported in a 1981 study in the *New England Journal of Medicine*, but it is unclear what constituent of coffee may be linked to cancer. Since the researchers were not attempting to link caffeine and pancreatic cancer, they stated more studies would be needed to establish a link. Other studies have not supported the conclusions found in the initial study.

Even though there is not conclusive evidence linking caffeine with these several health hazards, the FDA plans to remove caffeine from the Generally Regarded as Safe groups of substances and place it in an interim category while testing continues. Also, the FDA has recently made caffeine an optional, instead of mandatory, ingredient in cola drinks.

Until more is known about the effect of caffeine on our health, it would be wise to limit intake. Pregnant women should avoid caffeine altogether, as should people with high blood pressure.

CALCULATORS. *See Batteries, Button.*

CALDECORT. *See First-Aid Skin Ointments and Antiseptics.*

CALIFFO DELUX MOPED

1978, 1979, 1980 MODELS
Certain vehicles were equipped with mirrors that were inadequate for safe use.

CAMBRIDGE DIET, THE *(See also Diets)*

HAZARDS
The Cambridge Diet involves drinking three times a day a flavored powder mixed with water. The total daily caloric intake is 330 calories. Nutrition experts agree that diets of fewer than 800 calories a day should not be attempted without frequent medical supervision. Total dependence on as few as 330 calories per day for an extended period of time may result in serious adverse effects that require hospitalization. In fact, the FDA has investigated several cases associated with the Cambridge Diet in which acute illness developed, requiring hospitalization.

The FDA issued a public warning in 1977 concerning the hazards of low-calorie protein diets, such as the Cambridge Diet. The FDA proposed in 1982 that all such diets carry required warning labels concerning the potential health hazards associated with their use, although that regulation was never put into effect. The U.S. Postal Service brought suit against the distributors of the Cambridge Diet in the late 1970s, alleging their advertising claims to be fraudulent. In resolving the suit, the distributors agreed to remove claims of exaggerated weight loss and to include warning statements in their advertisements.

PRECAUTION
The use of the Cambridge Diet is not recommended.

CAMERA EQUIPMENT

HAZARDOUS MODEL
In May 1981, Consumers Union reported that J.C. Penney recalled 1,000 strobe flash attachments (catalog number 918-8137) for a potential shock hazard.

CAMERAS. *See Batteries, Button; Camera Equipment.*

CAMP COOKING AND HEATING EQUIPMENT

INJURIES

In 1974, 3,000 involved portable gas cooking stoves/grills, portable gasoline heating equipment; gasoline, kerosene, and propane lanterns and lamps; and portable grills.

HAZARDS

The majority of injuries are caused by portable gasoline cooking stoves/grills. Three-quarters of all injuries are burns; about one-fifth lacerations, contusions, or abrasions; 3 percent are poisonings. Burns are caused by the following: explosions, often when campers are trying to light equipment; ignition of gasoline vapors; ignition of a flammable fabric tent; and burns from contact with an outdoor gas grill or a kerosene heater.

Poisonings are usually caused by carbon monoxide emitted by lanterns, though they can also result from the use of barbecue grills indoors.

HAZARDOUS MODELS

In October 1979, the King Seeley Thermos Company recalled thousands of valves on portable gas grills. Some of the grills may have faulty valves that leak propane gas. The grills have been sold under the Structo brand name: model numbers 7962, 7963, 7964, 7965, and 7966.

CANDY. *See Food Colors, Artificial.*

CANDY, LICORICE. *See Drug and Food Interactions.*

CANNING, HOME *(See also Botulism)*

HAZARDS

Injuries occur during home canning. The major causes are:

- Exploding, cracking, or imploding jars, often caused during hot pack processes by lids that are too tight to allow escape of steam, by defects in the glass, or by sudden changes of temperature.

- Splashing of scalding water resulting from careless handling or tipping of canning boilers.

- Cuts or lacerations from inattentive or careless use of peelers, grinders, and juicers during food preparation.

Illness may result from consuming products of canning in which canning lids were not sealed properly, causing contamination and spoilage, or from failure to follow complete, correct food preparation and canning procedures.

PRECAUTIONS

In selecting equipment, the following precautions should be taken: examine canning lids for nicks, irregular surfaces, dents, and rust; check jars for cracks, chips, or bubbles; check the mouths of jars for uneven edges; and make certain the equipment comes with clear, detailed instructions.

In canning food, use only lids, seals, and jars manufactured specifically for home canning; do not reuse sealing lids; do not pour cold water over hot canning jars or set hot jars on cold surfaces; and test the seal according to instructions.

CAN OPENERS. *See Kitchen Appliances, Small.*

CARBON MONOXIDE *(See also Air Pollution, Indoor)*

HAZARDS

Each year, hundreds of people die of carbon monoxide poisoning. Thousands of others suffer dizziness, nausea, and convulsions. This gas is especially dangerous because it cannot be seen, tasted, or smelled. Many related accidents are caused by the following.

- Lack of ventilation in a car, either because the engine is running in a closed space like a garage or because the exhaust leaks into the passenger compartment.

- Using a charcoal grill for cooking or heating in houses, camping trailers, or mobile homes.

- Unvented space heaters, including gas ranges.

- Heating equipment with loose or cracked vent pipes and heat exchangers.

When a generous supply of fresh air is available, and the fuel is burning properly, there is little danger of carbon monoxide poisoning. But operating an internal combustion engine or improperly adjusted fuel-burning appliance in a closed area without fresh air can be fatal.

PRECAUTIONS
To help prevent carbon monoxide poisoning, watch for the symptoms. Mild cases produce sleepiness, headache dizziness, blurred vision, irritability, and inability to concentrate. Severe cases cause nausea and vomiting, shortness of breath, convulsions, unconsciousness, and death. The best first aid for poisoning is fresh air. For other precautions, refer to specific products that produce carbon monoxide.

CARDINAL BOAT TRAILER

1972 MODEL
The design of the axle may cause the locking nuts to fail to provide locking action. This could result in the lock nuts coming off.

CAR INTERIORS. *See Nitrites and Nitrosamines.*

CAROID AND BILE SALTS. *See Laxatives.*

CARPETS. *See Floors.*

CARRAGEENAN AND FURCELLERAN

These emulsifiers and stabilizers are derived from red seaweed and are used to keep mixtures from separating. They are also used as gelling agents and thickeners. Both additives are useful with milk protein, enabling the suspension of cocoa or chocolate in milk without settling or thickening.

HAZARDS

Short-term studies on pregnant mice and rats indicate that carrageenan and furcelleran may cause chromosomal changes and should be avoided during pregnancy until additional studies are conducted.

CARRIERS, BABY BACK. *See Baby Back Carriers.*

CARRIAGES, BABY. *See Baby Walkers, E-Z Roller Baby Stroller.*

CARS. *See Automobile Safety Defects; Automobile Transmissions; individual models.*

CASEIN

The major protein found in milk and milk products, casein can be converted to ammonium, calcium, magnesium, potassium, and sodium caseinates, which are used for various purposes in food. They act as binders and extenders in imitation sausage, soups, and stews; they serve as clarifying agents in wine; or they can be used in frozen desserts. Calcium caseinate also qualifies as a dietary supplement.

HAZARDS/PRECAUTIONS

Casein is a natural protein and does not represent a health hazard, except to persons who are allergic to it. But during the process used to extract casein and convert it to caseinate, a by-product can be formed that has been found to cause kidney damage in laboratory animals. Until further research demonstrates the safety of these products, it is advisable to limit consumption of food containing caseinates.

CATSUP. *See Salt.*

CAULKING COMPOUNDS

INJURIES
There were 13,000 injuries involving household chemicals, including caulking compounds, in 1980.

HAZARDS
Caulking compounds may contain strong irritants, and the vapors may damage the lungs.

HAZARDOUS MODELS
Avoid eye or skin contact with the following products: Dow Corning and Dow Corning Paintable, M.D. Silicone, G.E. Window & Door, G.E. Silicone, and Sherwin Williams. Avoid breathing vapors from the following: Sears Polyurethane, Dap Flexiseal C.W. 100. And avoid both types of contact with the following: Grocel Water Seal 100, UGL AC-88, Goodyear Plio-Seam, and Contech Easy Caulk.

CAUSTICS. *See Oven Cleaners; Toilet Bowl Cleaners.*

CEILINGS AND WALLS *(See also Asbestos)*

HAZARDS/PRECAUTIONS
Some ceilings and drywalls installed between 1945 and 1978 contain a crumbly asbestos material that was sprayed or troweled on. As with all asbestos-containing products, these ceilings and walls should be left alone if they are in good condition. If repair or removal is necessary, use a trained asbestos contractor and follow the general guidelines for handling asbestos products (*see* Asbestos). Once asbestos fibers are disturbed, they float in the air indefinitely and do not disperse. Inhaling asbestos fibers can cause cancer and other respiratory illness.

Walls and ceilings may also contain insulation made with asbestos, which can become exposed during renovations. Again, a trained asbestos contractor should be employed.

CEMENT. *See Air Pollution, Indoor; Asbestos.*

CENTRAX. *See Benzodiazepines.*

CEPACOL. *See Throat Medications.*

CEPASTAT. *See Throat Medications.*

CEREAL. *See Aspartame; Food Colors, Artificial; Nitrites and Nitrosamines.*

CHAIN SAWS

INJURIES
In 1981, there were 64,000 injuries and approximately 50 deaths.

HAZARDS
The most serious hazard is "kickback," the sudden and potentially violent rearward or upward movement caused by interference with the movement of the chain. This can occur if the saw chain at the tip of the guide bar touches any object, such as a nearby branch or log. It can also occur when the wood being cut closes in and pinches the saw chain at the top of the guide bar in the cut.

Other hazards include burns and electrocutions; loss of control either after completion of a cut or during one-hand use; and bouncing or skating on the surface of the wood being cut, sometimes cutting the hand of the operator or a helper.

PRECAUTIONS
Chain saws should be purchased with the following features:

- Good balance and comfort;

- Hand grips that are not near each other;

- A hand guard in front of the forward handle to prevent the left hand from slipping onto the chain;

- Anti-kickback features like guide bars and safety tips covering the chain as it passes around the nose of the guide bar;

- Chain brakes;

- Trigger or throttle lockouts and chain catchers; and

- Bumper spikes on the front of the engine or motor housing.

HAZARDOUS MODELS

In 1981 approximately 8,000 Electramac electric chain saws made by the Black and Decker Manufacturing Company and imported from Canada by the McCulloch Corporation (model numbers EM10, EM12A, and EM14A) were voluntarily recalled. These saws may spontaneously restart because of a failure in the on/off switch.

CHAIRS *(See also Folding Chairs; High Chairs)*

INJURIES

In 1980, 210,000 were reported.

HAZARDS

Thousands of these injuries, and some deaths, are caused by fires associated with upholstered furniture. Most of these injuries and deaths result not from burns, but from the inhalation of smoke and toxic gases in these fires. The most common cause of these fires is ignition by cigarettes. Once ignited, upholstered furniture may smolder for hours, producing smoke and toxic gases that may be fatal. With flaming ignition sources such as lighters or candles, the burning may be more rapid.

Most other injuries are fractures, contusions, or lacerations resulting from hitting, tripping over, or falling from chairs or sofas. Abnormal protuberances are especially hazardous. In addition, fingers and other extremities can be pinched or lacerated in the movement of rocking chairs or reclining chairs.

PRECAUTIONS

The content of the fabric is a major factor in the resistance of upholstery to smoldering cigarettes. In general, fabrics made of vinyl, wool, or those containing 50 percent or more polyolefin, nylon, acrylic, or polyester, or acetate fibers can resist smoldering cigarettes better than other fibers. The resistance of cotton, rayon, or linen fabrics depends on the weight of the fabric. The heavier the weight, the more likely it will burn.

CHEESE. *See Casein; Drug and Food Interactions; Food Colors, Artificial.*

CHEVROLET BIG 10

1978 MODEL
Rear-wheel mounting bolts may be defective, causing wheel to come off.

1979 MODEL
Front lap belts tend to ride up.

CHEVROLET CAMARO

1978 MODEL
Rear-wheel mounting bolts may be defective, causing wheel to come off. Seat belt is uncomfortable.

1979 MODEL
Incorrect lubricant may cause rear-brake stoplights to fail and cruise control to remain engaged.

1980 MODEL
Possibility of defective nut in steering mechanism may reduce control. Brakes may malfunction.

1981 MODEL
Rear seat belts may not lock in crash.

1982 MODEL
Gasoline may spurt from filler neck of fuel tank, possibly causing fire. Rear seat-belt anchorages may pull through the underbody in an accident. Handling is unsteady and unpredictable in hard turns.

Brakes may lock in stopping. Driver's view of instrument panel is restricted. Driver's view to the rear is restricted.

CHEVROLET CAPRICE

1977 MODEL
Child could become entrapped in rear side-storage compartment of wagon. Driver's side view is somewhat obstructed by wide center roof pillars.

1978 MODEL
Rear-wheel mounting bolts may be defective, causing wheel to come off. Front-seat adjustor assembly may be defective. Child could become entrapped in rear side-storage compartment of wagon.

1979 MODEL
Incorrect lubricant may cause rear-brake stoplights to fail and cruise control to remain engaged. Child could become entrapped in rear side-storage compartment of wagon. Front seat-belt anchorage could fail. Open trunk latch is hazardous to tall persons.

1980 MODEL
Front-brake pipe could wear through with loss of brake fluid and front brakes.

1981 model
Brake-pedal support bracket may be incorrect, possibly causing brake overheating and reduced effectiveness.

1982 MODEL
Injection pump may fail, causing throttle valve to remain open.

CHEVROLET CAVALIER

1982 MODEL
Fuel-hose clamps may fracture, causing fuel leakage and possibly fire. Head restraints restrict rear view of short drivers. Gauges are hard to read in daytime because of reflections.

1983 MODEL
On cars with two-liter engines, fuel system may leak at the throt-

tle-body injection-fuel-feed connection, creating a fire hazard. Gauges are hard to read in daytime because of reflections.

CHEVROLET CELEBRITY

1982 MODEL
Fuel-hose clamps may fracture, causing fuel leakage and possibly fire.

1983 MODEL
Power brakes somewhat difficult to modulate, and one of front wheels may lock in stopping.

CHEVROLET CHEVELLE

1978 MODEL
Rear-wheel mounting bolts may be defective, causing wheel to come off.

CHEVROLET CHEVETTE

1977 MODEL
Front seat belts tend to ride up. Fuel filler is vulnerable in side swipe. Open rear hatch is hazardous.

1978 MODEL
Rear-wheel mounting bolts may be defective, causing wheel to come off. Fuel tank and filler are vulnerable in a crash. Open rear hatch is hazardous. In the 4-door model, center roof pillar restricts visibility.

1980 MODEL
Rear seat belts may not lock in a crash. Carburetor fuel inlet housing plug may come out, causing fuel leakage and possibly a fire. Sharp corners on trunk lid are hazardous to tall persons.

1981 MODEL
Rear seat belts may not lock in a crash. Carburetor fuel inlet housing plug may come out, causing fuel leakage and possibly a fire. Sharp corners and latch may be dangerous when trunk lid is open. Response is sluggish in abrupt maneuvers. In hard, high-speed turns, control is difficult.

1982 MODEL
Carburetor fuel inlet housing plug may come out, causing fuel leakage and possibly a fire.

CHEVROLET CITATION

1980 MODEL
Brake pipe could fail, causing loss of brake fluid and partial loss of braking. Fuel hose could be incorrectly positioned, causing fuel leakage and possibly a fire. Rear control arm could be defective, damaging brake or fuel lines. Front suspension-coil spring could be defective, causing damage to brake hose and suspension. Transmission cooler-line hoses may be defective, causing leakage of fluid and possibly fire. Steering-gear mounting plate may develop fatigue cracks, causing partial loss of steering control. Rear hatch has sharp corners. Rear wheels have a tendency to lock up in moderate to hard breaking situations, sending the car out of control.

1981 MODEL
Engine-to-body ground cable may be defective, causing the headlights to dim. Metal coat hooks could be dangerous in a crash. Head restraints and wide center pillars obstruct driver's view. Power steering hose could deteriorate and leak fluid, possibly causing fire. Rear wheels have a tendency to lock up in moderate to hard breaking situations, sending the car out of control.

1982 MODEL
Fuel-hose clamps may fracture, causing fuel leakage and possibly fire. Clutch may rub against brake pipe, causing loss of brake fluid and partial loss of braking action.

CHEVROLET CORVETTE

1977 MODEL
Sunlight reflecting off horn button cap and lock lever may temporarily blind driver.

1978 MODEL
Rear-wheel mounting bolts may be defective, causing wheel to come off.

CHEVROLET EL CAMINO

1978 MODEL
Front-wheel bearing may fail, possibly causing loss of control. Lower-rear control-arm bolts may fracture, causing loss of control.

1979, 1980, 1981 MODELS
Lower-rear control-arm bolts may fracture, causing loss of control.

CHEVROLET IMPALA

1977 MODEL
Child could become entrapped in rear side-storage compartment of wagon.

1978 MODEL
Rear-wheel mounting bolts may be defective, causing wheel to come off. Front-seat adjuster assemblies may be defective. Child could become entrapped in rear side-storage compartment of wagon.

1979 MODEL
Incorrect lubricant may cause rear-brake stoplights to fail and cruise control to remain engaged. Child could become entrapped in rear side-storage compartment of wagon. Front seat-belt anchorage could fail. Occupant protection was rated as poor in a U.S. Department of Transportation 35-mph crash test of the 4-door model.

1980 MODEL
Front-brake pipe could wear through with loss of brake fluid and front brakes.

1981 MODEL
Brake-pedal support bracket may be incorrect, possibly causing brake overheating and reduced effectiveness.

1982 MODEL
Injection pump may fail, causing throttle valve to remain open. Occupant protection was rated poor in a U.S. Department of Transportation 35-mph crash test of a 4-door model.

CHEVROLET LUV

1978 MODEL
Rear-wheel mounting bolts may be defective, causing wheel to come off.

1979 MODEL
Tailgate clamps could injure fingers.

CHEVROLET MALIBU

1977 MODEL
Rear-axle shaft may be defective, causing separation of tire and wheel assembly.

1978 MODEL
Rear-wheel cylinder retainer may be improperly installed, causing loss of brake fluid and braking action. Rear-wheel mounting bolts may be defective, causing wheel to come off. Head restraints may be incorrect, possibly injuring rear-seat passengers in accident. Front-wheel bearing may fail, possibly causing loss of control. Lower-rear control-arm bolts may fracture, causing loss of control. Fan blade may separate. In low position, head restraints provide little protection for other than short persons. Rear metal coat hooks could be hazardous.

1979 MODEL
In wagon, defogger backlights may have defect that shatters glass. Lower control-arm bolts may fracture, causing loss of control.

1980 MODEL
In wagon, defogger backlights may have defect that shatters glass. Lower-rear control-arm bolts may fracture, causing loss of control.

1981 MODEL
Lower-rear control-arm bolts may fracture, causing loss of control.

1982 MODEL
Injection pump may fail, causing throttle valve to remain open.

CHEVROLET MONTE CARLO

1977 MODEL
Rear-axle shaft may be defective, allowing separation of tire and wheel assembly.

1978 MODEL
Lower-rear control-arm bolts may fracture, causing loss of control. Rear-wheel cylinder retainer may be improperly installed, causing loss of brake fluid and braking action. Rear-wheel mounting bolts may be defective, causing wheel to come off. Head restraints may be incorrect, possibly injuring rear-seat passengers in accident. Front-wheel bearing may fail, possibly causing loss of control. Fan blade may separate. In low position, head restraints only protect short persons. Open trunk lid is hazardous to tall persons.

1979 MODEL
Lower-rear control-arm bolts may fracture, causing loss of control. Uniroyal tires may fail. Incorrect lubricant may cause rear-brake stoplights to fail and cruise control to remain engaged.

1980 MODEL
Lower-rear control-arm bolts may fracture, causing loss of control. Power brakes may lock up.

1981 MODEL
Lower-rear control-arm bolts may fracture, causing loss of control.

1982 MODEL
Injection pump may fail, causing throttle valve to remain open.

CHEVROLET MONZA

1977 MODEL
Engine-mount bracket may contact steering mechanism, impeding steering.

1978 MODEL
Rear-wheel mounting bolts may be defective, causing wheel to come off. Steering-shaft coupling may be defective, causing loss of steering. Engine mount may contact steering mechanism, causing difficult steering.

1979 MODEL
Carburetor fuel-feed hose may rupture, causing fuel leak and possibly fire.

1980 MODEL
Rear seat belts may not lock in a crash. Rear end may fishtail.

CHEVROLET NOVA

1977 MODEL
Rear-axle shaft may be defective, causing loss of control.

1978 MODEL
Rear-axle shaft may be defective, causing loss of control. Rear-wheel mounting bolts may be defective, causing wheel to come off.

CHEVROLET SPORTVAN

1977 MODEL
Gauges are sometimes hard to read because of reflections.

1978 MODEL
Rear-wheel mounting bolts may be defective, causing wheel to come off.

CHEVROLET STATION WAGON

1978 MODEL
Rear-wheel mounting bolts may be defective, causing wheel to come off.

1979 MODEL
Rear storage compartment may trap children.

CHEVROLET VEGA

1978 MODEL
Rear-wheel mounting bolts may be defective, causing wheel to come off.

CHEWING GUM. *See Aspartame.*

CHILDREN'S ASPIRIN. *See Aspirin.*

CHILDREN'S SLEEPWEAR *(See also Clothing)*

HAZARDS

Each year, many children are burned while wearing sleepwear. Also, there are still children's clothes on the market that contain TRIS, a flame-retardant that causes skin cancer.

FEDERAL STANDARDS

The CPSC requires that all children's sleepwear through size 14, as well as yard goods intended or promoted for use in this sleepwear, be made from flame-resistant material. These materials must stop burning after the fire source is removed. Sleepwear is not required to carry a label indicating compliance with the standards, but must carry a label if the flame resistant is affected by laundering. Today, virtually all U.S. manufacturers meet the standard by using inherently flame-resistant fibers or through fabric construction, not by adding flame-retardant chemicals to the fabric. Daywear for infants and children, including diapers and underwear, are not required to meet the sleepwear standards even though children may sleep in this clothing.

In the late 1970s, the CPSC banned the use of TRIS in children's clothes.

PRECAUTIONS

To reduce the risk of purchasing children's clothes treated with TRIS, the CPSC urges consumers who are purchasing children's sleepwear to avoid purchasing any garments made from acetate, triacetate, or blends of these two materials. It also recommends not purchasing any children's sleepwear with labels removed.

HAZARDOUS MODELS

In 1981, the CPSC has filed administrative complaints against the following manufacturers and retailers of children's sleepwear that was treated with TRIS, which is believed to cause cancer:

- A&B Wiper Supply Company, which made available approximately 150,000 children's pajamas and nightgowns through Value Stores, a factory retail outlet, and four flea markets in Philadelphia, and through Family Dollar stores in nine southeastern states.

- John R. Lyman Company, which purchased an estimated 75,000 children's sleepwear garments. Roughly 25,000 of these garments were sold to consumers through the Lyman Mill Outlet in Chicopee, Massachusetts, between November 1979 and February 1981.

- S. Schwab Company, which sold about 1,200 children's garments to a Kansas retail outlet called The Store and shipped about 480 garments to an Oklahoma outlet known as Name Brands, Inc.

- Hollywood Needlecraft, Inc., which sold children's garments to Ely Finer Company, which then sold some of these to the Marshall's Department Store in Granada Hills, a Los Angeles suburb.

- Retailers—Odd Lot Trading and Bunnie Towne in New York City, Bargain Center Store and Swap-O-Rama in Chicago, United Factory Outlet in Detroit, Dollar General Store in Indianapolis, Thunderbird Drive-in in southern Florida, and Dollar General Stores in Atlanta.

As of May 1983, the Schwab and Hollywood Needlecraft complaints were still pending; the others have been settled.

CHILD SAFETY SEATS

Child safety seats provide essential protection to children riding in cars. All seats manufactured after January 1, 1981, must be certified as passing a prescribed and rigorous crash test. Consumers must make certain they are purchasing a safety seat with this certification. Possibly, there are still a few seats on the market that do not provide adequate protection to child riders.

Consumers must also make certain, however, that the certified seat they are purchasing is installed properly, is convenient enough so that it is used, and is sufficiently comfortable so that children will stay put. An article in the April 1982 issue of *Consumer Reports* provides a detailed evaluation of the restraining system, accommodations, and installation of 27 different child safety seats including infant seats, toddler seats, booster seats, and convertible seats.

PRECAUTIONS
- If the seat comes with a top leather strap, the strap must be properly affixed to the car in order for the seat to be effective.

- Over 40 states have passed child safety seat laws requiring that children by adequately protected in automobiles.

HAZARDS
Automobiles are the single largest killer of children after the first weeks of life.

CHIMNEYS *(See also Fireplaces)*

INJURIES
In 1980, 16,000 involved chimneys or fireplaces.

HAZARDS
Some of these injuries were burns, smoke inhalation, and related problems caused by fires. Major causes of fires in metal chimneys include installation too close to combustibles, use of a chimney unsuited for the wood-burning appliance, a creosote fire in the chimney, and chimney failure, primarily a buckling of the inner liner. Major causes of fires in masonry chimneys are improper construction or deterioration of the chimney and overheating from a creosote fire.
Chimney connectors that are improperly installed or used as the entire venting apparatus for a stove also contributed to fires, and these tended to cause more damage than other chimney-related fires.

CHINESE FOOD. *See Monosodium Glutamate.*

CHIPBOARD. *See Pressed-Wood Products.*

CHLORASEPTIC LOZENGES AND SPRAY. *See Throat Medications.*

CHLORDANE

Chlordane, a chlorinated hydrocarbon, is an insecticide that has been banned by the EPA, except for use against termites and fire ants.

HAZARDS

Recently, exposure to chlordane gas in homes treated with the chemical for termite control has become an important concern. Many homes have been measured at levels above the 0.5-microgram safety level established by the National Academy of Sciences. Many of the residents of these homes have developed symptoms of chlordane poisoning, including nausea, headaches, and irritability. Although no conclusive connection has been established linking these symptoms to chlordane exposure, the U.S. Air Force is now ordering the relocation of all personnel living in Air Force homes with levels at or above 0.5 microgram of chlordane gas.

The health effects of acute chlordane poisoning include nausea, vomiting, twitching, trembling, convulsions, coma, and death. Exposure can occur through inhalation or ingestion of the chemical. As a chronic hazard, chlordane is a proven carcinogen in laboratory animals.

PRECAUTIONS

The two most significant factors affecting chlordane gas levels in homes appears to be application techniques and home design. Chlordane should never be directly applied inside the home or be allowed to vent into the home heating system. The National Pest Control Association has recommended that chlordane also not be used on homes with plenums (crawl spaces used for convection in conjunction with heating ducts).

Alternatives to the use of chlordane should be investigated whenever possible. If chlordane is used, a licensed pest-control applicator should do the work, not an inexperienced homeowner.

CHLORINE. *See Water Contaminants.*

CHLORINE BLEACH. *(See also Bleachers)*

Household bleach is classified as a pesticide under the Federal Hazardous Substances Act because of its disinfectant claims. The normal concentration of chlorine in household products is 5 percent.

HAZARDS

The National Poison Prevention Center reports few instances of bleach being ingested, but mixing chlorine bleach with ammonia or vinegar can generate toxic fumes that can be fatal.

PRECAUTIONS

Care should be taken not to mix other cleaning fluids with high concentrations of chlorine bleach.

CHLOR-TRIMETON. *See Allergy Medications.*

CHOCOLATE MILK. *See Caffeine; Carrageenan and Furcelleran.*

CHOPPERS, FOOD. *See Kitchen Appliances, Small.*

CHRISTMAS DECORATIONS *(See also Christmas Lights; Christmas Trees)*

INJURIES

In 1973, 3,500 involved Christmas ornaments, lights, trees, and other decorations.

HAZARDS

Broken ornaments often cause cuts, and small ornaments or ornament parts can be easily swallowed by young children. In addition, many streamers and tinsel are combustible. All Christmas greenery, if dried out, can burst into flames when a lighted match, cigarette, or candle is nearby. Candles should not be placed amid dry greenery or near flammable furnishings such as curtains. In addition, certain popular Christmas greenery, such as mistletoe, yew, holly berries, are toxic if ingested by small children.

PRECAUTIONS

Be sure tinsel, silver and gold icicles, cotton and sparkle batting are all fireproof. Fireproof homemade decorations with a preservative of 1 cup ammonium sulfate, 1/2 cup boric acid, 2 tablespoons borax, and 8 tablespoons of 3 percent hydrogen peroxide. Spray this over the tree and pour some into the cup at the base of the tree. Also spray other decorations. These chemicals, however, are harmful if ingested, so keep out of reach of children.

CHRISTMAS LIGHTS *(See also Christmas Decorations)*

INJURIES
In 1973, 3,500 involved Christmas lights, trees, trimming, ornaments, and other decorations.

HAZARDS/PRECAUTIONS
The most serious hazard is fires caused by the following.

- Frayed wires, loose connections, broken or cracked branches, or curtains and other flammable materials.

- Overloading of extension cords. No more than three sets of lights should be placed on any one cord.

- Heated bulbs that come in contact with the needles or branches or curtains and other flammable materials.

- Wax candles placed on a tree. These should never be lit.

Also, hairlike wires exposed between the bulb holder and socket can cause shocks. These wires should be trimmed so they are not exposed. Shocks can also be caused by contacts that slide out of the bulb socket.

CHRISTMAS TREES *(See also Christmas Decorations)*

INJURIES
In 1973, 3,500 involved Christmas trees, lighting, trimming, ornaments, and other decorations.

HAZARDS
The most serious hazard in natural trees is fires caused by dryness. Metal trees present no fire hazard in themselves, but they can be the cause of electric shocks if electric lights are attached to the tree.

PRECAUTIONS
Trees will be less likely to dry out if they are kept outside as long

as possible, then once inside, their butt end is cut off higher and the base is kept in water. It is also important to keep trees away from heat sources. Dispose of them as soon as needles begin to fall off in large quantities.

CHRYSLER CORDOBA

1977 MODEL
Carburetor pump seal may be defective, causing stalling.

1978 MODEL
Tilt steering column may be defective.

1980 MODEL
Exhaust gas may enter passenger compartment. Throttle may not return to closed position when accelerator pedal is released. Original tires may be defective.

1981 MODEL
Solenoid may malfunction, causing stalling. Automatic-speed control switch may stick in "resume" position.

CHRYSLER E-CLASS

1983 MODEL
The hydraulic brake tubing routed to the left rear wheel may have been distorted during assembly, allowing interference between the tube and an exhaust-system hanger bolt, and a partial loss of braking.

CHRYSLER IMPERIAL

1981 MODEL
Automatic speed-control switch may stick in "resume" position.

CHRYSLER LE BARON

1977 MODEL
Brakes may fail because of brake-tube corrosion or brake-hose cracking.

1978 MODEL
Brakes may fail because of brake-tube corrosion or brake-hose cracking. Tilt steering column may be defective. Secondary catch system may be defective, possibly causing hood to fly open.

1979 MODEL
Fuel tank is not well protected. Response is sluggish in avoidance maneuvers. Occupant protection of the 2-door model was rated poor in a U.S. Department of Transportation 35-mph crash test. Stalling is chronic. Radial tires may fail.

1980 MODEL
Brake hose may abrade and fail, causing fire. The occupant protection of the 2-door model was rated poor in a U.S. Department of Transportation 35-mph crash test.

1981 MODEL
Solenoid may malfunction. Automatic-speed control switch may stick in "resume" position. Fuel filler is vulnerable in crash. Trunk latch could be hazardous when lid open.

1982 MODEL
Ball joint may separate from knuckle, causing loss of control. Responded sluggishly in abrupt maneuvers. View of instrument panel restricted for tall drivers. Sharp corners and sharp latch on open trunk lid are hazardous. Tinted band and rear-view mirror restrict the view of tall drivers. Wide rear roof pillars restrict the rear view of the driver.

1982 CONVERTIBLE MODEL
Occupant protection was rated poor in a U.S. Department of Transportation 35-mph crash test.

1983 MODEL
The hydraulic brake tubing routed to the left rear wheel may have been distorted during assembly, allowing interference between the tube and an exhaust system hanger bolt, and a partial loss of braking. Interference between the hydraulic tube and the rear-park brake cable may cause tube failure and partial loss of braking.

CHRYSLER MOTOR HOME

1970 M-300 CHASSIS MODEL
The master cylinder push rod end may come loose from the master

cylinder. This would result in complete loss of brakes.

1970 M-375 CHASSIS MODEL
Manufacturer may have misrouted brake lines that resulted in abrasion damage to the tubes. This could result in total brake failure.

1976, 1977 M3 AND M4 CHASSIS MODELS
Bolts in the front disc brakes may loosen. These loose bolts can interfere with the disc brakes, causing the wheels to lock up.

CHRYSLER NEWPORT

1981 MODEL
Solenoid may malfunction, causing stalling. Automatic-speed control switch may stick in "resume" position.

CHRYSLER NEW YORKER

1981 MODEL
Solenoid may malfunction, causing stalling. Automatic-speed control switch may stick in "resume" position.

CHRYSLER TOWN & COUNTRY

1982 MODEL
Ball joint may separate from knuckle, causing loss of control.

CIGARETTE LIGHTERS. *See Lighters.*

CIGARETTES *(See also Air Pollution, Indoor; Carbon Monoxide; Formaldehyde; Nitrites and Nitrosamines; Pregnancy and Drugs)*

HAZARDS
Smoking is not only linked to cancer and heart disease, but researchers have now found that cigarette smoke contains low-level

radiation and the radiation alone could account for roughly half of all cases of lung cancer. According to Dr. Joseph R. DiFranza of the University of Massachusetts, a person smoking one and a half packs of cigarettes a day for a year will get enough radiation on the bifurcation areas of the lungs to equal 300 chest x-rays.

Cigarette smoking causes cancer, heart disease, bronchial ailments, and several different allergies for the smoker. Secondhand smoke is also harmful to a nonsmoker and increases their risk of developing these diseases as well. Young children raised in smoke-filled homes are more apt to develop bronchitis or pneumonia early in life. Victims of heart and lung disease or of allergies are likely to suffer if exposed to tobacco smoke. A study published by the *New England Journal of Medicine* concludes that healthy workers suffered lung damage when exposed on the job to tobacco smoke for 20 years or more. Some of their lungs' tiny air tubes and sacs were scarred and their performance on breathing tests was impaired. Working in a smoke-filled environment seemed to have the same adverse effect as smoking one to ten cigarettes a day.

Inhaling the smoke from surrounding cigarettes—passive smoking—can also cause infants to develop food aversions. Researchers first observed this phenomenon in mice, which ordinarily craved sweetened water but rejected it after being exposed to cigarette smoke in concentrations that nonsmokers often involuntarily inhale. Infants are very sensitive to smoke because their physiologic protective mechanisms are still immature, and nicotine may concentrate more and stay longer in their bodies. Even very small doses of nicotine can nauseate infants, who may then associate nausea with the foods they consumed in a smoky atmosphere.

CIMATTI MOTORCYCLE

1975 MODEL
The certification labels contained erroneous weight information and failed to meet the requirements of federal law.

CIMETIDINE

HAZARDS
This prescription drug is used to treat duodenal ulcers and prevent their recurrence. The most common side effects of the medica-

tion include diarrhea, rash, dizziness, and muscle pain. In some cases, cimetidine can also cause serious blood disorders.

PRECAUTIONS

Let your doctor know if you are taking aspirin, arthritis drugs, anticoagulants, tranquilizers, anticonvulsants, Inderal, Lopressor, or Marax before beginning your treatment with cimetidine.

WARNING

Cimetidine can occasionally cause serious blood disorders. Call your doctor immediately if you suffer from tiredness, weakness, pale appearance, increased occurrence of infection, fever, sore throat, and easy bruising or bleeding. A few cases of kidney and liver disease have also been reported as a result of using this drug.

BRAND NAME: Tagamet

CIRCUIT BREAKERS *(See also Home Electrical System; Lamps)*

HAZARDOUS MODELS

In 1981, Reliance Electric announced that its Federal Pacific Electric Company would replace or modify several models of its molded case circuit breakers that can fail under certain conditions. There is a possible defect in the two-pole 220-volt breakers that allows them to trip open at relatively low overcurrent conditions. This offer applied to some 700,000 circuit breakers made from 1973 to 1979.

CIRCUIT INTERRUPTERS. *See Home Electrical System; Lamps.*

CITIZEN BAND ANTENNAS. *See Antennas.*

CITRATE OF MAGNESIA. *See Laxatives.*

CITRUS FRUITS. See *Drug and Food Interactions; Food Colors, Artificial.*

CLAMP LIGHTS. See *Work Lights.*

CLEANING AGENTS *(See also Bleachers; Drain Cleaners; Oven Cleaners; Soaps; Solvents; Toilet Bowl Cleaners; Upholstery Cleaners)*

HAZARDS
Cleaning agents contain a variety of hazardous chemicals.

- Lye (potassium hydroxide, sodium hydroxide) in oven and drain cleaners.

- Ammonia in oven, drain, and window cleaners, and wax removers.

- Sulfuric or hydrochloric acid in commercial grain and toilet cleaners.

- Phosphoric acid in many denture and metal cleaners, and polishes.

- Sodium tripolyphosphate in coffeepot cleaners.

- Sodium phosphatein in scouring powders.

- Sodium silicate and sodium metasilicate in dishwashing detergent.

- Sodium hypochlorite and calcium hypochlorate in chloride bleach.

- Sodium perborate in oxygen bleach and denture cleaners.

- Sodium dodecylbenzene sulfonate in most detergents.

Most of these chemicals can damage skin, eyes, and lungs. It is especially important that they never be mixed because chemical reactions can produce dangerous vapors.

CLEARASIL. *See Acne Medications, Nonprescription.*

CLINICORT. *See First-Aid Skin Ointments and Antiseptics.*

CLOFIBRATE

This drug is prescribed to lower the amount of fatty substances in blood, such as cholesterol and triglycerides, and to reduce the risk of heart disease. It should be used only if diet, exercise, or other methods of treatment have not worked. The serious side effects associated with clofibrate include: gallstones, tumors, angina (chest pains), and irregular heartbeat. Ulcers may also become worse. Regular blood tests are essential when taking the medication. If you are also taking a blood thinner, your doctor may have to reduce the dosage. Let your doctor know if you ever had jaundice or liver disease before taking the drug.

Although clofibrate has helped decrease nonfatal heart attacks, it has not been successful in reducing the incidence of fatal heart attacks. There is also evidence the drug may produce cancer in humans. The drug is not recommended for most patients because of the uncertain benefits and the high risk involved. Diabetics probably do not need the drug because the medications they take to control their diabetes seem to control cholesterol and triglycerides.

Less serious side effects associated with clofibrate include: muscle aches, soreness, cramping, nausea, vomiting, diarrhea, bloating, rash, itching, hair loss, headache, dizziness, increased appetite and weight gain, decreased sexual desire, painful urination, anemia, liver problems, and the decrease in white blood cells.

| WARNING |

Do not take this drug if you are nursing or pregnant. Stop use of the drug several months before trying to become pregnant.

BRAND NAME: Atromid-S.

CLOTHING *(See also Children's Sleepwear)*

HAZARDS
Each year there are thousands of injuries and deaths from burns associated with flammable fabrics.

FEDERAL STANDARDS
In recent years the federal government has acted to ensure that some fabrics are less flammable. Standards have been set for the flammability of general wearing apparel, carpets and rugs, mattresses and mattress pads, and children's sleepwear.

PRECAUTIONS
To reduce the danger of flammable fabrics:

- Purchase flame-resistant clothing for your children.

- Keep in mind that tightly woven, heavy fabrics will ignite and burn more slowly than those that are lightweight and loosely woven, smooth-surfaced fabrics more slowly than napped fabrics, and close-knit, low-pile fabrics more slowly than fluffy high-pile fabrics.

- In laundering flame-resistant fabrics, follow the instructions on the label. Most recommend the use of phosphate-based detergents. In addition, soaps may leave a fat deposit that may render the flame retardant finishes ineffective. Finally, use fabric softeners sparingly.

HAZARDOUS MODELS
In 1981, approximately 40,000 recreational sweatshirts made in mainland China and distributed by Grace International Apparel, Inc., were recalled. These items, which are fire hazards, were distributed by several stores including Korvettes.

In August 1979, the Edgewood Chenille Company recalled thousands of women's bathrobes, jackets, shorts, and tube tops sold under the Edgewood and Wrappers labels. The garments, which are made of 100 percent cotton chenille, are highly flammable. When tested by the CPSC, 7 of 10 failed to pass the federal flammability standard for adult wearing apparel.

In October 1981, Sears, Roebuck & Company recalled approximately 160,000 men's terry-cloth bathrobes. After repeated washing and drying, the cotton fabric may burn rapidly if ignited.

COACHMAN MOTOR HOME

1974, 1975, 1976 PRESIDENT, STATESMAN, AND VIP MODELS
The supports on the gasoline tanks are inadequate and the tank

may fall off the vehicle.

1976 LEPRECHAUN, JIMMY MODELS
The LP gas tanks may fall off due to the poor design of the mounting system.

1976, 1977 TRAVEL VAN "A" AND "B" MODELS
The "bay window" on the rear side of the vehicle has the potential of being forced outward under certain stress conditions. These are most likely to occur during a sudden turn or stress maneuver. Anyone near the window may, as a result, be ejected from the vehicle.

1978, 1979 CAMPER VAN MODELS
The two-burner Premier Range, Model SU-2, may have defective burner assemblies. The defect may cause the flame to go out and, therefore, release LP gas into the camper. In addition, small holes in the burner tube may allow gas to escape.

1979 JIMMY, GREENBRIAR (19 AND 21 FEET) MODELS
The mounting of the LP gas tanks was improperly done by the manufacturer. As a result, the tanks may drop to the ground during transit.

COAL-BURNING STOVES. *See Wood- and Coal-Burning Stoves.*

COFFEE. *See Caffeine; Coffee, Decaffeinated.*

COFFEE, DECAFFEINATED

HAZARDS
Methylene chloride, a chemical commonly used to decaffeinate coffee, has been shown to cause cancer in rats and mice in a study sponsored by the National Toxicology Program. As a result of this finding, several coffee producers have switched to other decaffeinating methods.
Folger and High Point now are using ethyl acetate, which appears to be safe. Nestlé uses a patented water spray "natural process" involving "something that occurs naturally in the beans." The Premium coffee company extracts caffeine by a water process. As of late 1982, most other coffee producers still used methylene chloride.

COFFEE, FREEZE DRIED. See Caffeine; Coffee, Decaffeinated.

COFFEE GRINDERS. See Coffee-making Equipment; Cooking Appliances, Small Electric.

COFFEE, INSTANT. See Caffeine; Coffee, Decaffeinated.

COFFEE MAKERS. See Coffee-making Equipment; Cooking Appliances, Small Electric.

COFFEE-MAKING EQUIPMENT *(See also Cooking Appliances, Small Electric.)*

INJURIES
In 1980, 6,000 involved small, electric cooking appliances including coffee grinders, percolators, and makers.

HAZARDS
Specific dangers of automatic drip coffee makers include breakable glass carafes, scalding from steam spewed out, and burns from the "warmer" plate.

HAZARDOUS MODELS
In October 1980, Regal Ware, Inc. recalled approximately 6,800 electric coffee makers. The 10-cup, stainless-steel percolators were insulated with a thermoplastic material that may deteriorate and permit bare wiring to conduct electrical current through the metal parts of the coffee pot.
In 1979, Corning Glass Works voluntarily recalled virtually all Corning Ware coffee percolators because the handle and metal band may separate without warning from the white glass-ceramic pot. Corning received approximately 7,000 separation complaints including reports of roughly 1,250 injuries between 1972 and 1979.
In January 1981, Consumers Union reported that the Varco MX228 grinder runs with its cover tilted open about 1 1/4 inches, which may allow contact with spinning blades. The Chemex ECG's ground-coffee exit is large enough to expose some moving parts.

Kitchenaid KCM lacked a shield over the grinding mechanism.

In October 1982, General Electric recalled approximately 200,000 drip coffee makers. GE received more than 400 reports of overheating, countertop damage, or fires caused by a thermal fuse malfunction. The models that may be defective are:

- B1–3385–0 and B1–3382–0 with date code between 634 and 717;

- B1–3390–0 with date code between 704 and 717, and B1; or

- B2–3387–0 with date code between 618 and 822.

In September 1982, the Continental Gourmet Corporation announced it would replace defective parts on its Pronto Caffee EM–1 Espresso/Cappuccino Beverage Makers manufactured through May 1980. According to the CPSC, the coffee basket in approximately 22,000 units may be difficult to secure.

COFFEE PERCOLATORS. *See Coffee-making Equipment; Cooking Appliances, Small Electric.)*

COLA. *See Drug and Food Interactions.*

COLACE. *See Laxatives.*

COLD CREAMS. *See Skin Moisturizers and Creams.*

COLD MEDICATIONS. *See Benzodiazepines; Digoxin.*

COLEMAN CAMPING TRAILER

1975 VALLEY FORGE MODEL 980
The original McCleary tires may have tread separation at speeds over 50 mph.

1981, 1982 SUN VALLEY, REDWOOD, REDWOOD 7, COLONIAL MODELS
In some cases, the manufacturer failed to tighten the nuts that hold the axle and wheel to the frame. As a result, the leaf springs may fail or break altogether, allowing the axle to come loose.

1982 CAMPING TRAILERS AND PICKUP CAMPERS
Defective gas-line union nuts were installed, which cause the line to leak.

COLOCTYL. *See Laxatives.*

COMPOZ. *See Sleeping Aids, Nonprescription.*

COMBS. *See Hair Accessories.*

CONCRETE. *See Asbestos; Air Pollution, Indoor.*

CONTACT. *See Decongestants, Oral.*

CONTACT LENS SOLUTION. *See Germicides and Disinfectants.*

CONTACT LENSES, SOFT

HAZARDS
Soft contact lenses are not as durable and generally not as sharp in focus as hard contact lenses. Furthermore, they provide more opportunities for bacterial buildup and subsequent infection than hard contact lenses. The FDA, responsible for regulating eyewear, has received numerous consumer complaints that soft contact lenses

also lose their prescription strength quickly. Soft contacts need replacement about once every year or two, although with some brands, replacement is needed much more frequently—as often as every three or four months.

PRECAUTIONS

Consumers should ask their physicians about the life expectancy of various lenses and instructions for care of the lenses to ensure maximum longevity. Wearers should always follow carefully the instructions for care and cleaning of soft contact lenses, since proper care reduces the risk of bacterial buildup that can lead to infection. Protein buildup is also a particular problem in extended-wear lenses.

CONTAINERS. *See Baby Powder Containers; Gasoline Containers; Waste Containers*

CONTEMPO CAMPERS

1973, 1974, 1975 MODELS

The rivets used to attach the camper tops to the trucks have a tendency to crack. As a result, a heavy wind or possibly highway speeds can cause the top to lift off the vehicle.

CONTRACEPTIVE SPONGE

HAZARDS

The FDA approved the over-the-counter sale of a new contraceptive sponge in June 1983, despite a call from consumer groups for further scientific studies to determine the safety of the new device. According to one group, the contraceptive, to be marketed under the brand name Today, is dangerous because it contains polyurethane. Studies conducted in 1979 by the World Health Organization (WHO) showed a high frequency of precancerous and cancerous lesions in mice receiving daily insertions of polyurethane sponge tampons. There is concern that the sponge, when inserted into the body, will become a breeding ground for bacteria and could lead to another toxic-shock-type epidemic. Some toxicologists are also concerned that the spermicide Nonoxynol-9, which is inserted into the sponge, can be dangerous as well.

PRECAUTIONS
Until the safety of this device has been determined through further testing, it would be prudent to avoid use of the contraceptive sponge.

COOKING APPLIANCES, SMALL ELECTRIC *(See also Coffee-making Equipment; Corn Poppers; Fondue Pots; Fry Pans, Electric; Hot Plates; Kettles, Electric; Pressure Cookers; Toasters.)*

INJURIES
In 1980, 6,000 involved deep fryers, food warmers, frying pans and skillets, griddles, waffle irons, rotisseries, slow cookers, kettles, hot pots, and other countertop cooking appliances.

HAZARDS
- Electrical problems. Fire, electric shocks, and even electrocutions can be caused by a defective or worn heating element, by a short circuit in the appliance or in the electrical outlet circuit, by overheating of the appliance or overloading of the circuits. In addition, shocks can occur when a metal utensil touches the heating element, as when a knife is inserted into a toaster to free a slice of bread.

- Electrical cord hazards. Children are the principal victims of accidents associated with electrical cords on appliances. They either pull on or become entangled in long, dangling cords, overturning the appliance and its contents on themselves.

- Burns from hot surfaces. Metal surfaces, plastic handles, and temperature selection dials can become hot enough to burn someone who touches them. In some appliances, the heating element may become exposed to the touch during use.

- Instability. Instability of the appliance or of the table it rests on can lead to an upset. Not only the heated appliance, but also the hot food and/or boiling liquid can burn the victim.

- Grease. It may ignite or splatter under excessively hot temperatures.

PRECAUTIONS
In purchasing countertop cooking appliances, look for the following.

- An on–off switch.

- A thermostat that will shut off the heating element if the appliance cooks dry.

- Three-prong grounded plugs on appliance cords to prevent shocks, or at least double-insulation to help protect against shocks.

- In electric coffee pots, a short or retractable cord.

- Stability and sturdiness. On coffee or tea pots, avoid heavy handles that can shift the weight to one side. Also, look for a short pot with a base wider than a top. Finally, short legs offer more stability than tall thin ones do.

- Small spouts on pots and tops that fit securely and thus lead to less hot liquid spilled in case of an upset.

- Sharp metal edges, sharp points, and broken glass that are potential hazards.

To use these appliances safely:

- Never insert a metal utensil in a toaster or similar appliance.

- Unplug them when they are not in use.

- Do not plug two heat-producing appliances into the same circuit at the same time.

- Unplug electrical appliances before filling with water.

- Do not heat sugar-topped or filled pastries in a toaster since the sugar can gum up the toaster and cause a fire, or become hot enough to burn your hand when you remove it.

- Plug in appliances above the counter or table level.

- Use only heavy-duty extension cords on appliances.

- Make sure the heating element is covered or guarded when in use.

- Keep cooking utensils away from flammable objects such as curtains.

HAZARDOUS MODELS

In February 1982, Consumers Union reported the following potential hazards in toaster oven/broilers:

- The Broil King 135 had removable elements that do not snap snugly into their sockets, exposing the elements' core that can be electrically live even when the appliance is switched off. Also, a slot on the side panel permits the insertion of metallic objects with a possible shock hazard, and some samples may have sharp edges. It was rated conditionally acceptable.

- Some samples of the Sunbeam 20560, J.C. Penney catalog number 2727, Proctor-Silex models, Sears catalog number 6344, and Toastmaster 320 and 340 may have sharp edges.

- The Norelco T04500 and Toastmaster 320 and 340 lack carrying handles.

In February 1982, Consumers Union reported the following potential hazards in broiler ovens:

- Some samples of the Munsey BB3 and the Broil King 320 and 560 may have sharp edges.

- The Toastmaster 7009 and Broil King 560 lack carrying handles.

- The doors of the J.C. Penney catalog number 1762, Sears catalog number 6921, Toastmaster 5242, Ward's catalog numbers 45297 and 45929, and Broil King 320 and 560 are ill-fitting and may come off their hinges when opened.

In addition to the hazards listed above, the Broil King 320 and 560 had removable elements that do not snap snugly into their sockets, exposing the elements' core, which can be electrically live even when the appliance is switched off. They were rated conditionally acceptable.

COOKING UTENSILS. *See Cookware; Food Poisoning.*

COOKWARE *(See also Food Poisoning)*

INJURIES
In 1980, 25,000 involved metal or nonmetal pots and pans.

HAZARDS

Most injuries result from burns that are caused by the following conditions.

- Contents spilled, splattered, or splashed because the pan or its contents are disturbed.

- Contents like grease or oil splashed or splattered when the pan is not disturbed.

- Hot, loose, or broken handles.

- Children pulling or upsetting heated pots.

- Ignition of grease or oil.

PRECAUTIONS

Pots and pans should be positioned on a stove so that the handle does not protrude over the front edge of the stove as a temptation to a child to grasp at or does not cross another burner so that it is unintentionally heated.

COOLER CHESTS. *See Coolers.*

COOLERS

INJURIES

In 1980, 8,000 involved camping and picnic equipment including portable food or beverage coolers and sleeping bags.

HAZARDOUS MODELS

In May 1979, Consumers Union reported that the hatch lid covers on the Coleman and Igloo 80 cooler chests are difficult to open from the inside, threatening entrapment of small children.

CO-OP MARK 4 TIRES. *See Uniroyal Tires.*

CO-OP MARK 74 TIRES. *See Uniroyal Tires.*

COPPER-7. *See Intrauterine Devices.*

COPPER-T. *See Intrauterine Devices.*

CORDOVAN SUPER HIGHWAY TIRES. *See Firestone Transport Tires.*

CORDS. *See Extension Cords; Home Electrical System.*

CORICIDIN and CORICIDIN-D. *See Decongestants, Oral.*

CORN. *See Health Foods; Monosodium Glutamate.*

CORNED BEEF. *See Nitrites and Nitrosamines.*

CORN POPPERS *(See also Cooking Appliances, Small Electric)*

HAZARDS
Most injuries consist of burns resulting from contact with hot portions of the popper or from oil splattering from the product. A problem with many poppers without thermostats is that the longer they are plugged in, the hotter they get.

CORN SYRUP. *See Botulism, Infant.*

CORTAID. *See First-Aid Skin Ointment and Antiseptics.*

CORTISONE. *See Digoxin; Spironolactone with Hydrochlorothiazide; Thiazides.*

CORTISONE-5. *See First-Aid Skin Ointments and Antiseptics.*

COSMETICS. *See Boric Acid; Bubble Bath; Deodorants and Antiperspirants; Deodorants, Genital; Douches; Formaldehyde; Hair Dyes; Hair Rinses; Nail Hardeners; Nitrites and Nitrosamines; Shampoos, Regular, Baby, and Dandruff; Skin Moisturizers and Creams; Talcum Powder.*

COTTAGE CHEESE. *See Salt.*

COUGH MEDICATIONS

There are two types of cough medications: suppressants and expectorants. Neither type is as effective as many advertisements claim.

HAZARDS/PRECAUTIONS

The active ingredients in cough suppressants are either codeine or dextromethorphan. Codeine commonly causes constipation and drowsiness and can be physically and psychologically addictive if taken for a prolonged period. Overdoses of codeine can cause an inability to breathe spontaneously, so patients with lung disease should avoid codeine drugs. Dextromethorphan can cause stomach upset or drowsiness, and large doses can cause disturbances in levels of consciousness.

Expectorants are of dubious value, according to the FDA. Using a vaporizer is more helpful, as well as drinking lots of fluids. Medications added to a vaporizer are ineffective.

Many cough medications contain extra ingredients (such as antihistamines or pain and fever reducers) that do little to relieve a cough. If these medications are needed, it is better to take them separately in the most effective dosage. Liquid cough medications often contain alcohol as well. At best, the alcohol helps relieve a tickle sensation in the throat. But alcohol is a central nervous system depressant and can increase the drowsiness associated with other ingredients in the medication, such as codeine or an antihistamine. Some cough medications, such as Broncho-Tussin, Creo-Terpin and Halls, contain more than 20 percent alcohol, which is more than twice the amount found in most table wines. According to Wigder's Guide to Over-the-Counter Drugs (Los Angeles: J. P. Tarcher, 1979), medications containing a decongestant and/or an antihistamine, and as much or more alcohol than wine, include: Nyquil (25 percent), Quiet-Nite (25 percent), Romilar CF (10 percent), Trind (15 percent), Tussar-SF (12 percent), Vicks Formula 44 (10 percent), and Vicks Formula 44D (10 percent).

Because sugar is also added to many cough preparations, diabetics should carefully check the ingredient label in order to choose a sugar-free product.

COUNTERTOP OVENS. See Cooking Appliances, Small Electric.

COUNTERTOPS. See Pressed-Wood Products.

CRADLES. See Cribs.

CRAFTS. See Hobbies and Crafts.

CREO-TERPIN. See Cough Medications.

CRIBS

INJURIES

In 12 months from 1973 to 1974, 9,000 full-size and 103 portable crib-related injuries occurred. More than two-thirds of these injuries were suffered by children under two years of age.

HAZARDS

- Suffocation can occur in a mesh-sided crib with the drop side down, forming a loose pocket that the infant can roll into.
- Falls causing contusions, lacerations, or fractures resulted from a defect in the crib, usually to the unintentional release of the locking mechanism.
- Suffocation or strangulation caused by broken, loose, or missing parts of the cribs including broken or loose metal guide rods and/or support brackets, missing screws, missing slats, and detachment of side rails from cribs.
- Injuries resulting from falls against the outside of the crib.

FEDERAL STANDARDS

Federal safety regulations are in effect requiring that spaces between the slats be no more than 2 3/8 inches to prevent the head of an infant from slipping between the slats. Minimum distance between the top of the mattress and the top of the side rail has also been set to help prevent children from climbing over the rail. Finally, hazardous cutout designs in crib ends and side panels have also been eliminated by the federal standard. These regulations apply to full-size cribs manufactured after February 1974 and non-full-size cribs made after 1976. If older cribs are used, it is important to use bumper pads, securely tied in place, to prevent falls between the slats.

HAZARDOUS MODELS

In August 1979, Questor Juvenile Furniture Company voluntarily recalled plastic brackets used to support the springs on approximately 34,000 full-sized Babyline cribs. In November 1981, they recalled an additional 54,000 units. The plastic brackets may break, causing the mattress and spring to drop slightly. Only cribs with the following date codes are involved: 677, 777, 877, 977, 1077, 1277, 178, 278, 378, 478, 578, 678, 778, 878, and 978.

In February 1980, the CPSC and Bassett Furniture Industries, Inc., reached a consent agreement about Candelite and Mandalay style cribs. As a result of the design, infants can strangle if they trap their heads between a corner post and the headboard or footboard as they stand on the crib mattress. Bassett agreed to modify the cribs. Mandalay crib models 5126-505, 5621-505, 5225-505 and Candelite models 5028-505, 5028-510, 5127-505, and 5127-510 are involved.

In October 1981, Questor Juvenile Furniture Company recalled approximately 17,000 portable cribs. Infants were in danger of falling to the floor because the soft vinyl crib "basket" could become unstitched from the net sides. The recall pertains only to model 320

Kantwet Trav-L-Cribs that do not contain a date code on the reverse side of the large white "law tag" attached to the crib mattress.

In October 1982, Graco Metal Products, Inc., recalled approximately 67,000 Swyngomatic Converta Cradles. The insufficient support for the cradle's masonite bottom board may allow infants to fall out of the cradle if the board is not positioned properly during assembly by the purchaser.

The CPSC warned that more than 1,000 Starlighter non-full-size baby cribs manufactured between 1975 and 1978 by Contemporary Times, Inc., present a neck entrapment hazard. In addition, a baby may fall out of the crib and sustain injury as a result of improper crib side height. The firm has declared bankruptcy and therefore is not recalling the cribs.

CROCK POTS. *See Cooking Appliances, Small Electric.*

CURLERS. *See Hair Accessories.*

CURLING IRONS. *See Hair Accessories.*

CULTIVATORS, POWER. *See Garden Equipment, Power.*

CUSHMAN THREE WHEELERS

1971 MODEL
Parts may have been omitted in the building of the master brake cylinder. The brakes on models 898–400,401,403,404,405, and 406–7110 may fail.

CUTLERY. *See Knives.*

CYCLAMATE *(See also Sweeteners, Artificial)*

Cyclamate was widely used for 20 years before being banned in 1970 because it caused cancer in laboratory animals. Like saccharin, cyclamate was in use before legislation passed in 1958 shifted the burden of proof of safety to the manufacturers.

In 1973, Abbott Laboratories, the manufacturer of cyclamate, petitioned the FDA, claiming that post-1970 studies showed that cyclamate was safe. However, the FDA informed them that their evidence did not show "to a reasonable certainty" that cyclamate was safe for human consumption. In 1980, the FDA rejected the 1973 petition.

Abbott Laboratories petitioned the FDA again in 1982 to hear more evidence, and the agency now is considering restoring approval of the artificial sweetener.

DAIRY PRODUCTS. *See Drug and Food Interactions; Food Colors, Artificial; Salt.*

DALKON SHIELD *(See also Intrauterine Devices)*

Dalkon Shields are an intrauterine birth-control device used by more than 2.2 million women between 1970 and 1974. This IUD was removed from the market voluntarily by A.H. Robins, the manufacturer, in 1974 because of repeated reports of pregnancy-related complications, but some devices may still be in use. The FDA advises all women still using the Dalkon Shield to have it removed.

In addition to the earlier links to pregnancy-related complications as a result of using the Dalkon Shield, a new study by Baltimore's Johns Hopkins Medical Institution shows women who use the IUD are 5 to 10 times more likely to suffer pelvic inflammatory disease (PID) as women who use other IUDs.

The danger presented by the Dalkon Shield lies in the "tail string," which enables a user to check that the device is still in place and allows possible nonsurgical removal by a physician. The shield's tail string is a multifilament string that can let bacteria ascend or "wick" between the filaments into the uterus via tiny holes in the nylon sheath encasing it. The study comparing the Dalkon Shield to other IUDs shows that it is the only IUD to use the multifilament tail string.

Nearly 86 percent of wearers of the Dalkon Shield carried the device for at least three years. Scientists involved in the study say the shield's wicking problem worsens as the sheath deteriorates over a long period of time, and they recommend that women who are still using the Dalkon Shield have it removed.

DALMANE. *See Sleeping Medications, Prescription.*

DANDRUFF SHAMPOOS. *See Shampoos, Dandruff.*

DARVOCET-N. *See Propoxyphene.*

DATSUN 200

1978 MODEL
Safety belts are awkward. Driver's rear view is restricted.

1981 MODEL
Safety belts may ride up to neck and abdomen. Head restraints are hazardous in a crash.

DATSUN 210

1978 MODEL
Safety belts are poorly designed. Driver's visibility is poor through rear window. Open trunk lid is hazardous.

1979 MODEL
Front lap belts tend to ride up. Catch on open trunk lid is hazardous to tall persons. The occupant protection of the 2-door model was rated poor in a U.S. Department of Transportation 35-mph crash test.

1980 MODEL
Front head restraints are hazardous in a crash.

1981 MODEL
Brakes are hazardous.

1982 MODEL
Frequent steering corrections are needed to stay on straight course. Brakes are hazardous.

1983 MODEL
See Nissan Sentra.

DATSUN 280 (ZX)

1977–1979 MODELS
Moisture accumulation in air regulator could cause high idle in cold weather.

1980 MODEL
Rear view is obstructed by head restraints. Front view is obstructed by mirror. Open hatch lid is hazardous to tall persons. Handling can be difficult in emergency maneuvers.

DATSUN 310

1980 MODEL
Main shaft locking nut may come loose, causing problems in shifting and possibly failure of transmission. Open hatch lid can be hazardous. The occupant protection of the 310GX 2-door hatchback was rated as poor in a U.S. Department of Transportation 35-mph crash test.

1982 MODEL
Power brakes feel heavy and somewhat hard to modulate.

DATSUN 510

1978 MODEL
Seat belts tend to ride up. Driver's visibility is restricted. Open trunk lid can be hazardous.

1980 MODEL
Seat belts may not pull out of the retractor. Handling could be difficult in emergency maneuvers. Front head restraints could be hazardous in a crash. Open hatch lid is hazardous.

DATSUN 810 (MAXIMA)

1977 MODEL
Open trunk lid can be hazardous. Moisture accumulation in air regulator could cause high idle in cold weather.

1978 MODEL
Moisture accumulation in air regulator could cause high idle in cold weather.

1979 MODEL
Moisture accumulation in air regulator could cause high idle in cold weather.

1981 MODEL
Open trunk lid can be hazardous. Head restraints may be hazardous in a crash.

DAYTON SUPER EMT II TIRES. *See Firestone Transport Tires.*

DAYTON THOROBRED DUALOAD SUPER EMT TIRES. *See Firestone Transport Tires.*

DECAFFEINATED COFFEE. *See Coffee, Decaffeinated.*

DECONGESTANTS, ORAL *(See also Belladonna Alkaloids and Barbiturates; Caffeine)*

Colds are caused by viruses. Although over 100 types of cold viruses are known, they are all treated with decongestants. Your physician cannot prescribe a more potent medicine for the common cold than you can buy without a prescription. If you have a bacterial infection, your symptoms will probably be more painful and more localized than those of a virus. A sinus infection caused by bacteria should be treated with prescription antibiotics.

While usually safe if taken in the correct dosage, the side effects of oral decongestants include nervousness, insomnia, headaches, rapid heart beat, palpitations, rise in blood pressure and blood sugar. If you are being treated for overactive thyroid glands, ischemic heart disease or angina, hypertension or poorly controlled diabetes mellitus, be sure to consult your physician before using these drugs.

Oral decongestants also interact with many other medications, but because the effects are usually mild they often go unnoticed. The medications that are affected by oral decongestants include heart medications, blood pressure pills, and some antidepressants. Consult your doctor if you are on any of these medications before taking a decongestant.

When choosing a decongestant, avoid combinations that contain an antihistamine, aspirin or acetaminophen, caffeine, or belladonna. The dosage levels in combination drugs are often too low to be effective or have side effects that constitute an unnecessary risk if you do not need that particular ingredient. Antihistamines have a mild drying effect and cause drowsiness. In addition, they are totally ineffective in treating the symptoms of the common cold. Fever relievers such as aspirin and acetaminophen should be taken only when you actually have a fever, not to treat a runny nose. Caffeine does not treat any cold symptom. Belladonna dries secretions, but so does your decongestant ingredient. Belladonna alkaloids also cause urine retention in elderly males with prostate enlargement and exacerbate glaucoma.

Among the combination drug products on the market containing both antihistamine and a decongestant, and often other undesirable ingredients, are Alka-Seltzer Plus Cold Medicine, Contac, Coricidin and Coricidin-D, Dristan, Fedahist, Novahistine, Nyquil, Sinarest, Sine-off, Sinutabs, and Triaminic.

Some of these drug products are also time-release medications, which are ineffective because they do not always deliver a steady dose of medication into the bloodstream, but can either "dump" all the medication in at once or delay for hours before releasing it.

Oral decongestants containing phenylpropanolamine and phenylephrine should also be avoided as they greatly increase blood pressure and are so rapidly destroyed in the stomach and intestines that it is impossible to maintain adequate dosage levels. The recommended ingredient in oral decongestants is pseudoephedrine, a much more effective drug. Among the common oral decongestants (not containing an antihistamine) are D-Feda, Novafed, Ornex, Sinutab-II, and Sudafed.

DEEP FRYERS. *See Cooking Appliances, Small Electric.*

DE LOREAN AUTOMOBILES

1981 MODEL
Stabilizer bar or lower ball joints may detach. Throttle may stick in cold weather.

DELTA RADIAL II TIRES. *See Uniroyal Tires.*

DEMAZIN. *See Allergy Medications.*

DEMULEN. *See Oral Contraceptives.*

DENTURE CLEANERS. *See Cleaning Agents.*

DEODORANTS AND ANTIPERSPIRANTS *(See also Aerosol Containers)*

HAZARDS

Although deodorants and antiperspirants are among the most useful cosmetics, they do entail risks for users. Eight main ingredients commonly used in these products have been banned over the past decade by the FDA. A number of other ingredients have been voluntarily removed by manufacturers because too many consumer complaints were received.

The most common adverse reaction to deodorants and antiperspirants is skin irritation. Often this irritation can be severe, including skin outbreaks that require medical attention.

Most antiperspirant products are based on astringent salts such as aluminum chloride or aluminum chlorhydrate, which retard the flow of sweat. These salts are very acidic when mixed with perspiration and can cause skin irritation. Most of the antiperspirants not based on an aluminum salt contain a zirconium compound. The FDA has banned the use of zirconium compounds in aerosol products, however, because of the risk of cancer from inhaling the compound.

Deodorants that do not have an antiperspirant—or antisweat—effect do no contain either aluminum salts or zirconium compounds.

The bactericide in most of these products is triclosan. Although triclosan seems to be a low irritant, there are indications that it can cause liver damage when absorbed into the body through the skin.

Aerosol products have the most serious potential for harm and should be avoided. Most injuries related to aerosols occur when the eye is burned or injured when the product is accidentally sprayed into the eyes. Although permanent damage rarely occurs, an antiperspirant spray can cause temporary loss of vision, conjunctivitis, or much discomfort.

PRECAUTIONS

If you don't have a problem with body odor or if you do not perspire excessively, it is best to avoid the use of these products. Baking soda is a good and safe substitute.

DEODORANTS, GENITAL

HAZARDS

Skin irritation is common with use of genital deodorants. The products should be avoided, especially prior to intercourse when the product is carried into the more sensitive mucous membrane of the vagina. Males may also suffer skin problems if their partner uses a genital deodorant prior to intercourse. These irritations can be painful and may have side effects that persist for months. Urinary tract infections can also be caused in women if the urethra is narrowed, causing retention of urine within the bladder. Itching, burning, and swelling may occur. Allergic reactions may even cause large lumps to develop.

PRECAUTIONS

If you experience a disagreeable genital odor, you may have an infection and should consult a physician.

DEODORANT SOAPS. *See Soaps.*

DEODORANT TAMPONS. *See Tampons, Deodorant.*

DEPO-PROVERA. See *Medroxyprogesterone Acetate.*

DERBI MOPEDS

1977–1980 MODELS
Improperly sized mirrors were attached to many of these vehicles.

DES. See *Diethylstilbestrol.*

DESKS. See *Pressed-Wood Products.*

DESSERTS, FROZEN. See *Casein; Food Colors, Artificial.*

DESSERT TOPPINGS. See *Aspartame.*

DETERGENTS. See *Soaps; Water Contaminants.*

DEXATRIM. See *Diet Aids, Nonprescription.*

DEXEDRINE. See *Sleeping Aids, Nonprescription.*

D-FEDA. See *Decongestants, Oral.*

DIABINESE. See *Antidiabetic Agents, Oral.*

DIA-QUEL. *See Diarrhea Medications.*

DIARRHEA MEDICATIONS *(See also Digoxin)*

HAZARDS

Opium and paregoric are the only recognized effective treatments for diarrhea, but in most states these drugs are available only by prescription because of their addictive nature. Most over-the-counter diarrhea medications are ineffective. Some also contain anticholinergic ingredients that should not be used by people with glaucoma or enlarged prostate gland. They also can cause dry mouth, blurred vision, and heart palpitations. Among the anticholinergic drug products available are Donnagel, Donnagel-PG, and DIA-quel.

PRECAUTIONS

Prolonged use of diarrhea medications containing opium or paregoric should be avoided because opiates are habit-forming, and overdosage can result in sedation and even cessation of unaided breathing (respiratory depression).

DIAZEPAM. *See Benzodiazepines.*

DIESEL FUELS. *See Fuels, Liquid.*

DIETAC. *See Diet Aids, Nonprescription.*

DIET AIDS, NONPRESCRIPTION

Diet aids assist in weight loss by suppressing the appetite. They are intended to help a dieter reduce caloric intake. The active ingredient is usually phenylpropanolamine-hydrochloride (PPAH), which is similar to amphetamine. Some brands also include caffeine, which accentuates the "jitteriness" caused by the pills. Vitamins are also added to some of the products.

HAZARDS

The most common side effects of these products are nausea, anxiety, irritability, dizziness, headache, lack of coordination, heart palpitations, and high blood pressure. PPAH also has the potential to alter brain functions, and may trigger psychotic behavior, hallucinations, seizures, or even stroke. The products are the center of controversy, since their safety has not been established and their long-term effectiveness is in doubt. Most public-interest health groups warn against their use. Changing eating habits and reducing caloric intake are a much safer and more effective means of weight loss.

One study found PPAH dieters gained back 63 percent of lost weight within a year of concluding their diet compared to behavior modification dieters who regained only 17 percent of their weight loss.

In addition, 10,000 reports of PPAH poisoning were made in 1980 to the National Clearing House for the FDA's poison control centers. There have been cases of psychotic behavior, paralysis due to stroke, and child mortality, all associated with use of PPAH. It is also easy to take an overdose of PPAH without realizing it because the drug is used in certain cough, cold, and allergy remedies that a dieter may be using simultaneously with the diet aids. For young children, three diet pills may constitute a fatal overdose. Consumers of over-the-counter drugs may assume these products are harmless, but there is always the possibility that these drugs used in combination with either prescription drugs or other over-the-counter drugs can be dangerous.

The FDA allows the sale of PPAH diet aids with instructions for dosage of up to 75 milligrams a day, while it is continuing to test the effects of larger doses. The Center for Science in the Public Interest, citing the long-term ineffectiveness of the drugs and the potentially dangerous side effects, is working to have the FDA ban the over-the-counter sales of the diet aids.

PRECAUTIONS

If you are being treated for high blood pressure, depression, diabetes, or thyroid disease, do not use these products because the drugs used for the treatment of your disease react badly with them.

Do not use these diet aids if you are pregnant or may become pregnant.

BRAND NAMES: Ayds; Appedrine; Control; Dexatrim; Dietac; Hungrex; Odrinex; Prolamine.

DIETARY SUPPLEMENT. *See Casein.*

DIETHYLSTILBESTROL

HAZARDS

Diethylstilbestrol is a drug that used to be prescribed to prevent miscarriage. It was widely used in the 1950s and usage continued through the 1960s and into the early 1970s. The drug was then discovered to be ineffective for the purpose of miscarriage prevention. It was also found to increase the chance of breast cancer and other endocrine-related cancers in mothers who used it. Daughters of these mothers share the same risks as their mothers, and sons are often born with birth defects as well.

The use of diethylstilbestrol greatly heightens the risk of early cancer. The drug decreases the latency period for cancer growth by substantial amounts and increases the rate of death from breast cancer and related cancers.

Diethylstilbestrol and other estrogens were previously used as additives for cattlefeed as well as for miscarriage prevention. However, the FDA is removing these additives from the food supply.

PRECAUTIONS

Women exposed to diethylstilbestrol, as well as their children, should frequently have examinations for cancer to prevent possible future medical complications. All women who have the drug and their daughters should have frequent breast and vaginal examinations.

BRAND NAME: DES

DIETS *(See also individual plans by name)*

Although the FDA is responsible for assuring the safety of foods and their appropriate labeling, they cannot assure the same criteria for claims made in articles or books about dieting. Without any government regulation, writers can make dietary claims that appear credible, but are more often written to sell their books rather than to educate.

The FDA advises consumers to consult a physician, dietitian, or nutritionist before beginning any diet. Consumers can also educate themselves by reading nutritional texts and material available in libraries. Weight loss requires a reduction in caloric intake over a period of time. The most effective way to lose weight and to maintain the lower weight is to initiate a program of moderate exercise as well as to eat a balanced diet consisting of smaller amounts of ordinary foods. A physician should advise the dieter how safely and effectively to alter his/her diet.

The FDA has also proposed labeling on certain diet products warning that misuse may be fatal. Under the proposal, food products deriving more than 50 percent of their calories from protein and promoted for weight reduction would be required to carry the label—"*Warning:* Very low calorie protein diets (below 400 calories per day) may cause serious illness or death. *Do not use for weight reduction without medical supervision.* Not for use by infants, children, and pregnant or nursing women."

DIGITALIS HEART MEDICATIONS. *See Thiazides.*

DIGOXIN

This drug is prescribed for patients with heart problems to strengthen and regulate the heartbeat. Before taking the drug, be sure to inform your physician if you have ever had liver, kidney, or thyroid disorders. If you are taking antacids, antibiotics, cortisone-like steroid drugs, cough or cold preparations, laxatives or diarrhea drugs, quinidine or diuretics, your doctor will need to adjust your medication. Check your pulse every day while resting *before* taking digoxin. When starting treatment or changing dosage, be sure to inform your physician of any problems. There is only a small difference between helpful and harmful amounts of digoxin in your body.

Call your doctor immediately if you notice any signs of digoxin toxicity: loss of appetite, stomach ache, nausea, vomiting, diarrhea, blurry vision, seeing spots, halos, yellow vision, or weakness. Call your doctor immediately if you have a change of 20 beats or more per minute from your normal pulse. Symptoms of heart failure should also be immediately reported to your doctor: fatigue, difficulty breathing, swelling of feet or ankles, and rapid, or "galloping," heartbeats.

| WARNING |

Digoxin should never be used in weight loss. It is dangerous and may cause death. It should always be closely monitored by a physician.

BRAND NAMES: Lanoxin, Digoxin Tablets, Digoxin Ampul, SK-Digoxin Tablets.

DIGOXIN AMPUL. *See Digoxin.*

DIGOXIN TABLETS. *See Digoxin.*

DILANTIN. *See Warfarin Potassium/Sodium.*

DIMETANE. *See Allergy Medications.*

DIMETHYL SULFOXIDE

This prescription drug is approved by the FDA only for treatment of a bladder condition called chronic intestinal cystitis. Its unapproved use in the treatment of arthritis and bursitis has precipitated a storm of controversy because of the serious side effects associated with the drug and its potential for harm. Although tests are now underway to determine its effectiveness in treating sprains, strains, scleroderma, arthritis, bursitis, and joint and spinal cord injuries, public-interest health groups warn against its use because of the risks involved.

HAZARDS

Because DMSO is a by-product of the paper industry and is widely used as an industrial solvent, it is readily available. The industrial-grade dimethyl sulfoxide is not pure enough for human use, and since it is a "carrier" chemical, a dangerous substance in the mixture or even on your skin can be spread throughout your body by contact with the mixture. The most serious side effects include eye damage, vision impairment, nausea, headache, chemical irritation type burns, or skin rash. Although your physician can legally prescribe dimethyl sulfoxide for treatment of arthritis or bursitis, health groups and the Arthritis Foundation warn against such use. FDA investigations in the use of dimethyl sulfoxide for the treatment of arthritis are expected to be completed in 1983.

> WARNING

Do not use this drug without a doctor's prescription. The industrial-grade chemical is not pure enough for human use. Do not try to treat yourself with dimethyl sulfoxide or buy the chemical through the mail, from a store or any commercial source because you cannot be sure of the purity of the drug or the correct dosage.

BRAND NAME: DMSO

DINETTE SETS. *See Pressed-Wood Products.*

DIOXIN

Dioxin is a term referring to a group of 75 separate compounds. There is a wide variance in the level of toxicity among the different dioxins. The most toxic dioxin is TCDD (tetrachlorodoi-benzo-p-dioxin), which occurs as a trace contaminant in many commercial herbicides and wood preservatives, such as 2,4,5-T, Silvex and Pentaclorophenol.

HAZARDS

The acute or short-term effects of TCDD poisoning include cloracne—a painful scarring skin disorder occurring on the face, neck, and back; increased miscarriages; loss of sensation to the extremities; extreme fatigue; anorexia and depression.

Although the chronic effects of TCDD are not documented in humans, TCDD is a proven carcinogen and teratogen in laboratory animals.

In the environment, dioxins are very stable compounds when not exposed to direct sunlight. However, since their most common use is as a herbicide, they are often exposed to direct sunlight. In the food chain, dioxins are stored in the fatty tissues of organisms and consequently accumulate in foods.

At present, a ban on 2,4,5-T exists only in areas where the herbicide application corresponded with higher than normal miscarriage rates. The Environmental Protection Agency is currently reviewing 2,4,5-T and other dioxin-containing herbicides for possible regulatory action.

PRECAUTIONS

Until regulatory action is taken, it is essential to avoid use of herbicides and preservatives containing these dioxins.

DIPLOMAT TIRES. See *Uniroyal Tires.*

DISHWASHER DETERGENTS. See *Soaps.*

DISHWASHING LIQUIDS. See *Soaps.*

DISINFECTANTS. See *Germicides and Disinfectants.*

DISONATE. See *Laxatives.*

DIURETICS. See *Caffeine; Digoxin; Drug and Food Interactions.*

DIURIL. See *Thiazides.*

DMSO. See *Dimethyl Sulfoxide.*

DODGE ARIES

1981 MODEL
Brake warning lights may fail. Automatic-speed control switch may stick in "resume" position. Engine-cooling fan has no protective shroud. Side vision partially obstructed by wide center pillars in 4-door sedan and wagon. Sharp metal edge on dashboard and sharp-edged handles for rear vent windows could be hazardous.

1982 MODEL
Ball joint may separate from knuckle, causing loss of control. Sharp metal edge on dashboard.

1983 MODEL
The hydraulic brake tubing routed to the left rear wheel may have been distorted during assembly, allowing interference between the tube and an exhaust-system hanger bolt and a partial loss of braking. The hydraulic brake tube may allow interference between the tube and the rear-park brake cable, which may cause tube failure and a partial loss of braking.

DODGE ASPEN

1977 MODEL
Secondary catch system may be defective, possibly causing hood to fly open. Brakes may fail because of brake tube corrosion or brake hose cracking. Carburetor may be defective, possibly causing stalling. Catalytic converter flange may crack.

1978 MODEL
Brakes may fail because of brake tube corrosion or brake hose cracking. Tilt steering column may be defective. Secondary catch system may be defective, possibly causing hood to fly open. Front suspension may be defective, possibly causing loss of control. Catalytic converter flange may crack.

1979 MODEL
Catalytic converter flange may crack. Fuel-filler cap is vulnerable in sideswipe. Jack and lug wrench have sharp edges.

1980 MODEL
Brake hose may abrade and leak fluid, causing fire. Fuel tank is vulnerable in sideswipe. Strong spring on trunk lid could be hazardous.

DODGE CHALLENGER

1978 model
Fuel may leak near engine, causing fire.

1980 MODEL
Ashtray bulb socket may overheat and cause fire.

DODGE CHARGER

1977 MODEL
Carburetor pump seal may be defective, causing stalling.

1978 MODEL
Tilt steering column may be defective.

1982 MODEL
Sharp corners on open trunk lid could be hazardous. Fast-back styling obscures driver's rear view.

DODGE COLT

1977 MODEL
Front-brake hose assembly may be defective. Control may be difficult in emergency maneuvers. Driver's seat belt tends to ride up. Fuel tank and filler are vulnerable in a crash.

1978 MODEL
Fuel may leak near engine, causing fire.

1979 MODEL
Fuel tank and filler are vulnerable in a crash. Front seat belts tend to ride up. Open hatch latch is hazardous to tall persons.

1980 MODEL
Ashtray bulb socket may overheat and cause fire.

1982 MODEL
The occupant protection of the 4-door hatchback in a U.S. Department of Transportation 35-mph crash test was rated as poor.

DODGE CORONET

1977 MODEL
Carburetor pump seal may be defective, causing stalling.

DODGE DART

1977 MODEL
Carburetor may be defective, causing stalling.

DODGE DIPLOMAT

1977 MODEL
Brakes may fail because of brake tube corrosion or brake hose cracking. Secondary catch system may be defective, possibly causing hood to fly open.

1978 MODEL
Brakes may fail because of brake tube corrosion or brake hose cracking. Secondary catch system may be defective, possibly causing hood to fly open. Tilt steering may be defective. Fuel filler is vulnerable in side swipe.

1981 MODEL
Solenoid may malfunction, causing stalling. Automatic-speed control switch may stick in "resume" position.

DODGE MAGNUM

1978 MODEL
Handling is unpredictable during emergency maneuvers. Controls are hidden and hard to reach. Front seatback may jam. Visibility is restricted. Open trunk lid is hazardous to tall persons.

DODGE MIRADA

1980 MODEL
Exhaust gas may enter passenger compartment. Throttle may not return to closed position when accelerator pedal released.

1981 MODEL
Solenoid may malfunction, causing stalling. Automatic speed-control switch may stick in "resume" position.

DODGE MONACO

1977 MODEL
Potential damage to shift linkage bushings may cause transmission to be in a gear position other than that indicated. Carburetor pump seal may be defective, causing stalling. Accident avoidance is poor to fair. Rear view is obstructed.

1978 MODEL
Tilt steering column may be defective.

DODGE OMNI

1978 MODEL
Alternator may fail, causing loss of battery charging. Steering coupling may be oversized, possibly causing loss of control. Front suspension may be defective, possibly causing loss of control. Fuel tube may have been misrouted, possibly causing fuel leakage and fire. Lower control arm may crack, possibly causing loss of control. Hub nuts may loosen, loosening front wheel. Fuel tank may leak when full, creating a fire hazard. Fuel return hose may chafe and leak, possibly causing fire. Unpredictable and possibly dangerous handling during abrupt maneuvers. Seat belts are uncomfortable.

1979 MODEL
Fuel-line hose may fail, causing fuel leakage and fire. Torque steer pulls car to right during acceleration.

1980 MODEL
Secondary catch system may fail, causing hood to open. Ball joint may separate from arm, causing loss of control.

1981 MODEL
Automatic speed-control switch may stick in "resume" position.

1982 MODEL
Ball joint may separate from knuckle, causing loss of control.

DODGE ST. REGIS

1979 MODEL
Windshield defroster may be inadequate. Stalling is chronic.

Open trunk lid latch is hazardous. The occupant protection of the 4-door model in the U.S. Department of Transportation 35-mph crash tests was rated as poor.

1981 MODEL
Solenoid may malfunction, causing stalling. Automatic-speed control switch may stick in "resume" position.

DODGE TRUCK MOTOR HOME

1973 CHASSIS NUMBERS RM 300, 350, 400 MODELS
On motor homes with tilt-steering wheels, the electrical lines may become disconnected when the wheel is in the full-rear position. This can result in the loss of turn signals, hazard lights, and possibly disconnect the ignition that would cause the loss of power while driving or the inability to start the engine.

1976 CHASSIS NUMBER M5 MODEL
Wheels come apart at the original weld and separate from the vehicle.

1978 CHASSIS NUMBERS M3, M4, M5, M6 MODELS
The clamps on the carburetor fuel inlet hose may have been installed incorrectly. As a result, leakage can occur, causing an under the hood fire.

1979 CHASSIS NUMBERS M3, M4, M5 MODELS
These vehicles were equipped with a plastic fuel tank. The tank is not far enough away from the drive shaft and, as a result, the universal joint may penetrate the tank.

DODGE 400

1982 MODEL
Ball joint may separate from knuckle, causing loss of control.

1983 MODEL
The hydraulic brake tubing routed to the left rear wheel may have been distorted during assembly, allowing interference between the tube and an exhaust system hanger bolt, and a partial loss of braking.

The hydraulic brake tube may allow interference between the tube and the rear-park brake cable, which may cause tube failure and a partial loss of braking. Driver's view to right rear is restricted by wide rear roof pillars and partially blanked rear-door windows. Design of trunk lid is such that when open it can be hazardous.

DODGE 600

1983 MODEL

The hydraulic brake tubing routed to the left rear wheel may have been distorted during assembly, allowing interference between the tube and an exhaust system hanger bolt, and a partial loss of braking.

DOG SHAMPOO. *See Kwell Shampoo and Cream.*

DOLENE. *See Propoxyphene.*

DONNAGEL AND DONNAGEL-PG. *See Diarrhea Medications.*

DONNATAL. *See Belladonna Alkaloids and Barbiturates.*

DOORS *(See also Glass Doors and Windows)*

INJURIES

In 1980, 57,000 involved nonglass doors and panels.

HAZARDS

Most injuries are caused by a combination of human inattention and some hazardous element in the planning, design, or installation of the door such as the following.

• Poor location. Doors that open into a hallway or other frequently used locations are hazardous. So are doors opening over a flight of stairs, especially when the door swings out over the stairs. Also, doors should be planned so that two do not hit when open.

• Swinging doors, which increase the chances of collisions and may trap small children and pets.

• Improperly hung doors, which bind or stick. Not only can these cause collisions, but they also may cause falls when a door that will not open finally does release.

• Sharp edges, including worn metal weatherstripping on the edge of a door.

• Glass in doors.

• Door return devices, especially those using chains or sliding devices with springs, which may cause the door to rebound and strike the victim.

• Door stops, especially those that are rigid and attached to the door.

• Clothes hooks mounted on doors at eye level.

PRECAUTIONS
Garage doors using counter-balancing systems are safer than those using a long coil spring on each side of the door that is attached by a hook-shaped bend in the spring end. In the latter, great stress is placed on the hook, which may cause metal fatigue and failure. Sectional garage doors can crush fingers, especially when there is only one handle. Handles should be installed on several panels of the door.

DORIDEN. *See Sleeping Medications, Prescription.*

DORMIN. *See Sleeping Aids, Nonprescription.*

DOUCHES

Most physicians think routine douching is unnecessary and ill-advised for healthy women. Use of a douche as a contraceptive measure is also completely useless. Whereas little benefit is to be gained from douching, there are a number of hazards.

HAZARDS

Irritation and allergic reactions are commonly associated with douching. Douche solutions containing strong chemicals can produce "chemical vaginitis" by irritating the tissues of the vagina. Douche solutions can also irritate external tissues, producing swelling or inflammation of the vulva or a dermatitis of the inner thighs.

Since any douche is likely to be irritating if the solution is too strong, concentrations that are measured and mixed by the user may be hazardous. Some ingredients in commercial douches are also irritating because they dry out the tissues.

Certain chemical ingredients in douches are also toxic when absorbed internally in sufficient quantity. One of these ingredients, boric acid, is absorbed through the skin as well.

Regardless of what chemicals are used in douches, there is an added risk from the actual process of douching. Pelvic infection can occur if too much pressure is used and the douche fluid enters the uterus. There is, of course, a risk of infection if the douching apparatus is not clean or the douching solution is contaminated.

DOXYLAMINE AND PYRIDOXINE

HAZARDS

There is growing concern over the use of this drug product, prescribed to treat nausea and vomiting in pregnancy, because of the number of birth defects associated with its use. Despite strong pressure from many health and public-interest organizations, the FDA has refused to ban the drug, saying evidence is not yet conclusive linking the drug to birth defects. The FDA has, however, required stern warnings to be distributed to women who use the drug and has warned physicians to prescribe the drug only after all more conservative treatments have failed and only when the patients' symptoms require extreme action. An FDA advisory panel said it is concerned that Bendectin may be prescribed unnecessarily, increasing the risk to the fetus.

WARNING

In the view of a number of health and public-interest organizations, there is sufficient evidence to link this drug, prescribed during pregnancy, to birth defects in infants. It is wise to avoid the use of this drug under all circumstances.

BRAND NAME: Bendectin

DRAIN CLEANERS *(See also Cleaning Agents)*

INJURIES
In 1980, 12,000 involved drain cleaners, oven cleaners, and other caustics.

HAZARDS
Most injuries are related to the highly corrosive chemicals used in these products. These chemicals can injure the skin or eyes and can be very destructive if swallowed.

PRECAUTIONS
To prevent these injuries, in purchasing drain cleaners:

• Buy a child-resistant package if small children live in or frequently visit your home.

• Keep in mind that a granular drain cleaner is somewhat less hazardous than a liquid drain cleaner because it can be brushed off dry skin before damage results.

• Remember that flexible plastic containers can increase the chance of an injury because, when grabbed, the force of the grip could shoot a stream of the chemical out of the container.

DRAMAMINE. *See Nausea Medications.*

DRISTAN. *See Decongestants, Oral.*

DRISTAN NASAL MIST. *See Nasal Sprays and Decongestants.*

DRUG AND FOOD INTERACTIONS

Thousands of people lose the full benefit of drugs they take because they consume food or drink that inactivates the medication or slows its absorption. There are so many drugs that physicians sometimes have difficulty keeping up with the safety rules for taking them. It is important for the patient to ask the doctor and the pharmacist how each drug should be taken and what food, if any, should be avoided. While on medication, if any unusual symptom occurs after eating a particular food, be sure to inform your physician (see Table below).

DRUGS AND FOOD THAT DO NOT MIX

FOOD	INCOMPATIBLE DRUG	POSSIBLE EFFECT OF COMBINING
Fruit juices, Citrus fruits, Tomatoes, Vinegar, Cola, Pickles	Antibiotics, such as penicillin, ampicillin, and erythromycin	Decreases drug action
Dairy products, Sardines	Tetracycline	Reduces effectiveness of drug
Acidic foods such as fruit juices, citrus fruits, pickles, tomatoes, cola, or vinegar	Aspirin and aspirin combinations	Intensifies irritating effect on stomach and may result in ulcers or serious gastric bleeding
Monosodium glutamate (MSG)	Diuretics	May eliminate too much sodium from body
Brussels sprouts, cabbage, cauliflower, kale, rutabaga, mustard greens, soy beans, or turnips	Thyroid hormones	Interferes with hormones and may lead to goiter
Green leafy vegetables, asparagus, bacon, broccoli, brussels sprouts, or beef liver	Anticoagulants	Cancels blood-thinning effects

Excessive licorice (artificial licorice does not produce harmful effects)	Any drug that affects heart or blood pressure	Excessive potassium loss, which can result in fatigue; also can cause headache, high blood pressure, and even heart failure
Vitamin B_6-rich foods (wheat germ, liver, pork, or beef)	Levodopa (Larodopa), a drug for parkinsonism	Blocks drug effects
Foods containing sugar	Antidiabetics	Blocks drug action

DRUG INTERACTIONS WITH OTHER DRUGS *(See also Drug and Food Interactions; Drugs and Alcohol)*

HAZARDS
When more than one kind of prescription or nonprescription drug is being taken simultaneously, an adverse reaction may occur.

PRECAUTION
When getting a prescription, patients should tell the physician all the drugs they are taking so that the physician may determine if the new drug is incompatible with other medications being used.

DRUGS AND ALCOHOL *(See also Drug and Food Interactions; Drug Interactions with Other Drugs)*

HAZARDS
Adverse reactions occur when alcohol is combined with any of more than 100 drugs. Some of these reactions are so severe they can cause death. Less severe reactions include nausea, vomiting, headache, stomach cramps, and drowsiness.

PRECAUTIONS
Alcohol should not be consumed with any medication, whether it is purchased over-the-counter or prescribed by a physician, unless given explicit physician approval.

DRUGS AND ELDERLY PEOPLE

The incorrect use of drugs by senior citizens poses a major, but little-recognized threat. Although the elderly compose about one-tenth of the population in the United States, they consume up to one-third of all medications purchased each year. Not only are they more likely to receive drugs for acute problems, but the medication they take for chronic disorders will often be with them for the rest of their lives.

The physiology of the aged adds to the risks of improper medication. Because of deteriorating vision, older people may have difficulty reading instructions that come with their drugs. They may have trouble remembering at what times to take medicine or whether to take it with food or on an empty stomach. The livers of elderly persons are less efficient in metabolizing drugs, their intestinal tracts do not absorb medications as readily, and their kidneys are 50 percent less efficient in excreting chemicals than when they were younger—all of which increase the chance of ill effects. Furthermore, for all patients, including the elderly, it is essential to inform the physician of all drugs currently being taken before a new prescription is issued.

Studies have shown that 25 percent of older people in hospitals and nursing homes suffer from drug-related ailments. Very often the elderly may aggravate existing medical problems by mixing prescribed drugs with over-the-counter medicine. Some older people even swap drugs among themselves without considering the harmful consequences. Also, poor eating habits may cause symptoms that physicians attribute to disease and for which they then prescribe unnecessary drugs.

Physicians must become more aware of the multiple and chronic problems of old age rather than simply prescribing a drug for each disease they diagnose. They must consider the problems that hamper an older citizen's proper use of drugs.

DRY CELL BATTERIES. *See Batteries, Dry Cell.*

DRYERS

INJURIES
In 1980, 12,000 involved dryers and washers.

HAZARDS
The most frequent injuries are cuts and bruises from falling against the dryers, but other more serious accidents also occur.

- Child entrapment. This is more likely to happen in old dryers without safety buttons on the control panel which must be pushed after the door has been closed to start the dryer, yet children can still get trapped in the newer machines.

- Fire. Failure to clean the lint trap can permit lint to accumulate and, if sufficiently heated, to ignite. Recently, the use of antistatic compounds has contributed to some fire hazards. If sprayed on electric coils in dryers, they may result in excessive lint buildup.

- Carbon monoxide poisoning. In case of gas model dryers, faulty exhaust piping, piping with obstructions, or piping that has several turns can permit lint to block the exhaust pipes, causing carbon monoxide to accumulate. Faulty piping can also cause leaks to develop, permitting poisonous gases to get into the laundry room or other rooms.

- Electric shock. If dryers are not properly grounded, a current leak or short circuit can give you an electric shock. This risk is increased in the laundry room because you are likely to be working near plumbing or other grounded metal objects. There may also be water on the floor that can conduct electric current through the user more easily.

PRECAUTIONS

Make certain any dryer you purchase has the following features:

- A safety start button on the control panel that must be pushed after the door is closed to start the dryer. Since 1972, voluntary standards have recommended this feature.

- A door that can be opened easily from the inside. Avoid those with doors that can be opened only by a latch from the outside.

To use a dryer safely:

- Do not spray antistatic compounds on or near the electric coils.

- Vent all gas dryers directly to the outside, not to a chimney. Avoid turns in the piping because they can permit lint accumulation.

- Do not overload a dryer since heavy, wet laundry can impede the motion of the drum and cause overheating.

- Be sure that both electric and gas dryers are grounded by a three-prong plug and a properly grounded outlet, or by other means.

- With an older gas dryer, to light a pilot light, strike the match before turning on the gas.

- Do not dry items that have been used with flammable liquids because they could ignite and cause a fire. Items containing plastic or foam rubber should not be dried in a dryer.

- Keep the lint trap clean.

DULCOLAX. *See Laxatives.*

DUMPSTERS. *See Waste Containers.*

DUNLOP MOTORCYCLE TIRES

QUALIFIER K127C MODELS
The size M130/90-16 tire failed to meet the federal government's endurance standards. It is used on the rear of a motorcycle. The tire was recalled on February 3, 1982. The M140/90-16 size tire was recalled on August 23, 1982. These tires may have a ply ending in the lower sidewall sufficiently misplaced as to cause flex fatigue in the lower sidewall and premature failure. For more information on tire recalls, see TIRES.

DUST *(See also Aerosols; Asbestos; Gasoline; Hobbies and Crafts; Lead; Paint; Solvents)*

HAZARDS
There are many sources of toxic substances lingering in our homes—chemical residues from aerosol products, house mites that lodge in furniture and bedding, human and animal danders, and bacteria that breed and are transported by air-conditioning and home heating systems. All these substances can be found in household dust and can cause allergic reactions. While most allergic reactions involve the respiratory system, they can also cause rashes or Meriere's disease, which causes impairment of the inner ear.

Ordinary house dust burns into charcoal at 325°F.—well below the average furnace temperature—releasing minute quantities of such toxic gases as phosgene and cyanide, which reduce the lungs' access to the available oxygen supply. Children are especially susceptible because their lungs are forced to handle a proportionately high amount of air impurities. Toxic ozone concentrations at three feet—the height of a child—are four times the concentration at six feet. In addition, children breathe more air per unit of body weight than adults and have respiration rates of up to 10 times the adult rate.

PRECAUTION

To reduce dust levels in the home, it is essential to reduce the use of spray chemicals, clean and vacuum regularly, and clean air system filters and vents regularly. In addition, keep humidifying systems free from sediment and bacteria buildup. Place non-polyvinyl chloride plastic covers on mattresses and pillows as well as over the open bottoms of chairs and sofas to lighten the dust load for an allergy-prone family member. Fabrics can be coated with emulsified oil compounds, which serve as dust seals. Always vent stoves directly outside. Cover or store outside any work clothes that are contaminated by chemicals or toxic dusts.

For more information on the health hazards associated with dust, see *The Household Pollutants Guide*, Center for Science in the Public Interest (Garden City, NY: Anchor Books, 1978, $3.50).

DYMELOR. *See Antidiabetic Agents, Oral.*

EASY TRAIL TRAVEL TRAILER

1975, 1976 MODELS
The manufacturer failed to properly install the lighting system required by the federal government.

EDGERS. *See Garden Tools, Power.*

EFFERSYLLIUM INSTANT MIX. *See Laxatives.*

EGGS AND EGG-RICH FOODS *(See also Food Poisoning)*

PRECAUTIONS
Use only clean, unbroken, odor-free eggs when making soft-cooked eggs, poached eggs, scrambled eggs, omelets, uncooked salad dressings, ice cream, or soft custard. Cracked or soiled eggs can contain harmful bacteria and should be used only in recipes calling for thorough cooking, such as hard-boiled eggs, baked goods, and casseroles. Hot foods with a high egg content should be served hot to avoid possible food poisoning. Egg-rich foods to be served cold should be refrigerated as soon as possible and remain refrigerated until serving time.

ELECTRA STEEL-BELTED RADIAL TIRES. See *General Tires.*

ELECTRICAL CORDS. See *Extension Cords; Home Electrical System.*

ELECTRICAL PLUGS. See *Home Electrical System.*

ELECTRICAL SYSTEM, HOME. See *Home Electrical System.*

ELECTRICAL TEST METERS *(See also Home Electrical System)*

HAZARDOUS MODELS
In February 1981, Radio Shack recalled more than 150,000 lead kits for electrical test meters. The two probes are designed in such a way that metal remains exposed even when it is fully inserted into the lead wire tips, posing a potential shock hazard. The kits were sold for $4.99 and can be identified by catalog number 270–332.

ELECTRICAL WIRING. See *Aluminum Wiring; Home Electrical System.*

ELECTRIC BASEBOARD HEATERS

HAZARDS
Though safer than gas or oil heaters because they do not have open flames, electric baseboard heaters can start fires and cause burns. Injuries are often caused by the following.

• Children reaching into the heater and touching the hot coil or other hot surfaces.

• Ignition of drapes, bedding, shag rugs, and furniture located too close to the heaters.

• Short-circuits caused by heaters burning through the insulation of nearby appliance cords.

- Combustion of dust, dirt, and other debris allowed to accumulate around the baseboard.

- Cuts caused by sharp edges on unguarded metal fins around the heating elements.

PRECAUTIONS

- Keep drapes, bedding, shag rugs, toys, and other combustible objects away from heaters.

- Keep all electric cords away from heaters.

- Clean the heater frequently.

- Keep infants away from the heaters and teach children that the heaters may be hot enough to burn them.

ELECTRIC BLANKETS

INJURIES
An estimate of 16 deaths and 875 injuries in 1979.

HAZARDS
Cord and cord/blanket junction failures include flexural failure at the cord connector or failure within the cord connector body.
Thermostat failures sometimes occur after water has leaked into the thermostat during laundering.
Heat entrapment resulting from folding or bunching of the blanket.

ELECTRIC BROOMS. *See Home Cleaning Equipment.*

ELECTRIC CAN OPENERS. *See Kitchen Appliances.*

ELECTRIC COMBS. *See Hair Accessories.*

ELECTRIC FANS. *See Fans, Electric.*

ELECTRIC FOOD CHOPPERS. *See Kitchen Appliances, Small.*

ELECTRIC FOOD GRINDERS. *See Kitchen Appliances, Small.*

ELECTRIC FRYING PANS. *See Cooking Appliances, Small Electric; Frying Pans, Electric.*

ELECTRIC GRIDDLES. *See Cooking Appliances, Small Electric.*

ELECTRIC HAIR CURLERS. *See Hair Accessories.*

ELECTRIC HEATING PADS. *See Heating Pads.*

ELECTRIC ICE CRUSHERS. *See Kitchen Appliances, Small.*

ELECTRIC JUICERS. *See Kitchen Appliances, Small.*

ELECTRIC KETTLES. *See Cooking Appliances, Small Electric; Kettles, Electric.*

ELECTRIC KNIFE SHARPENERS. *See Kitchen Appliances, Small.*

ELECTRIC KNIVES. *See Knives.*

ELECTRIC OVENS. *See Ranges.*

ELECTRIC PAINT REMOVERS

HAZARDOUS MODELS
In June 1979, Consumers Union reported the following heaters pose a fire hazard:

- Hyde-Lectric Paint Remover HE–100

- Hyde-Lectric Painter Remover and Putty Softener HE–200

- Magna 252 Super Tool

- Red Devil Electric Paint Remover 3401

- Sears Electric Paint Remover catalog number 44792

- Smith-Victor Torchlamp TL2

- Wards Electric Paint Remover catalog number 75–537600

- Warner Electric Paint Burner 384

ELECTRIC RANGES. *See Ranges.*

ELECTRIC SKILLETS. *See Cooking Appliances, Small Electric; Fry Pans, Electric.*

ELECTRIC SLICERS. *See Kitchen Appliances, Small.*

ELECTRIC WOKS. *See Cooking Appliances, Small Electric.*

ELECTRONICALLY OPERATED TOYS. *See Toys, Electronically Operated; Toys, General.*

EL PASO PICKLED HOT JALAPENO PEPPERS. *See Sulfites.*

EMETROL. *See Nausea Medications.*

EMPCO TIRES. *See Tires.*

ENO. *See Antacid Medications.*

ENOVID. *See Oral Contraceptives.*

EQUAL. *See Aspartame.*

ERYTHROMYCIN ESTOLATE

HAZARDS

Since 1962 this drug has carried a label warning of the increased risk of hepatotoxicity associated with its use. A stronger boxed warning was added in 1973. In 1979 the FDA initiated formal procedures to remove the drug from the market because of evidence in adults of greater risk of hepatotoxicity with estolate than with other forms of erythromycin and disputed evidence of better bioavailability. On recommendation of an advisory committee, however, the FDA withdrew the proposal on the basis that the drug's benefits outweighed its risks. FDA recommends that the drug should be used with extreme caution, however, at the discretion of the physician.

BRAND NAME: Ilosone

ESIDRIX. *See Thiazides.*

ESTROGEN *(See also Oral Contraceptives)*

Estrogens are prescribed to treat some symptoms of surgical or natural menopause, cancers in men and women, and the prevention of the painful swelling of breasts of a mother not nursing her infant.

HAZARDS

The proper use of estrogens in menopause is usually short term, and over half the population of women never need to take them. Unfortunately, because many physicians have prescribed estrogen haphazardly, the use of the drug during menopause has become so common that not prescribing it is often viewed as unfair to the patient. But while long-term treatment has questionable benefits, it does carry serious risks. Endometrial (lining of uterus) cancer is more likely to develop with longer and the larger doses. Breast and other cancers may also be more likely, but the evidence is not yet conclusive. Gall bladder disease is known to be more likely.

If you have had a heart attack, stroke, or angina pectoris, you should avoid using estrogens if possible. Your risk of blood clotting may be increased, especially if you are taking large doses (as women often do) to prevent painful breast swelling or severe menopause symptoms. Other side effects may include nausea, vomiting, breast tenderness, enlargement, or secretion of liquid—which is not dangerous—from the breast, and growth of fibroid tumors in the uterus. Excess fluid retention may also occur, making certain other conditions worse, such as asthma, epilepsy, migraine, heart disease, or kidney disease. Jaundice has also resulted from taking estrogens, as have the growth of liver tumors.

Estrogen is also used in treating diseases of the bones and symptoms of senility and mental disorders. It is believed, however, that the high risk of cancer is not worth the minor benefits estrogen may provide for these ailments.

PRECAUTIONS

Be alert to the following symptoms and if they occur, discontinue use of the drug as soon as possible and see a physician: abnormal vaginal bleeding, pains in calf or chest, sudden shortness of breath, coughing blood, severe headache, dizziness, faintness or change in vision, breast lumps, jaundice (yellowing of the skin and eyes), or mental depression.

WARNING

Do not take estrogens if you are pregnant. Estrogen increases the risk of child birth defects, and a female child will be more likely to develop cancer of the vagina or cervix later in life.

BRAND NAMES: Premarin (tablets and cream for vaginal use); Premarin with methyltestosterone (tablet); PMB Premarin with meprobamate (a tranquilizer in tablet form); Premarin Intravenous estrogenic substance (estrone) for intramuscular injection.

ESTROGENIC SUBSTANCE. *See Estrogen.*

EXCEDRIN. *See Aspirin; Caffeine.*

EXECUTIVE MOTOR HOME

1971, 1972, 1973 25- AND 28-FOOT MOTOR HOMES MODELS

The regulator installed on the propane gas tank may collect moisture. In the event of freezing, the regulator will not function properly. Either too much gas will be released, causing a dangerous condition inside the home, or too little gas will be released.

EXERCISE EQUIPMENT

INJURIES
In 1980, 45,000 cases were reported.

HAZARDS
Injuries included sprains, fractures, contusions, and lacerations from falls from or against equipment and from equipment that was falling or in operation. Moving parts and sharp edges increase the risk of injury.

Exercise bikes, one of the most popular kinds of exercise equipment, can be dangerous if the spokes are uncovered, allowing limbs to get caught in the moving wheel.

HAZARDOUS MODELS
In 1981, 120,000 Beacon Scandia model 462 and Sears model 2930 exercise bikes manufactured from August 1976 through July 1980 were recalled because improper assembly could allow the seat post to puncture the seat and injure the user.

EX-LAX. *See Laxatives.*

EXTENDED-WEAR CONTACT LENSES. *See Contact Lenses, Soft.*

EXTENSION CORDS *(See also Home Electrical System; Lamps)*

INJURIES
Approximately 1,500 annually, of which roughly one-third involve children under ten years of age, and most of these are under five years old. Electrical burns to the mouth are the most common injury.

HAZARDS
A large number of electrical fires are caused by short circuits and the overloading and misuse of extension cords. The main causes of injuries involving these cords are children putting extension cords in their mouths, overloaded cords, worn or damaged cords, and tripping over cords.

STANDARDS

Electrical contractors are required to follow either the National Electrical Code (NEC) or local electrical codes. The NEC requires that electrical outlets be not more than 12 feet apart along a wall so that no point along a wall will be more than 6 feet from an outlet. The NEC also requires that portable and other types of lamps be equipped with polarized or grounding type plugs. (In polarized plugs, one blade is slightly wider than the other.) Polarization and grounding ensure that the lamp socket is connected to the neutral, or grounded, side of the circuit, thereby reducing the risk of shock or electrocution. Voluntary safety standards now require that general-use extension cords have safety closures, warning labels, current rating information, and other features protecting consumers.

PRECAUTIONS

Consumers should buy and use extension cords with safety closures and other safety features. They should also purchase only three-wire extension cords for appliances with three-prong plugs.

EXTENSION WORK LIGHTS. *See Work Lights.*

EXXON TIRES. *See Uniroyal Tires.*

EYE DROPS. *See Eye Medications, Nonprescription; Germicides and Disinfectants.*

EYE-GENE. *See Eye Medications, Nonprescription.*

EYE MEDICATIONS, NONPRESCRIPTION

Over-the-counter products to relieve eye strain do little but reduce redness in the eyes. The products are safe but ineffective in relieving eye strain. Although they do reduce redness in the eyes, if overused they may increase the redness. Washing your eyes with cold water is as effective as any over-the-counter treatment in soothing the eyes.

> **WARNING**

Consult a physician if you experience eye pain, headache, change in vision, or pain from exposure to light.

E-Z ANT TRAPS. *See Insecticides, Household.*

EZ LOADER TRAILER

1981 MODEL
On certain vehicles, the spindles that connect the axle to the wheels may break when subjected to jolting or stress. This will cause the wheel and tires to fall off.

E-Z ROLLER BABY STROLLER

HAZARDOUS MODELS 6620, 6020
These strollers are manufactured by Graco Children's Products, Inc. While the stroller is being unfolded for use, children have put their fingers in the main hinges on each side of the stroller. In order to prevent injury, the company is providing free plastic hinge guards for the owners of these models. If you own one of these strollers you can contact the company at (800) 345-4109 between 9 A.M. and 4 P.M. eastern standard time. Pennsylvania residents can write: Graco, Box 100, Elverson, Pa. 19520.

FACIAL CREAMS. *See Skin Moisturizers and Creams.*

FANS, ELECTRIC

INJURIES

In 1980, 14,000 were reported.

HAZARDS/PRECAUTIONS

Most injuries are burns, lacerations, or amputations caused, respectively, by fires resulting from the motor overheating or by contact of hands with moving blades. To help prevent the former, do not operate fans in or even near a window when it is raining.

HAZARDOUS MODELS

In July 1979, Consumers Union reported that the Lakewood S223, Edison 204001 and 204005, Lasko 4713, Kool King FK 53, Wards catalog number 48108, Sears catalog number 8131, and Superlectric 2072 had sharp corners on the frame. The window-mounting panels on Frigid models P20B and SP20R also had sharp edges where they support the fan.

In June 1981, Consumers Union reported that the Frigid HV362 whole-house fan lacked thermal-overload protection.

In July 1982, Consumers Union reported the following potential hazards in portable fans: the frame of Edison 204007B and 204014A, Eagle Aire EA203, Galaxy 3713, 3714, and 3746, and Sears catalog number 8120 and 8121 had pointed corners.

FANS, GENERAL ELECTRIC

HAZARDOUS MODEL

General Electric has recalled their 9-inch fan model F1-OF-9A, which is a portable two-speed oscillating fan.

General Electric is warning owners that a potential fire hazard exists in some units. If you own one of these fans, you should call the GE Answer Center at (800) 626-2000 and ask for Department 25. There is no charge for this call and the line is open 24 hours a day.

FEBRINOL. *See Acetaminophen.*

FEDAHIST. *See Decongestants, Oral.*

FEEN-A-MINT. *See Laxatives.*

FEMCAPS CAPSULES. *See Caffeine; Menstrual Pain Medications.*

FEMIRON. *See Iron and Iron Supplements.*

FENCES

INJURIES

In 1980, 95,000 involved all fences. In 1976, 5,000 involved non-electric chain link fences.

HAZARDS

Injuries occur mainly to children who typically suffer fractures, lacerations, or punctures when climbing over, falling against, running into, or jumping over a fence. A few injuries are suffered by snowmobilers who run into fences, while others are caused by swinging gates.

PRECAUTIONS

Consumers should make certain that link fences have the following:

- Knuckle-to-knuckle barbs on top and bottom so that the sharp end is turned downward or into the fence rather than up and out.

- Self-closing gates with latches at least three feet above the ground, if the fence is intended to keep toddlers in or out.

FENDON. *See Acetaminophen.*

FERRARI 308

1977–1979 MODELS
Fuel hoses may fail, possibly causing fire.

FIAT LANCIA

1977 MODEL
Electrically powered windows may be operated when ignition is off creating the potential for injury to small children.

FIAT STRADA

1979 MODEL
Fuel lines could wear through, causing fuel to leak into passenger

compartment with the possibility of fire. Infiltration of water and dirt may cause tail lights to fail. Fuel tank and fuel filler are vulnerable in a crash. Controls and displays are confusing. Driver's rear view is obstructed by wide rear roof pillar. Windshield wipers block driver's view to right front.

1982 MODEL
Controls and displays are confusing.

FIAT SUPER BRAVA

1978 MODEL
Heater fan switch may be defective, creating fire hazard.

FIAT X1/9

1979 MODEL
Loosening bolts may cause axle shafts to detach from the differential or rear wheel hubs.

1980 MODEL
Driver's outside rear-view mirror may lack proper magnification.

FIAT 124 SPORT SPIDER

1977–1979 MODELS
Water accumulation may deteriorate brake line, causing loss of efficiency in braking and possible failure of brakes.

FIAT 131 SEDAN

1977 MODEL
Lack of lubrication may cause excessive wear of drive shaft, possibly resulting in sudden loss of power and impaired handling.

FIBERBOARD. *See Pressed-Wood Products.*

FIRE ANT TREATMENTS. *See Chlordane.*

FIRE EXTINGUISHERS

INJURIES
There were 1,624 in 1972-73. Lacerations, contusions, abrasions, and fractures accounted for 71 percent of all these injuries, chemical burns and thermal burns for 8 percent and 6 percent, respectively.

HAZARDS
- The inhalation of poisonous by-products of extinguishers.

- Chemical burns caused by extinguishants.

- Rupture of the pressurized container.

HAZARDOUS MODEL
In October 1979, Consumers Union reported that people with weak hands might have difficulty activating two Pem All models, PA27ABC and PA50-2-ABC. In January 1981, after testing additional units, Consumers Union judged that, while there was general improvement, some samples of these units may still be difficult to activate for people with weak hands.

FIREPLACE WATER HEATER

HAZARDOUS MODELS
In November 1982, the CPSC warned consumers of an explosion hazard with fireplace-powered water heaters sold under the brand names Hydrohearth, Hydroplace, and Aqua Grate. The manufacturers of these units are no longer in business. Plumbing connects the unit to the hot-water heating system of the home. If the flow of water through the unit is slowed or stopped, and it does not have an adequate pressure relief device, the buildup of pressure can cause an explosion.

FIREPLACES *(See also Chimneys)*

INJURIES

In 1980, 16,000 involved fireplaces or chimneys.

HAZARDS

Most injuries are cuts or bruises caused by handling wood, andirons, or other equipment. Some of the most serious, however, are burns to children.

Many fireplace accidents are caused by clothing caught on fire from the open flames; sparks from the fire landing on flammable material; flammable liquids used to kindle or rekindle the fire; and carbon monoxide poisoning caused by inadequate venting.

PRECAUTIONS

- Do not use gasoline or other flammable liquids anywhere near the fire.

- Have the chimney inspected for creosote buildup before each heating season.

- Burn only one artificial log at a time since these produce intense heat.

- Always use a screen that completely covers the fireplace opening.

- Keep the damper and other vents working and open when the fuel is burning.

- Use chimney guards to prevent birds and animals from blocking the flue.

FIRESTONE 500 TIRES

This tire was part of one of the most massive recalls in the history of the industry. Premature failure was due to a manufacturing defect. This tire was recalled on July 16, 1980 (there was also an earlier Firestone 500 recall), and included such brand names as K-Mart Radial 40, Ward's Grappler II, Atlas Glodenaire II, National Steel Belted Radial and Union tires. The recall included both the 5 and 7 rib models. See TIRES for more information on tire recalls.

FIRESTONE LONGHAULER TIRES. *See Firestone Transport Tires.*

FIRESTONE TRANSPORT TIRES

These tires were recalled on February 15, 1982 because tires developed a condition known as socketing. This condition could lead to separation of the plys in the tread area or parts of the tread surface coming off. The tire was also sold under the following names: Trans Hiway, Montgomery Ward Road Guard HD, Firestone Longhauler, Dayton Super EMT II, Super Highway II, Multi Mile Super Highway, Cordovan Super Highway, Firestone Transport Duplex, and Dayton Thorobred Duaload Super EMT. See TIRES for more information on tire recalls.

FIREWORKS

INJURIES
The 9,000 injuries in 1980—many to children and many very serious—included blindings, amputations, severe burns—even deaths.

HAZARDS
Injuries can be inflicted by exploding fireworks or by a container or other object that is fragmented by the firework. Even sparklers, considered by many as the ideal "safe" firework for the young, burn at very high temperatures and can easily ignite clothing.

FEDERAL STANDARDS
Under the Federal Hazardous Substances Act, the government prohibits the sale to consumers of the most dangerous types of fireworks, including cherry bombs and aerial bombs. In 1976 the CPSC imposed a more stringent regulation lowering the permissible charge to no more than 50 milligrams of powder and providing performance specifications for fireworks intended for consumer use including a requirement that fuses burn between three and six seconds.

PRECAUTIONS

Young children should never be allowed to play with fireworks. Users should never try to relight or handle malfunctioning fireworks, but should soak them in water and throw them away. Also, never ignite fireworks in a container, especially one of glass or metal.

FIRST-AID SKIN OINTMENTS AND ANTISEPTICS *(See also Boric Acid; Neomycin)*

There are a variety of topical ointments and antiseptics available without a prescription to treat small cuts, abrasions, and burns. Many of these medications may contain ingredients that can complicate or aggravate existing conditions.

HAZARDS/PRECAUTIONS

Iodine and povidone iodine are effective antiseptics, but they may cause skin irritation, especially if combined with alcohol. B.F.I. Powder, a widely marketed antiseptic, contains boric acid and should not be used to treat open cuts, burns, or abrasions because it is quickly absorbed through broken or damaged skin and can cause nausea, vomiting, diarrhea, skin rash, kidney damage, or shock. Products containing neomycin should also be used cautiously. Neomycin can cause allergic reactions in some people, and its use may mask the presence of a more serious infection. In addition, use of neomycin can build up an immunity in patients to other more important antibiotics, rendering them useless in future treatment. Cortisone is now available without prescription to treat itching and rash. It should not be used, however to treat skin disorders, because it can mask the evidence of infection or actually cause the infection to spread.

FISH. *See Seafood.*

FISH, PROCESSED. *See Seafood.*

FISH STICKS. *See Seafood.*

FISK TIRES. *See Uniroyal Tires.*

FIZRIN. *See Antacid Medications.*

FLATWARE. *See Tableware.*

FLEA POWDERS. *See Kwell Shampoo and Cream.*

FLEET. *See Laxatives.*

FLEETWOOD TRAVEL TRAILER

1968, 1969, 1970 MODELS
   Loading more than 500 pounds of cargo to the trailer can cause the wheels to fail.

1971 MODEL
   The electric brakes contain a defective electromagnet that will cause one or more of the brakes to fail.

1974, 1975, 1976 MODELS
   The undercarriage was assembled in the reverse direction on some models. The result is that the brakes may lock up. In addition wheel runoff may occur because the wheel lugs are not self-tightening.

1976 KENSKILL MODEL
   Some of these trailers lack an electrical ground wire. In addition, the fuse wires to the furnace are too small and could cause a fire.

1977 WILDERNESS, TAURUS, TERRY MODEL
When the manufacturer installed the refrigerator, the LP gas shut-off valve was damaged on some models, which has caused leakage into the refrigerator compartment with the associated potential fire hazard.

1979 TAURUS MODEL
On some models the flu outlet to the furnace is not long enough to provide connection of the insulating sleeve to the furnace outer case. This condition could cause fire and serious injury.

FLETCHER'S CASTORIA. *See Laxatives.*

FLOOR POLISHES

HAZARDS
Although the polishing ingredients may not be toxic, the solvents used to liquefy the polishes might be, and are combustible as well.

PRECAUTIONS
When using waxes for wood floors, be certain to ventilate the area adequately because the waxes contain petroleum solvents such as naphtha, which emit toxic fumes. Wear rubber gloves when applying furniture polish with a cloth; do not use polishes near fire or flame; and if swallowed, do not induce vomiting.

HAZARDOUS MODELS
According to labels, two polishes for nonwood floors, Armstrong Suncoat and Johnson Wax Brite, contain eye irritants. Consumers Union judged one regular resilient flooring polish—Scotch Buy Cleans & Shines—and most polishes for wood flooring it tested—Bruce Clean & Wax, Bruce Dark Tone, Johnson Wax Beautiflor, Wood Preen, Johnson Wax Klear Wood Floor Wax, and Bruce One Step—to leave floors more slippery than others tested.

FLOORS

INJURIES
In 1975, 84,000 involved floors and flooring materials.

HAZARDS

Most injuries resulted from falls caused by slipping or tripping. Specific hazards include the following.

- Slippery surfaces resulting from spilled fluids or washing and waxing.

- Small rugs, runners, and similar items that are not anchored to the floor.

- Raised edges of linoleum or carpeting, or objects on the floor that cause tripping.

- Rain or snow on porch or terrace floors.

- Oil spills on carports or garage floors.

PRECAUTIONS

In washing and waxing, block off the room until the floor is dry, avoid laying down excessive wax, buff paste wax thoroughly, and use different mops or sponges to wash and wax.

Anchor small rugs or runners with double-faced carpet tape or something similar.

Add sand or similar abrasive material to paint that will be used to cover a porch or terrace floor.

Look for protrusions that might cause a fall inside or outside the house. Tack, tape, or glue down carpet and tile edges. Draw attention to irregularities in the floor with bright paint.

FLOOR TILES. *See Vinyl Floor Tiles and Vinyl Sheet Flooring.*

FLOWAWAY WATER 100's. *See Caffeine; Menstrual Pain Medications.*

FLUORESCENT LIGHTS *(See also Black Lights; Home Electrical System; Lamps)*

HAZARDS

A recent New York University study showed that people exposed to fluorescent light an average of 35 hours a week for five years had an 87 percent greater risk of developing malignant melanoma, a rare and often fatal skin cancer characterized by dark skin nodules, than people not exposed to fluorescent lighting. Other scientists disagree with the linking of fluorescent light to the increased risk of cancer.

One theory is that office workers are more susceptible to melanoma because they spend most of their time indoors and go outside to the bright sunlight at noon. Melanoma can also be caused by the continued sudden exposure of untanned skin to intense ultraviolet (UV) light such as sun rays. Severe sunburn is considered a contributor to the instance of melanoma. According to one study, fluorescent lights were found to emit only 1/3000th as much UV light as the noonday sun does on a typical autumn day in New York.

HAZARDOUS MODELS

In August 1979, the American Electric Corporation voluntarily recalled more than 20,000 Brite Bar fluorescent light fixtures. The power cord could create a risk of fire if damaged, altered, or used in a manner contrary to the instructions accompanying the unit. The product under recall is the model 9500 "Brite Bar" slim-line, fluorescent light fixture.

FLU SHOTS

Flu shots are considered essential today for the elderly population but unnecessary for healthy children and adults. Because of age and chronic ailments, the elderly are more susceptible than the normal population to severe illness and complications from an attack of flu, such as pneumonia, encephalitis, and kidney failure. Medical authorities recommend that seniors and anyone with a chronic illness should take the preventive flu vaccine, available since the early 1960s. Medicare funds are not currently available for flu inoculations, although there is pressure in Congress to reverse that policy.

Adverse reactions and occasionally death have been reported in the past in connection with flu inoculations, particularly during the massive vaccination campaign against "swine flu" in 1976, but the percentage of adverse reactions was minuscule compared to the millions of vaccinations administered.

FLY CONTROL DEVICES

HAZARDOUS MODELS

In January 1979, Pestolite, Inc., voluntarily recalled 1,005 Commercial Fly Control Devices, model SK-4. If too many dead insects accumulate and block the centrifugal fan, the unit may overheat and create a fire hazard.

FMC MOTOR HOME

1973, 1974, 1975, 1976 A,J,L,V,R MODELS

The brake tubes on some models are not able to stand up under some climatic conditions. The tubes can become perforated, causing the loss of brake fluid. These models come with a dual-braking system, so the failure will result in reduced braking capacity and a warning light on the dash.

FOLDING CHAIRS *(See also Chairs)*

INJURIES

In 1980, 8,000 involved beach chairs or other folding chairs.

HAZARDS

The most important types and causes of injuries are contusions, sprains, or lacerations resulting from the folding or collapse of the chair; contusions, lacerations, amputations from entrapment of fingers; and lacerations from falls from or against these chairs, or from contact with sharp edges.

FOLGER'S DECAFFEINATED COFFEE. *See Coffee, Decaffeinated.*

FONDUE POTS *(See also Cooking Appliances, Small Electric)*

INJURIES

Hundreds annually.

HAZARDS

Splattering or spilling hot oil can be injurious after the fondue starts bubbling as the pot is being moved from the stove to the table. Handles may get so hot that the pots cannot be carried without dropping them, and sometimes the handles loosen or fall off.

Ignition of clothing may occur by the open flame of the alcohol burner under the pot, or ignition of the fuel itself, denatured alcohol or alcohol impregnated solids.

PRECAUTIONS

In purchasing a fondue pot, keep the following in mind.

- The handles should be securely fastened, well insulated, and fire-resistant.

- The pot and stand should have broad bases for increased stability.

- A deep pot that slopes inward toward the top will reduce the chance of splattering of oil.

- Solid fuel is much safer than liquid alcohol as a fuel because it cannot spill. Electricity is even safer because it has no flame.

To use a fondue pot safely:

- Be sure that the flame is completely extinguished and the burner has cooled for at least 15 minutes before refilling a liquid alcohol burner. A burner's heated vapors could cause ignition of the fuel used to refill the burner and burning fuel could be spilled on you.

- Never hold a burner in your hand to light it. Place it in the stand.

- Keep it as close to the outlet as possible so that people will not trip over the cord.

- Reduce splattering when cooking meat by adding one teaspoon of salt to three cups of oil and also by blotting the meat dry before adding to the pot.

- Do not use ceramic pots for meat fondue because they are not designed to withstand high temperatures.

- If the oil begins to smoke or catches fire, turn off the heat and cover the pot to smother the flames. Do not try to move the pot.

FOOD ADDITIVES *See Food Colors, Artificial; Food Colors, Natural; Food Flavoring Additives; Food and Hyperactivity.*

A food additive is any substance that becomes part of a food product when added either directly or indirectly. At the present time, about 2,800 substances are intentionally added to foods to maintain or improve nutritional value, maintain freshness, help in processing or preparation, or make food more appealing.

HAZARDS

Food additives are more strictly regulated today than in earlier years, but questions remain about the safety of many of these additives. The consumer should keep current on this subject by reading newspaper and magazine articles on food additives. Information about recent studies involving food additives will also help the consumer get the benefits and avoid the risks of food additives. Even if an additive has been banned, foods containing it may not be recalled; in such cases food manufacturers would only be prevented from using the additive in the future.

PRECAUTIONS

A sound, balanced, and diversified diet containing adequate amounts of fresh foods and little or no junk food will prevent overexposure to food additives.

FOOD COLORS, ARTIFICIAL *(See also Food Colors, Natural; Food and Hyperactivity)*

Artificial colorings are added to foods to make them look more appealing and desirable. Rarely do these additives contribute to nutrition. Color additives are used in beverages, candy and confections, cereals, ice cream, butter and cheese, sausage casings and meats, baked foods, snack foods, gravies, jams and jellies, nuts, salad dressings, and many other foods.

HAZARDS

There are two major areas of concern with regard to the health implications of colorings: One relates to their possible effect on the behavior of children and the other to their toxicology as revealed by experimental testing.

A connection between diet and hyperactivity in children has been suggested by Dr. Benjamin Feingold, a San Francisco allergist. His theory, implicating many food additives, has prompted numerous experimental studies. Results have been inconclusive, although hyperactive youngsters have had improvement in their behavior when additives were eliminated from their diets. Parents suspecting that additives may be affecting their children's behavior should discuss the problem with their family doctor in order to decide if an additive-free diet would be wise.

Studies of the safety of artificial colorings contained in products already on the market have been ongoing for more than 20 years. The FDA allows these additives to be used by industry while testing continues. Completed studies have indicated that some of the artificial colors may be harmful, but they have not been removed from the market.

Several consumer groups charge that the FDA has permitted the testing to continue for too many years and also that the agency is reluctant to remove certain artificial colors from the market even if evidence exists that they are dangerous. The safety of nine artificial colorings has been questioned, but they are still permitted. Two are restricted to use in a single product.

- FD & C Blue No. 2.. Industry studies have shown an increase in brain tumors among rats fed the additive used in baked goods, pet foods, and beverage powders.

- Citrus Red No. 2. It is restricted to coloring orange skins not used for processing and has induced cancer in animals.

- Orange B. This coloring is restricted to casings and surfaces of frankfurters and sausages, and has a similar chemical structure to amaranth, which is banned because of research linking it to cancer.

- FD & C Red No. 3. Some evidence exists that this additive may be harmful, but clear evidence is lacking. It has shown adverse effects on blood and may also cause mutation of the genes.

- FD & C Red No. 40. This coloring may have induced cancer in animals, but evidence is lacking.

- FD & C Yellow No. 5. This additive has been found to cause allergic reactions. As of July 1, 1982, manufacturers are required to list this additive on labels of food that contain it. Most people allergic to this coloring are also allergic to aspirin. It is used in candy, desserts, cereals, and dairy products.

- FD & C Green No. 6. While this food coloring is apparently safe, it contains P-toluidine, an impurity that is a by-product of the manufacturing process. P-toluidine has been linked to cancer.

- FD & C Blue No. 1, FD & C Green No. 3, and FD & C Yellow No. 6. No evidence of hazard has been found in these last three additives, but there has been criticism of the inadequacy of research done on them.

PRECAUTIONS

Food manufacturers are not required to list artificial colors on the ingredient label and they seldom do so. But the color of a food may suggest to the consumer that an artificial color has been used. Artificial colors usually serve only a cosmetic purpose in food and should be avoided whenever possible. Testing is inadequate on many of these additives, and once a food color is approved, the FDA is reluctant to change the additive's classification even if serious health concerns are raised or additional testing shows a potential hazard.

FOOD COLORS, NATURAL

Natural color additives may appear as individual items on labels or just be identified as "natural color(s)." Natural colors come from pigment in plants, animals, small organisms, and minerals. Some of these can also be produced synthetically, but in that case, the additive must be listed on the label as an artificial coloring.

Natural colorings are used for the same reasons as artificial colors—to make foods look as acceptable and desirable as possible. Some of the natural colorings are also used as flavorings and a few as vitamin sources.

It cannot be assumed, however, that because a food additive is natural, it is safe. Safrole, a natural additive derived from sassafras and formerly used in root beer, was banned because it caused liver cancer. Caffeine and MSG are also natural and their safety is being questioned. Research at times into the safety of natural additives, including natural color additives, has been inadequate and questions of safety remain.

The following group of natural color additives are probably safe, but research is incomplete or nonexistent. Further studies are needed.

- Annatto (bixin). Extracted from seeds of a tropical tree. Research so far has shown no adverse effects, but data is incomplete.

- Beet red. A normal ingredient in the diet, unlikely to be harmful. However, research studies have been inadequate.

- Carrot oil, fruit juce, grape skin extract, toasted defatted cottonseed flour and vegetable juice. Components of food in the normal diet are probably safe although research is nonexistent.

- Saffron. Available data on this natural color is inadequate for assessing possible hazards. It provides an orange-red color.

PRECAUTIONS

It is difficult to assess the safety of most natural food colors, but one should not assume the products are therefore safe. More research is urgently needed in this area, and consumers should regard natural colorings with skepticism until such testing is completed.

FOOD FLAVORING ADDITIVES

There are more flavor additives used in foods than all other types of additives combined (perhaps 1,700 flavoring agents). Some come from natural ingredients; others are produced synthetically.

Flavoring agents used before 1958 were permitted to remain in use unless challenged by scientists using data available at that time. The research available was inadequate by today's standards and the vast majority of flavors remained unchallenged. Since then, laboratory studies have discovered a few flavoring agents that were harmful, and they have been banned from further use. Only recently have more intensive studies begun. Flavorings that have come into existence since 1958 must undergo thorough scientific testing before they can be approved for use.

The FDA does not require manufacturers to list individual chemical components composing a flavoring, but only state "artificial flavors," "imitation flavors," or "natural flavors" on the label. Even this labeling is not required for some products. Often a combination of several flavorings are used, making the evaluation of safety of flavoring agents in a particular product difficult.

FOOD GRINDERS. *See Kitchen Appliances, Small.*

FOOD POISONING *(See also Eggs and Egg-Rich Foods; Meat and Poultry)*

HAZARDS

Food poisoning can disguise itself as an upset stomach, headache, or nausea. Many people who think they have a "flu bug" actually have a minor case of food poisoning. Food poisoning can be serious but there are some easy rules to avoid its occurrence.

PRECAUTIONS

Food should not stand at room temperature for more than two hours because bacteria may start to multiply. Always refrigerate cooked food at once, being sure food is thoroughly cooked to kill bacteria. Despite common misconceptions, germs seldom change the taste, odor, or appearance of food.

Use clean utensils, platters, and countertops to ward off germs that might contaminate meat, poultry, and dairy products.

Be sure to bandage cuts and sores on your hands before you handle food. Keep pets out of areas where food is prepared. Teach children to wash their hands before touching food.

Bacteria that cause food poisoning are most commonly found in raw meat, poultry, eggs, dairy products, and vegetables. Always handle these foods properly. Another bacteria source can be found in stews, soups, and gravies when they are improperly stored or left at room temperature for long periods of time. Staphylococcus organisms, which occur normally on human skin and in the nose and throat, can be transmitted to food by handling and can infect others who eat the food. Persons with a staph infection should not handle food.

FOOD PROCESSORS

INJURIES

In 1980, 8,000 involved food processors, mixers, or blenders.

HAZARDOUS MODELS

In September 1981, Consumers Union reported that the interlock system of the Sanyo SKM 1200 tended to stick, allowing continued operation with the bowl lid removed.

FOOD AND HYPERACTIVITY *(See also Sugar)*

Many people know that a poor diet can lead to health problems such as vitamin deficiencies, dental cavities, obesity, skin problems, and heart disease, but most people are surprised to learn that their diet might affect their behavior.

This theory was first advanced in 1971 by Dr. Benjamin Feingold, an allergist in San Francisco, who claimed that artificial colorings and other chemicals in food could cause learning difficulties and hyperactivity in children. More recent scientific studies to test Feingold's theory do not support the dramatic improvement vouched for by the parents of some hyperactive children; however, some children do show improvement when placed on an additive-free diet.

If you suspect your child might be hyperactive, discuss possible treatment plans with your physician. Some parents may wish to try the Feingold diet, which still has many advocates, before placing their children on amphetamines. This decision should be made only after careful consideration of the alternatives and after consultation with a physician.

FOODS, CANNED *(See also Botulism; Canning, Home; Lead)*

HAZARDS

For most adult Americans, as well as many children, diet is the largest source of lead exposure. Acording to government-commissioned surveys, many children, particularly heavy eaters, exceed the recognized safe levels of lead intake from food alone, not including exposure to lead from such other sources as air, water, soil, and household paint.

Although few deaths are currently attributable to lead poisoning, exposure can cause convulsions and, more frequently, brain damage or mental retardation. Even low levels of lead exposure can lead to learning impairment or neurobehavioral impairment. For adults, lead exposure can cause peripheral nervous system disorders or disruption of reproductive capacity in both men and women. At all ages, lead overdoses can cause kidney damage and anemia, and even normal exposure can interfere with normal blood formation.

Lead enters the food chain through the soil, air, and water, as well as the use of lead-based pesticides. Lead also enters foods during canning and processing. The FDA has estimated that canned foods contribute approximately 20 percent of the lead found in the average person's diet. Much of this lead contamination comes from the lead solder used in can seams.

PRECAUTIONS

The Center for Science in the Public Interest has petitioned the FDA to require labeling on all canned food to read: "Important: This food should not be stored in the can or in any other metal container after opening."

Not only does lead contaminate all canned food, but the contamination is significantly increased if food is stored in the can. Acidic foods, in particular, absorb the lead from the soldered seams quickly once the can is opened and the contents are exposed to the air. This includes orange and other fruit juices, tomatoes and tomato paste, and most fruits. Always transfer the contents of a can into a nonmetal container before storing.

FOOD WARMERS. *See Cooking Appliances, Small Electric.*

FORD AUTOMATIC TRANSMISSIONS. *See Automobile Transmissions.*

FORD COUNTRY SQUIRE

1979 MODEL
Horn and wiper controls are inconvenient. Defrosting is spotty. Driver's visibility is somewhat restricted.

FORD COURIER

1979 MODEL
Sluggish, sloppy handling in emergency maneuvers. Inside mirror interferes with tall driver's view. Seat belts tend to ride up.

FORD ECONOLINE CLUB WAGON

1975, 1976, 1977 MODELS
Many models were equipped with an unpadded instrument panel made of a material that can be broken if an occupant were to hit it in an accident situation. The broken panel itself can inflict serious injury on the occupant.

FORD ESCORT

1981 MODEL
Wiring harness may overheat, possibly causing fire. Rear-brake backing-plate attachment bolts may have inadequate torque, possibly causing loss of braking. Metal fasteners may penetrate fuel tank, causing loss of fuel and fire hazard. Power brake boosters may be defective, possibly causing loss of service brakes. Fuel inlet may be ungrounded, possibly causing fire during refueling. Speed control may be activated unexpectedly by vacuum leak.

1983 MODEL
The 3-door hatchbacks may not be in compliance with FMVSS301-75, Fuel System Integrity, because excess fuel may leak in rollover tests. Right front power brake locks prematurely in stopping. Controls are inconvenient to operate. Hatch lid latch is hazardous to tall persons.

FORD EXP

1982 MODEL
In U.S. Department of Transportation 35-mph crash tests, the occupant protection was rated low.

FORD FAIRMONT

1978 MODEL
Pushrod could disengage from pedal, causing loss of service brakes. Front disc brakes may be defective, causing brake pull. Parking gear may not engage when placed in "park" position, causing the car to roll free. Wiring may chafe, possibly causing loss of electrical power control. Wiper system may fail. Air reed valve may fail, possibly causing engine to stall. In low position, head restraints protect only short persons. Poorly designed horn and wiper controls.

1979 MODEL
Rear lamp sockets may be incorrect. Certification label may list incorrect weight. Brake retaining pin may be defective. Poor occupant protection in the 4-door model when crash tested at 35 mph by the U.S. Department of Transportation.

1980 MODEL
Brake assembly may be incorrect, causing slow stopping. Open trunk lid is hazardous to tall persons.

1981 MODEL
Pushrod could disengage from pedal, causing loss of service brakes.

FORD FAIRMONT

1982 (FUTURA) MODEL
Excessive slack in shoulder harness. Power steering feels numb. Somewhat difficult to control on rough roads. In cars with C-3 automatic transmissions, column-mounted gear-shift levers may contain defective transmission park actuating lever rod springs, allowing the vehicle to roll when the gear-shift lever is in the "park" position.

1983 (FUTURA) MODEL
In cars with C-3 automatic transmissions, column-mounted gear-shift levers may contain defective transmission park actuating lever rod springs, allowing the vehicle to roll when the gear-shift lever is in the "park" position. Transmission-control selector tube may be defective, which could cause the gear-shift-selector-level indicator to incorrectly indicate the actual gear position. Horn and windshield-wiper controls are awkward to operate.

FORD FIESTA

1978 MODEL
Blower motor wires may be improperly located, possibly causing fire. Valve stem holes could be mislocated, causing loss of air in tire. Controls are illogical and awkward to operate.

1979 MODEL
Rear lamp sockets may be incorrect. Placard lists incorrect information about tires. The occupant protection of the 2-door model in

the U.S. Department of Transportation 35-mph crash-test program was poor.

FORD FUTURA

1978 MODEL
Poorly designed horn and wiper controls. Wide side pillars may block driver's sight. Open trunk lid is hazardous to tall persons.

1979 MODEL
Rear lamp sockets may be incorrect.

1982, 1983 MODELS *See Ford Fairmont.*

FORD GRANADA

1977 MODEL
Transmission selector pointer may be mispositioned, possibly causing forward motion and accident when car is started. Excessive fuel may spill in rollover, causing fire hazard. Cooling fan may crack and separate into fragments. Fuel tank and filler are vulnerable in a crash.

1978 MODEL
Steering-gear balls may fracture, causing a loss of steering.

1979 MODEL
Rear lamp sockets may be incorrect. Pushrod could disengage from pedal, causing loss of service brakes. Rear-window defroster is inadequate. Rear seat belts may be too short. The occupant protection of the 4-door model in the U.S. Department of Transportation 35-mph crash test was poor.

1981 MODEL
Excessive slack in front shoulder harness. Driver's view is obstructed by wide rear roof pillars and long hood.

1982 MODEL
Tire placards may list incorrect information. Unpredictable handling in emergency maneuvers. Power steering is sluggish. Daytime

reflections obscure speedometer. At night, instrument-panel lights reflect in windshield. Position of horn, on end of turn-signal lever, is unsafe. Excessive slack in shoulder portion of front safety belts.

FORD LTD

1978 MODEL
Seat belt is uncomfortable and may fail to lock.

1979 MODEL
Rear lamp sockets may be incorrect. Coupling rivet pins may be defective, possibly causing loss of steering. Fan blade could come loose and be thrown. The word "light" is omitted from the instrument panel. Front brake hoses may be misindexed, possibly causing braking loss. Brake valves may be incorrect, possibly causing rear wheel lockup. Pushrod could disengage from pedal, causing loss of service brakes. Fuel filler pipe is vulnerable in sideswipe. Horn and wiper controls are inconvenient. Occupant protection in the U.S. Department of Transportation 35-mph crash test was rated as poor.

1981 MODEL
Start switch may malfunction and allow starting in reverse. Rear bumper on station wagons could corrode and detach.

1982 MODEL
Incorrect insulator may have been installed in steering column shift cane lever, causing failure of shift.

1983 MODEL
Transmission control selector tube may be defective, which could cause the gearshift-selector-level indicator to indicate the actual gear position incorrectly. Cam retainer pins in parking pawl actuating rod assemblies may be defective, which could result in the parking pawl not engaging the parking gear when the shift selector is in the "park" position, allowing the vehicle to roll. Driver's forward view is restricted by a high hood and exposed wipers. Front safety belts allow excessive slack in the shoulder straps.

FORD LTD II

1977 MODEL
Transmission selector pointer may be mispositioned, possibly caus-

ing forward motion and accident when car is started. Cooling fan may crack and separate. Engine may leak fuel at rubber hose connecting fuel inlet tube and fuel filter, possibly causing a fire.

1979 MODEL

Power steering gears may be defective, causing loss of steering. Nuts may be stripped, causing seat to slide along track. In a 35-mph crash test conducted by the U.S. Department of Transportation, severe injury to the legs of the driver was noted.

FORD MAVERICK

1977 MODEL

Left-door lock assemblies may be defective, possibly causing door to open while car is moving. Steering-gear balls may fracture, causing loss of steering. Gas tank may be defective. Radial tires may be defective.

1979 MODEL

Rear lamp sockets may be incorrect.

FORD MOTOR HOME

1973, 1974 CHASSIS 450, 500 MODELS

The bolt used to fasten the brake master cylinder to the brake pedal assembly was too short on many models. As a result, the brake pedal becomes disconnected from the brake system and the operator loses the ability to stop the vehicle.

The spring that returns the master cylinder to its primary position may actually cause the parts of the brake to break into small pieces. If the fragments become lodged within the cylinder, gradual lockup of the brakes could occur.

The left-front-brake hose can contact the brake pedal bracket, which will result in damage to the hose, loss of fluid, and eventual loss of brakes.

FORD MUSTANG

1977 MODEL

Cooling fan blades could crack and separate. Fuel filler and tank are vulnerable in a sideswipe. Tail lights may be defective. Driver's view to front and rear is restricted.

1978 MODEL
Rear seat belts may fail to lock. Cooling fan blades could crack and separate. Seat belts are uncomfortable.

1979 MODEL
Rear lamp sockets may be incorrect. Cooling fan may crack and throw fragments. Steering gear coupling flanges may be incorrect, possibly causing loss of steering. Plastic engine-fan finger guards may contact fan and shatter. Pushrod could disengage from pedal, causing loss of service brakes. Open hatch lid is hazardous to tall persons. Driver's view is obstructed. Seat release levers and door handle are difficult to locate. Horn and windshield-wiper controls are inconvenient.

1980 MODEL
Driver's front and rear view are obstructed. Fuel tank and filler are vulnerable in a crash. Open hatch lid is hazardous. Horn and windshield-wiper controls are inconvenient and confusing.

1981 MODEL
Driver-seat back latch may be defective, allowing seat to fall back into a reclined position.

1982 MODEL
GL ran too wide in hard turns and was difficult to control in abrupt maneuvers. Sharp corners and latch on open trunk lid are hazardous. Driver's view to rear is restricted. Gauges are difficult to read.

1983 MODEL
Horn and windshield-wiper controls are poorly designed.

FORD PINTO

1977 MODEL
Incorrect nuts may puncture fuel tank causing an explosion or fire.

1978 MODEL
Rear seat belts may fail to lock.

1979 MODEL
Rear lamp sockets may be incorrect.

FORD THUNDERBIRD

1977 MODEL
Transmission selector pointer may be mispositioned, possibly causing forward motion and accident when car is started. Engine may leak fuel at rubber hose connecting fuel-inlet tube and fuel filter, possibly causing a fire. Cooling fan could crack and separate. Runs very wide during hard cornering. In a crash, head restraints could be hazardous. Gauges are difficult to read because of reflections. Open trunk lid is hazardous to tall persons.

1978 MODEL
Front seat belts may fail to lock.

1979 MODEL
Rear lamp sockets may be incorrect. Power-steering gears may be defective, causing loss of steering. Nuts may be stripped, causing seat to slide along track. Pushrod could disengage from pedal, causing loss of service brakes. Wheel rim or tire may chafe front brake hose, possibly causing brakes to malfunction.

1980 MODEL
Brake assembly may be incorrect, causing slow stopping.

1983 MODEL
Fuel tank may have inadequately welded front seams, possibly causing fuel leakage and a fire. Cam retainer pins in parking pawl actuating rod assemblies may be defective, which could result in the parking pawl not engaging the parking gear when the shift selector is in the "park" position, allowing the vehicle to roll.

FORD TORINO

1979 MODEL
Rear lamp sockets may be incorrect.

FORD F150

1979 MODEL
Rear lamp sockets may be incorrect. Fuel tank and filler are vulnerable in a crash. Seat latches have sharp edges. Fair handling in accident avoidance. Front seat belts tend to ride up.

FORMALDEHYDE *(See also Air Pollution, Indoor; Mobile Homes; Pressed-Wood Products; Urea-Formaldehyde Foam Insulation)*

This chemical is used in thousands of consumer products from toothpaste to shampoo to felt-tip pens. Products containing formaldehyde represent 8 percent of the gross national product of the United States.

As a preservative, formaldehyde is used in hundreds of cosmetic preparations. It gives many paper products such as bags and towels added strength. It is used in many synthetic fabrics, both in clothing and upholstery fabrics, for its permanent press qualities.

As a resin, formaldehyde is used in pressed-wood products including furniture, paneling, plywood, and masonite. (Other products containing formaldehyde are listed below.)

The use of formaldehyde as a resin in foam insulation has been banned by the CPSC since 1982, although a U.S. Circuit Court recently overturned the ban. The Commission is now working with the pressed-wood and formaldehyde industries to reduce the level of formaldehyde "off-gasing" from pressed-wood products.

The Department of Housing and Urban Development, which has jurisdiction over mobile homes, has also established standards for reducing the formaldehyde emission levels in these units.

HAZARDS

Exposure to formaldehyde can cause irritation to eyes, nose, throat, and skin; nausea, headaches, nosebleeds, dizziness, memory loss, shortness of breath, and asthmatic-like symptoms. People with respiratory problems such as asthma, emphysema, or allergies often have a more serious reaction to formaldehyde, although some people with no previous history of these problems develop them after exposure to formaldehyde.

Reactions to formaldehyde may be temporary, and may be relieved by leaving the source of exposure, or can become chronic like a sensitized allergy. People who become sensitized to formaldehyde often experience a severe reaction when they come in contact with even small amounts of it in products such as newspapers, perfumes, or telephones. In experiments with laboratory animals, formaldehyde vapors have been shown to cause cancer. Many scientists believe formaldehyde increases the risk of cancer for humans as well.

The formaldehyde products with the highest levels of off-gasing are urea-formaldehyde foam insulation and pressed-wood products. Pressed-wood products—including plywood, particleboard, and fiberboard—are used extensively in mobile homes, new home construction, and in the remodeling and renovation of existing homes. These products are also extensively used in the construction of mobile housing, where the high ratio of products to the size of the mobile home and the low air-ventilation rate make the problem more severe.

PRECAUTIONS

If you suspect a problem with formaldehyde off-gasing, contact the Consumer Product Safety Hotline (800–638–CPSC) for a list of laboratories in your area to test your home. The CPSC can also give you information on reducing formaldehyde levels through the use of sealants and ventilation. If you suspect a problem with formaldehyde, contact your local or state health department. An inexpensive, commercial formaldehyde monitor is available from 3M Labs, which you can use yourself in your home to get an approximate level of off-gasing. Write 3M Corporation, P.O. Box 13457, St. Paul, MN 55164.

PRODUCTS CONTAINING FORMALDEHYDE

Particleboard
Urea-formaldehyde foam insulation
Wax and butcher wet-strength paper
Permapress cotton
Plastic
Plywood
Molding compounds
Fiberglass and mineral wool insulation binders
Formica
Pressed-wood furniture
Brake drums
Plastic parts for vehicles
Plumbing fixtures
Hardware
Lawn and garden equipment
Sporting goods
Counter- and tabletops
Melamine tableware
Resins and oil-based paints
Explosives
Vinyl resins
Electrical insulation parts
Nitrogen fertilizers
Phenolic termasetting resins
Rubber tires
Insecticides
Pharmaceuticals
Textile-treating agents
Detergents

Mascara and other cosmetics
Barber and beauty-shop disinfectants
Air fresheners
Dry cleaners for disinfectant
Fiberboard
Air and furnace filters
Furniture adhesives
Binding on paperbag seams
Plaster of paris castings
Orthopedic casts and bandages
Binders for sand foundry cores
Coated papers used for cartons and labels
Coatings for appliances
Primer coats for automobiles
Paint and wood finishes
Housings for electric shavers and mixers
Electronic equipment
Soap dispensers
Stove and refrigerator hardware
Toilet seats
Knobs and buttons
Utensil handles
Shampoo
Nail polish
Mildew preventatives
Synthetic lubricants
Textile waterproofing
Flour preservative
Wheat grains and agricultural seeds

PRODUCTS CONTAINING FORMALDEHYDE

Water-softening chemicals	Facial tissues and napkins
Urethane coatings and resins	Hospital bedsheets
Antihistamines	Examining-table paper rolls
Aerosol insecticides	Dental bibs
Dyes for textile industry	Diaper liners
Embalming agents	Some filter papers
Antiperspirant formations	Rayon
Oral hexamethylenetetramine medication	Drapery and upholstery fabrics
	Carpet and upholstery latex backing
Drinking milk	Nonwoven binders and flock adhesives
Dental filling	Softeners and lubricants
Dust-sterilizing solutions	Flame retardants
Hair-waving preparations	Antislip agents
Deodorants	Antistatic agents
Nail hardeners	Bactericides and napping agents
Glues	Sanforized cottons
Acrylic	Leather tanning
Wool	Preservatives
Nylon fibers	Vaccines
Photochemical smog	Automotive exhaust
Cigarette smoke	Water filters

FREE SPIRIT II MOPED

1978 MODEL
Sold by Sears. The front brake assembly is prone to failure and causes grabbing when applied.

FREEZE-DRIED COFFEE. *See Caffeine; Coffee, Decaffeinated.*

FRENCH'S IDAHO MASHED POTATOES. *See Sulfites.*

FRUIT, CANNED. *See Foods, Canned.*

FRUIT-FLAVORED BEVERAGES. See *Brominated Vegetable Oil (BVO); Food Colors, Artificial; Food Colors, Natural; Food Flavoring Additives.*

FRUIT, FRESH. See *Botulism; Botulism, Infant; Canning, Home; Drug and Food Interactions; Individual Fruits.*

FRUIT JUICES. See *Drug and Food Interactions.*

FRYERS. See *Cooking Appliances, Small Electric.*

FRY PANS, ELECTRIC *(See also Cooking Appliances, Small Electric)*

HAZARDS

Most injuries involving electric fry pans or skillets are:

• Electric shocks occurring when one hand is on the appliance and the other hand on metal such as a sink, stove, or other electric appliance.

• Burns resulting from contact with hot liquid when the appliance is knocked over.

• Burns resulting from contact with the hot appliance, especially from the glass lids on larger frying pans.

FUELS, LIQUID *(See also Gasoline; Gasoline Containers)*

INJURIES

In 1980, 29,000 involved liquid fuels including gasoline, lighter fluids, diesel fuels, kerosene, and lamp oils.

HAZARDS

Most injuries are burns caused by accidental or improper ignition of the fuels spilled on clothing or the body or added to an existing fire. Some injuries occurring mainly to children involve poisoning from accidental ingestion of the fuels.

FUEL STORAGE TANKS. *See Fuels, Liquid; Gasoline Containers.*

FURCELLERAN. *See Carrageenan and Furcelleran.*

FURNACES *(See also Air Pollution, Indoor; Carbon Monoxide)*

INJURIES
There were 12,000 in 1980.

HAZARDS
The following hazards occurred with furnaces.

- Contact with hot metal grates and other hot surfaces, especially by children.

- Carbon monoxide poisoning in oil, gas, coal, or wood furnaces starved of their necessary intake air, especially when clogged or cracked exhaust lines allow carbon monoxide to leak into the house.

- Ignition of accumulated fuel vapors, sometimes when an attempt is being made to light a pilot light.

PRECAUTIONS
Gas furnaces should have a "safety pilot" that automatically stops the flow of fuel when the pilot light goes out. They should be installed according to local codes, which usually specify the air intake and exhaust requirements for safe operation. In addition, metal furnace grates should be covered with metal screens, the air intake should not be blocked, and flammable liquids should be kept away. It is wise to ask a professional to do all major servicing of furnaces.

HAZARDOUS MODELS
In 1981, the Home Division of Lear Siegler, Inc., began a program to repair approximately 55,000 liquid propane and natural gas furnaces used in mobile homes. The furnaces may pose a risk of death or poisoning by leaking carbon monoxide if portions of the vent system corrode. The furnaces contain the Miller brand name on the top of the louvered door.

FURNITURE. See Beds, Bunk; Chairs; Folding Chairs; Stools; Pressed-Wood Products

FURNITURE POLISHES *(See also Aerosol Containers; Poisons)*

The three types of commercial furniture polish are solvents, emulsions, and aerosol sprays. In each, the principal ingredients are oil and wax. Petroleum or mineral spirits solvents dissolve the oil (conditioner) or wax (protector) ingredients for easy and even application. When the solvent dries, it leaves the protective coating of oil or wax. Emulsion products are liquid mediums with the active ingredients suspended in them and may contain other ingredients to help make the application smoother.

Aerosol sprays allow quick application of oil and wax, but their health and environmental dangers outweigh the benefits of faster application. Polish-spray propellants can also decompose into harmful gases when in contact with heated surfaces.

HAZARDS

The health dangers of furniture polishes include poisoning, acute ingestion of the solvent or emulsion polishes by children, and the inhalation of fumes and vapors in homes where fresh air is usually lacking. Some kerosene-like substances, when ingested, enter the lungs and saturate them so that they cannot function. There is no way to rid the body of the poison or to reverse its effect. Most polishes are flammable and can be ignited by active smoke. Some, such as petroleum, can cause skin irritation and, among some individuals, skin photosensitization (sensitivity to light). Naphtha can induce death by cardiac arrest; nitrobenzene and dinitrobenzene are highly poisonous when ingested; and oil of cedarwood is a nervous stimulant that has been used to induce abortions. They are all contained in some polishes.

For more information on the health hazards of furniture polishes, see *The Household Pollutants Guide* by the Center for Science in the Public Interest (Garden City, N.Y.: Anchor Books, 1978, $3.50).

FUSES. See Home Electrical System.

G

GAMES, BATTERY-POWERED. *See Batteries, Button.*

GARAGE DOORS. *See Doors.*

GARBAGE DISPOSERS

HAZARDS
Most injuries are lacerations, fractures, avulsions, or amputations resulting from the victim's hand contacting the disposal's blades.

PRECAUTIONS
Users should try to avoid ever putting their hands into a disposal and, if they must, they should make certain the unit is off and the blades are no longer spinning.

GARDEN EQUIPMENT, POWER *(See also Garden Tools, Power; Snowblowers)*

INJURIES
In 1980, 13,000 involved large garden equipment including tractors, power tillers or cultivators, power leaf mulchers and

grinders, lawn vacuums, logsplitters, snowthrowers, or snowblowers.

HAZARDOUS MODELS

In February 1982, the CPSC issued a complaint against Sears, Roebuck & Company and Roper Corporation over 220,000 Rotospader roto-tillers that Roper manufactured and Sears sold. The roto-tillers could become locked in reverse and mutilate the legs of the user. Model number beginning "917," distributed between 1963 and 1979, was alleged to be hazardous. Several thousand roto-tillers sold by Roper through independent dealers were also involved. The complaint has been settled.

GARDEN TOOLS, POWER

INJURIES

In 1980, 11,000 involved power lawn trimmers or edgers, power hedge trimmers, leaf blowers, and other small power garden tools. In 1979, 6,900 involved power hedge trimmers.

HAZARDS

Most injuries were cuts caused by the following:

- Changing positions of the hands while the trimmer is running.

- Moving branches out of the way while cutting.

- Trying to hold the cord away from the blade.

- Dropping the trimmer because of a violent deflection when the blade contacts fence wire, posts, or heavy branches.

- Tripping or falling and catching the trimmer by the moving blade.

- Pulling the trimmer through a hedge by the cord, causing the switch to be tripped "on."

- Picking up the trimmer by the blade.

Some injuries were electrical shocks caused by the failure to use three-hole extension cords with three-prong plugs.

PRECAUTIONS

Trimmers should be purchased with the following features:

- Cutting teeth and guards that are close together;

- Two handles; the forward handle should be wide and high above the cutting blades;

- Light enough in weight so that it can be controlled easily; and

- Double-insulated or grounded with a three-wire cord.

HAZARDOUS MODELS

In September 1981, Consumers Union reported that the blade on the Black & Decker hedge trimmers, model numbers 8118, 8124, 8134, 8144, and 8155, may continue running if the operator loses his grip on the handle. It also reported that the Little Wonder D1000 failed to meet new safety standards for Underwriters Laboratories' approval. Finally, it noted that the Disston Dual Power 2060 was not double-insulated.

In August 1982, Consumers Union reported that the following string trimmers may be hazardous:

- The Lawn Boy LB60E4 and LB30E4 and K&S Trim All TA1017 and TA953 are not double-insulated.

- The K&S Trim All TA1017's helper handle has a sharp edge.

GARDEN TRACTORS

INJURIES
In 1978, 3,000 were reported.

HAZARDS
Garden tractors could be hazardous in the following ways:

- Overturning when driving over uneven terrain, steep slopes, or embankments.

- Running over someone standing behind the vehicle (this happens most often to young children) when the tractor goes in reverse.

- Ignition of flammable liquids such as gasoline.

- Falls from going too fast or abrupt shifts in speed.

Make certain to buy a garden tractor with the following features: safety guards for all moving parts to reduce the hazard of touching belts, chains, pulleys, and gears; and a throttle, gears, and brakes that are accessible and can be operated smoothly and with minimum effort.

Take the following precautions when operating tractors:

• Never allow children to operate them.

• Wear sturdy, rough-soled work shoes and close-fitting slacks and shirts to avoid entanglement in moving parts.

• Clear the area before you drive over it.

• Always turn off the tractor and wait for moving parts to stop before leaving it.

• Always turn off the machine and disconnect the spark plug wire before adjusting the machine.

• Drive up and down, rather than across, slopes.

• Never refuel a tractor when it is running or the engine is hot.

• Never refuel a tractor indoors because unseen vapors may be ignited by a spark or pilot light.

• Start the garden tractor outdoors, not in the garage where carbon monoxide gas can collect.

GAS CONTROL VALVES *(See also Furnaces; Gas Connector Valves)*

PRECAUTIONS

Exercise caution when attempting to locate the gas valve. To locate the valve, remove the access panel on the front of the heating appliance. If any odor of leaking gas is present, do not attempt to locate the valve, but immediately contact the gas supplier for assistance. When looking for the valve and model number, be careful not to use matches or other ignition sources, which could cause any accumulated gas to explode.

HAZARDOUS MODELS

In 1982, more than 200,000 gas control valves used in heating appliances fueled by liquid propane gas were recalled because of an explosion hazard. The combination valves, made by Honeywell, Inc., serve the dual purpose of regulating the gas supplied to the appliance and shutting off the gas supply when the pilot light is extinguished. But the valves may allow the LP gas to leak, possibly exposing it to an ignition source, such as electric sparks or matches, and cause an explosion. The valves with the following model numbers were recalled: C5133, C5134, CS5133, CS5134, V4136, V4146, V5118, V5189, V7284, V8129, V8136, V8139, V8146, VS8133, VS8138, and VS8141.

GAS HEATERS. *See Air Pollution, Indoor; Carbon Monoxide; Space Heaters.*

GASOLINE *(See also Air Pollution, Indoor; Fuels, Liquid; Gasoline Containers; Lead)*

HAZARDS

The lead content of gasoline contributes significantly to the continuing problem of lead poisoning in the United States. Since 1977, the use of lead in gasoline has decreased as gasoline additive regulations have gone into effect. However, health officials feel the levels of lead in gas still represent a major concern, especially when combined with other sources of lead contamination including pollution, paint, and lead in dust and dirt.

Unleaded gas also has harmful properties. An estimated 40 percent of unleaded gas contains MMT, a manganese additive that increases hydrocarbon emissions. MMT also plugs up some catalytic devices on autos, and is extremely toxic to humans. Chronic manganese poisoning causes many neurologic symptoms, including Parkinson's disease.

Other common additives found in gasoline include anti-knock agents, which can be fatal in very small doses; scavengers to remove lead oxides, which can cause liver damage and may cause cancer; anti-rust agents, about which the toxicity is unknown; anti-oxidants, which are added to stored gasoline to prevent decomposition and can cause burns to the eyes and skin; and metal deactivators, which are extremely toxic substances added to gasoline to counter the oxidizing effect of metals found in gas. Modifiers, dyes, and de-icers are other harmful additives.

Emission pollutants from automobile engines—including carbon monoxide—invade building interiors, especially in congested city areas. Cleaner-burning engines and catalytic converters have lowered pollution levels somewhat and, as stricter fuel standards reduce the amount of gasoline cars use, auto pollution levels will be further reduced.

GASOLINE CONTAINERS *(See also Fuels, Liquid; Lighters)*

HAZARDS

Because it is highly flammable and its vapor is explosive when mixed with air, gasoline is difficult to store safely. Glass jugs can shatter too easily. Plastic bottles may split, be porous enough to allow gas vapors to escape, or may even be dissolved. Even containers supposedly designed for storing gasoline can be unsafe. In addition, most containers do not have a flame arrestor—a fine wire mesh in the pour opening—to prevent flames racing up the stream of fuel being poured and causing an explosion.

PRECAUTIONS

To use gasoline and its containers safely, Consumers Union recommends following these rules.

- Store gasoline only in a container specifically designed for it, and with a flame arrestor.

- Do not fill container to the top. Leave an inch or two for expansion.

- Do not carry a filled container in your car, except to bring it home from the service station.

- Store gasoline in a separate garage or outbuilding, or leave it outdoors under a shelter.

- Keep a full container out of direct sunlight and away from heat.

- Cap all openings, including vent holes, when not using.

- Do not use a stopper on a pouring extension when storing.

- Do not empty a container. A small amount of liquid can form vapor rich enough to explode.

- If someone swallows gasoline, do not induce vomiting, but call for medical help immediately.

- Keep container out of the reach of children.

HAZARDOUS MODELS

In March 1981, Consumers Union judged the following containers to be potentially unsafe.

- Eagle 1001, Huffy 4612, Stancan 032321, and Stancan 032331, which leaked in Consumers Union's pressure test.

- Brookins 699, Delphos 325D, and Huffy Tanker 4690, which leaked when pouring.

- Delphos 401 and Huffy 4624, which leaked in Consumers Union's pressure test and when pouring.

GAS OVENS. *See Air Pollution, Indoor; Ranges.*

GAS RANGES. *See Air Pollution, Indoor; Ranges.*

GAS STOVES. *See Air Pollution, Indoor; Ranges.*

GAS WATER HEATERS

INJURIES

In 1978, 1,100 were reported.

HAZARDS

Many accidents occur because victims forget about their water heater. Other accidents occur when a flammable liquid is used in the vicinity. The heavier-than-air vapors of a liquid such as gasoline can flow along the floor and be explosively ignited by the flame of the water heater's pilot light or burner. More accidents occur when clogged burners and vents cause carbon monoxide poisoning.

PRECAUTIONS

In purchasing a gas water heater, make sure there is:

• An automatic thermostat that turns the burner on and off, and keeps the water from rising above a set temperature.

• A safety relief device to take over should the regular thermostat fail.

• A cut-off device that will shut off the gas if the pilot light goes out or if the water temperature rises too high.

In installing and maintaining a heater:

• Install the temperature and pressure-relief valve at the same time.

• Do not repair a defective valve. Any time a water heater is replaced, the valve should also be replaced.

HAZARDOUS MODELS

In 1980, more than 600,000 liquid-petroleum-gas water heaters sold between 1961 and 1980 by the A.O. Smith Corporation, by Sears, Roebuck & Company, and by other retailers were recalled. The defect was in thermostats that became damaged and permitted LP gas to escape, which created the danger of explosion. The thermostat was manufactured by Emerson Electric Company. (See the list below of water heaters possibly containing the defective thermostats.)

In June 1982, the CPSC filed an administrative complaint against the Robertshaw Controls Company for failing to report, in 1974, the estimated 47 deaths and 93 injuries associated with a defect in Unitrol 110 and Unitrol 200 gas water heater controls manufactured by the company. More than 300,000 of these controls were installed in liquid-petroleum-gas water heaters between December 1954 and March 1957. The complaint alleges that when the pilot is extinguished, the automatic pilot function of the control may fail to operate by failing to stop the continuing flow of unburned gas to the main burner of the water heater, thereby creating a fire and explosion hazard. As of May 1983, the complaint was still pending.

GATOR ROACH HIVES. *See Insecticides, Household.*

GELATIN. *See Aspartame.*

WATER HEATERS POSSIBLY HAVING WHITE-ROGERS THERMOSTATS

A.O. SMITH COMPANY
A.O. Smith
American Standard
Arcoglas
Arcoglas Classic
Conservationist
Continental
Energy Saver 5
Energy Saver 10
Fuel Saver 10
Fuel Saver 1
Futura
Gas 1
Gas 2
Gas 3
Glascote
Kee
Minnegasco
National
Permaglas
Signet

SEARS
Economiser
Homart
Honor Bilt
Powermiser
Sears series (15 up to 600)

RHEEN MANUFACTURING COMPANY
Right
Right 10
Right Miser
Right Miser 10
Montgomery Ward
    (MODELS 33032, 33158, 33166, 33376)

W.L. JACKSON MANUFACTURING COMPANY
Big O
Gibson
Hermitage
Jackson
Marathon
Metermiser
Plum Easy
Presto
Simonson
Tempmaster
Tip Top

STATE INDUSTRIES
Ambassador
Aqua-Lux
Censible
Coop
Courier
Economaster
Imperial Citation
Master Service
Mission
Modern
President
Ready-Hot
Sentry
Superlife
Sutherlite
Thermo-King

GENERAL ELECTRIC OSCILLATING FAN. *See Fans, General Electric.*

GENERIC DRUGS

      Every drug has a generic name and one or more brand names. A brand name is given to a drug by the company that manufactures it.

The generic name, given by the FDA, is usually a contraction of the drug's chemical name.

Aspirin is the generic name of a pain killer that is marketed under several brand names. Manufacturers attempt to convince consumers that there are significant differences in competing brands, but the law requires that both generic- and brand-name drugs meet the same standards of safety, strength, purity, and effectiveness. They are expected to behave the same way in the body; only taste, color, shape, and packaging may differ.

Some instances have come to light where products containing the same active ingredient, made by different manufacturers, are absorbed at different rates by the body. Thus, they differ in the rate at which the drug does its work. Where such differences exist, one drug should not be substituted for another. The FDA has issued a list of drugs that are therapeutically equivalent. Most pharmacists have a list to help them substitute generic drugs for their brand-name versions. Because of difficulties in developing scientific equipment and sensitive tests to determine these equivalencies such data is not yet available for all brand name drugs and their generic counterparts.

The real difference between brand-name and generic drugs is most often price. Brand-name drugs usually cost considerably more than their generic counterparts.

Some drugs do not have a generic version as there is a law that prohibits their sale until the 17-year patent on the original brand-name drug has expired. Only about one-fourth of the most often prescribed drugs have generic substitutes.

When a physician writes a prescription, either the generic or brand name of a drug may be specified. If a brand name is used and a generic equivalent is available, the pharmacist may choose to substitute the generic drug, unless the physician has indicated on the prescription that there should be no substitute.

Both prescription and over-the-counter generic drugs are as good as their brand-name versions, when the drugs have been approved by the FDA for safety and effectiveness. They are usually much less expensive and will save the consumer money.

GENITAL DEODORANTS. *See Deodorants, Genital.*

GEORGIE BOY CRUISE-AIR MOTOR HOME

1973 25-FOOT MODEL

The exhaust pipe over the rear axle may be too close to the floor, possibly resulting in damage to the floor or fire.

GERIPLEX FS. *See Laxatives.*

GERITOL. *See Iron and Iron Supplements.*

GERMICIDES AND DISINFECTANTS *(See also Aerosol Containers; Formaldehyde)*

Commercial air fresheners get rid of odors from sources including pets, cooking, the bathroom, the furnace, smoking, or people in four different ways: by exchanging one odor for another, by deadening the sense of smell with a chemical that affects the nerve, by coating nasal passages with an oily film, or by deodorizing—deactivating the unwanted odor.

HAZARDS

Some air fresheners contaminate the air with foreign substances such as carbolic acid, a toxic chemical that can cause serious burns and tissue destruction when allowed to come in contact with the skin. Many air fresheners also contain formaldehyde.

Disinfectants do not sterilize. They can reduce but not kill offending germs. Soon after disinfecting, germs will again be present in large numbers, as opposed to sterilizing in which drastic measures, such as high temperatures, are used to remove all microbial life.

True disinfectants are usually toxic chemicals. The most common household bactericide and germicide is cresol. Cresol is a caustic that poisons the nervous system, liver, and kidneys and may also injure the lungs, pancreas, and spleen. It may be absorbed through the skin and mucous membranes of the respiratory tract. Cresol, also called paracresol, can be found in common compounds such as dyes, pigments, antioxidants, resins, plasticizer vaporizers, tricresyl, soaps, lotions, perfumes, detergents, creams, and tobacco smoke.

Benzalkonium chloride is a preservative and a bactericide found in products such as contact lens solutions and is the most commonly used eye-drop preservative. However, studies indicate benzalkonium may damage the cellular components of the cornea.

For more information about the health hazards of germicides

and disinfectants, see *The Household Pollutants Guide* by the Center for Science in the Public Interest (Garden City, N.Y.: Anchor Books, 1978, $3.50).

GLASS DOORS AND WINDOWS *(See also Doors)*

INJURIES

In 1980, 196,000 involved glass doors or windows.

HAZARDS

• Walking or running into, or falling against, sliding glass doors, often when the victim was unaware the door was closed.

• Pushing on the glass portion to open or close storm doors, losing one's balance and falling against the glass in these doors, or opening or closing the doors against a person in the flow of traffic.

• Slipping and falling against glass bathtub and shower enclosures.

• Walking into, running into, or pushing on glazed panels next to doors, typically because the victim was unaware of their presence or mistook them for doors.

• Striking the glass when opening or closing windows; removing or installing windows; falling, knocking, or pushing against windows; contacting unmounted glass or storm windows in storage or broken glass in windows.

GOVERNMENT STANDARDS

The CPSC developed a mandatory safety standard for any glazing materials in doors, sidelights, bath and shower doors, requiring that glazing materials either do not break, or break in a way unlikely to cause injury. The standard applied to materials used and manufactured after July 6, 1977. Over 30 states had previously passed similar laws to improve safety in glazing materials.

PRECAUTIONS

In purchasing glass doors or replacing glass in doors or panels, select a glazing material that is less hazardous than regular glass. Tempered glass, laminated glass, and rigid plastic are all safer. Make certain the door is hung properly to resist shocks from slamming and minor collisions.

To make existing glass doors safer, place decals or colored tape on them to show that glass is present, install safety bars at doorhandle level to prevent contact with the glass, and install protective screens or grilles over the glass in storm doors. It is also wise to place furniture or a large planter in front of large glass enclosures like a picture window.

GLASS JARS. *See Bottles.*

GLASS PANELS. *See Glass Doors and Windows.*

GMC CABALLERO

1978–1980 MODELS
Lower-rear control-arm bolts may fracture, causing loss of control.

1981 MODEL
Lower-rear control-arm bolts may fracture, causing loss of control.

GMC MOTOR HOMES

1973 MODEL
Fuel line has a tendency to crack, which will cause leakage when the tank is completely full.
Seat belts in living quarters may have been installed with inadequately locking seat-belt anchor fasteners. These fasteners may vibrate loose, rendering the seat belt ineffective.
In some models the pin that connects the brake pedal to the braking system is missing. If so, the brakes will not work.

1973, 1974 MODELS
TZE-063: The wheels installed on the vehicle are not compatible with radial tires. Radial tires cause excessive stresses on the wheel and could crack the rim. A cracked rim will result in sudden loss of air and the driver could lose control of the steering.
ZEO-500: The rear-suspension outer-wheel bearings may fail, causing the rear wheel to separate from the vehicle. Alo, water can

enter the accelerator cable sheath and freeze. If this were to occur, the throttle could be prevented from returning to idle position.

1975 P-30 SERIES MODEL

The rear-axle stabilizer bar can break. If both brackets break, the stabilizer bar can fall down and dig into the road. Depending on the speed of the vehicle, this action could cause a serious accident.

1976, 1977 G-30 CUTAWAY VAN, P-30 MODELS

The master brake cylinder was assembled with improperly manufactured bolts. Many of these bolts are extremely brittle and will easily break. If breakage were to occur, the master cylinder would develop a leak and loss of brake fluid would render the brakes inoperable.

1976, 1977 ZEO-6582 AND ZEO-6583 MODELS

On models equipped with the Onan 6.0KW motor generator, the 110-volt AC conduit on the generator can contact the positive battery terminal or starter solenoid post, resulting in a short circuit. Also, the 110-volt AC conduit and cable insulation may wear out from contact with the negative battery terminal, causing a short circuit. Such shorting can cause a fire, and can burn the fuel supply hose to the generator, resulting in a gasoline-fed fire.

GOOD SEASONS SALAD DRESSING MIX. *See Sulfites.*

GRAINS. *See Beer Additives.*

GRANT'S ANT OR ROACH TRAPS. *See Insecticides, Household.*

GRAPEFRUIT. *See Drug and Food Interactions.*

GRAVIES. *See Food Poisoning.*

GRAVIES, PREPARED. *See Food Colors, Artificial.*

GREENS. *See Produce.*

GRIDDLES, ELECTRIC. *See Cooking Appliances, Small Electric.*

GRILLS. *See Camping Cooking and Heating Equipment.*

GROCERY CARTS. *See Shopping Carts.*

GUNS, BB

INJURIES
In 1980, 53,000 were reported.

HAZARDOUS MODELS
In April 1979, Daisy Manufacturing Company recalled approximately 19,100 BB guns. After several thousand normal shots have been fired, the safety mechanism may malfunction, allowing the gun to be fired with the safety on. The guns involved are model numbers 105A, 1938A, and 111A and were manufactured in 1978.

GUNS, SPEAR

HAZARDOUS MODELS
In October 1979, AMF voluntarily recalled more than 1,800 underwater spear guns. A defect in the guns' "trigger shock-line retainers" can cause unintentional firing if the shock lines are wrapped too tightly around the retainer, or if the taut lines and gun barrel are held together. The following model numbers and brand names are affected: 5300 Long Tom, 5302 Sharp Shooter, 6334108 Supersten, 63333503 Competizione, 5304 Californian, 5306 Frontiersman, 5308 Shortie, 5310 Snub Nose, 6334009 Sten, 6333008 Medisten, 6331006 Ministen, 6330005 Miniministen.

In 1980, AMF Voit, Inc., issued a warning about an estimated 97,300 spear guns. These guns may contain defective triggers and may fire accidentally even though their safety catches are engaged.

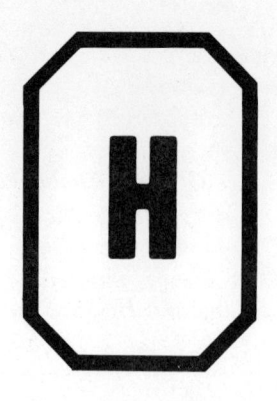

HAIR ACCESSORIES *(See also Hair Dryers)*

INJURIES
In 1980, 13,000 involved hair dryers, hair curlers, electric combs, nonelectric combs or hairbrushes, electric hair curlers, curling irons, hair clips, or hair pins.

HAZARDS
Hot irons touching the scalp or other skin, sharp edges on adjustable foil barrels, and electrical accidents involving short circuiting through contact with wet surfaces.

HAIR CURLERS. *See Hair Accessories.*

HAIR DRYERS

INJURIES
In 1974, 1,000 cases were reported.

HAZARDS
Burns, which can be caused by skin contact with hot parts of the appliance, particularly on dryer/stylers where there are metal components that become extremely hot and can cause serious burns on

contact or on bonnet-type dryers, where an air hose becomes very hot and can burn bare skin.

Electric shocks can be caused by plugging in or turning on a hair dryer with wet hands or by faulty wiring even when hands are dry.

Overheating can occur if the air intake vents are covered by clothing, a towel, lint, hands, hair, or if the dryer is run for very long periods of time, or if the thermostat fails.

Inhalation of asbestos fibers has been linked in scientific studies to asbestosis, lung cancer, mesothelioma, and other diseases. Many hair dryers manufactured before 1980 contain asbestos liners. When it was discovered these dryers were releasing asbestos fibers into the air, manufacturers voluntarily recalled the products.

PRECAUTIONS

In purchasing a hair dryer:

• Make sure there it a cut-off device to turn off the dryer if the appliance begins to overheat. There usually is either a heat-activated switch that turns the dryer back on when it gets cooler, or a fuse that blows when the appliance overheats.

• In salon-type dryers, make sure the hood is large enough to accommodate head plug rollers easily. To avoid neck strain, make sure the angle of the hood is comfortable.

• Make sure it can be held easily without covering the air intake vents with your hand.

• Make sure there are no exposed metal strips close to where the hot air comes out.

• Make certain the hair dryer does not contain asbestos fibers. If you are concerned about your pre-1980 model, contact its manufacturer to find out if it contains asbestos.

To use a hair dryer safely, keep air intake vents clear of towels, clothing, lint, hair, and other obstructions and never use them in the bathtub or immerse a hair dryer in water. If a dryer is accidentally dropped into water while it is plugged in, be sure to unplug it before touching it.

HAIR DYES *(See also Hair Rinses)*

HAZARDS

Studies have shown that hair dyes contain certain chemicals that cause cancer in laboratory animals and may cause cancer in humans. No matter how hazardous the chemicals used in hair dyes may be, the FDA has no power to ban them because of a 1938 law exempting hair dyes from regulation. The agency's only recourse is to require that the products containing the suspect chemical bear a warning label.

Unfortunately, cosmetic companies are able to avoid these warning labels by "reformulating" the hair dyes so that the cancer-causing chemical is no longer included. The problem is that the new chemical is similar in structure to the original one and may be just as dangerous.

This is exactly what happened when the FDA proposed that a warning label be put on all products containing the chemical 4-methoxy-m-phenylenediamine sulfate (abbreviated as 4-MMPD). It was removed from the hair dyes and replaced with the chemical 4-ethoxy-m-phenylenediamine sulfate (4-EMPD). Some cancer investigators believe this chemical has the same potential for causing cancer, although scientific opinion is mixed. The FDA cannot propose a cancer-warning label for the reformulated chemical until years of testing are completed.

In addition to the risk of cancer, there are many acute health hazards associated with the use of hair dyes, including skin irritation and sensitization, as well as gastrointestinal and neurological symptoms. Permanent eye damage or blindness may also result if the dyes come in contact with the eyes. Do not use hair dyes to color eyebrows or eyelashes.

PRECAUTIONS

Although it has not been proved that chemicals used in hair dyes cause cancer in humans, it would be wise to avoid use of these products. But if these products are used, certain precautions are essential. Risk is related to the amount of chemical used and the length of exposure. Dyes should not be used or left on the head longer than necessary. The scalp should be rinsed thoroughly with water after use. Always patch test before using a hair dye, and never dye eyebrows or eyelashes.

HAIR RINSES *(See also Hair Dyes)*

Temporary hair dyes are also known as hair rinses. Coal-tar dyes that are suspected to cause cancer in laboratory animals are present in these rinses as well as in permanent hair dyes. The difference between these two products is that the coal-tar dyes in the rinses coat rather than penetrate the hair shaft as they do in the permanent dyes. This coating is generally removed with the next shampooing.

The FDA is unable to determine if these rinses are safe because the manufacturers are allowed to keep the identities of many of the ingredients secret. However, studies have shown that chemicals containing coal-tar dyes cause cancer in laboratory animals. One coloring agent that is known to be in some rinses is Direct Blue 6, which is one of the seven hair-dye chemicals that caused cancer in animal studies conducted by the National Cancer Institute.

PRECAUTIONS
Until further information about the chemical composition of these rinses is ascertained and the safety question resolved, it would be wise not to use hair rinses or dyes.

HALLS. *See Cough Medications.*

HAM. *See Nitrites and Nitrosamines.*

HAMBURGER *(See also Food Poisoning)*

Ground meat must be handled carefully to avoid food poisoning. The meat should always be cooked until it is at least brownish-pink in the center. Never serve it raw. Ground meat requires special care because when it is ground, germs on the surface are spread throughout the meat.

HAMBURGER HELPER, BETTY CROCKER. *See Sulfites.*

HAMMERS

INJURIES
In 1980, 50,000 cases were reported.

HAZARDS
The most common injuries are cuts or bruises resulting from hitting the thumb or fingers while hammering a nail. Other injuries are caused by pieces of metal chipping off the head of a hammer or the head flying off because it is loose or the handle is cracked.

PRECAUTIONS
In selecting a hammer, avoid fragile cast-iron head hammers for anything but very light tasks. Also, the hammer face should be larger than the head of the object being struck. When using masonry hammers, wear ear protectors and eyeglasses (or goggles).

HASSOCKS. *See Stools.*

HEALTH FOODS

Claims that "health," "organic," and "natural" foods are safer and more nutritious than conventionally grown and processed foods are not supported by scientific evidence. These terms are often used interchangeably and are difficult to define. To add to the confusion, the FDA has taken no position on their use in food labeling and states that they have not attempted to arrive at a legal definition of these terms for food labels because enforcement would be very difficult and costly. One thing all "health," "organic," and "natural" foods seem to have in common is that they cost the consumer more than conventional foods.

Proponents of these "health" foods claim they are more nutritious, but studies have shown no differences between these natural foods and foods treated with manufactured fertilizers and pesticides. Of course, the mere absence of chemicals is claimed as an advantage for such foods, but the claim is often false. Many of these foods do contain pesticide residues. Even if no pesticide was used on a particular crop, residues may remain in the soil from the last application. Also, drifting sprays and dusts or rainfall runoff may settle on the plants. Traces of pesticides may be found in both organic and conventional foods, but usually these residues are within federal tolerance levels. Since the appearance of chemically and organically grown foods do not differ, it is difficult to be sure if a product labeled "organically grown" is accurate.

Many people buy "health" foods because they wrongly believe that since these products are "natural," they are safe. Hundreds of poisons occur naturally in foods. Sassafras tea has been banned by the FDA because it contains safrole, which produces liver cancer in laboratory animals. Kelp, a seaweed, can have a high arsenic content. Aflatoxin, a known cancer-causing substance, can grow on improperly stored peanuts, corn, and grains.

Many commonly used foods, "health" or conventional, contain low levels of toxic substances. Health foods would be a preferable alternative if they were in fact "healthy foods." Because there are no regulations in this area, the consumer has no way of knowing the manufacturer's definition of "natural" or "health" food.

HEARING AIDS. *See Batteries, Button.*

HEART MEDICATIONS. *See Drug and Food Interactions.*

HEAT GUNS

HAZARDOUS MODELS

In June 1979, Consumers Union reported that the following heaters pose a fire hazard.

- Hyde-Lectric Paint Remover HE-100

- Hyde-Lectric Painter Remover and Putty Softener HE-200

- Magna 252 Supertool

- Red Devil Electric Paint Remover 3401

- Sears Electric Paint Remover catalog number 44792

- Smith-Victor Torchlamp TL2

- Ward's Electric Paint Remover catalog number 75-5376000

- Warner Electric Paint Burner 384

In April 1980, Top Flite Models, Inc., began a program to repair approximately 20,000 heat guns used by model airplane hobbyists. The guns, which contain asbestos heat shields in the barrel, emit asbestos fibers during use. They were made between 1974 and 1977. Top Flite is trying to replace the asbestos shields with mica liners.

HEATING PADS

HAZARDS

Most injuries are burns caused by prolonged exposure at high temperatures or fires resulting from malfunctioning of the appliance.

PRECAUTIONS

To avoid burns, it is especially important that users avoid lying on heating pads. In addition, pads should not be used when sleeping; should not be used by people with insensitive skin or poor blood circulation; should never be used on skin treated with a liniment, salve, or ointment containing heat-producing ingredients; should not be used over a recent wound; and should not be used by the elderly, by diabetics, or by people who are taking cortisone or similar medications.

HAZARDOUS MODELS

In March 1981, Consumers Union reported that it had rated the wrap-around Kax 44MH "not acceptable" because it uses insulation that is not waterproof on its heating wires. Consumers Union also reported that most of the models it tested have pointed levers that can stab fingers.

HEAT LAMPS. *See Sunlamps.*

HEDGE TRIMMERS. *See Garden Tools, Power.*

HELMETS. *See Motorcycle Helmets.*

HEMORRHOID MEDICATIONS

Hemorrhoids, or "piles," are inflamed veins surrounding the rectum. Apart from surgery there is no real cure, but temporary symptomatic relief is available.

If you have hemorrhoids, do not treat yourself but consult a physician for a correct diagnosis. The physician may prescribe a steroid drug that is more effective than over-the-counter medications, most of which contain astringents or anesthetics.

HERPES SIMPLEX INFECTION. *See Smallpox Vaccination.*

HIDE KILLS CRAWLING INSECTS. *See Insecticides, Household.*

HIGH CHAIRS

INJURIES
In 1980, 8,000 involved high chairs and youth chairs. Most occurred to children under four years of age, and nearly 25 percent involved children under one year old.

HAZARDS
Falls from the chair result from safety devices not being used or secured, or when children sitting in a chair are not closely supervised. On many older high chairs, the crotch strap running between the child's legs to prevent slipping under the tray frequently is attached to the tray. Thus, if the tray is removed, the strap offers no protection. Many newer chairs are manufactured to meet a voluntary standard requiring, among other things, a system of retaining straps functioning independently of the tray. High chairs in compliance with this standard are identified by a label.

Falling or collapsing of a high chair can happen when the child in the chair is boisterous, or a second child attempts to climb on the chair, or a child tries to climb into an empty chair unassisted. A folding high chair can collapse when the locking device fails or is released accidentally because of poor construction or deterioration of the locking device, failure to lock the chair properly, violent rocking of the chair, or kicking of the device itself. The collapsing chair can cause pinching and entrapment of the child.

PRECAUTIONS
In purchasing a high chair, look for the following: sturdy, undamaged straps and belts that work correctly and a sturdy chair with a wide base for stability.

In older chairs, make certain there are adequate safety straps and that these are in good condition.

HIGH POINT DECAFFEINATED COFFEE. See *Coffee, Decaffeinated.*

HILLS BROTHERS DECAFFEINATED COFFEE. See *Coffee, Decaffeinated.*

HOBBIES AND CRAFTS

HAZARDS
Metalwork, sculpture, pottery, plasticrafts, jewelry making, lapidary work, and woodwork may be harmful because they generate dust and fumes. Dust from the crafts may contain chemicals, such as lye, hydrosulfite, and asbestos in powder form. Paint pigments contain several toxic substances—lead, cadmium, mercury, and selenium. Breathing these particles can result in scarred lung tissue, impaired respiration, and chronic respiratory diseases like bronchitis, emphysema, or pulmonary fibrosis.

Fumes from volatile toxic chemicals, such as solvents used in photography, printing, furniture refinishing, etc., can cause headaches, drowsiness, chemical intoxification, impaired motor response, and death. The firing of glazed pottery, soldering, and welding can produce lead vapors and carbon monoxide; metalworking can give off noxious nitrogen oxides and metallic vapors; heating plastics can cause toxic gases to be released. Recirculating air systems in homes allow rapid buildup of airborne particles and fumes, and dust can be tracked or carried to all parts of the house. Sweeping may aggravate the problem.

Many chemicals—such as acids, lye, and other alkalies—cause severe burns and eye damage. Solvents used in adhesives, varnishes, lacquers, oil paints, and paint thinners can irritate exposed parts of the body and penetrate the skin by dissolving natural oils. Some of these probably cause cancer. Goggles can protect eyes from toxic substances such as the ultraviolet radiation produced in welding. Soft contact lenses with properties for retaining medication can also hold strong vapors against the eyes, rather than allowing tears to wash the substances away. Fast-drying adhesives bond so rapidly and strongly that it is very easy to accidentally bond fingers together, or to bond a finger to an eye.

PRECAUTIONS

Sometimes even the most minuscule amounts of craft-related chemicals can be poisonous. Mealtime hazards abound both in and outside the workshop. Food can be contaminated by dusts, filings, vapors, and spilled chemicals or toxic residues on clothes, beards, hands, fingernails, and hair. Ingestive hazards exist in the finished product as well. Make sure any product that is made to go in the mouth—eating utensils, pipes, whistles, etc.—are free of contaminants. Do not use toxic glues in laminated cutting boards and bowls, lead or leaded solder in metal food and beverage containers, or certain poisonous species of wood in objects to be used in storing, serving, or eating food.

For more information on health hazards associated with hobbies and crafts, see *The Household Pollutants Guide* by the Center for Science in the Public Interest (Garden City, N.Y.: Anchor Books, 1978, $3.50).

HOLIDAY RAMBLER TRAILER

1965, 1966, 1967, 1968 MODELS

The wheel rims were poorly designed and may break under loaded conditions. Models include 22R-433,212; 22T-41,123; 190R-71,36; 210R-136,91; 220R-82,83; 190T-126,301; 210T-117,129; 220T-70.

1970, 1971, 1972 MODELS

Fittings on gas supply hose located at pressure regulator in front of trailer may develop cracks.

1975-1978 FREE SPIRIT, WIDE WORLD AND MONITOR MODELS

Vehicles with center bath may have misrouted LP gas hose. It is possible that the gas hose may contact the suspension system or the exhaust shield. Such contact could rupture the hose and because of the proximity to the exhaust, the propane could easily explode.

1977, 1978 RAMBLETTE, RAMBLER 1000, 3000, 5000 MODELS

The location of the LP gas supply line is very close to the kitchen-sink drawer. Repeated opening and closing of the drawer could rupture the line and because of the proximity to the furnace, an explosion could result.

HOME BUILDING. *See Air Pollution, Indoor; Formaldehyde; Pressed-Wood Products.*

HOME BUILDING MATERIALS. *See Air Pollution, Indoor; Asbestos; Formaldehyde; Pressed-Wood Products.*

HOME CANNING. *See Botulism; Canning, Home.*

HOME ELECTRICAL SYSTEM *(See also Aluminum Wiring; Antennas; Bulb Reflectors; Circuit Breakers; Extension Cords; Fluorescent Lights; Lamps; Night Lights; Wall Outlets)*

INJURIES
More than 700 deaths and 10,000 injuries annually.

HAZARDS
The electrical distribution system includes circuit wiring, lighting fixtures, fuses or circuit breakers, receptacles, switches, cords and plugs. When a part of this network fails or is misused, a fire can result. Specific causes of fires include:

• Insulation on wiring that has deteriorated or worn away, exposing wires carrying an electric current. Deterioration or other damage can occur when a cord is placed under carpeting or furniture, or coiled up during use.

• Using bulbs of higher wattage than is recommended in light fixtures and lamps. "Overlamping" may lead to overheating and can cause fires.

• Using fuses with higher amperage than the circuit is designed for. "Overfusing" may cause the circuit to overheat and can lead to fire.

- "Old technology" aluminum wiring, which can cause overheating and fires. Houses built between 1965 and 1973 may contain this kind of wire.

- Overloading a wall receptacle with too many appliances.

- Overloading an electrical circuit.

- Overloading extension cords, which may lead to overheating of the circuit or of the cord.

- Thermal insulation installed around faulty wiring or lighting fixtures, which retains heat and so creates a fire hazard.

The most important danger signals for faulty wiring are:

- Wires or circuit breakers that buzz, indicating that lines carrying current are loose in the system.

- Fuses that constantly burn out.

- The presence of heat at a receptacle or wall switch, which means that current is spilling outside of the lines.

- An acrid smell when you turn on an appliance or a lamp.

- Lights that dim when you turn on an appliance.

PRECAUTIONS

To determine whether a circuit is being overloaded: Add the wattage of each appliance plugged in to the circuit and divide the sum by 120. The result tells you how many amperes of current are flowing in the circuit. If the number is greater than the amperage of the fuse, then the circuit is overloaded.

Sometimes, however, fuses blow and breakers shut down when only one or two appliances or lights are turned on. That could mean there is a short inside the appliance, which is drawing an abnormal amount of current.

Before working with the electrical system, make certain the power has been turned off by using an electrical tester. These testers, which are inexpensive, have two metal probes connected to a tiny bulb.

HOME INSULATION *(See also Asbestos; Foam Insulation, Urea-Formaldehyde)*

HAZARDS

Home insulation can increase the chance of fires. The hazard varies depending on the material.

• Fibrous glass is naturally fire resistant, but the paper vapor barriers used in some fibrous glass insulation products and the resins used in the manufacturing process are flammable.

• Plastic foam insulation is usually treated with flame retardant chemicals to make it less combustible.

• Cellulose insulation manufactured with improper amounts and kinds of fire retardants, may present a flammability hazard or cause corrosion problems. That is why Congress required the CPSC to issue a mandatory safety standard for cellulose insulation prescribing a material's resistance to surface burning, the potential for sustained smoldering, and tests for corrosion.

The addition of thermal insulation to deficient electrical systems may increase the risk of fire. Such deficiencies include loose junction points such as screws, wire nuts, or fuse boxes; surface-mounted lights; and overfused wires. Covering any of these with thermal insulation can generate enough heat to start a fire.

Urea-formaldehyde foam insulation can release vapors into the home which cause a variety of health problems.

PRECAUTIONS

Insulation should be kept at least three inches away from the sides of recessed light fixtures and should not be placed in such a way as to trap heat. It should also be kept away from exhaust flues or furnaces, water heaters, space heaters, or other heat-producing devices. To help ensure this, a barrier should be installed to maintain permanently clearance around these items. Finally, insulation should not be installed over enclosed surface-mounted ceiling light fixtures with two or more bulbs.

HONDA ACCORD

1977 MODEL

Road salt may corrode undercarriage components. Fuel filler is vulnerable in sideswipe.

1978 MODEL

Road salt may corrode undercarriage components. Fuel filler is vulnerable in a crash.

1979 MODEL
Road salt may corrode undercarriage components.

1980 MODEL
Seat belts ride up. Fuel filler is vulnerable in a sideswipe. Front view for tall persons is obstructed by mirror. Handling is difficult in emergency maneuvers.

1982 MODEL
Corners and latch striker of open trunk lid are hazardous. Rear head restraints restrict driver's view.

HONDA CIVIC

1977 MODEL
Choke override mechanism may short-circuit, causing fire. Seam in muffler may split, causing leakage of gas that may overheat rear storage compartment floor. Road salt may corrode undercarriage components.

1978 MODEL
Seat belts tend to ride up. Fuel filler is vulnerable in sideswipe. Road salt may corrode undercarriage components.

1979 MODEL
Road salt may corrode undercarriage components. Occupant protection was rated poor in the U.S. Department of Transportation's 35-mph crash-test program for the 2-door model.

1980 MODEL
Front view is obstructed by mirror. Fuel filler is vulnerable in sideswipe. Open hatch is hazardous. Occupant protection of the 2-door model was rated poor in the U.S. Department of Transportation's 35-mph crash-test program.

1981 MODEL
Handling is difficult in accident avoidance. Corners of open hatch lid are hazardous to tall persons. The occupant protection of the 4-door model was rated poor in the U.S. Department of Transportation's 35-mph crash-test program.

1982 MODEL
Rear-view mirror restricts view of tall drivers.

HONDA PRELUDE

1979 MODEL
Road salt may corrode undercarriage components.

1980 MODEL
The occupant protection of the 2-door model was rated poor in the U.S. Department of Transportation's 35-mph crash-test program.

1981 MODEL
Seat belts may ride up on neck and abdomen and may be too short for large persons.

HONEY. *See Botulism, Infant.*

HOT CHOCOLATE MIXES. *See Carrageenan and Furcelleran.*

HOT DOGS *(See also Bone Meal; Food Colors, Artificial; Lead; Nitrites and Nitrosamines; Salt)*

HAZARDS
Hot dogs have been labeled "unguided missiles" by one health group because of their hazards and the lack of government regulation. A major concern with hot dogs and cold cuts is their high sodium content. Too much sodium can aggravate high blood pressure and contribute to stroke or heart attack. Nitrites are also used as preservatives in hot dogs and luncheon meats, and can combine with naturally occurring amines during the storage or cooking process, or in the body, to form cancer-causing nitrosamines. Hot dogs and luncheon meats are also high in cholesterol.

Because luncheon meats and hot dogs are made from residues of meat left on the bones, slivers of bone often are ground up with the meat and enter the product. At one time, these products were required to indicate "mechanically deboned meat" on the label to indicate the presence of bone, but now manufacturers can merely list calcium as present in the ingredient labeling list. Bone contains lead from the animals' diet. The bone tissue of animals retains the lead, and it is passed on to the consumer. Lead poisoning can lead to mental retardation, anemia, learning impairment, and death.

PRECAUTIONS
Because children are more susceptible to lead poisoning than adults and because they are exposed to lead from so many sources in our environment, it is wise to limit intake of lead from hot dogs and luncheon meats as much as possible.

HOT SHOT ROACH INSECTICIDE. *See Insecticides, Household.*

HOT PLATES *(See also Cooking Appliances, Small Electric)*

HAZARDS
Injuries involving hot plates and warmers are usually burns resulting from ignition of clothing or other combustibles, or from accidental touching of hot portions of these appliances.

HOT POTS. *See Cooking Appliances, Small Electric.*

HOT TUBS *(See also Bathtubs)*

HAZARDOUS MODELS
Hydro Air Industries, Inc., voluntarily recalled approximately 125,000 suction drain cover fittings for spas, hot tubs, and whirlpools because of the danger of hair entrapment. When several young girls put their heads under water, their long hair became entangled in the suction drain cover fitting. Two incidents resulted in death by drowning.

HOUSEHOLD CHEMICALS. *See Adhesives; Aerosol Containers; Auto Body Kits; Bleachers; Caulking Compounds; Cleaning Agents; Drain*

Cleaners; Floor Polishes; Fuels, Liquid; Insect Repellents; Oven Cleaners; Paints; Soaps; Solvents; Spray Starches; Toilet Bowl Cleaners; Upholstery Cleaners.

HOUSEHOLD CLEANERS. *See Cleaning Agents; Water Contaminants.*

HUNGREX. *See Diet Aids, Nonprescription.*

HUNTING KNIVES. *See Knives.*

HYDROCORTISONE. *See First-Aid Skin Ointments and Antiseptics.*

HYDRODIURIL. *See Thiazides.*

HYGROTON. *See Thiazides.*

IBUPROPHEN *(See also Arthritis Medications)*

This analgesic/anti-inflammatory drug is used to control symptoms in acute or short-term arthritis and to relieve moderate pain from swollen joints and morning stiffness accompanying various types of arthritis, including rheumatoid and osteoarthritis. It is also sometimes used to treat pain other than arthritis pain. Ibuprophen should not be taken with aspirin, anticoagulants (blood thinners), cortisone-like steroid drugs, or other arthritis drugs. Contraindications include a history of dizziness, allergic reaction to aspirin, bronchospasm, liver disease, hypertension or heart disease, nasal polyps, stomach ulcer, or any intestinal bleeding. Side effects should be immediately reported to your physician, including nausea, vomiting, stomach cramps or pain, constipation, continuing diarrhea, heartburn, stiff neck, headache, fever, dizziness, ringing in the ears, mental depression, difficulty sleeping, skin rash, blurred or decreased vision, or swelling of the hands or legs.

WARNING

Contact your physician immediately if you have any bleeding, black tarry bowels, or vomiting of blood.

BRAND NAMES: Motrin, Rufen

ICE CREAM. *See Casein; Food Colors, Artificial; Meat and Poultry.*

ICE CREAM MAKERS. *See Kitchen Appliances, Small.*

ICE CRUSHERS. *See Kitchen Appliances, Small.*

ILOSONE. *See Erythromycin Estolate.*

IMIBICOLL WITH VITAMIN B$_{1f20p100lr20}$*See Laxatives.*

INDERAL. *See Cimetidine.*

INDOCIN. *See Spironolactone with Hydrochlorothiazide.*

INFANT FORMULA

HAZARDS

Infant formula will curdle when stored improperly at temperatures above 72°, or when formula containers are damaged. When infant formula curdles, it separates into a yellow fat/oil layer on top and a water/protein layer on the bottom, which will not remix entirely. If you suspect that an infant formula is curdled, do not use it. Curdled formula can cause mild upset stomach and diarrhea or vomiting, or it can cause more serious illness if the formula has become contaminated with airborne microorganisms.

PRECAUTION

In storage, infant formula cans must be kept cool and undamaged. If you find any problem with a can of infant formula, notify the store and the FDA immediately.

INSECTICIDES, HOUSEHOLD

HAZARDS/PRECAUTIONS

All household insecticides are poisonous and should be used with extreme caution, especially if there are children or pets in the home. Some of the pesticides on the market work effectively without presenting an unnecessary risk, while other products are so hazardous they should not be used in the home. All household insecticides, however, should be used according to directions. Also, these products should not be used in homes where any occupants have allergies or asthma.

All insecticide sprays come in aerosols and are extremely flammable and should not be used near an open flame. Some aerosols, such as Hot Shot Roach, are more flammable than others.

Consumers should check the chemical contents in household insecticides and avoid those containing kepone (decachloroocta-hydro-1,3,4-metheno-cyclobuta[cd]pentalen-2-one), diazinon (0,-0-diethyl 0-[2-isopropyl-6-methyl-4-pyrimidinyl] phosphorothioate or 0,0-diethyl 0-[2-isopropyl-4-methyl-6-pyrimidinyl] phosphorothioate), and dichlorvos—DDVP, which is listed on labels as 2,2-dichlorovinyl dimethyl phosphate.

Although kepone is an effective insecticide, it was discovered to be carcinogenic in laboratory animals. As of 1980, kepone was found in such products as Black Leaf Ant Traps, E-Z Ant Traps, Grant's Ant Traps, Grant's Roach Traps, Judd Ringer Ant Packs, Lucky-Mack Roach, Waterbug and Ant Killer, Magi-Kill Ant Traps, and Tat Ant Traps.

Diazinon is very toxic and is usually found in preparations along with a much more poisonous substance, sulfotepp. Six products that contained diazinon as of 1980 are Hide Kills Crawling Insects, Johnston's No-Roach, Real-Kill Ant and Roach Killer, Spectracide Professional Home Pest Control Pressurized, and Walgreens Ant and Roach Killer.

Dichlorvos (DDVP) is a common chemical in household insecticides and is under continuing study because of suspected adverse effects from chronic exposure to even trace amounts. Until these studies are complete, it is advisable not to use products containing DDVP.

Insecticides containing arsenates should also be avoided because they are extremely poisonous and, when mixed with food bait, may not taste unpleasant to children or pets. These compounds were present as of 1980 in Gator Roach Hives, Terro Ant Killer, and Vinson Roach Killer.

INSECT REPELLENTS

HAZARDS

Deet (N,N-diethyl-meta-toluamide), which is the major active ingredient in 12 of the 15 insect repellents examined by Consumers Union, has been found by the federal government to be safe and effective for general use. However, a Canadian hospital reported the death of a child with a metabolic disease who had sprayed herself with a repellent containing deet. Moreover, the active ingredient may produce irritation if sprayed into eyes or onto sensitive skin.

PRECAUTIONS

No one should spray insect repellents into eyes, mouth, or onto sensitive skin. So that children avoid doing this, keep repellents out of their reach.

Those who are known or suspected to have metabolic defects should avoid using repellents if deet is the active ingredient.

INSECT SPRAYS. *See Insect Repellents; Kwell Shampoo and Cream.*

INSTANT PUDDING. *See Food Colors, Artificial; Salt.*

INTERFERON

Interferon has been proclaimed as the "miracle cure" for cancer as well as several other ailments. Unfortunately, early reports were too optimistic. How and if interferon works remains to be established. Many studies are currently under way, but the FDA will not give approval for general use until these studies are completed.

Interferon is a protein produced by the body in response to a stimulus, such as a virus. It helps cells prepare to fight off the virus by stimulating the production of antiviral proteins. Interferon also seems to increase the activity of white blood cells, which kill foreign cells without involving other parts of the immune system.

Interferon is in very short supply and extremely expensive to produce. The body itself produces only small amounts. Interferon produced in other animal species is not effective in humans. Within the last few years scientists have developed several ways of producing interferon. This has added to the supply of interferon on the market, but it takes large amounts of interferon to achieve appreciable effects.

Short-term studies with cancer patients have been promising, but long-term results are as yet unavailable. It is too early to know whether interferon will be effective in preventing virus infections or have any long-term negative effects.

INTERNATIONAL HARVESTER SCOUT

1969 MODEL

The accelerator rod beneath the accelerator pedal could become lodged on the carpeting and prevent the return of the accelerator to the idle position.

1974, 1975 MODELS

The front-axle steering knuckle may have been improperly heat-treated. This can decrease the life of the knuckle and failure will result in loss of steering.

1978 MODEL

Because of the design of the fuel system, specifically the placement of the fuel line, the fuel line could be severed by the front fender in an accident. This greatly increases the potential for a gasoline fire.

1977, 1978, 1979 MODELS

The design of the seats is such that parts of the frame may actually sever the safety belts in an accident. This renders the seat belts practically useless.

1980 MODEL

During the assembly process, some wheel-mounting studs were not properly installed. This can result in the wheel actually coming off the vehicle while in motion.

INTERNATIONAL HARVESTER 1510 MOTORHOME

1970, 1971, 1972, 1973 MODELS

The drag link between the pitman arm and steering arm may be adjusted too tightly. This may result in stud breakage and loss of steering.

INTRAUTERINE DEVICE *(See also Dalkon Shield; Progestasert)*

HAZARDS

Women using intrauterine devices have an increased risk of developing pelvic inflammatory disease (PID), according to the FDA. PID includes a group of several pelvic infections that may affect the uterus, fallopian tubes, or fallopian tubes and ovaries. Women who develop PID have an increased chance of infertility. At a particular risk are women under the age of twenty-six who use IUDs, women having multiple sex partners, and women with a prior medical history of PID who use IUDs. Early warning signs are low-grade abdominal pain, abnormal discharge, often accompanied by an unpleasant odor, and an irregular menstrual cycle. If you experience any of these symptoms, check with your doctor immediately. The scar tissue that forms with PID increases the chance of ectopic pregnancy and the inability to have children.

Of 100 women who use an IUD for one year, between one and six will become pregnant, according to the FDA Women wearing an IUD should have the device checked once a year by a physician to ensure that it is still in place. An IUD can be expelled without the user's knowledge. If an IUD user suspects she may be pregnant, should consult her doctor immediately, and if the pregnancy is confirmed, have the IUD removed. If a pregnancy occurs while using an IUD, blood poisoning, miscarriage, and even death can result. Other infrequent complications with the use of an IUD include anemia, pregnancy outside the uterus, septic abortion, and perforation of the uterus or cervix. Although rare, an IUD can pierce the wall of the uterus when inserted, requiring surgery to remove it.

PRECAUTIONS

Before having an IUD inserted, tell your doctor if you have ever had cancer or other abnormalities or the uterus or cervix; bleeding between periods or a heavy menstrual flow; infections of the uterus, cervix, or pelvis, including pus in the fallopian tubes; recent pregnancy, abortion, or miscarriage; uterine surgery; history of venereal disease; severe menstrual cramps; allergy to copper; history of anemia or fainting attacks; unexplained genital or vaginal discharge, or any suspicious or abnormal Pap smear.

Consult your doctor immediately if you experience heavy or unusual bleeding. The IUD should be removed to prevent anemia from developing. If you wear an IUD containing copper (Copper-T, Copper-7), it should be replaced every three years. An IUD containing progesterone (Progestasert) should be replaced every year. If you have gonnorrhea or may be exposed to it, you should not use an IUD.

IRON AND IRON SUPPLEMENTS *(See also Minerals)*

Iron is an essential mineral that carries oxygen to human cells and enables the cells to make use of the oxygen. Iron is abundant in the diet of most people, and a supplement is unnecessary unless you are losing a significant amount of blood through heavy menstruation, ulcers, hemorrhoids, intestinal bleeding, or stomach bleeding.

HAZARDS

Large doses of iron can cause damage to the liver, pancreas or heart. Pregnant women, children six months to five years, girls beginning to menstruate, strict vegetarians, and dieters may need extra iron, but consult your physician before taking an iron supplement. Overdosage of iron can cause nausea, dizziness, and constipation or diarrhea.

PRECAUTIONS

Iron can be fatal to young children. Hospital emergency rooms report a significant number of cases of iron poisoning, often when a child eats a bottle of flavored children's vitamins with iron added. Be sure to keep all medications, including vitamins and iron supplements, out of the reach of small children.

> WARNING

If for any reason you are bleeding abnormally, do not take an iron supplement, but see a doctor for control of the bleeding and for any necessary replacement therapy.

IRONS

INJURIES
In 1980, 12,000 cases were reported.

HAZARDS
Most of the serious injuries are burns caused by the following:

- Pulling or tripping on the cord. Since irons are used in exposed traffic areas, the electric cords are more accessible to children.

- Knocking over the iron. Some irons have resting bases that are unstable, and a slight push will tip them over. If they do, you may be burned by hot water or the hot face of the iron itself.

- A child climbing on a chair and touching the hot iron.

- Water spilling on parts carrying electric current, causing an electric shock.

- Irons designed for right-handed people can increase the chances of injury to left-handers.

PRECAUTIONS

Irons that are purchased should have the following features:

- A cord that can be moved in order to accommodate left- or right-handed people. An iron with a cord permanently centered at the rear of the handle is satisfactory for all users.

- A wide resting base so that it will not tip over easily.

- A large water opening so that it will be easy to fill, thus minimizing the chance of spilling water on electrical components.

To use an iron properly:

- Use demineralized or distilled water in a steam iron because normal tap water may leave mineral deposits, which can clog steam and vent openings, although some newer irons will take tap water.

- Unplug a steam iron when filling it with water to eliminate the chance of electric shock if water spills on live lecrical components.

- Always unplug the iron and put it out of reach of children even if you leave for just a few minutes.

- Place the ironing board as close as possible to a wall and the outlet.

ISOPHRIN NOSE SPRAY. *See Nasal Sprays and Decongestants.*

ISOTRETINOIN

This prescription drug was recently approved by the FDA for the treatment of severe cystic acne which is unresponsive to conventional therapy. Although initial testing shows the drug to be effective, there are significant adverse reactions associated with use of Accutane, and the FDA recommends its use be limited to patients with "severe recalcitrant" cystic acne only. The FDA also recommends that a second course of therapy should be delayed at least eight weeks after the completion of the first course because patients may continue to improve after stopping use of the drug.

HAZARDS

The most frequent adverse reaction to the drug is lip inflammation which occurred in more than 90 percent of patients tested. Up to 80 percent also experienced dryness of skin or mucous membranes. Some patients also developed conjunctivitis, rash, thinning of hair, or musculoskeletal symptoms. Approximately 5 percent of the patients tested developed either peeling of palms and soles, skin infections, gastrointestinal symptoms, fatigue, headache, or increased susceptibility to sunburn. The drug has also been associated with birth defects, and test of 170 humanpatients showed the drug can cause chemical abnormalities in the liver, skin infections, inflammation of eye membranes and increse sensitivity to the sun.

PRECAUTIONS

Use of this drug is contraindicated in patients sensitive to parabens which are used as preservatives in the formulation. Patients should not take Vitamin A or a vitamin supplement containing Vitamin A while taking this drug because it increases the possibility of side effects. Dosage should be individualized according to the patient's body weight and severity of the disease.

WARNING

This drug should not be used by women who are pregnant or may become pregnant. Isotretinon has caused birth defects in experiments with laboratory animals. Hoffman-LaRoche, Inc., the drug's manufacturer, voluntarily strengthened warnings on the new acne medication in July 1983, after three women who took the drug gave birth to deformed infants. Because it is not known whether the drug is excreted in human milk, it should not be taken by nursng mothers.

BRAND NAME: Accutane

IUDs. *See Intrauterine Devices; specific makes.*

J

JAGUAR XJS

1977 MODEL
Fuel pipe may chafe through, causing fuel leakage and possibly fire. Overaxle fuel pipes may tear, causing loss of fuel and possibly fire.

1978 MODEL
Fuel pipe may chafe through, causing fuel leakage and possibly fire.

1980–1982 MODELS
Fuel-hose connections may deteriorate, possibly causing fuel leakage into engine compartment and fire.

JAGUAR XJ6

1977 MODEL
Exhaust gas recirculation manifold core plug may be defective, causing stalling. Windshield-washer pump motor may malfunction.

1978 MODEL
Catalyst downpipe units may be defective. Icing may prevent throttle from returning to idle position. Gear selector may indicate park when car is in gear.

1979 MODEL
Catalyst downpipe units may be defective. Icing may prevent throttle from returning to idle position. Gear selector may indicate park when car is in gear. Fuel filter may be scored, causing fuel leakage.

1980–1982 MODELS
Fuel-hose connections may deteriorate, possibly causing fuel leakage into engine compartment and fire.

JAGUAR XJ12

1977 MODEL
Windshield-washer pump motor may malfunction. Fuel pipe may chafe through, causing fuel leakage and fire hazard.

1978 MODEL
Fuel pipe may chafe through, causing fuel leakage and fire hazard.

JAM. *See Food Colors, Artificial.*

JARS. *See Bottles.*

JELLY. *See Food Colors, Artificial.*

JEWELRY MAKING. *See Hobbies and Crafts.*

JUDD RINGER ANT PACKS. *See Insecticides, Household.*

JUICE, CANNED. *See Foods, Canned; Lead.*

JUICERS. *See Kitchen Appliances, Small.*

KAOPECTATE. *See Diarrhea Medications.*

KELP. *See Health Foods.*

KEROSENE. *See Fuels, Liquid; Ranges; Space Heaters.*

KEROSENE HEATERS *(See also Air Pollution, Indoor; Space Heaters)*

INJURIES

In 1981, there were about 900 portable kerosene heater fires, resulting in 210 reported injuries and 30 deaths. As a result of increased use, reports of contact burns from kerosene heaters have jumped from 230 in 1978 to 6,800 in 1982.

HAZARDS

Kerosene heaters are better designed in the 1980s than they were in the mid-1950s, when they caused numerous fatal fires. But many concerns still remain, including: the danger of fire should the heater tip over; the use of gasoline rather than kerosene; the risk of burns, especially to children, from accidental contact with the hot surfaces on the heater; and the potentially hazardous level of pollutants, such as nitrogen dioxide and sulfur dioxide, emitted by the heater. An additional hazard is the handling and storing of the kerosene used in the heaters. Although liquid kerosene is hard to ignite, it burns readily if absorbed by a rug, which then acts as a wick. Care should be taken in refueling the heaters, and models should be avoided that might easily tip over and spill out kerosene.

PRECAUTIONS

The CPSC is working with the kerosene heater industry on voluntary safety standards and is also mounting a consumer awareness program to educate users.

Some safety tips to remember are:

- In using a kerosene heater, always keep a window open to avoid the buildup of toxic emissions. Use the heater only on an occasional basis to avoid accumulation of indoor air pollution.

- Only use good-quality 1K kerrosene in your heater. 1K kerosene is low in sulfur and less polluting than 2K kerosene. *Never* use gasoline or home heating fuel, and store the kerosene in a cool, well-ventilated area away from the garage or living area.

- Always refuel your heater out of doors, and *never* refuel a heater when it is hot or operating.

For more information on kerosene heaters, write: Public Information, Consumer Product Safety Commission, Washington, DC 20207.

KETOCONAZOLE

HAZARDS

Ketoconazole is the only prescription drug approved by the FDA for oral treatment of systemic fungal infections. However, since the drug was approved in 1981, several cases of fatal, massive hepatic necrosis and numerous cases of liver injury (usually with jaundice) have been reported to the FDA in patients using the drug.

PRECAUTIONS

The FDA has now proposed a warning on the drug to read: "One user of Nizoral [brand name] in 10,000 may suffer liver damage. In all likelihood, this figure represents some degree of underreporting." Doctors have been alerted by the FDA that potentially fatal liver disorders may occur with use of this drug. Patients taking it should be closely monitored by their physician. Proper dosage of ketoconazole is critical for minimizing possible harmful effects, especially with children.

> WARNING

Symptoms of liver dysfunction, including unusual fatigue, nausea or vomiting, jaundice, dark urine or pale stools, should be reported to a physician immediately.

BRAND NAME: Nizoral

KETTLES, ELECTRIC *(See also Cooking Appliances, Small Electric)*

HAZARDS
Injuries resulting from use of crock pots and other electric kettles include electric shocks, burns, and lacerations from electrical malfunctions, explosions, and spilled contents.

KITCHEN APPLIANCES, SMALL

INJURIES
In 1980, 9,000 involved the following kitchen appliances: ice crushers, juicers, ice cream makers, knife sharpeners, slicers or choppers, can openers, or food grinders.

HAZARDS
Injuries include electric shocks caused by malfunctioning equipment and lacerations caused by contact of moving parts with hands.

HAZARDOUS MODELS
In July 1979, Consumers Union reported that numerous models of can openers left a sharp point inside open cans, gouged slivers, and/or jammed slivers. Check *Consumer Reports* for these models.

KITCHEN CABINETS. *See Pressed-Wood Products.*

KITCHEN SOAPS AND DETERGENTS. See Soaps.

KNIFE SHARPENERS. See Kitchen Appliances, Small.

KNIVES

INJURIES

In 1980, 143,000 involved cutlery or unpowered knives including switchblades and pocketknives, but excluding hunting and fishing knives. Most injuries were cuts on fingers, hands, and arms which could have been avoided.

HAZARDS

Most injuries are caused by:

- Improper use, that is, cutting toward instead of away from fingers, directing the knife up instead of downward on a cutting board, using the wrong kind of knife for a particular job.

- Improper storage so that persons reaching into a drawer, box, or sink unexpectedly come into contact with the knife.

- Distraction and haste, which may cause the knife to slip or inadvertently lacerate a finger or hand.

PRECAUTIONS

In purchasing a knife, consumers should make certain it is sturdily made. The tang of the knife, the portion extending into the handle to which the handle is attached, should be at least one-third of the length of the handle. The handle should be riveted to the blade in at least two places. The knife should feel comfortable: The balance of the weight of a small paring knife should be in the handle, but the balance of the weight of larger knives should be in the blade.

KNIVES, ELECTRIC

HAZARDS

Most injuries involve lacerations caused by the user's finger contacting the cutting edge or electric shocks caused by malfunctioning equipment, especially when the user is in contact with wet surfaces.

KONSYL. *See Laxatives.*

KWELL SHAMPOO AND CREAM

HAZARDS

This prescription shampoo contains lindane, a pesticide closely related to DDT. It is used to treat head and pubic lice and scabies. Many studies have linked lindane to cancer in rats.

Lindane is easily absorbed into the bloodstream, and may also have direct effects on the human nervous system ranging from headaches to convulsions. Children seem to be more susceptible to these effects than adults.

The cream form of this product, used to treat scabies, is especially unadvised since it must be applied and left on for 24 hours.

Lindane is also found in insect sprays, flea powders, and dog shampoos where it is listed as gamma benzene hexachloride (GBH) or hexachlorcychlohexane (HCH).

The U.S. Food and Drug Administration and the U.S. Environmental Protection Agency both have regulations under consideration to restrict lindane, but at present, neither of these measures have been approved. Consumers Union has also petitioned the FDA to withdraw approval of Kwell as a lice treatment and to require a warning label on the scabies cream.

PRECAUTIONS

Women who are pregnant, are contemplating pregnancy, or are at risk of becoming pregnant, should not use this product because it has been linked to fetal abnormalities and stillbirths.

Children with lice should use one of the other treatments available for treating lice, such as RID or A-200 Pyrinate, although hay fever sufferers may be allergic to these products since they are made from chrysanthemums.

> **WARNING**

This product causes cancer in rats. It is especially toxic for children and unborn fetuses. If you are pregnant or if there is a possibility you may become pregnant, do not use this product. Lindane can cause fetal abnormalities and stillbirths. Use of this product is not reccommended.

LADDERS

INJURIES

In 1980, 89,000 involved ladders and step stools.

HAZARDS

Most injuries are caused by falls, though some result from electrocution when a metal ladder touches power lines.

PRECAUTIONS

In purchasing ladders, consumers should look for the following features.

- Length sufficient for any use to which they might be put.

- Absence of sharp edges, dents, bent steps, rungs, or rails on metal ladders. Absence of splits, cracks, chips, and all but small tight knots on wooden ladders.

- On wooden stepladders, reinforcement of steps with metal rods or metal angle-braces.

- Slip-resistant rubber or plastic feet on metal ladders.

- Slip-resistant steps on metal stepladders.

To prevent electrocution, it is important to use only double-insulated or properly grounded electrical tools on metal ladders.

HAZARDOUS MODELS

In September 1981, Consumers Union reported the following safety hazards in aluminum stepladders.

• The Whitemetal Wonderlight failed the step-bending test and had sharp edges.

• The Howard 3506, J.C. Penney catalog number 0036, and Werner Saf-T-Master 366 failed the leg-bending and walking tests.

• Daymond HH56/U556 failed the leg-bending and step-attachment tests and had sharp edges.

• Sears catalog number 42386 and 42056, Whitemetal Heartsavers, and Howard 5506 had sharp edges.

• Scranton Star failed the walking test and had sharp edges.

• Keller Greenline 706 failed the twist test and had sharp edges, including one at the spreader hinge.

Consumers Union reported the following safety hazards in wooden stepladders.

• Sears catalog number 40196 and Rich 260 Acme had spreader handles that could jam and metal braces riveted to front rails that could interfere with footing at the top step.

• Wards catalog numbers 6778 and 6782 failed the leg-bending test, and the 6782 has metal braces riveted to front rails that could interfere with footing at the top step.

L.A. FORMULA. *See Laxatives.*

LAMPS *(See also Black Lights; Christmas Lights; Extension Cords; Fluorescent Lights; Home Electrical System; Night Lights)*

245 / LAWN MOWERS, POWER

INJURIES
In 1980, 32,000 involved lamps, electric fixtures, and associated equipment such as light bulbs, wiring systems, lamp cords, extension cords, circuit breakers, and ground-fault circuit interrupters.

LANACORT. *See First-Aid Skin Ointments and Antiseptics.*

LANOXIN. *See Digoxin.*

LAPIDARY WORK. *See Hobbies and Crafts.*

LAUNDRY BOOSTERS. *See Bleachers.*

LAUNDRY SOAPS. *See Soaps.*

LAWN EDGERS. *See Garden Tools, Power.*

LAWN MOWERS, POWER

INJURIES
In 1980, 63,000 involved power lawn mowers, hand lawn mowers, grass and leaf catchers, snowthrowers, or blowers.

HAZARDS
Injuries from power lawn mowers are usually caused by the following.

• Contact with the rotating blade, often when the victim is clearing the discharge chute of grass clippings, especially when the grass is wet; when the victim adjusts the machine without turning it off and waiting for the blade to stop; or when the machine hits an obstacle such as a rock and the user's foot slips under the housing.

• Propelled objects such as wire, rocks, or twigs that are shot out either through the discharge chute or from under the housing.

- Overturning, which occurs primarily when riding mowers are used on steep slopes or embankments.

- Mower running over the victim, which often occurs when a riding mower or garden tractor is being driven in reverse, and sometimes occurs when the operator pulls the mower backward over the foot.

PRECAUTIONS

CPSC staff says that reel lawn mowers are safer than rotary lawn mowers, mainly because their blades move more slowly. However, rotary mowers are often preferred because they cut down tall grass more efficiently.

Mowers should be purchased with the following features.

- A rear guard to prevent extremities from contacting the rotating blade.

- A discharge opening that is aimed downward.

- A "deadman" release on the wheel drive.

- Handles with "upstops" to prevent them from rising up when the machine hits an obstacle.

- Insulated spark-plug connector.

- Engine exhaust not directed at the grass-catching bag because sparks from a backfiring engine could ignite the bag.

- A grass-catching bag positioned so that it cannot come into contact with the muffler during use.

- On rear-baggers, a mechanism that prevents operation with the grass chute open.

- Appropriate warning labels.

Take the following precautions when operating.

- Never allow young children to operate the lawn mower.

- Wear sturdy, rough-soled work shoes and close-fitting slacks and shirts.

- Clear the area you plan to mow of wires, cans, and debris.

- Never mow a wet lawn because you might slip or be tempted to try to clear the machine without turning it off.

- Always turn off the machine and disconnect the spark plug wire or electric plug when you need to unclog or adjust the machine.

- Mow across the slope when using a hand power mower, up and down with a riding mower.

- Wait at least 30 seconds after shutting off the engine to make certain the blades have stopped.

- Never refuel a mower while it is running or the engine is hot.

- Never refuel a mower indoors because vapors may be ignited by a spark.

- Start the mower outdoors, so carbon monoxide gas cannot collect.

- Do not smoke near the mower because gasoline fumes may ignite.

HAZARDOUS MODELS

The Black & Decker Manufacturing Company recalled approximately 18,000 model number 8055 19-inch Battery Powered (Cordless) Lawn Mowers. When the lawn mower battery is not in use and is either being recharged or is unattended, there may be an unexpected discharge that could cause a fire.

In June 1981, Consumers Union rated the following self-propelled lawn mowers as unsafe because they could propel themselves unattended or because the rear-bagging chute was judged unsafe when the grass catcher was removed: Allis-Chalmers 1690562, Bolens 8548, International Harvester 3342, Lawn-Boy Mulch-R-Catch 8671, Lawn-Boy R8237, Ryan B851, Simplicity 1221PP, and Snapper 21400P.

LAWN TRIMMERS. *See Garden Tools, Power.*

LAWN VACUUMS. See Garden Equipment, Power.

LAXATIVES (See also Digoxin; Pregnancy and Drugs)

HAZARDS

There are four types of laxative products available without a prescription: bulk formers, stool softeners, saline (salt) cathartics, and stimulants. Any laxative can be habit-forming and should be used only occasionally. The side effects from chronic use of any laxative include constipation, anal fissures, loss of potassium, abdominal cramps, interference with the absorption of some vitamins, diarrhea, and excessive salt intake.

There are numerous laxatives on the market, but the FDA requires them to carry this warning: "Prolonged or continued use of this product can lead to laxative dependency and loss of normal bowel function. Serious side effects from prolonged use or overuse may occur."

Unless directed by a physician to do so, avoid use of bowel stimulant drugs such as phenolphthalein (Ex-Lax, Feen-a-mint), senna (Fletcher's Castoria, Senokot), bisacodyl (Dulcolax), and cascara (Cas-Evac). All these agents stimulate peristalsis and are capable of producing severe and painful cramping, according to the FDA. Enemas are particularly habit-forming and should be avoided if they contain a laxative.

Another class of laxatives that also works by increasing peristalsis is the saline or salt cathartics. The most common salts are magnesium citrate (citrate of magnesia), magnesium hydroxide (milk of magnesium), and sodium phosphate (buffered laxative, Fleet, Sal Hepatica). Patients with chronic kidney disease may have difficulty excreting magnesium and should be wary of using milk of magnesia. Patients on salt-restricted diets should also avoid using the preparations containing sodium.

For occasional use, the best laxatives are bulk-producing laxatives or stool softeners. According to the FDA, "bulk-forming laxatives are among the safest of laxatives." Psyllium bulk preparations include Effersyllium Instant Mix, Konsyl, L.A. Formula, Mucilose Flakes and Granules, and the Metamucil products. Those on a salt-restricted diet should avoid Metamucil Instant Mix, however, as it contains a considerable amount of sodium.

For some people stool softeners—such as Colace, Coloctyl, and Disonate—are effective, whereas for other patients, they provide little relief. Mineral oil is popular among the elderly, but use over time, especially by the elderly or disabled, can lead to lipid pneumonia, a chronic condition sometimes caused by inhalation of oil into the lungs.

PRECAUTIONS

Tension, pregnancy, change in eating habits, and certain medications can all cause constipation. If the condition continues, consult a physician.

LEAD *(See also Bone Meal; Foods, Canned; Gasoline; Paint; Water Contaminants)*

A government study has found lead affects 4 percent of all young children, more than are affected by measles, mumps, rubella, and every major childhood disease combined. Black and inner-city children are affected the most. Scientists speculate exposure to lead for this high-risk population from peeling paint and auto exhaust is much higher than that of middle-class children.

HAZARDS

Children are exposed to lead from food stored in cans, from air, water, and soil, as well as from lead-based paints. They can absorb lead by eating contaminated paint chips, by drinking formula from a leaded can, by eating dirt containing lead, by chewing on toys covered with lead-contaminated dust, by playing with pets covered with lead dust, by drinking tap water or breathing air that is contaminated with lead from gasoline emissions or industrial emissions.

Although polluted air is not usually the major source of contamination for children, it is an important contributing source. It is estimated that 90 percent of the lead found in fresh vegetables comes from air pollution. Other sources of lead exposure in the home include: heated solder in metalworking; lead glazes in pottery; tobacco smoke (present in small quantities); leaded water pipes; leaded dinnerware; leaded candlewicks; and yellow lacquer in pencils.

Young children absorb about four times more lead per unit ingested than adults, and because their developing brains are more sensitive to the effects of even small amounts of lead, the damage to small children is much greater than among adults. Although the number of deaths resulting from lead poisoning has been drastically reduced since the government instituted its lead-screening program, irreversible brain damage, blindness, and mental retardation still result. Most commonly, lead poisoning is responsible for learning impairment among inner-city children.

PRECAUTIONS

One of the most troublesome problems with lead exposure is that it comes simultaneously from multiple sources, so it is very easy for a child to exceed the daily "safe" limit. Early signs of lead poisoning include irritability, headaches, and general malaise. Unfortunately, these symptoms are often overlooked in small children. A simple, inexpensive blood test is available to assess lead levels in children before obvious signs of illness appear. If found in time, a lead-poisoned child can be treated with drugs called chelating agents, which remove lead from the body.

LEAF BLOWERS. *See Garden Tools, Power.*

LEAF GRINDERS, POWER. *See Garden Equipment, Power.*

LEAF MULCHERS, POWER. *See Garden Equipment, Power.*

LETTUCE. *See Produce.*

LEVODOPA (LARODOPA). *See Drug and Food Interactions.*

LIBRIUM. *See Benzodiazepines; Sleep Medications, Prescription.*

LICE SHAMPOO. *See Kwell Shampoo and Cream.*

LIFE JACKETS

There are three types of life jackets approved by the U.S. Coast Guard.

- Type I. A vest or a "horse-collar" bib is bulky and offers the greatest protection but is confining.

- Type II. A bib or "horse collar" that does not provide as much buoyancy as the first type, but is not as bulky and cumbersome.

- Type III. Foam-filled vests that zip up the front and have straps or drawstrings to keep them snug.

Most recreational boaters use either type II or III, but most of those models tested by Consumers Union did not consistently turn wearers face up. Of type III vests, the Sears Helmsman catalog number 63146 was the only adult model, and the Kent 4350-35 the only child's vest that held wearers in a vertical, slightly backward position in the water. The APCO 51300 was the only adult vest of the tested type II models that turned most wearers face up in two tests. Of type II vests and bibs for children, Consumers Union judged the Sears catalog number 63165, the Stearns Heads-Up PW002, and the Sears catalog number 63116 to be acceptable.

LIGHT BULBS. *See Home Electrical System; Lamps.*

LIGHTER FLUID. *See Fuels, Liquid; Lighters.*

LIGHTERS *(See also Fuels, Liquid; Gasoline Containers)*

INJURIES
Nearly 6,000 injuries in 1976 involved lighters or lighter fluid.

HAZARDS
The following are causes of injuries from lighters.

- Children playing with them.

- Product failures, including unexpectedly high flame heights and failure to extinguish properly.

- Spilled lighter fluid that is ignited by a spark or flame from the lighter. Children and the elderly are frequently involved in these accidents.

STANDARDS

In 1975, the American Society for Testing and Materials published a voluntary standard for cigarette lighters that set safety standards and provided for limits on the maximum flame height.

PRECAUTIONS

In purchasing lighters, look for those that are self-extinguishing, that are easy to fill, and that burn with a low flame.

LIGHTING FIXTURES. *See Home Electrical System; Lamps; Night Lights.*

LIGHTS. *See Black Lights; Christmas Lights; Extension Cords; Fluorescent Lights; Home Electrical System; Lamps; Night Lights; Work Lights.*

LINCOLN AUTOMATIC TRANSMISSIONS. *See Automobile Transmissions.*

LINCOLN CONTINENTAL

1979 MODEL
Parking pawl could malfunction, causing the car to roll free.

1980 MODEL
Original tires may be defective.

1982 MODEL
Seal may be inadequate, possibly allowing fuel leakage and fire.

1983 MODEL
Transmission-control selector tube may be defective, which could cause the gearshift selector level indicator to indicate the actual gear position incorrectly. Cam retainer pins in parking pawl actuating rod assemblies may be defective, which could result in the parking pawl not engaging the parking gear when the shift selector is in the "park" position, allowing the vehicle to roll.

LINCOLN MARK V AND VI

1977 MODEL
Transmission selector pointer may be mispositioned, possibly causing forward motion and accident when car is started. Aluminum rear-bumper reinforcement could detach.

1978 MODEL
Parking gear may malfunction, causing the car to roll free. Aluminum rear-bumper reinforcement could detach.

1979 MODEL
Parking pawl may malfunction, causing the car to roll free.

1980 MODEL
Pinched wire could cause overheating and fire, even when vehicle is not in use. Stop lamp may be contaminated and malfunction.

1981 MODEL
Start switch may malfunction and allow starting in reverse. Electrical relays may be susceptible to water leakage, possibly causing a fire.

1983 MODEL
In Mark VI, transmission-control selector tube may be defective, which could cause the gearshift-selector-level indicator to incorrectly indicate the actual gear position. Cam retainer pins in parking pawl actuating rod assemblies may be defective, which could result in the parking pawl not engaging the parking gear when the shift selector is in the "park" position, allowing the vehicle to roll.

LINCOLN TOWN CAR

1983 MODEL
Transmission-control selector-tube retaining clips may be defective, which could cause the gearshift selector level indicator to indicate the actual gear position incorrectly. Cam retainer pins in parking pawl actuating rod assemblies may be defective, which could result in the parking pawl not engaging the parking gear when the shift selector is in the "park" position, allowing the vehicle to roll.

LINCOLN VERSAILLES

1977 MODEL
Transmission-selector pointer may be mispositioned, possibly causing forward motion and accident when car is started.

1978 MODEL
Wiring harness may be misrouted, preventing the shutting off of the speed-control system.

1979 MODEL
Parking pawl could malfunction, causing the car to roll free.

1980 MODEL
Original tires may be defective.

LINOLEUM. *See Asbestos; Vinyl Floor Tiles and Vinyl Sheet Flooring.*

LIPPES LOOP. *See Intrauterine Devices.*

LISTERINE MOUTHWASH. *See Throat Medications.*

LITHIUM CARBONATE. *See Spironolactone with Hydrochlorothiazide; Thiazides.*

LOESTRIN. *See Oral Contraceptives.*

LOGSPLITTERS, POWER. *See Garden Equipment, Power.*

LONITEN. *See Minoxidil.*

LO/OVRAL. *See Oral Contraceptives.*

LOPRESSOR. *See Cimetidine.*

LORAZEPAM. *See Benzodiazepines.*

LOROXIDE. *See Acne Medications, Nonprescription.*

LOTUS ESPRIT

>1978, 1979 MODELS
>Fuel may leak from joint in pressure fuel system, creating fire hazard.

LUCKY MACK ROACH, WATERBUG AND ANT KILLER. *See Insecticides, Household.*

LUNCHEON MEAT. *See Food Colors, Artificial; Hot Dogs; Lead; Nitrites and Nitrosamines.*

MAGI-KILL ANT TRAPS. *See Insecticides, Household.*

MASERATI MERAKS

1977, 1978, 1979 MODELS
Clutch and brake pedal could become spongy because of temporary vaporization of fluids.

MASONITE. *See Pressed-Wood Products.*

MATCHES

INJURIES
In 1980, 7,000 involved matches and matchbooks.

HAZARDS
Most injuries are caused by children playing with matches and the elderly using them, or product failures such as fragmentation caused by nonuniform and improper application of ignition compounds to the match tips. Other injuries involved old-fashioned "friction matches," which can ignite by being rubbed against a rough surface and igniting an entire open matchbook.

FEDERAL STANDARD

The CPSC issued a mandatory safety standard for matchbooks manufactured after May 4, 1978, which requires, among other features, that the striker strip be placed on the back of the matchbook, that the staple holding the matchbook together be elsewhere than on the striking surface, that the ignition delay be no more than two seconds, and that the match cannot glow more than five seconds after the flame goes out nor re-ignite.

PRECAUTION

To reduce related hazards, purchase safety matches rather than friction matches.

MATTRESSES

INJURIES

In 1980, 6,000 involved mattresses or other bedding.

HAZARDS

Most injuries are caused by fires from burning cigarettes. Many injuries and deaths result, not from burns, but from the inhalation of smoke and toxic gases in these fires.

FEDERAL STANDARDS

Federal regulations require that a minimum of nine cigarettes be allowed to burn on the smooth, tape edge and quilted or tufted locations of a bare mattress. The char length on the mattress surface must not be more than 2 inches in any direction from any cigarette.

MAYO DIET, THE *(See also Diets)*

This plan instructs dieters to eat grapefruit before each meal, then eat as much bacon, eggs, meat, fish, and vegetables as they wish. The Mayo Diet, according to the FDA, is based on the erroneous theory that grapefruit contains enzymes that somehow subtract calories by increasing the fat-burning process. This diet provides no credible advice for weight reduction, and the dieter does not lose any body fat. At best, the grapefruit eaten before a meal will cut the dieter's appetite and help him/her to eat less. Because grapefruits are high in acid, the plan may lead to stomach irritation.

MAZDA GLC

1978 MODEL
Front seat belts ride up.

1979 MODEL
Fuel tank and fuel filler are vulnerable in a crash. Front seat belts tend to ride up. Open hatch is hazardous.

1980 MODEL
Fuel filler is vulnerable in a sideswipe.

1981 MODEL
Handling is difficult in accident avoidance. Fuel filler is vulnerable to sideswipe. Head restraints may be hazardous in a crash. Front seat belts ride up.

1982 MODEL
Head restraints offer marginal protection to tall persons. Rear window quickly accumulates grime in rainy weather.

MAZDA RX-4

1977 MODEL
Rear brakes lock prematurely. Open trunk lid is hazardous to tall persons.

MAZDA 626

1980 MODEL
Fuel tank and filler are vulnerable in a sideswipe. Head restraints may be hazardous in a crash. Brakes could pull to one side. The occupant protection of the 2-door model in the U.S. Department of Transportation's 35-mph crash-test program was rated poor.

1981 MODEL
Head restraints may be hazardous in a crash.

1982 MODEL
The occupant protection of the 4-door model in the U.S. Department of Transportation's 35-mph crash test was rated poor.

MEDROXYPROGESTERONE ACETATE

This prescription drug is a progestin used to treat menstrual disorders, to test if the body is producing certain hormones, and also to treat some forms of cancer in women. Although it has been prescribed to prevent miscarriage and to test for pregnancy, it is no longer approved for these purposes because of the greatly increased risk of birth defects.

HAZARDS

This drug has also been marketed in the U.S. and abroad under the brand name Depo-Provera, as both an oral and injectable contraceptive. In its injectable form, Depo-Provera is effective in preventing conception for up to three months. The drug was removed from the market, however, in the early 1970s when laboratory studies linked it to breast tumors in dogs and monkeys. The Upjohn Company, the manufacturer of Depo-Provera, is currently seeking a reevaluation and reapproval of the drug by the FDA. Many health officials and women's health groups oppose the remarketing of Depo-Provera because of the risks involved. In addition, synthetic progestins, such as Depo-Provera, have been found in both animal and human studies to cause masculinization of the fetus. Progestins, or estrogen and progestin compounds, have been associated with other birth defects as well. The FDA withdrew all approval of pregnancy-related uses of progestins in 1973 because of the evidence of terato-genicity.

BRAND NAME: Depo-Provera.

MEAT AND POULTRY *(See also Food Colors, Artificial; Food Poisoning; Hamburger; Hot Dogs)*

HAZARDS

According to the federal government, there are 140 pesticides and contaminants "likely to leave residues" in meat and poultry products, but the USDA tests for only 60. The number of pesticides and contaminants tested has decreased in the past few years, although the USDA's inspection budget has increased. More of the budget is now going into educating farmers on the use of pesticides, rather than testing for residues in meat and poultry. In addition, the USDA has decided not to publicize the findings of its inspections, so when violations do occur and residues are present in meat and poultry products, consumers have no way of knowing which products are hazardous.

Salmonella poisoning can also occur by eating turkey, beef, pork, chicken, and homemade ice cream that has been contaminated through improper handling by producers. No federal action has been taken to reduce the amount of salmonella bacteria in raw meat, although most other developed countries have much stricter salmonella controls.

PRECAUTIONS

Meat and poultry may not only come contaminated from the store; they can also be contaminated in the home. Contrary to popular belief, food poisoning can occur with little change in the color, odor, or taste of a product. Chicken, turkey, and duck should always be cooked thoroughly, as should ground meat. All meat products should be refrigerated within two hours after cooking.

In preparing a stuffed turkey or chicken, stuff the bird right before roasting. Refrigerate the stuffing and bird separately. Do not stuff the bird in advance, and do not store the stuffing in the bird.

MECHANICS LIGHTS. *See Work Lights.*

MENSTRUAL PAIN MEDICATIONS *(See also Caffeine)*

Nonprescription drugs marketed for the relief of menstrual pain and related distress are no more effective than plain aspirin or acetaminophen (Tylenol). Some of the other ingredients found in menstrual medications include antihistamines, which have a mild sedative effect; decongestants, which are a mild stimulant; caffeine, which is a mild diuretic and stimulant; diuretics to treat water retention, and aspirin or acetaminophen for pain. Most of the ingredients in these medications are unnecessary. In addition, caffeine has been linked to birth defects, breast disease, and pancreatic cancer.

MERCEDES-BENZ 69

1977, 1978 MODELS
Fuel-tank ventilation system could malfunction, causing fuel leakage and possibly fire.

MERCEDES-BENZ 230

1977, 1978 MODELS
Fuel-tank ventilation system could malfunction, causing fuel leakage and fire hazard.

MERCEDES-BENZ 240 D

1980 MODEL
The occupant protection of the 4-door model was poor in a 35-mph crash test conducted by the U.S. Department of Transportation.

MERCEDES-BENZ 280

1977, 1978 MODELS
Fuel-tank ventilation system could malfunction, causing fuel leakage and fire hazard.

MERCEDES-BENZ 300SD

1978, 1979 MODELS
Crankshaft pulley could separate from mounting plate, causing failure of water pump, power-steering pump, and alternator.

MERCEDES-BENZ 450

1977, 1978 MODELS
Fuel-tank ventilation system could malfunction, causing fuel leakage and fire hazard.

MERCEDES-BENZ 3000

1979 MODEL
Seat belts may ride up. Open trunk lid is hazardous to tall persons.

MERCURY AUTOMATIC TRANSMISSIONS. *See Automatic Transmissions.*

MERCURY BOBCAT

1977 MODEL
Handling is unpredictable in accident avoidance.

1978 MODEL
Rear seat belts may fail to lock.

1979 MODEL
Rear lamp sockets may be incorrect. The occupant protection of the 2-door hatchback in a 35-mph crash test conducted by the U.S. Department of Transportation was poor.

MERCURY CAPRI

1977 MODEL
Gear shift lever may break during use. In Capri II, handling is unpredictable in emergency handling.

1979 MODEL
Steering-gear coupling flanges may be incorrect, possibly causing loss of steering. Rear lamp sockets may be incorrect. Cooling fan may crack and throw fragments. Plastic engine-fan finger guards may contact fan and shatter. Pushrod could disengage from pedal, causing loss of service brakes.

1981 MODEL
Driver-seat back latch may be defective, allowing seat to fall back into a reclined position.

1982 MODEL
Steering response is somewhat unpredictable.

MERCURY COMET

1977 MODEL
Left-door-lock assemblies may be defective, possibly causing door

to open while car is moving. Steering-gear balls may fracture, causing a loss of steering.

1979 MODEL
Rear lamp sockets may be incorrect.

MERCURY COUGAR

1977 MODEL
Engine may leak fuel at rubber hose connecting fuel-inlet tube and fuel filter, possibly causing a fire. Transmission-selector pointer may be mispositioned, possibly causing forward motion and accident when car is started. Cooling fan could crack and separate. Fuel filler is vulnerable to sideswipe. Steering is sluggish in accident avoidance. Dashboard controls can be confusing.

1978 MODEL
Handling is sluggish in emergency maneuvers.

1979 MODEL
Rear lamp sockets may be incorrect. Nuts may be stripped, causing seat to slide along track. Pushrod could disengage from pedal, causing loss of service brakes. Rear seat belts may be too short. Handling is sluggish in emergency maneuvers. Power steering may be defective, causing loss of steering.

1980 MODEL
Brake assembly may be incorrect, causing slow stopping. Original tires may fail prematurely.

1982 MODEL
Tire placard may list incorrect information.

1983 MODEL
Fuel tanks may have inadequately welded front seams, possibly causing fuel leakage and a fire. Cam retainer pins in parking pawl actuating rod assemblies may be defective, which could result in the parking pawl not engaging the parking gear when the shift selector is in the "park" position, allowing the vehicle to roll.

MERCURY LYNX

1979 MODEL
Rear lamp sockets may be incorrect.

1981 MODEL
Wiring harness may overheat, possibly causing fire. Rear-brake backing-plate attachment bolts may have inadequate torque, possibly causing loss of braking. Metal fasteners may penetrate fuel tank, causing loss of fuel. Vacuum leak may develop and inadvertently activate speed control servo. Power-brake boosters may be defective, possibly causing loss of service brakes. Fuel inlet may be ungrounded, possibly causing a fire during refueling.

1982 MODEL
Open hatch latch is hazardous to tall persons. Front-wheel-drive model overresponded to steering in abrupt maneuvers. Controls are inconveniently located.

1983 MODEL
The 3-door hatchbacks may not be in compliance with the federal standard (FMVSS301-75) that limits the amount of fuel leakage in a crash.

MERCURY MARQUIS

1979 MODEL
Pushrod could disengage from pedal, causing loss of service brakes. Wrong circuit breakers may have been installed, causing failure of windshield wipers and washers. Front-brake hoses may wear, possibly causing loss of brakes. Rear lamp sockets may be incorrect. Coupling rivet pins may be defective, possibly causing loss of steering. Front-brake hoses may be misindexed, possibly causing braking loss. Open trunk latch is hazardous. Gauges are hard to read. Horn and wiper controls are inconvenient. The occupant protection in a 35-mph crash test conducted by the U.S. Department of Transportation was poor for the 2-door model.

1981 MODEL
Start switch may malfunction and allow starting in reverse.

1983 MODEL
Transmission control selector tube may be defective, which could cause the gearshift selector level indicator to indicate the actual gear

position incorrectly. Cam retainer pins in parking pawl actuating rod assemblies may be defective, which could result in the parking pawl not engaging the parking gear when the shift selector is in the park position, allowing the vehicle to roll.

MERCURY MONARCH

1977 MODEL
Transmission selector pointer may be mispositioned, possibly causing forward motion and accident when car is started. Steering-gear balls may fracture, causing a loss of steering. Cooling fan could crack and separate into fragments. Handling is unpredictable during emergency maneuvers. Fuel tank and filler are vulnerable in a crash.

1978 MODEL
Handling is sluggish and sloppy in hard turns.

1979 MODEL
Rear lamp sockets may be incorrect. Pushrod could disengage from pedal, causing loss of service brakes. Rear-window defroster is inadequate.

MERCURY VAPOR LAMPS. *See Black Lights.*

MERCURY ZEPHYR

1978 MODEL
Front disc brakes may be defective, causing brake pull. Parking gear may not engage when placed in "park" position, causing the car to roll free. Wiring may chafe, possibly causing loss of electrical power control. Wiper system may fail. Air reed valve may fail, possibly causing engine to stall. Horn and wiper controls are poorly designed.

1979 MODEL
Pushrod could disengage from pedal, causing loss of service brakes. Rear lamp sockets may be incorrect. Certification labels may list incorrect weight. Open trunk sill is hazardous to tall persons. Jack handle has sharp corners. Horn and wiper controls are inconvenient.

1980 MODEL
Brake assembly may be incorrect, causing slow stopping. Firestone 720 tires may be defective.

1981 MODEL
Pushrod could disengage from pedal, causing loss of service brakes.

1982 MODEL
In cars with C-3 automatic transmission, column-mounted gear-shift levers may contain defective transmission park-actuating-lever rod springs, allowing the vehicle to roll when the gear-shift lever is in the "park" position.

1983 MODEL
In cars with C-3 automatic transmissions, column-mounted gear-shift levers may contain defective transmission park-actuating-lever rod springs, allowing the vehicle to roll when the gear-shift lever is in the "park" position. Transmission control selector tube may be defective, which could cause the gear-shift selector-level indicator to indicate the actual gear position incorrectly.

METAL CLEANERS. *See Cleaning Agents.*

METALWORK. *See Hobbies and Crafts.*

METAMUCIL. *See Laxatives.*

METAPREL. *See Asthma Inhalers.*

METHOXSALEN. *See PUVA.*

METHYL ALCOHOL. *See Solvents.*

METOCLOPRAMIDE HYDROCHLORIDE (REGLAN INJECTABLE).
See *Sulfites.*

MGB

1977, 1978 MODELS
Gasoline may leak from float chamber gasket, creating fire hazard. Overdrive wiring harness may chafe, causing short circuit and fire hazard.

MG MIDGET

1978 MODEL
Fuel hose may be incorrect, possibly causing fuel leakage and fire.

MICRONEFRIN. See *Sulfites.*

MICROWAVE OVENS *(See also Ranges)*

HAZARDS
Short-term exposure to microwaves can cause painful burns, cataracts, or temporary sterility. Microwaves can also interfere with electric and electronic items, including old pacemakers (new pacemakers shield against electrical interference). But what health effects long-term exposure to low levels of microwaves has to humans is as yet undetermined. Leakage of microwaves from ovens may result from defective oven design or construction; faulty safety features that fail to ensure a closed door before oven operation; abused or dirty door seals; worn-out door latches, hinges, and locks.

PRECAUTIONS
To avoid possible low-level exposure to microwaves from leaky ovens, service and replace door hinges, latches, safety locks, and seals regularly; make sure oven does not operate with the door open; and do not stand directly against the oven while it is operating.

MIDAS INTERNATIONAL MOTORHOME

1977 29-FOOT MODEL
The spare tire bracket was improperly welded to the vehicle. The tire may fall off in transit.

MIDLAND-ROSS AIRSTREAM TRAILER

1977 MODEL
The hydraulic piston in the braking system was improperly assembled. A snap ring may have been incorrectly installed, resulting in the pushrod being separated from the hydraulic piston and causing the loss of brakes.

MIDOL. *See Caffeine; Menstrual Pain Medications.*

MILK *(See also Casein; Drug and Food Interactions; Salt)*

HAZARDS
Although milk is a nutritious food, it contains two potential hazards. Milk is often high in sodium—frequently much higher than stated on the carton, according to a Consumers Union survey. Whole milk is also high in fat and cholesterol—up to 3.25 percent milk fat. Many studies have shown a link between saturated fat—cholesterol as found in milk fat—and heart disease.

PRECAUTIONS
Generally, adults should not drink whole milk. Low-fat milk, which may contain from 0.5 to 2.5 percent milk fat or skim milk, which contains less than 0.5 percent milk fat, are much healthier for most adults and provide all the nutritional benefits of whole milk. Calories can also be reduced by drinking low-fat or skim milk. Skim milk has only about 86 calories per eight-ounce glass, compared to 121 in low-fat milk and about 151 in whole milk.

MILK CHOCOLATE. *See Caffeine; Food Colors, Artificial.*

MILK OF MAGNESIA. *See Laxatives.*

MILK PRODUCTS. *See Casein; Drug and Food Interactions; Food Colors, Artificial.*

MINERAL OIL. *See Laxatives.*

MINERALS *(See also Iron and Iron Supplements)*

Minerals, such as calcium, phosphorus, sodium, chloride, potassium, magnesium, and sulfur, are necessary in relatively large amounts in our diet, while only trace amounts of other minerals are needed. Lead, mercury, and cadmium, which are found in the diet, are regarded as harmful. However, even minerals needed by the body are harmful if we absorb too much of them.

If all the potassium required by the body in one day were taken in a single concentrated dose, severe illness could result. Many children under five years of age are hospitalized each year due to iron poisoning caused by accidental ingestion of multiple daily dietary supplements. Other minerals can cause adverse health effects if as little as twice the minimum daily requirement is taken.

Taking too much of one essential mineral may upset the balance and function of other minerals in the body and can contribute to such health problems are anemia, bone demineralization and breakage, neurologic disease, and fetal abnormalities. The risks, according to the FDA, are greatest for the very young, pregnant and breast-feeding women, the elderly, and those with inadequate diets or chronic disease.

Below is a table of the USDA Recommended Daily Allowance (RDA) for certain key minerals. So little is known of some other minerals that RDAs have not been established for them.

USDA RECOMMENDED DAILY ALLOWANCE FOR MINERALS BY AGE GROUPS

	UNIT*	INFANTS (0–12 MONTHS)	CHILDREN UNDER 4 YEARS OF AGE	ADULTS AND CHILDREN OVER 4 YEARS OF AGE	PREGNANT OR LACTATING WOMEN
Calcium	g	0.6	0.8	1	1.3
Iron	mg	15	10	18	18
Phosphorus	g	0.5	0.8	1	1.3
Iodine	mcg	45	70	150	150
Magnesium	mg	70	200	400	450
Zinc	mg	5	8	15	15
Copper	mg	0.6	1	2	2.0

KEY: g = gram; mg = milligram; mcg = microgram; 1,000 mcg (microgram = 1 mg; 1,000 mg (milligram) = 1 g

*To understand the relative amounts needed, it may be useful to know that 1 level teaspoon of white sugar weighs about 4 g.

MINI-BIKES *(See also Bicycles)*

INJURIES

In 1974, 31,000 involved these two-wheeled, gasoline-driven vehicles.

HAZARDS

The four most common causes of injuries are:

1. Mechanical and structural problems, including throttles that stick; instability; chain breakage; poorly located exhaust pipes; and loose, missing, or broken parts.
2. Poor riding conditions.
3. Contact with parts. Chain sprocket mechanisms can catch clothing, toes, and fingers, causing painful injuries, even amputations. Riders can also be lacerated on sharp edges and by loose or protruding parts such as kickstands or pedals.
4. Misuse by riders.

PRECAUTIONS

In purchasing a bike:

• Look for large wheels, which are more stable than small ones.

• Look for exhaust pipes that point rearward, away from the legs of drivers.

• Make certain there are footbrakes, even if there are handbrakes.

• Check the bike for sharp edges by running your hand along fenders and other metal parts.

• Make certain there are chain guards.

MINOXIDIL

HAZARDS

This drug is prescribed for hypertension. It reduces high blood pressure by relaxing and enlarging small blood vessels to allow blood to flow more easily. But severe side effects may occur, including increased heart rate, rapid weight gain or swelling, increased difficulty in breathing, new or worsened chest pain, arm or shoulder pains, or severe indigestion. Less severe side effects include increased hair growth, rash, or tenderness of the breasts.

PRECAUTIONS

Minoxidil should be used with caution, and only if your high blood pressure is severe and other medications have not worked effectively. If side effects appear, consult your physician before stopping the medication, even if the side effects are bothersome.

Medications to lower blood pressure with a diuretic and prevent heart palpitations are usually prescribed to supplement this medication. Dosage instructions should be carefully followed. If you miss a dose, wait until the next dose.

MITSUBISHI TREDIA

1983 MODEL
Certain vehicles do not comply with FMVSS301, Fuel System Integrity, because excess fuel may leak in rollover tests after a crash.

MIXERS

INJURIES
In 1980, 8,000 cases involved mixers, blenders, or food processors.

HAZARDS
Injuries include lacerations caused by contact between moving blades and fingers, and electric shocks caused by malfunctioning equipment.

HAZARDOUS MODELS
In July 1980, Consumers Union reported that of the 23 mixers tested, *only* the General Electric M74 had a safety interlock to keep people from removing the beaters unless the speed selector was in the "off" position.

MOBILE HOMES, RECREATIONAL VEHICLES (See also Formaldehyde; specific makes)

HAZARDS
There are a number of safety concerns associated with mobile homes and recreational vehicles (RVs). The most serious is fire, because of the numerous ignition sources. Between 1968 and 1972, most mobile homes were wired with aluminum, which has been associated with many residential fires. Many mobile homes have faulty furnaces or heaters, which may have misaligned flues. This can direct hot air at flammable materials or release harmful fumes into the home. When fires do start, they spread rapidly because of the low ceilings, narrow halls, and abundance of flammable materials. Many times faulty or blocked exits can make it difficult for the occupants to escape.

Formaldehyde is a chemical used in many of the items in a mobile home. Recently, complaints about adverse reactions to formaldehyde have arisen. Formaldehyde is present in plywood and particleboard, which are used extensively in the construction of mobile homes. Over time, the formaldehyde breaks down and releases vapors into the air. These vapors can be harmful. This process is called out- or off-gassing, and can last for two to five years.

PRECAUTIONS

Many mobile home and RV dealers sell products such as Off, Gone, or Hyde-Away to deodorize the smell of formaldehyde off-gassing. These products simply cover up the odor. The best precaution is to ensure that the home is well ventilated. Ironically, better-insulated homes are the ones with the greatest risk of trapped fumes.

The following are important considerations when buying a mobile home or recreational vehicle. (The answer to each question should be yes.):

- Is there fire-stopping material between the walls and partitions?

- Are there two exit doors?

- Is there at least one outside window in each bedroom and one smoke detector outside each sleeping area?

- Are there no more than two LP gas tanks, and do they have safety release valves?

- Are the gas tanks inaccessible from the inside?

- Is the oil tank vented at the bottom and inaccessible from the inside?

- Do all fuel-burning appliances (except ranges, lights, and clothes dryers) have their combustion systems accessible only from the outside?

- Are all heat-producing appliances located away from the doors, drapes, and other combustible materials?

- Is the tire pressure and rim size adequate for your expected loads?

MOBILE TRAVELER MOTOR HOME

1975, 1976, 1977 MODELS

On mobile homes equipped with Suburban LP gas furnaces the copper gas line extends across the top of the furnace. Normal vibration can cause the line to rub on the furnace and cause a leak in the line. This condition would subject the occupants to a dangerous fire or explosion.

1976 MODEL
During the assembly of the motorhome body on the Dodge chassis, there was the possibility that holes were drilled into the plastic gas tank. If the holes are not repaired or the tank not replaced, gas leakage and fire could result.

MODICON. *See Oral Contraceptives.*

MONITOR COACH TRAVEL TRAILERS

1965, 1966, 1967 17- AND 19-FOOT MODELS
The rated capacity of the suspension system may be inadequate for normal use, which will result in sagging springs or wheel breakage. It may be necessary to replace the entire suspension system and wheels.

MONKEY BOARDS. *See Playground Equipment.*

MONOSODIUM GLUTAMATE (MSG) *(See also Drug and Food Interactions; Salt)*

Monosodium glutamate is added to foods to improve or enhance flavor. It accounts for 99 percent of the glutamates used as food additives.

HAZARDS
Several studies have found that MSG caused central nervous system damage to several types of laboratory animals during the first ten days of life. Persons who are sensitive to MSG may experience headaches, burning sensations, or facial and chest pressure after consuming foods containing this additive.

PRECAUTIONS:
Anyone sensitive to sugar beets, corn, or wheat should avoid MSG since it is derived from these products. In addition, anyone with vascular illness, brain edema, eye inflammation, or acute hyperten-

sion as well as those undergoing eye surgery should restrict their intake of MSG. Although few infant foods contain MSG, those containing the enhancer should be avoided. It is also advisable for young children to avoid or strictly limit their intake of this substance.

MONTGOMERY WARD ROAD GUARD HD TIRES. *See Firestone Transport Tires.*

MOPEDS (*See also Mini-Bikes*)

INJURIES

In 1980, 58,000 involved motor scooters, mini-bikes, mopeds, or trail bikes.

HAZARDS

Mopeds are so slow they cannot be used on many highways, bridges, or tunnels. Moreover, all two-wheelers are dangerous to ride in rain or snow.

HAZARDOUS MODELS

In May 1981, Consumers Union rated the Solex 4600 as poor in handling because it headed into tighter turns than the rider intended and required considerable skill to control. It was also noted that the levers on the following motorized bikes used to engage the engine were inconvenient and hazardous: Bike Bug QBM-23, Sears catalog number 48851, and Tas Spitz QBM-23. The Columbia Commuter 2220 and 2240 mopeds have brakes that were dangerously unresponsive. The following mopeds were also poor in handling moderate bumps: Yamaha QT50G, Puch Sport MK II, and Peugeot 103LVS-U3.

MOTION-SICKNESS MEDICATIONS. *See Nausea Medications.*

MOTOBECANE MOPEDS

1974–1978 VELOSOLEX 4600 MODELS
The manual choke was not identified as required by federal law.

1975–1980 MOBYLETTE MODELS
Many of these vehicles may not be in compliance with the federal law which prohibits speeds in excess of 30 mph.

1977, 1978, 1979 MOBYLETTE AND VELOSOLEX 4600 MODELS
Many of these vehicles were imported without the tire, rim, and inflation pressure labels as required by law.

MOTORCYCLE HELMETS

FEDERAL STANDARD
Motorcycle helmets must meet a federal standard for resistance to impact and penetration and for the strength of their chinstrap assembly.

PRECAUTIONS
Wearing a helmet reduces the risk of serious injury tremendously when one is riding a motorcycle. Interestingly, researchers have found that expensive helmets do not provide significantly more protection in traffic accidents than inexpensive ones, but those helmets with an integral chin section offer considerably more protection.

HAZARDOUS MODELS
In June 1981, Consumers Union reported that the bubble-shaped shield of the Western Auto 8042 distorted vision somewhat, and that the chin section of the Javelin 6601 and Sears catalog number 75276 tended to block the view of the cycle's gauges. In addition, nearly all the full-face models had ventilation problems: Breath fogged their face shields occasionally. Finally, the extra foam inserts in the Simpson 30 and 61 lowered sound levels too much to be safe.

MOTOR OILS

HAZARDS
Motor oil is less toxic than gasoline, but it can still be harmful if swallowed. Some motor oils contain TCP (tricresyl phosphate), a very toxic additive that can cause paralysis if ingested.
Waste oil is a major ecological problem because millions of pounds are dumped into the environment each year. The detergents

contained in motor oil are a particular environmental problem. Oil recycling has never become very popular because traditional recycling techniques do not generate a high-quality motor oil.

MOTOR SCOOTERS

INJURIES
In 1980, 58,000 cases involved motor scooters, mini-bikes, mopeds, or trail bikes.

HAZARDOUS MODELS
In June 1981, Consumers Union rated the Lambretta Grand Prix 150 as not acceptable and judged the Vespa P125X as far harder to control than a motorcycle. After hitting a moderate bump in a gentle turn, the steering of the Lambretta scooter began to oscillate wider and wider because there was not enough clearance between the handlebar and the rider's leg. Both scooters were judged poor in nearly all CU handling tests.

MOTRIN. *See Ibuprophen.*

MOXALACTAM DISODIUM

HAZARDS
Moxalactam disodium is an antibiotic manufactured by the Eli Lilly Company under the trade name Moxam. It is used in treating life-threatening infections where bleeding is common. A recent study linked moxalactam, and other antibiotics like it, to serious bleeding problems. Only moxalactam was linked to deaths during the study. The FDA is currently considering strengthening the label wording on the drug, although the manufacturer denies there is a problem of increased bleeding with moxalactam.

BRAND NAME: Moxam

MOXAM. *See Moxalactam Disodium.*

MUCILOSE FLAKES AND GRANULES. *See Laxatives.*

MULTI MILE SUPER HIGHWAY TIRES. *See Firestone Transport Tires.*

MURINE. *See Eye Medications, Nonprescription: Germicides and Disinfectants.*

MUSCLE STIMULATORS, ELECTRIC

HAZARDS

These machines, originally designed to help stroke patients, are now often advertised as "passive exercisers." The claims made for "sweatless" exercise are exaggerated according to most health professionals, and the FDA fears life-threatening accidents may occur with unsupervised use. The hazards include serious shocks and burns. In addition, the prescription stimulating devices should never be used by heart patients wearing pacemakers or by epileptics.

MYCITRACIN. *See First-Aid Skin Ointments and Antiseptics; Neomycin.*

NAIL HARDENERS *(See also Formaldehyde)*

HAZARDS

Nail hardeners often contain formaldehyde as a preservative, sometimes in concentrations in excess of 5 percent. Although the FDA has no official standards for the regulation of formaldehyde in these products, the agency does encourage companies to keep formaldehyde content below 5 percent. The Cosmetic Industry Review, an industry-funded panel of scientific experts, has issued a report stating that formaldehyde is safe in cosmetic products only at concentration levels up to .2 percent. The panel stated that available data are not adequate to determine that nail hardeners containing up to 5 percent formaldehyde are safe.

According to the FDA, there are few reported adverse reactions to the formaldehyde in nail hardeners, but because the chemical is corrosive, toxic, and allergenic, as well as skin sensitizing, some people develop severe allergic reactions. The number of adverse reactions increases as the percentage of formaldehyde increases. Many more reactions are reported dealing with products containing a 5 percent concentration than in products where the formaldehyde content is lower. In addition to possible serious skin irritations, formaldehyde at these levels can cause permanent damage to the nail and even cause the nail to lift off from the nail bed completely.

PRECAUTIONS

The FDA has no plans to formally regulate nail hardeners because they represent such a small share of the cosmetic market and because adverse reactions are relatively low. The agency does require, however, that explicit directions for use be included with these products and that the products contain safety shields. Always follow the directions carefully when using nail hardeners and be sure to keep the solution off your skin. General use of these products is not recommended.

> WARNING

Keep these products out of reach of children. If spilled on the skin, they can severely irritate or cause burns.

NANKANG TIRES

5.70–8, 6 PLY TUBELESS N–36, 4.80–8,6 TUBELESS N–36 MODELS
Factory surveillance revealed that the tires were produced with inadequate postinflation pressure, resulting in channel cracking in tread area in the later life of the tire. In certain conditions these cracks could result in a blowout. The recall occurred on April 28, 1981. See TIRES for more information on tire recalls.

NASAL SPRAYS AND DECONGESTANTS

HAZARDS

Inhalers and nose sprays are effective in quickly reducing congestion, but overuse is common and results in rebound congestion, or worsening of the congestion. This creates a vicious cycle because the more the user employs the spray, the more congested he/she becomes and the more often the spray is needed.

PRECAUTIONS

Avoid use of brands that contain antihistamine because it is ineffective in treating the common cold and it may promote the development of an allergy to the antihistamine used. Also avoid Isophrin hydrochloride 1 percent and Neosynephrine hydrochloride 1 percent because they are too strong and can be irritating.

NATIONAL STEEL BELTED RADIAL TIRES. *See Firestone 500 Tires.*

NAUSEA MEDICATIONS

HAZARDS

Over-the-counter, motion-sickness drugs are often effective for conditions of nausea caused by motion. They are not, however, effective in treating flu, indigestion, or gastroenteritis. The most common side effect of these medications is drowsiness, so care should be taken when driving or operating machinery. If you have glaucoma or an enlarged prostate gland, consult your doctor before using these drugs.

Both adults and children may safely use brands containing dimenhydrinate or cyclizene, such as Dramamine, Marezine, or Trav-arex. But Bonine and Vertrol should only be used by people over 12 years of age.

Two brands of medication are sold for the relief of nausea and vomiting not associated with motion sickness: Pepto-Bismol liquid or tablets and Emetrol liquid. These drugs have not been approved as effective by the FDA. Emetrol also has a high sugar content and should not be taken by diabetics.

NECTA SWEET. *See Saccharin.*

NEMBUTAL. *See Sleep Medications, Prescription.*

NEOMYCIN

HAZARDS

This antibiotic is sometimes used in topical ointments for the treatment of various skin disorders complicated by bacterial infection. It should never be used on open wounds. An advisory panel to the FDA believes there is no harm in using neomycin, but recommends it should not be used on large areas of skin. Other evidence indicates that neomycin commonly causes skin rashes and can sensitize people to other more important antibiotics, rendering them ineffective in future treatments. In addition, long-term use of neomycin greatly increases the risk of developing an allergy to the medication, and its use can often mask a more serious infection.

NEO-POLYCIN. *See First-Aid Skin Ointments and Antiseptics; Neomycin.*

NEOSPORIN. *See First-Aid Skin Ointments and Antiseptics; Neomycin.*

NEO-SYNEPHRINE NOSE SPRAY. *See Nasal Sprays and Decongestants.*

NERVINE CAPSULES, LIQUID, AND EFFERVESCENT TABLETS. *See Sleeping Aids, Nonprescription.*

NESTLÉ DECAFFEINATED COFFEE. *See Coffee, Decaffeinated.*

NIGHT LIGHTS *(See also Home Electrical System; Lamps)*

HAZARDOUS MODELS
In April 1980, Danara International, Ltd., recalled approximately 55,000 Winnie-the-Pooh plastic night lights. Some of the lights were manufactured with insufficient amount of glue, permitting the front cover to detach from the light assembly, thereby exposing the interior electrical wiring. Sears, Roebuck & Company sold most of the lights.

NIMROD CAMPING TRAILERS

1972 MODEL
On some models, the springs were improperly installed. As a result, the springs could be torn loose during normal usage.

1972, 1973 MODELS
The welding of the A frame and front lateral section of the trailers may be inadequate due to poor workmanship and excess welding temperatures. The frame should be reinforced for safe usage.

NISSAN SENTRA

1983 MODEL
On Deluxe, sharp corners of the trunk lid and protruding latch are hazardous.

NISSAN STANZA

1982 MODEL
Brake pedal may be adjusted too low, which may cause longer stopping distances.

NITE REST CAPSULES. *See Sleeping Aids, Nonprescription.*

NITRITES AND NITROSAMINES *(See also Salt; Shampoos; Skin Moisturizers and Creams)*

Nitrite is a chemical used widely as a preservative in cured meats such as hot dogs, bacon, bologna, ham, and corned beef. The use of nitrite in food has the beneficial effect of preventing the formation of the toxin that can cause botulism, a deadly form of food poisoning. Nitrite is also used to give cured meats their red coloring.

Cured meats are only one source of creating nitrosamines in a person. According to the NRC, National Research Council, cigarette smoking is by far the greatest source. Inhaling fumes from interiors of new cars is second. Beer drinking is third; but recent changes in processing have reduced the amount of nitrosamines in beer. Some cosmetics also contain nitrites, which can be absorbed through the skin in greater quantities than nitrites consumed in foods. Baked goods, cereals, and vegetables also provide nitrites in the body. It is estimated by the NRC that the amount of nitrosamine formed in the body is roughly equal to what a person gets from sources outside the body.

HAZARDS
Studies questioning the safety of nitrites in cured meats stirred a controversy in the late 1970s when the USDA considered banning the preservative because of a suspected link to cancer. A 1978 MIT study raised concerns over the health risks associated with nitrites. Although nitrites themselves are not apparently toxic, they contribute

to an increased risk of cancer because they can combine with naturally occurring substances called amines to form nitrosamines, which are known cancer-causing substances. The chemical reaction with amines can occur in storage, during cooking, or once in contact with amines in our bodies. Nitrites were not banned, however, because industry argued there was no available substitute preservative for use in cured meats, and because a government panel of scientists felt the health data was incomplete.

PRECAUTIONS

According to the NRC, the search should continue for other methods of curing meats that do not involve nitrite. In the meantime, the amount of nitrite you consume should be reduced as much as possible. For those who wish to avoid any risk associated with nitrite-cured meat, it would be best to avoid these foods or consume nitrite-free versions of them.

NIZORAL. See Ketoconazole.

NO DOZ. See Caffeine; Stimulants.

NODULAR. See Sleeping Medications, Prescription.

NONOXYNOL-9. See Contraceptive Sponge.

NORINYL. See Oral Contraceptives.

NORLESTRIN. See Oral Contraceptives.

NORTON TRIUMPH MOTORCYCLES

1968, 1969 COMMANDO 750CC MODELS
Due to improper crating and warehousing procedures the large

diameter top tube of the main frame may fracture during normal usage.

1971 COMMANDO, ROADSTER, FASTBACK MODELS
The drive pegs in the rear brake drum may work loose due to the incorrect brazing of the pegs. Loose pegs can cause considerable damage to the vehicle. The kickstart pawl may sheer off during normal use because of the use of incorrect materials.

1972, 1973 COMMANDO 750cc, 850cc MODELS
The top or bottom Girling rear suspension unit may detach in service because of an improper bonding of the rubber to metal inner sleeves of insufficient length.

1974 COMMANDO MODELS
The plastic fuel line used on some models may be incompatible with gasoline and may disintegrate.

1974, 1975 TRIDENT T160 MODELS
The rear footbrake pedal levers may have been manufactured with incorrect material and may fail during normal use.

1975 COMMANDO 850cc MK3 MODEL
Excess weld buildup on suspension unit may foul rear hydraulic brake mounting bracket. This could result in the fracture of the suspension system.

NO-TEARS SHAMPOOS. *See Shampoo, Baby.*

NOVAFED. *See Decongestants, Oral.*

NOVAHISTINE. *See Decongestants, Oral.*

NUPERCAINAL OINTMENT, CREAM, SUPPOSITORIES. *See Hemorrhoid Medications.*

NURENBERGER HERCULES MOPED

1977, 1978 P1, P4 MODELS
Many of these vehicles do not have a federally required rear-view mirror.

NUTRA SWEET. *See Aspartame.*

NUTS. *See Aflatoxin; Food Colors, Artificial.*

NYQUIL. *See Cough Medications; Decongestants, Oral.*

O

ODRINEX. *See Diet Aids, Nonprescription.*

ODRINIL. *See Caffeine; Menstrual Pain Medications.*

OFFICE FURNITURE. *See Pressed-Wood Products.*

OLDSMOBILE CUTLASS

1977 MODEL
　　In lowest position, head restraints provide inadequate protection. Runs very wide in hard cornering. Rear-axle shaft may be defective, allowing separation of tire and wheel.

1978 MODEL
　　Lower-rear control-arm bolts may fracture, causing loss of control. Rear-wheel mounting bolts may be defective, causing wheel to come off. Front-wheel bearing may fail, possibly causing loss of control. Fan blade may separate. Open trunk lid is hazardous to tall persons.

1979 MODEL
　　Incorrect lubricant may cause rear-brake stoplights to fail and

cruise control to remain engaged. In wagon, defogger backlights may have defect that shatters glass. Lower-rear control-arm bolts may fracture, causing loss of control. Lap belts tend to ride up. Rear view obstructed by high rear windowsill. Open trunk and latch is hazardous to tall persons.

1980 MODEL
In wagon, defogger backlights may have defect that shatters glass. Lower-rear control-arm bolts may fracture, causing loss of control. The occupant protection in the 4-door model in a 35-mph U.S. Department of Transportation crash test was poor.

1981 MODEL
Lower-rear control-arm bolts may fracture, causing loss of control.

1982 model.
Fuel-hose clamps may fracture, causing fuel leakage and possibly fire. Daytime reflections on the instrument panel.

OLDSMOBILE DELTA 88

1978 MODEL
Rear-wheel mounting bolts may be defective, causing wheel to come off.

1979 MODEL
Front seat-belt anchorage could fail. Uniroyal tires may be defective.

1980 MODEL
Tire placard label may be incorrect.

1982 MODEL
Injection pump may fail, causing throttle valve to remain open.

OLDSMOBILE FIRENZA

1982 MODEL
Fuel-hose clamps may fracture, causing fuel leakage and possibly fire.

1983 MODEL
On cars with two-liter engines, fuel system may leak at the throttle body injection fuel feed connection, creating a fire hazard.

OLDSMOBILE OMEGA

1977 MODEL
Rear-axle shaft may be defective, causing loss of control.

1978 MODEL
Rear-axle shaft may be defective, causing loss of control. Rear-wheel mounting bolts may be defective, causing wheel to come off. Fan blade may separate. Uniroyal tires may be defective.

1979 MODEL
Gauges are hard to read. Fuel filler is vulnerable in sideswipe. Driver's visibility is restricted.

1980 MODEL
Brake pipe could fail, causing loss of brake fluid and partial loss of braking. Fuel hose may be incorrectly positioned, causing fuel leakage and possibly fire. Front-suspension coil spring could be defective, causing damage to brake hose and suspension. Transmission cooler-line hoses may be defective, causing leakage of fluid and possibly fire. Steering-gear mounting plate may develop fatigue cracks, causing partial loss of steering control. Rear brakes may lock up. Brake lock up may occur during moderate to heavy braking and cause the car to spin out of control.

1981 MODEL
Power-steering hose could deteriorate and leak fluid, possibly causing fire. Engine-to-body ground cable may be defective, causing headlights to dim.

1982 MODEL
Fuel-hose clamps may fracture, causing fuel leakage and possibly fire. Clutch may rub against brake pipe, causing loss of brake fluid and partial loss of braking action.

OLDSMOBILE STARFIRE

1977 MODEL

Engine mount bracket may contact steering mechanism, causing difficult steering.

1978 MODEL
Rear-wheel mounting bolts may be defective, causing wheel to come off. Steering-shaft coupling may be defective, causing loss of steering. Engine-mount bracket may contact steering mechanism, causing difficult steering. Front safety belts are awkward. Fuel tank and filler are vulnerable in crash. Open hatch is hazardous to tall persons.

1979 MODEL
Electrical short in engine oil pressure switch may start engine when ignition is in "on" position. Carburetor fuel-feed hose may rupture, causing fuel leak and possibly fire.

OLDSMOBILE TORONADO

1977 MODEL
When transmission shift level shifted to park, parking pawl may not engage and car could roll freely.

1978 MODEL
Rear-wheel mounting bolts may be defective, causing wheel to come off.

1980 MODEL
Tire placard label may be incorrect. Electrical short may occur in exhaust-gas recirculation wiring harness, causing fire.

1981 MODEL
Front left upper-control-arm nuts may come off, causing loss of control.

1982 MODEL
Injection pump may fail, causing throttle valve to remain open.

OLDSMOBILE WAGON

1977, 1978, 1979 MODELS
Child could become entrapped in rear side storage compartment.

OLDSMOBILE 98

1977 MODEL
Tires may be defective. Catalytic converter may be defective. Power brake booster may fail.

1978 MODEL
Rear-wheel mounting bolts may be defective, causing wheel to come off. Seat belts are uncomfortable. Brakes may fail.

1979 MODEL
Front seat-belt anchorage could fail. The occupant protection in the 4-door model was rated poor in a 35-mph U.S. Department of Transportation crash test.

1980 MODEL
Tire placard label may be incorrect.

1982 MODEL
Injection pump may fail, causing throttle valve to remain open.

OMNI STEEL BELTED RADIAL TIRES. *See Tires.*

OMNIPEN. *See Ampicillin.*

ONE-A-DAY PLUS IRON. *See Iron and Iron Supplements.*

OPEN ROAD MOTOR HOME

1970 MODEL
The door locks and latches do not meet the minimum standards set by the federal government. As a result, the doors may inadvertently open.

1970, 1971, 1972 22- AND 23-FOOT MODEL
There is the possibility that the 22- and 23-foot motorhome bodies were installed on a chassis system that was too small, and resulted in

the vehicle not having the correct center of gravity. Too much weight is placed on the front suspension system, making normal handling of the vehicle very dangerous. This situation can be corrected only by extending the rear walls, roof, and floor by 32 inches in the rear and relocating the components in the vehicle.

1973 STATESMEN 21-, 23-, AND 25-FOOT MODELS

In many cases the furnaces were not properly secured to the floor with screws. The normal operation of the vehicle will result in movement of the furnace and separation of the furnace from the flue. Deadly fumes could escape into the vehicle.

1974 MODEL

The plastic shower curtain in many of these vehicles not meet the minimum federal safety standards and could be a fire hazard.

ORAL CONTRACEPTIVES

HAZARDS

Although the "pill" is an effective birth control method, numerous serious risks and side effects are associated with its use, and for many women the use of oral contraceptives is contraindicated altogether.

You should *not* use the pill if you have any personal or family history of blood clots in the legs or lungs; angina pectoris (chest pain); heart attack; known or suspected cancer of the breast or sex organs; unusual vaginal bleeding that has not been diagnosed; or known or suspected pregnancy. If your mother took the drug DES during pregnancy, you have an increased risk of a rare form of cancer, and that risk is increased significantly by use of the pill.

A new study by the Division of Reproductive Health, Center for Disease Control (CDC) in Atlanta, raises questions about the increased risk of cancer with the use of oral contraceptives. Researchers found that the risk of ovarian and endometrial cancer actually decreased with the use of birth control pills. According to the study, 1,700 cases of ovarian cancer and 2,000 cases of endometrial cancer are averted each year in the U.S. with the use of oral contraceptives. In a related finding, the researchers discovered use of an oral contraceptive before a woman's first pregnancy did not increase her risk of breast cancer more significantly than other methods of birth control. The study, which also provided no support for the theory that oral contraceptive use increases the risk of breast cancer, found use of the pill did not increase the risk of cancer among women with benign breast disease or a family history of cancer.

Some oral contraceptives contain estrogen, others a combination of estrogen and progesterone, and still others contain progesterone only. Although evidence of the increased risk of cancer in women who take the pill has never been documented, animal studies have linked cancer of the breast, sex organs, and liver to estrogen use. Until further studies confirm the findings of the CDC research, it would be prudent to use oral contraceptives cautiously.

A number of studies show that developing fetuses have an increased risk of heart and limb defects if the mother takes oral contraceptives just before or during pregnancy. Miscarriage may also be more likely if regular use of the pill was discontinued just prior to becoming pregnant.

The risk of a possibly fatal heart attack or stroke associated with use of the pill is increased if you have any family history of blood clots or heart attack, or if you are over 35 and/or smoke. It has also been found that older-type birth control pills, which are high in estrogen, have a beneficial effect on cholesterol levels, whereas the newer brands of pills containing high levels of progestin have the opposite effect on cholesterol levels, increasing the risk of heart disease.

There are two types of cholesterol in a woman's body affected by estrogen and progestin in birth control pills. LDL cholesterol is considered bad and linked with heart disease, while HDL cholesterol is considered good and helps prevent heart attack. Estrogen pills have been found to reduce the levels of LDL and increase the levels of HDL, while progestin pills increase the LDL levels and decrease levels of HDL. Prolonged use of high-level progestin pills may not be wise a better balance between estrogen and progestin is more desirable.

Gallbladder disease, requiring surgery, has also been identified as a possible side effect of the pill. Less serious side effects include tender breasts, nausea, vomiting, weight loss or gain, swollen ankles, spotty darkening of the face, and changes in menstrual period, particularly in use of the all-progestin mini-pill or pills low in estrogen.

More severe problems associated with the use of oral contraceptives include worsening migraine, asthma, epilepsy, heart disease, and kidney disease (as a result of water retention). Oral contraceptives may also promote the growth of fibroid tumors in the uterus, mental depression, and suicidal impulses. Some women also develop high blood pressure while using the pill, although blood pressure returns to normal when use of the pill is discontinued. Liver tumors have been reported as well by pill users. If a tumor ruptures, it can cause fatal bleeding.

A patient package insert describing the side effects and contraindications of oral contraceptives should come with your prescription. Be sure to read the information carefully. Also talk to your physician about other forms of contraception, such as the diaphragm and intrauterine devices.

> **WARNING**

Be alert to symptoms that may indicate a problem with use of the pill and call your physician immediately.

- Sharp or crushing chest pain
- Coughing blood
- Sudden shortness of breath
- Pain in the calf
- Severe headache, vomiting, dizziness, or fainting
- Disturbance of vision or speech
- Weakness
- Numbness
- Breast lumps
- Severe abdominal pain (liver tumor)
- Severe depression
- Yellowing of skin

Do not smoke while using the pill. *Do not take* the pill after age 40.

ORAL HYPOGLYCEMIC AGENTS. *See Antidiabetic Agents, Oral.*

ORANGES. *See Drug and Food Interactions; Food Colors, Artificial.*

ORINASE. *See Antidiabetic Agents, Oral.*

ORNEX. *See Decongestants, Oral.*

ORTHO-NOVUM. *See Oral Contraceptives.*

OTTOMANS. *See Stools*

OVCON. *See Oral Contraceptives*

OVEN CLEANERS *(See also Cleaning Agents)*

INJURIES
In 1980, 12,000 involved oven cleaners, drain cleaners, and other caustics.

HAZARDS
The most common of these injuries were chemical burns to the face and hands caused sometimes by spraying the cleaner the wrong way. Others were poisonings resulting from children ingesting the cleaners. Finally, some were caused by the inhalation of ammonia gas some cleaners produce.

FEDERAL STANDARD
Oven cleaners containing more than 2 percent of certain caustic substances must be packaged in child-resistant containers.

PRECAUTIONS
When using them, open the windows and make sure that children are out of the room.

OVENS. *See Microwave Ovens; Ranges.*

OVENS, COUNTERTOP. *See Cooking Appliances, Small Electric*

OVRAL. See Oral Contraceptives.

OVULEN. See Oral Contraceptives.

OXAZEPAM. See Benzodiazepines.

OXSORALEN CAPSULES. See PUVA.

OXY-5, OXY-10. See Acne Medications, Nonprescription.

P

PACE ARROW MOTORHOME

1971 F, G, H, K, X MODELS
In some models, the windshields installed in the motorhomes did not meet the minimum standards as required by law.

1973 MODEL
The exhaust pipe is mounted very close to the floor of the motorhome. As a result, heat can build up causing damage to the floor.

1977 MODEL
The certification label on some models shows the incorrect tire size and inflation pressure. Inflating the tires to the pressure indicated on the incorrect label is a significant safety hazard.

PACEMAKERS *(See also Microwave Ovens)*

Pacemakers are cigarette-lighter-size electrical devices implanted in the heart to deliver a stream of electrical impulses to stimulate or steady the heartbeat of a diseased heart, or to reestablish the rhythm of an arrested heart.

HAZARDS
Recent U.S. Senate studies by the Special Committee on Aging

show that doctors are implanting, monitoring, and replacing pacemakers in growing numbers, and often unnecessarily. The committee unearthed questionable practices on the part of the pacemaker industry, some salesmen, hospitals, and doctors, including kickbacks and other illegal or "improper inducements," "deceptive" and "dishonored" warranties, and the excessive prices Medicare is billed for the devices. The studies allege that pacemakers costing $600 to $900 to manufacture are sold to hospitals for $2,000 to $5,000 each. The hospital in turn marks this price up by another 50 to 150 percent when they apply for Medicare reimbursement.

The committee report further charged that pacemakers guaranteed for 10 years begin to wear out in three years or less, and that hundreds of pacemaker salesmen, who work on a commission, not only have to train physicians to implant the pacemaker (often in the operating room during surgery), but also train them how to monitor the devices and bill Medicare.

PACIFIERS *(See also Toys, General)*

INJURIES
Between 1973 and 1975, 200 cases were reported.

HAZARDS
Almost all injuries were suffocation or strangulation to children less than 18 months old. Children were able to break or pull apart the pacifier, swallowing the parts. Others were asphyxiated by the string used to tie the pacifier around the baby's neck.

FEDERAL STANDARDS
Government regulations require that pacifiers be large enough to prevent choking and must not come apart in small pieces.

PRECAUTIONS
Never tie a pacifier to a string around a baby's neck.

PAIN KILLERS. *See Acetaminophen; Aspirin; Benzodiazepines.*

PAINTS

INJURIES
In 1980, 20,000 injuries involved paints, solvents, or lubricants.

In addition, the National Bureau of Standards (NBS) estimates that 600,000 children may have unduly high levels of lead in their blood.

HAZARDS

Lead paint is a hazard to small children who like to eat paint chips. One small chip, half an inch square, can contain more than one milligram of lead—10 times more than the maximum "safe" daily dose of lead. A child who eats paint chips can accumulate an excessive amount of lead in a very short time. Lead poisoning can adversely affect health, intelligence, and behavior. Whereas adults absorb only about 10 percent of the lead they ingest, children absorb up to 50 percent in their bones and soft tissues and retain a much greater percentage of the lead they absorb. If untreated, lead poisoning can result in blindness, brain damage, mental retardation, and even death. In the U.S. it is a major contributor to learning disabilities in children.

Flaking paint is not only hazardous because a child might eat the chips, but is often the major source of lead in house dust and soil near outdoor painted surfaces. When combined with the other sources of lead—in food, water, canned goods, soil, and from industrial and auto emissions in the air—it can build up to a toxic dose.

Many interior latex paints still contain mercury, which is a source of indoor air pollution. Mercury-contaminated vapors can remain in the indoor atmosphere for some time after a room is painted, sometimes causing "mercurialism." Mercurialism occurs when low-level exposure builds up over time. It can cause symptoms ranging from fatigue, headache, and irritability to tremor, numbness of limbs, difficulty swallowing, deafness, blurred vision, and loss of muscle coordination.

FEDERAL STANDARDS

Since 1973, the CPSC has banned paints for household use containing more than 0.5 percent lead and toys and other children's articles containing such paint. In 1978, the commission further lowered the permissible lead content in paint to which children could be exposed to 0.06 percent. However, many older houses still have the old, often peeling lead paints. Sometimes the older layers of paint are covered by newer nonlead paint, but the U.S. Department of Housing estimates that 60 percent of homes built before 1969 and 30 percent built between 1940 and 1960 still have some surfaces coated with potentially hazardous amounts of lead paint.

PRECAUTIONS

Children who have lead poisoning may show the following

symptoms: unusual irritability, poor appetite, stomach pains and vomiting, persistent constipation, sluggishness or drowsiness. Unfortunately, many victims show no symptoms until it is too late for effective treatment. Further, diagnosis may be difficult because these same symptoms may indicate other illnesses.

HAZARDOUS MODELS

A Consumers Union study found Dutch Boy Paints had the highest mercury content among the latex paints surveyed, but its mildew resistance was little better than that of Sherwin-Williams paints, which contained no detectable amount of mercury.

PAINT SPRAY GUNS

HAZARDS

Airless paint spray guns can be dangerous because their contents are expelled under very high pressure, which can penetrate the skin. Sometimes the amputation of injured limbs is necessary.

PRECAUTIONS

It is important that any spray guns purchased should have a nozzle guard extending 3/4 to 1 1/8 inches beyond the spray jet. It is also important that they have a trigger guard to prevent discharge in case the gun is dropped. Finally, users should never attempt to unclog the nozzle with a finger or attempt to disassemble a gun before the pump is shut off and pressure in the hose is released.

HAZARDOUS MODELS

In late 1979, Sears, Roebuck & Company announced a repair program to correct a potential electrical shock hazard in 2,800 airless sprayers, model number 165.1555571.

PANELING. *See Pressed-Wood Products.*

PANELS. *See Doors; Glass Doors and Windows.*

PANS. *See Cookware.*

PANWARFIN. *See Warfarin Potassium/Sodium.*

PATCHING COMPOUNDS AND TEXTURED PAINTS *(See also Asbestos)*

HAZARDS
Before 1978, these products often contained asbestos, which is now linked to lung cancer and to other serious health disorders. In 1977, the CPSC banned asbestos patching compound material, but many older homes still contain these products.

PRECAUTIONS
If patching compound or textured paint was used in your home prior to the ban, it should not be removed unless absolutely necessary. If the compounds are in poor condition and need repair or removal, follow the precautions listed under general guidelines for handling asbestos products (*see* Asbestos) before doing any work.

PARTICLEBOARD. *See Pressed-Wood Products.*

PEANUT BUTTER. *See Aflatoxin; Food Colors, Artificial; Health Foods.*

PEANUTS. *See Aflatoxin; Food Colors, Artificial; Foods, Natural.*

PEERLESS TIRES. *See Uniroyal Tires.*

PELVIMETRY. *See X-ray, Pregnancy.*

PENICILLIN. *See Ampicillin; Drug and Food Interactions.*

PENTON MOPEDS

1975 KTM MODEL
Many of these vehicles do not have the proper lighting or certification labels as required by federal law.

PEPTO-BISMOL. *See Nausea Medications.*

PERCOLATORS, COFFEE. *See Coffee-Making Equipment; Cooking Appliances, Small Electric.*

PET FOODS. *See Food Colors, Artificial.*

PEUGEOT MOPEDS

1976 103 MODEL
The fuel tank shut-off valve was not identified as required by federal law.

1977, 1978, 1979 103–U3 MODEL
Certain vehicles may not be in compliance with the federal law that prohibits speeds in excess of 30 mph.

1978, 1979 103 SP U3, 103 LVS U3, 103 L2 U3 MODELS
Tire, rim, and inflation labels were not affixed to these vehicles as required by law.

PEUGEOT STATION WAGON

1979, 1980 MODELS
Air conditioner may short-circuit, causing fire.

PEUGEOT 504

1979 MODEL
Air conditioner may short-circuit, causing fire. Front seat belts ride up. Head restraints are hazardous in a crash. Fuel filler is vulner-

able to sideswipe. Operating controls are confusing. The occupant protection of the 4-door model in a U.S. Department of Transportation 35-mph crash test was rated poor.

1980 MODEL
Air conditioner may short-circuit, causing fire.

PEUGEOT 505

1982 MODEL
Handling is sluggish in emergency maneuvers.

1983 MODEL
In Diesel and Turbodiesel, horn control is inconvenient.

PEUGEOT 604 SL

1977 MODEL
Front-brake line may be defective, resulting in loss of front braking.

1978 MODEL
Handling is clumsy during accident-avoidance maneuvers. Controls and displays are confusing. Front seat belts ride up. Rear view is restricted.

PHENOBARBITAL. *See Spironolactone with Hydrochlorothiazide.*

PHENYLBUTAZONE. *See Warfarin Potassium/Sodium.*

PICNIC EQUIPMENT. *See Camp Cooking and Heating Equipment.*

PICKLES. *See Drug and Food Interactions.*

PILLOWS. *See Dust.*

PILLSBURY APRICOT NUT QUICK BREAD MIX. *See Sulfites.*

PILLSBURY PLUS CARROT 'N SPICE CAKE MIX. *See Sulfites.*

PINTO II MOPED

1978 MODEL SOLD BY J.C. PENNY
The front brake assembly is prone to failure and may cause grabbing when applied.

PIPE INSULATION *(See also Asbestos)*

HAZARDS
In some homes, hot water and steam pipes may be covered with asbestos-containing materials or asbestos paper tape. It is best to leave these materials alone whenever possible because once asbestos fibers are released in the air they do not disperse. Inhaling asbestos fibers has been shown to cause cancer and other respiratory illnesses.

PRECAUTIONS
If the material is damaged and must be repaired, it is best to wrap the material with wide duct tape or utilize some other commercial pipe covering that will prevent dissemination of the asbestos fibers. Try to avoid removal of the pipe or insulation. Before working with these products, consult the general guidelines for handling asbestos products *(see* Asbestos).

PLACIDYL. *See Sleep Medications, Prescription.*

PLANTS, HOUSEHOLD *(See also Poisons)*

HAZARDS

According to the National Poison Control Center, poisonings from household plants have increased 50 percent in the past five years. Household plants can often be toxic if ingested, touched, or inhaled. Reactions can be as mild as a stomach upset, skin rash, or nasal congestion, or as serious as depression of the circulatory and central nervous systems, violent vomiting, kidney inflammation, convulsions, heart failure, and even death (see table below).

English ivy, philodendron, and daffodils are common household plants that are quite toxic. Just by touching the dieffenbachia, a person can pick up toxic sap which, if transferred to the mouth, can cause severe burning and choking. The leaves of tomato and rhubarb plants are also poisonous, as are elderberry shoots and Irish potatoes if eaten green.

Children are often attracted to colorful berries and flowers, and sometimes confuse toxic leaves, stored bulbs, and seeds with safe foods.

PRECAUTIONS

Children should be cautioned against eating any plants, and poisonous plants should be placed out of their reach. In case of an accidental poisoning, contact your nearest poison control center.

For a list of local poison control centers see POISONS.

COMMON HARMFUL PLANTS*

CULTIVATED HOUSE AND GARDEN PLANTS	TOXIC PARTS	SYMPTOMS PRODUCED
Caladium Fancy-leaf caladium	All parts (toxic substance: calcium oxalate crystals)	Intense irritation to mucous membranes, producing swelling of tongue, lips, and palate
Colocasia Elephant ear, Dasheen	Same as above	Same as above

Dieffenbachia Dumb cane, Elephant ear	Same as above	Same as above
Monstera Swiss-cheese plant, Ceriman	Same as above	Same as above
Philodendron Elephant ear	Same as above	Same as above
Ricinus Communis Castor bean, Castor oil plant, Palma Christi	Seed, if chewed (toxic substance: ricin)	Burning sensation in the mouth, nausea, vomiting, abdominal pain, thirst, blurred vision, dizziness, convulsions
Lantana Lantana	All parts, especially the green berries (toxic substance: lantadene A)	Vomiting, diarrhea, weakness, ataxia, visual disturbances and lethargy
Hens-and-Chicks	Same as above	Same as above
Bunchberry	Same as above	Same as above
Hedera Helix English ivy	All parts (toxic substance: hederagenin, or steroidal saponin)	Local irritation, excess salivation, nausea, vomiting, thirst, severe diarrhea, abdominal pain
Digitalis Foxglove	Leaves, seeds, flowers (toxic substances: cardioactive glycosides—digitoxin, digoxin, gitoxin, and others)	Local irritation of mouth and stomach, vomiting, abdominal pain, diarrhea, cardiac disturbances
Ilex	Bright red berries (toxic substance: unidentified)	Nausea, vomiting, abdominal pain, and diarrhea
Iris	Rootstalk or rhizome (toxic substance: unidentified)	Nausea, vomiting, abdominal pain, and diarrhea
Ligustrum Common privet Waxed-leaf ligustrum	Leaves and berries (toxic substance: unidentified)	Nausea, vomiting, abdominal pain, and diarrhea

307 / PLANTS

Narcissus 　Narcissus 　Daffodil 　Jonquil	Bulb (toxic substance: unidentified)	Nausea, vomiting, abdominal pain, and diarrhea
Poinciana Gilliesii 　Poinciana 　Bird-of-Paradise	Green seed pods (toxic substance: unidentified)	Nausea, vomiting, abdominal pain, and diarrhea
Wisteria 　Wisteria	Whole pods or seeds (toxic substances: resin and glycoside wisterin)	Nausea, vomiting, abdominal pain, and diarrhea
Nerum Oleander 　Oleander	Leaves, stems, and flowers (toxic substances: cardioactive glycosides—oleandroside, oleandrin, and nerioside)	Local irritation to mouth and stomach, vomiting, abdominal pain, diarrhea, and cardiac disturbances
Taxus 　Japanese yew	Seeds and leaves (toxic substance: alkaloid toxine)	Gastroenteritis and cardiac disturbances
Prunus Americana 　American plum 　Wild plum	Leaves, stems, bark, and seed pits (toxic substances: cyanogenic glycosides)	Nausea, vomiting, abdominal pain, diarrhea, difficulty in breathing, muscular weakness, dizziness, stupor, and convulsions
Prunus Armeniaca 　Apricot	Leaves, stem, bark, and seed pits (toxic substances: cyanogenic glycosides)	Nausea, vomiting, abdominal pain, diarrhea, difficulty in breathing, muscular weakness, dizziness, stupor, and convulsions
Prunus Virginiana 　Choke cherry	Leaves, stems, bark, and seed pits (toxic substances: cyanogenic glycosides)	Nausea, vomiting, abdominal pain, diarrhea, difficulty in breathing, muscular weakness, stupor, and convulsions
Solanum 　*Pseudocapsicum* 　Jerusalem cherry 　Natal cherry	All parts (toxic substances: leaves contain cardioactive substance solanocapsine; berries contain	Cardiac depression

	glycoalkaloid solanine and related glycoalkaloids)	
Daphne Mezereum Daphne	All parts, especially berries, bark, and leaves (toxic substance: daphnin)	Local irritation to mouth and stomach, nausea, vomiting, and diarrhea
Rheum Raponticum Rhubard	Leaf blade (toxic substance: oxalic acid)	Corrosive action on the gastrointestinal tract
Arisaema Triphyllum Jack-in-the-Pulpit Indian turnip	Leaves (toxic substance: calcium oxalate acid)	Corrosive action to gastrointestinal tract, producing swelling of tongue, lips, and palate
Podophyllum Peltatum Mayapple Mandrake Ground lemon	Rootstalk, leaves, stems, and green fruit (toxic substance: podophylloresin)	Abdominal pain, vomiting, diarrhea, and pulse irregularities
Cicuta Maculata Water hemlock Spotted cowbane Poison parsnip	Root and rootstalk (toxic substance: cicutoxin)	Increased salivation, abodominal pain, nausea, vomiting, tremors, muscle spasms, and convulsions
Parthenocissus Quinquefolia Virginia creeper American ivy	Berries and leaves (toxic substance: oxalic acid)	Corrosive action to gastrointestinal tract, nausea, vomiting, abdominal pain, diarrhea, and headache
Conium Maculatum Poison hemlock Fool's parsley False parsley	All parts (toxic substances: lambda-coniceine, coniine, n-methyl coniine)	Gastrointestinal distress, muscular weakness, convulsions, and respiratory distress
Dartura Meteloides Moonflower Angel's trumpet Locoweed	Leaves, flowers, nectar, seeds (toxic substances: belladonna alkaloids)	Dilated pupils, dry mouth, increased body temperature, intense thirst, confusion, delirium, hallucinations, and pulse disturbances
Datura Stramonium Jimsonweed Jamestown weed Thorn apple Angel's trumpet	Same as above	Same as above

Robinia Pseudoacacia Black locust White locust	Young leaves, inner bark, seeds (toxic substances: robin and robitin)	Nausea, vomiting, and abdominal pain
Phytolacca Americana Pokeweed Pokeroot Poke salad Inkberry	All parts, especially the root, leaves, and green berries (toxic substance: tannin)	Oral burning sensation, sore throat, nausea, vomiting, and blurred vision
Gelsemium Sempervirens Yellow jessamine Carolina jessamine	All parts (toxic substances: alkaloids—gelsemine, gelsemicine)	Cardiac depression, visual disturbances, dizziness, headache, and dryness of mouth
Solanum Dulcamara European bittersweet Climbing nightshade	Leaves and berries (toxic substance: solanine)	Vomiting, diarrhea, abdominal pain, drowsiness, tremors, weakness, and difficulty in breathing
Atropa Belladonna Deadly nightshade	All parts (toxic substances: tropane alkaloids, atropine, and hyoscyamina)	Fever, visual disturbances, burning of mouth, thirst, dry skin, headache, and confusion

*National Poison Center Network

PLASTICRAFTS. *See Hobbies and Crafts.*

PLASTICS

HAZARDS

Plastics are widely used in home products including furniture stuffing and covering; carpeting and carpeting pads; insulation; paneling and appliances; and in the interior of cars, planes, and mobile homes. Like many of the traditional materials they replace, they are combustible; once ignited, they give off heat, smoke, and toxic gases. The many different types of plastics have a variety of combustibility characteristics. However, all are associated with at least one of the following hazards.

- Rapid flame spread.

- Extreme heat.

- Large amounts of dense smoke, especially in plastics which contain flame retardants.

- Toxic gases, particularly carbon monoxide, but also toxic combustion gases such as aldehydes, hydrogen cyanide, or hydrogen chloride.

In most cases, people die from smoke and carbon-monoxide gas inhalation before the flames reach them.

FEDERAL STANDARDS

Several federal agencies have responsibility for plastics' flammability. The National Highway Traffic Safety Administration has set standards for the flammability of materials used in automobiles. The Federal Trade Commission has ordered 26 members of the cellular plastics industry to discontinue marketing products through use of the terms "self-extinguishing" or "nonburning," to disclose the hazards associated with unsafe uses of the products, and to investigate more fully the combustibility of cellular plastics. The CPSC has responsibility for the flammability of interior furnishings in homes and has developed standards for upholstered furniture, carpets, rugs, and mattresses.

PLAYGROUND EQUIPMENT

INJURIES

In 1981, 162,000 cases involved treehouses, slides, sliding boards, seesaws, monkey bars, swings, and other playground equipment, resulting in injuries mainly to children between the ages of 5 and 10.

HAZARDS

Many injuries are caused by the following.

- Equipment that tips over because of nonexistent or faulty anchoring devices.

- Exposed screws and bolts.

- Open-ended hooks, especially S-hooks.

- Moving parts that pinch or crush fingers.

- Sharp edges or rough surfaces.

- Rings with a diameter between 5 and 10 inches that may trap children's heads.

- Falls onto hard surfaces such as concrete.

- Falls onto other playground equipment.

- Equipment that fails because nuts, bolts, and clamps loosen or nuts and bolts, chains, swings, or tubing rust through.

PRECAUTIONS

In purchasing playground equipment, consumers should make sure exposed bolts or screws are capped, there are good anchoring devices, and there are no open-ended hooks, sharp edges, or rough surfaces, or rings between 5 and 10 inches. Consumers should install this equipment over sand, earth, or other soft surfaces at least six feet from obstructions such as fences and walls or other equipment, and they should regularly check for loose connections and rust.

PLAYHOUSES. *See Playground Equipment.*

PLAYPENS

INJURIES

In 1980, 10,000 involved playpens, cribs, and baby gates.

HAZARDS

- Suffocation in a mesh-sided playpen with the drop side down, forming a loose pocket which the infant can roll into.

- Falls while the child was climbing out of the playpen.

- Finger entrapment when the side was being raised or lowered or in the locking mechanism.

- Falls onto a playpen part like the frame, wooden rail, or metal brace.

- Snagging of a body part or clothing on structure of the playpen causing choking, laceration, fracture, or other injuries.

HAZARDOUS MODELS
In August 1981, Consumers Union reported the following potential hazards in specific crib models.

- Ward's catalog number 5519 has gaps on the top rail near the folding mechanism that could pinch the child; its irregularly spaced spindles could trap an arm or a leg; and its top rail has sharp edges.

- The Cosco 310 and Strolee 376 lack padding on the top rail.

- Sears catalog number 36121, Cosco 310, Bilt-Rite 317, J.C. Penney catalog number 0034, Pride-Trimble 758, and Cosco 87 lack padding on the legs.

- The staples used to attach the draft strip on the Cosco 310 and 330 and the Welsh 263 models may create gaps that could trap fingers or hands; also the staples could pop out.

PLUGS. *See Home Electrical System.*

PLYMOUTH ARROW

1977 MODEL
Front-brake hose assembly may be defective. Control is difficult in accident avoidance. Fuel filler is vulnerable to sideswipe damage. Open trunk lid is hazardous to tall persons.

1978 MODEL
Fuel may leak near engine, causing fire.

PLYMOUTH CHAMP

1979 MODEL
The occupant protection of the 2-door hatchback in the 35-mph

U.S. Department of Transportation crash test was rated poor.

1980 MODEL
Ashtray bulb socket may overheat and cause fire.

1981 MODEL
Open hatch lid is hazardous. Front view for tall drivers is obstructed by rear-view mirror.

1982 MODEL
Premature wheel lockup lengthened stopping distances.

PLYMOUTH FURY

1977 MODEL
Potential damage to shift linkage bushings may cause transmission to be in a gear position other than that indicated. Carburetor pump seal may be defective, causing stalling. Ran very wide in hard cornering.

1978 MODEL
Tilt-steering column may be defective.

PLYMOUTH HORIZON

1978 MODEL
Steering coupling may be oversized, possibly causing loss of control. Fuel return hose may chafe and leak, possibly causing fire. Fuel tube may have been misrouted, possibly causing fuel leakage and fire. Lower control arm may crack, possibly causing loss of control. Hub nuts may loosen, loosening front wheel. Fuel tank may leak when full, causing fire hazard. Front suspension may be defective, possibly causing loss of control. Unpredictable and possibly dangerous handling during some emergency maneuvers. Front seat belts ride up.

1979 MODEL
Alternator may fail, causing loss of battery charging. Handling is poor to fair in emergency maneuvers. Front seat belts ride up. Front-seat release may jam. Rear view is obstructed by head restraints and

wide rear roof pillars. Open hatch lid in coupe is hazardous to tall persons.

1980 MODEL
Secondary catch system may fail, causing hood to open. Fuel-line hose may fail, causing fuel leakage and fire. Ball joint may separate from arm, causing loss of control.

1981 MODEL
Automatic speed-control switch may stick in "resume" position. Handling is sloppy in emergency maneuvers. Front seat belts tend to ride up.

1982 MODEL
Ball joint may separate from knuckle, causing loss of control. Some difficulty controlling in emergency maneuvers. Rear window quickly accumulates grime in rainy weather.

1983 MODEL
Handling is somewhat unpredictable in emergency maneuvers.

PLYMOUTH RELIANT

1981 MODEL
Stop-brake warning lights may fail. Automatic speed-control switch may stick in "resume" position. Sharp-edged handles for rear vent windows may be hazardous. Engine-cooling fan has no protective shroud. Side vision partially obstructed by wide center pillars in 4-door sedan and wagon. Sharp metal edge on dashboard. The occupant protection of the 4-door model in the U.S. Department of Transportation 35-mph crash test was rated poor.

1982 MODEL
Ball joint may separate from knuckle, causing loss of control.

1983 MODEL
The hydraulic brake tubing routed to the left rear wheel may have been distorted during assembly, allowing interference between the tube and an exhaust-system hanger bolt and a partial loss of braking. The hydraulic brake tube may allow interference between the tube and the rear-park brake cable, which may cause tube failure and a partial loss of braking.

PLYMOUTH SAPPORO

1978 MODEL
Fuel may leak near engine, causing fire. Brakes are prone to fade. Safety belts are uncomfortable. Fuel filler is vulnerable to sideswipe. Driver's view is restricted. Open hatch is hazardous to tall persons.

1980 MODEL
Ashtray bulb socket may overheat and cause fire.

PLYMOUTH VOLARE

1977 MODEL
Brakes may fail because of brake-tube corrosion or brake-hose cracking. Front suspension may be defective, possibly causing loss of control. Front seat belts ride up. Fuel filler is vulnerable to sideswipe. Trunk lid may shut in light breeze.

1978 MODEL
Brakes may fail because of brake-tube corrosion or brake-hose cracking. Tilt steering column may be defective. Fuel filler is vulnerable in sideswipe.

1979 MODEL
Steering is sloppy during emergency maneuvers. The occupant protection of the 2-door model in a U.S. Department of Transportation 35-mph crash test was rated poor.

1980 MODEL
Brake hose may fail, causing braking loss.

PLYMOUTH VOYAGER VAN

1977 MODEL
Runs very wide and unsteadily on hard turns. Fuel filler is vulnerable in a sideswipe. Rear door may slam shut in gentle breeze.

PLYWOOD. *See Pressed-Wood Products.*

PMB PREMARIN WITH MEPROBAMATE. *See Estrogen.*

POISONS *(See also Plants, Household; household products by name)*

HAZARDS
As many as 100,000 American children are accidentally poisoned each year. Most of the poisonings result from adult carelessness about common household substances, according to the CPSC. Until the CPSC required child-resistant caps on many over-the-counter drugs, aspirin was the most common cause of childhood poisonings. More recently, poisonous household plants have been the cause of the greatest number of reports of child poisonings. Detergents, cleaners, and soaps rank second, and vitamin/mineral preparations rank third. Parents often do not perceive common household liquids, such as furniture polish, liniments, and paint thinner, to be poisonous, and often do not take care in using and storing them.

PRECAUTIONS
Important reminders from the CPSC include: buy and use products with child-resistant caps and closures, and keep products in their original containers with the warning labels intact. The safety commission also warns that a child-resistant cap is no good if it is not used—be sure to resecure the container properly. They also advise that the closures are only child-resistant, not child-proof, so keep all poisons out of reach of small children, and keep the telephone numbers of the nearest poison control center and rescue service nearby in case of an accidental poisoning.

According to the National Poison Prevention Center, many accidental poisonings occur when young children are visiting in homes without small children, where no precautions against accidental poisoning have been taken. When visiting a friend or relative or when grandparents come to visit, put medications away and watch your child carefully. (See listing below of the NPC network.)

DIRECTORY OF THE NATIONAL POISON CENTER NETWORK

ALASKA
Anchorage Poison Center
Providence Hospital
Anchorage AK 99504
(907) 274-6535

NEW YORK
Southern Tier Poison Center
Binghamton General Hospital
Binghamton NY 13903
(607) 723-8929

SOUTH DAKOTA
Dakota Midland Poison Center
Dakota Midland Hospital
Aberdeen SD 57401
(605) 225-1880

Fairbanks Poison
  Center
Fairbanks Memorial
  Hospital
Fairbanks AK 99701
(907) 452-8181

DISTRICT OF COLUMBIA
National Capital Poison
  Center
Georgetown University
  Hospital
3800 Reservoir Road
Washington DC 20007
(202) 625-3333

FLORIDA
Gulf Region Poison
  Center
Baptist Hospital
Pensacola FL 32501
(904) 434-4611

IDAHO
Idaho Poison Center
  System
Department of Health
  and Welfare
Boise ID 83702
(800) 632-8000

ILLINOIS
Rush-Presbyterian
St. Luke's Poison Center
Rush-Presbyterian-
  St. Luke's Medical
  Center
Chicago IL 60613
(312) 942-6969

Peoria Poison Center
St. Francis Hospital-
  Medical Center
Peoria IL 61637
(800) 322-5330
Residents only
(309) 672-2334

INDIANA
Indiana Poison Center

WNY Poison Center
Children's Hospital of
  Buffalo
Buffalo NY 14222
(716) 878-7654

Hudson Valley Poison
  Center
Nyack Hospital
Nyack NY 10960
(914) 353-1000

NORTH CAROLINA
Triad Poison Center
Moses H. Cone Mem.
  Hosp.
1200 W. Elm Street
Greensboro NC 27401
(919) 379-4105

NORTH DAKOTA
St. Luke's Poison Center
St. Luke's Hospitals
Fifth Street at Mills
  Avenue
Fargo ND 58122
(701) 280-5575

OHIO
Central Ohio Poison
  Center
Children's Hospital
Columbus OH 43205
(614) 288-1323

Mahoning Valley Poison
  Center
St. Elizabeth Hospital
Youngstown OH 44505
(216) 746-2222

OREGON
Providence Poison
  Center
Providence Hospital
Medford OR 97501
(503) 773-6611

Oregon Poison Center
University of Oregon

McKennan Poison Center
McKennan Hospital
800 East 21st Street
Sioux Falls SD 57101
(605) 336-3878

TENNESSEE
Southern Poison Center
The University of
  Tennessee
College of Pharmacy
Memphis TN 38163
(901) 528-6048

TEXAS
Cook Poison Center—Fort
  Worth
Cook Children's Hospital
Forth Worth TX 76102
(617) 336-6611

Southeast Texas Poison
  Center
The University of Texas
  Medical Branch
Galveston TX 77550
(713) 765-1420

VERMONT
Vermont Poison Center
Medical Center Hospital of
  Vermont
Burlington VT 05401
(802) 658-3456

VIRGINIA
Blue Ridge Poison Center
University of Virginia
  Hospital
Box 484
Charlottesville VA 22908
(804) 524-6308

Central Virginia Poison
  Center
Medical College of
  Virginia
Virginia Commonwealth
  University
Richmond VA 23298
(804) 786-9213

Wisherd Memorial
  Hospital
Indianapolis IN 46202
(317) 630-7351

KANSAS
Northeast Kansas Poison
  Center
St. Francis Hospital &
  Med. Ctr.
1700 W. 7th Street
Topeka KS 66606
(913) 295-8093

MARYLAND
Maryland Poison Center
University of Maryland
  at Baltimore
Baltimore MD 21201
(301) 528-7701

Tri-State Poison Center
Sacred Heart Hospital
Cumberland MD 21502
(301) 722-6677

MICHIGAN
Midwest Poison Center
Borgess Hospital
Kalamazoo MI 49001
(616) 383-7070

Saginaw Region Poison
  Center
Saginaw General
  Hospital
Saginaw MI 48602
(517) 755-1111

MINNESOTA
Hennepin Poison Center
Hennepin County
  General Hospital
Minneapolis MN 56415
(612) 347-3147)

Health Sciences
  Center
Portland OR 97201
(503) 225-8968

Douglas Community
  Poison Center
Douglas Community
  Hospital
Roseburg OR 97470
(503) 673-6641

PENNSYLVANIA
Lehigh Valley Poison
  Center
The Allentown Hospital
Allentown PA 18102
(215) 433-2311

Keystone Region Poison
  Center
Mercy Hospital of
  Altoona
Altoona PA 16603
(814) 946-3711

Susquehanna Poison
  Center
Geisinger Medical
  Center
Danville PA 17821
(717) 275-6116

Northwest Poison
  Center
St. Vincent Health
  Center
Erie PA 16513
(814) 452-3232

Capital Poison Center
The Milton S. Hershey
  Medical Center
Hershey PA 17033
(717) 534-8955

Laurel Highlands
  Poison Center
Lee Hospital
Johnstown PA 15901
(814) 536-0037

Southwest Virginia Poison
  Center
Roanoke Memorial
  Hospital
Bellevue at Jefferson Street
Roanoke VA 24033
(703) 981-7336

WASHINGTON
COHMC Poison Center
Children's Orthopedic
  Hospital and
  Medical Center
Seattle WA 98105
(206) 526-2121

Spokane Poison Center
Deaconess Hospital
Spokane WA 99210
(509) 747-1077

Mary Bridge Poison Center
Mary Bridge Hospital
Tacoma WA 98405
(206) 272-1281

Pediatric Clinic
Madigan Army Medical
  Center
Tacoma WA 98431
(206) 967-6972

Central Washington Poison
  Center
Yakima Valley Memorial
  Hospital
2811 Tieton Drive
Yakima WA 98902
(509) 248-4400

WEST VIRGINIA
The West Virginia Poison
  Center
West Virginia University
School of Pharmacy
Charleston WV 25304
(304) 348-4211

319 / PONTIAC CATALINA

MISSOURI
CGMH St. Louis Poison Center
Cardinal Glennon Memorial Hospital for Children
St. Louis MO 63104
(314) 772-5200

NEW MEXICO
New Mexico Poison, Drug Information and Medical Crisis Center
The University of New Mexico
Albuquerque NM 87131
(505) 843-2551

Pittsburgh Poison Center
Children's Hospital of Pittsburgh
Pittsburgh PA 15213
(412) 681-6689

RHODE ISLAND
Rhode Island Poison Center
Rhode Island Hospital
Annex Bldg. 422
593 Eddy Street
Providence RI 02902
(401) 277-5727

SOUTH CAROLINA
Palmetto Poison Center
Richland Memorial Hospital
Columbia SC 29206
(803) 765-7359

WISCONSIN
Eau Claire Poison Center
Luther Hospital
Eau Claire WI 54701
(715) 835-1515

Green Bay Poison Center
St. Vincent Hospital
Green Bay WI 54305
(414) 433-8100

LaCrosse Area Poison Center
St. Francis Hospital
LaCrosse WI 54601
(608) 784-3971

Poison Center-Madison Area
University of Wisconsin Hospital
Madison WI 53792
(608) 262-3702

Milwaukee Poison Center
Milwaukee Children's Hospital
Milwaukee WI 53233
(414) 931-4114

POLYCILLIN. See *Ampicillin.*

PONTIAC BONNEVILLE

1978 MODEL
    Rear-wheel mounting bolts may be defective, causing wheels to fly off. Fan blade may separate.

1979 MODEL
    Front seat-belt anchorage could fail.

1982 MODEL
    Injection pump may fail, causing throttle valve to remain open.

PONTIAC CATALINA

1978 MODEL
Rear-wheel mounting bolts may be defective, causing wheels to fly off. Fan blade may separate.

1979 MODEL
Front seat-belt anchorage could fail.

1982 MODEL
Injection pump may fail, causing throttle valve to remain open.

PONTIAC FIREBIRD

1978 MODEL
Rear-wheel mounting bolts may be defective, causing wheels to fly off. Fan blade may separate.

1979 MODEL
Incorrect lubricant may cause rear-brake stoplights to fail and cruise control to remain engaged. Uniroyal tires may be defective. The occupant protection in a 35-mph U.S. Department of Transportation crash test was rated as poor.

1980 MODEL
Defective nut may exist in steering mechanism, reducing control. Catalytic converter may overheat.

1981 MODEL
Rear seat belts may not lock in a crash.

1982 MODEL
Gasoline may spurt from filler neck of full tank, possibly causing fire. Rear seat-belt anchorages may pull through underbody in a crash.

PONTIAC GRAND PRIX

1977 MODEL
Front-seat release latches threaten shins of rear-seat passengers. Gauges are difficult to read because of reflections.

1978 MODEL
Rear-wheel mounting bolts may be defective, causing wheels to fly off. Rear-axle shaft may be defective, allowing separation of tire and wheel assembly. Front-wheel bearing may fail, possibly causing loss of control. Uniroyal tires may be defective. Lower-rear control-arm bolts may fracture, causing loss of control.

1979 MODEL
Lower-rear control-arm bolts may fracture, causing loss of control.

1980 MODEL
Lower-rear control-arm bolts may fracture, causing loss of control.

1981 MODEL
Lower-rear control-arm bolts may fracture, causing loss of control.

1982 MODEL
Injection pump may fail, causing throttle valve to remain open.

PONTIAC J2000

1978 MODEL
Rear-wheel mounting bolts may be defective, causing wheels to fly off.

1982 MODEL
Handling is poor in emergency maneuvers. Rear view is obstructed for short drivers. Fuel-hose clamps may fracture, causing fuel leakage and possibly fire.

1983 MODEL
On cars with two-liter engines, fuel system may leak at the throttle-body injection-fuel-feed connection, creating a fire hazard.

PONTIAC LE MANS

1977 MODEL
Rear-axle shaft may be defective, allowing separation of tire and wheel assembly.

1978 MODEL
Rear-wheel cylinder retainer may be improperly installed, causing loss of brake fluid and braking action. Rear-wheel mounting bolts may be defective, causing wheels to fly off. Head restraints may be incorrect, possibly injuring rear-seat passengers in accident. Front-wheel bearing may fail, possibly causing loss of control. Fan blade may separate. Lower-rear control-arm bolts may fracture, causing loss of control.

1979 MODEL
In wagon, defogger backlights may have defect that shatters glass. Lower-rear control-arm bolts may fracture, causing loss of control.

1980 MODEL
In wagon, defogger backlights may have defect that shatters glass. Lower-rear control-arm bolts may fracture, causing loss of control.

1981 MODEL
Lower-rear control-arm bolts may fracture, causing loss of control.

PONTIAC PHOENIX

1978 MODEL
Rear-wheel mounting bolts may be defective, causing wheels to fly off. Fan blade may separate. Seat belts are poorly designed. Visibility is poor, especially when raining. In low position, head restraints provide little protection. Control is difficult in emergency maneuvers.

1979 MODEL
Control is difficult in emergency maneuvers. Driver's visibility is restricted. Fuel filler is vulnerable in sideswipe.

1980 MODEL
Brake pipe may fail, causing loss of brake fluid and partial loss of braking. Fuel hose may be incorrectly positioned, causing fuel leakage and possibly fire. Defect could exist in rear control arm, causing damage to brake or fuel lines. Front-suspension coil spring could be defective, causing damage to brake hose and suspension. Transmission cooler line hoses may be defective, causing leakage of fluid and possibly fire. Steering-gear mounting plate may develop fatigue cracks, causing partial loss of steering control. Rear brakes may lock up. Rear end may fishtail. In heavy to moderate and heavy braking situations, rear brakes could lock up causing car to spin out of control.

1981 MODEL
Power steering hose could deteriorate and leak fluid, possibly causing fire. Engine-to-body ground cable may be defective, causing headlights to dim. In heavy to moderate and heavy braking situations, rear brakes could lock up causing car to spin out of control.

1982 MODEL
Open hatchback is hazardous to tall persons. Fuel-hose clamps may fracture, causing fuel leakage and possibly fire. Clutch may rub

against brake pipe, causing loss of brake fluid and partial loss of braking action. View of short drivers is restricted.

PONTIAC SAFARI

1977, 1978, 1979 MODELS
Child could become entrapped in rear-side storage compartment.

PONTIAC SUNBIRD

1977 MODEL
Engine-mount bracket may contact steering mechanism, impeding steering. Front-seat levers are difficult for rear-seat passengers to reach. Driver's front and rear views are obstructed. Fuel filler is vulnerable in accident. Open hatch lid is hazardous to tall persons.

1978 MODEL
Rear-wheel mounting bolts may be defective, causing wheels to fly off. Steering-shaft coupling may be defective, causing loss of steering. Engine-mount bracket may contact steering mechanism, causing difficult steering.

1979 MODEL
Electrical short in engine oil pressure switch may start engine when ignition is in "on" position. Carburetor fuel-feed hose may rupture, causing fuel leak and possibly fire. Rear axle hopped severely during panic stops. Front safety belts are awkward.

1980 MODEL
Rear seat belts may not lock in a crash.

PONTIAC VENTURA

1977 MODEL
Radial tires may be defective. Catalytic converter may be defective. Power brake booster may fail.

1978 MODEL
Rear-axle shaft may be defective, causing loss of control. Rear-wheel mounting bolts may be defective, causing wheels to fly off.

POOLS, SWIMMING. See Swimming Pools.

PORK. See Meat and Poultry.

PORSCHE 911

1977 MODEL
Heater hose may be incorrect, creating a fire hazard. Functions of speed-control system may not be properly identified.

1978 MODEL
Functions of speed-control system may not be properly identified.

PORSCHE 928

1978, 1979, 1980 MODELS
Universal joint may be improperly positioned, possibly causing excessive steering-wheel free play.

POTATO CHIPS. See Food Additives; Salt.

POTS. See Cookware.

POTTERY. See Hobbies and Crafts.

POWER MOWERS. See Lawn Mowers, Power.

PRAZEPAM. See Benzodiazepines.

PREGNANCY AND DRUGS

HAZARDS

The use of any prescription or over-the-counter drug during pregnancy should be considered hazardous, especially during the first twelve weeks. The fourth through the eighth weeks of pregnancy are the critical period of major organ development in the embryo. Permanent birth defects may be caused by drugs acting adversely on the embryo during this period.

Some risk of injury to the fetus continues during the fourth through ninth months of pregnancy. The normal development of the brain, the nervous system, or the external genital organs may be impaired by the use of drugs during this period. Certain drugs within the fetus at the time of birth may have serious adverse effects because the newborn infant is unable to process and eliminate drugs rapidly and effectively.

Studies have shown that antinausea drugs often prescribed in early pregnancy may cause birth defects. Common drugs such as aspirin, antacids, tranquilizers, and laxatives may also be harmful. Even large doses of vitamins C or D may be dangerous. Nicotine (tobacco) and alcohol should be completely avoided. Recent studies regarding the use of alcohol by pregnant women indicate that alcohol, even used in moderation, can cause serious birth defects by temporarily cutting off oxygen to the developing unborn child. Drinking as little as one to two ounces of alcohol daily during the earliest part of pregnancy or a single episode of heavy drinking can produce serious changes in the development of the embryo.

PRECAUTION

Our present knowledge indicates it is advisable to avoid all drugs during pregnancy unless prescribed by an informed physician.

PRELUDIN. *See Sleeping Aids, Nonprescription.*

PREMARIN. *See Estrogen.*

PREMARIN INTRAVENOUS. *See Estrogen.*

PREMARIN WITH METHYLTESTOSTERONE. *See Estrogen.*

PRE-MENS FORTE. *See Caffeine; Menstrual Pain Medications.*

PREMIUM COMPANY DECAFFEINATED COFFEE. *See Coffee, Decaffeinated.*

PREPARATION H. *See Hemorrhoid Medications.*

PRESERVATIVES. *See Salt.*

PRESSED-WOOD PRODUCTS *(See also Formaldehyde)*

Pressed-wood products such as particleboard, plywood, chipboard, masonite, and medium-density fiberboard are used extensively in home building, mobile-home construction, and home remodeling. They are also used in numerous consumer products such as countertops, kitchen and bathroom cabinets, paneling, and a wide range of home and office furniture including desks, bookcases, sofas, dinette sets, end tables, and bedroom sets.

HAZARDS

Formaldehyde, which is used as a resin or glue in these products, "off-gases" over time and releases toxic formaldehyde fumes. Inhaling formaldehyde fumes has been shown to cause cancer in laboratory animals. More commonly, it causes a wide range of acute effects such as headaches, nausea, eye, nose and throat irritation, memory loss and other neurologic dysfunctions, nosebleeds, shortness of breath, and many asthmalike symptoms.

PRECAUTIONS

To reduce the release and buildup of formaldehyde in the home, pressed-wood products can be sealed with varnish, polyurethane, insulating paint, or other commercial sealants. Ventilation is also important, and as much outdoor air as possible should be circulated through the home. For persons extremely sensitive to formaldehyde, these techniques will be of little value, but they will help reduce the level of off-gasing somewhat. The U.S. Consumer Product Safety Commission is currently working with the pressed-wood industry to reduce emission levels in these products to the lowest feasible levels. In the meantime, consumers should limit their exposure as much as possible.

For more information call the CPSC Hotline, (800) 638–CPSC.

PRESSURE COOKERS *(See also Cooking Appliances, Small Electric)*

INJURIES
In 1975, 2,800 cases were reported.

HAZARDS
Most injuries are burns caused by steam. The most common hazards are:

- Forcing open the pressure cooker before it has cooled and thoroughly depressurized.

- Opening the pressure cooker when it registers low pressure.

- Misaligning the handles so that hot liquid escapes once pressure builds up inside the cooker.

- Dropping these heavy utensils, spilling scalding liquid.

PRECAUTIONS
In purchasing a pressure cooker, look for one with the following features:

- An emergency pressure relief device in addition to the regular pressure relief valve.

- Certification by an independent testing laboratory as meeting voluntary safety standards.

- An audible pressure control or a pressure gauge that shows precise pounds per square inch.

- A visible plunger that shows whether the cooker is still pressurized.

- Handles on both sides of a large cooker to give you a better grip when carrying.

When using pressure cookers:

- Do not open until all internal pressure has been released. If the handles are difficult to push apart, the cooker is still pressurized.

- Do not cook apple sauce, rhubarb, split peas, cranberries, spaghetti, and cereal because they can foam, sputter, and clog the steam vent of the pressure cooker.

- When the normal operating pressure (approximately 15 pounds per square inch) is reached, turn down the heat so that all the water that creates the steam does not evaporate.

- Carry the pressure cooker with oven mitts or potholders.

HAZARDOUS MODELS

In June 1982, Consumers Union reported that the escaping steam following the release of the safety plug could be followed by scalding hot liquid. In five Mirro models tested, this could take the form of a hot geyser, in nine Presto models tested, a spattering.

PRESSURIZED CONTAINERS. *See Aerosol Containers.*

PRETZELS. *See Salt.*

PRINCIPEN. *See Ampicillin.*

PRISTEEN. *See Deodorants, Genital.*

PRITIKIN DIET, THE *(See also Diets)*

A food plan published by Nathan Pritikin is almost the exact opposite of the Stillman high-protein diet. Pritikin's plan is aimed at the prevention or treatment of high blood pressure, diabetes, and other diseases. It includes a 1,000-calorie-a-day diet with very limited protein. It is high in complex carbohydrates and low in fats, cholesterol, sugar, salt, coffee, tea, and alcohol. The scientific community appears to be divided in its opinion of the Pritikin plan. Much of the diet is based on sound nutritional advice, but its value in losing weight has not been determined. Most physicians think, however, that 1,000 calories a day for any sustained period is too low.

PROCESSED FOODS. *See Monosodium Glutamate; Salt.*

PROCESSED FOOD, CANNED. *See Foods, Canned.*

PROCESSORS, FOOD. *See Food Processors.*

PRODUCE *(See also Drug and Food Interactions)*

HAZARDS
Unwashed fruit and vegetables may be hazardous because of pesticide residue. The FDA tests for less than half of the commonly used pesticides in produce because of budgetary limitations. Furthermore, only a small fraction of all produce sold is tested at all. Moreover, many pesticides commonly used on produce have never been tested for safety by the Environmental Protection Agency. Instead, the EPA sets tolerance levels and enforcement procedures with little scientific data to support these decisions.

PRECAUTION
Always wash fruit and vegetables thoroughly before eating.

PROGESTASERT *(See also Intrauterine Devices)*

Progestasert is an intrauterine device containing progesterone. The drug is released slowly from the device over a period of a year and acts as additional contraceptive protection. The advantages of this device are lower pregnancy rates and better toleration by women who have never had children. There are, however, serious adverse reactions associated with this IUD: spontaneous abortion, prolongation of menstrual flow, unexplained genital bleeding, and ectopic pregnancies.

PROLAMINE. *See Diet Aids, Nonprescription.*

PROPA P.H. *See Acne Medications, Nonprescription.*

PROPOXYPHENE

HAZARDS

Considerable controversy has arisen in recent years concerning the overprescription of this drug. Prescribed to relieve mild or moderate pain, propoxyphene is addictive if larger than recommended doses are taken. Consequently, propoxyphene should not be prescribed for chronic use. Overdose symptoms and even death can also occur with use of propoxyphene if other drugs, including tranquilizers, sleep aids, antidepressants, antihistamines, or alcohol are being taken at the same time.

Although side effects of this drug are infrequently reported, they include drowsiness, dizziness, nausea, and vomiting. Also reported are constipation, abdominal pain, skin rash, light-headedness, headache, weakness, visual disturbances, and feelings of excitement or discomfort.

PRECAUTIONS

Use of propoxyphene should be avoided because the risks outweigh the benefits. Propoxyphene products tend to be expensive, have dangerous consequences for many patients, including the risk of addiction, and are no more effective than regular aspirin, according to Consumers Union. Specific groups are at special risk: those with ulcers or asthma who are taking a blood thinner, children under 12, and mothers who are pregnant or breast feeding.

> WARNING

Do not use during pregnancy or while breast feeding. Get emergency help if you suspect an overdose. Restrict alcohol use when taking the drug. Do not drive or use possibly dangerous appliances or machines until you see how your body reacts to the drug. Use only intermittently and with caution because of the risk of addiction.

BRAND NAMES: Darvon, Darvocet-N, Dolene, SK-65, Wygesic

PUCH MOPEDS

1977, 1978 STEYR DAIMLER, MAXI SPORT, SPORT, SPORT MK II, MAGNUM MKII MODELS
On these models there exists the possibility of front brake failure or grabbing of the brakes when applied.

1978, 1979 STEYR DAIMLER, MAGNUM MK II MODELS
The wheel support cradle on the lower end of the front fork could separate allowing the front wheel to rotate in an unstable manner.

PUVA

A treatment that uses the drug methoxsalen in combination with ultraviolet A light, UVA is prescribed for the symptomatic control of severe psoriasis. The treatment, which was recently approved by the FDA, should be limited to severe, recalcitrant, and disabling psoriasis which has not been responsive to other forms of therapy.

The FDA has been monitoring the treatment since 1974, and it warns that while the drug is highly effective in treating severely debilitating cases of psoriasis, it is not a cure; the symptoms may reappear if maintenance treatment is not continued.

HAZARDS
Common acute side effects of the treatment include nausea and itching as well as transient, mild erythema. Moderate or severe burns may also occur, and the FDA warns that careful patient monitoring is essential.

Treatment with UVA also carries a number of long-term risks, including premature aging of the skin and skin cancer. The increased risk of cataracts is also of concern, but has not been thoroughly documented.

PRECAUTIONS

Patients with hepatic insufficiency should use UVA therapy only with caution, and patients with cardiac disease should not be treated in a vertical UVA chamber.

Patients should wear special highly absorbing protective eyewear during the UVA treatment and for 24 hours after taking methoxsalen to prevent cataract formation. An eye examination prior to beginning therapy and yearly afterward is recommended. Taking methoxsalen with meals is recommended to avoid nausea.

WARNING

Pregnant or nursing women should avoid UVA treatment because its effect on the fetus and mother's milk are unknown.

Q

QUAALUDE. *See Sleep Medications, Prescription.*

QUIET-NITE. *See Cough Medications.*

QUIET WORLD TABLETS. *See Sleeping Aids, Nonprescription.*

QUINIDINE. *See Digoxin.*

RADIATION. *See Microwave Ovens; Television Sets; X-Ray, Pregnancy.*

RADIOS. *See Sound Equipment.*

RANGES *(See also Air Pollution, Indoor; Microwave Ovens)*

INJURIES

In 1980, 37,000 involved cooking ranges, ovens, and related equipment. In 1978, 11,000 involved gas and electric kitchen ranges.

HAZARDS

Ranges are the primary ignition source for accidents experienced by the elderly. Most injuries result from:

• Leaning over or against the range.

• Reaching over or across the range. A burner can easily ignite a dangling sleeve or a towel used to move a pot.

• Climbing on or around the range, mainly by young children.

• Flammable vapor fires from contact cement, kerosene, and gasoline that are ignited by a pilot light or burner.

- Natural gas explosions. If the oven has no pilot light, or if the pilot light goes out, gas can accumulate and be ignited by a match or other ignition sources.

- A pan of grease left unattended can burst into flame. Often, instead of trying to cover the pan, a person will try to carry the grease to the sink, spilling the grease and igniting a garment.

- Any curtains, dishtowels, or other fabric near the stove that can catch on fire.

Gas stove emissions substantially degrade the quality of air in the home by producing noxious gases such as carbon monoxide and nitrogen oxides. These are emitted even when only the pilot lights are on. Buildup of carbon monoxide levels in the blood create increased stress on the heart, impair reflex coordination, and is fatal in large quantities. Nitrogen oxides are extremely irritating to the eyes and linings of the upper respiratory tract. High doses cause coughing and chest pains immediately, whereas lower concentrations produce only mild discomforts. High doses of nitrogen dioxide cause pulmonary edema and chronic low doses can cause chronic bronchitis. The incidence of illness is significantly higher among asthma sufferers, heavy smokers, people whose occupations expose them to high pollutant counts, and those that live in all-gas homes.

PRECAUTIONS

Look for the following before purchasing ranges.

- Knobs should be difficult for children to turn on.

- Controls should be arranged to eliminate the need to reach over the burners to turn the range on or off.

- Signal lamps showing when a burner is on should be on electric ranges.

- Pilot lights for the burners and the oven should be present on gas ranges.

In using gas ranges, take the following precautions.

- If the oven has no pilot light, do not turn on the gas until you have a match lit.

- Turn off the pilot when you use an oven cleaner because the spray could be ignited by the flame.

- Never use flammable liquids around a gas range.

- Keep all air vents open so that the gas gets enough oxygen to burn properly.

HAZARDOUS MODELS

In August 1979, Consumers Union reported that Sears catalog number 73881 and Magic Chef 348-W34HK have a door-locking lever that could pinch a hand or finger if the oven door is closed carelessly. O'Keefe & Merritt 31-6456, Tappan 31-2456, and Wards catalog number 4366 have hot bake elements with which potholders can easily come in contact, possibly causing a fire.

RATTLES. *See Baby Rattles.*

RAUTRAX. *See Reserpine.*

RAUTRAX-N. *See Reserpine.*

RAUTRAX-N MODIFIED. *See Reserpine.*

REAL-KILL ANT AND ROACH KILLER. *See Insecticides, Household.*

REALEMON LEMON JUICE CONCENTRATE. *See Sulfites.*

RECLINERS. *See Chairs.*

RECREATIONAL VEHICLES. *See Formaldehyde; Mobile Homes.*

RECORD PLAYERS. *See Sound Equipment.*

REFRIGERATORS

INJURIES
In 1980, 23,000 involoved refrigerators or freezers.

HAZARDS
Most injuries are caused by the following:

- Lacerations, contusions, or sprains caused by a hand caught in a refrigerator door or a head bumping the freezer door, or handle, or by moving the refrigerator.

- Asphyxiation of children trapped inside an old refrigerator.

- Electric shocks caused by a malfunction in the refrigerator such as a shorted-out compressor or damaged wires in the doors.
- Poisoning resulting from the emission of freon refrigerants used in the thermal systems. Refrigerants most commonly used are the same as those used as aerosol spray propellants (fluorocarbons) and therefore add to the atmospheric ozone-depletion problem. Fluorocarbons are invisible and odorless and normally leak at a very slow rate. Severe leakage from damaged systems can cause fluorocarbon inhalation, or it can decompose into highly toxic chemicals (hydrochloric acid, hydrofluoric acid, and phosgene) when it contacts heated surfaces, sparks, or flames of a furnace or fireplace.

FEDERAL STANDARDS
The Refrigerator Safety Act requires all household refrigerators manufactured after October 1958 to have a door that must open easily from the inside. However, regardless of the age, when a refrigerator is discarded, the door should be removed, the latch should be removed, or the door should be chained and padlocked.

REFUSE BINS. *See Waste Containers.*

REGROTON. *See Reserpine.*

RELAX-U-CAPS. *See Sleeping Aids, Nonprescription.*

RENAULT ALLIANCE DL

1983 MODEL
Operating controls are confusing.

RENAULT FUEGO

1982 MODEL
The occupant protection in the 2-door model in a 35-mph U.S. Department of Transportation crash test was rated as poor.

RENAULT LE CAR

1978 MODEL
Controls are confusing.

1980 MODEL
Fuel filler cap may be unseated by rear collision. Spare tire may fly into passenger compartment in a crash. Controls may be confusing. The occupant protection of the 2-door hatchback in the 35-mph U.S. Department of Transportation crash test was rated as poor.

1981 MODEL
Spare tire may fly into passenger compartment in a crash.

1982 MODEL
Front-wheel drive model handles vaguely in emergency maneuvers.

RENAULT 5

1977 MODEL
Without main spring, throttle may not close quickly. Controls may be confusing.

1978 MODEL
Without main spring, throttle may not close quickly.

1980, 1981 MODELS
Spare tire may fly into passenger compartment in a crash.

RENAULT 12

1977 MODEL
Without main spring, throttle may not close quickly. Response to steering is poor in emergency maneuvers.

1978 MODEL
Without main spring, throttle may not close quickly.

RENAULT 15

1977, 1978 MODELS
Without main spring, throttle may not close quickly.

RENAULT 17

1977, 1978 MODELS
Without main spring, throttle may not close quickly.

RENAULT 18i

1981 MODEL
Fuel leak may develop near engine. Brakes may be dangerous during break-in period. Controls may be confusing. The occupant protection of the 4-door model in the 35-mph crash-test program conducted by the U.S. Department of Transportation was rated as poor.

1982 MODEL
Brakes are poor.

REVCON MOTORHOME

1970–1976 SERIES 220,250,280 MODELS:
The bolts used in part of the steering system were not strong enough to withstand regular usage. As a result, these bolts may shear, causing partial or total loss of steering control.

RESERPINE

This prescription drug is produced by several companies in various strengths to treat mild forms of hypertension.

HAZARDS

Though reserpine has been proven to be effective, it has numerous side effects including: nausea, vomiting, diarrhea, muscular aches, headaches, dizziness, nasal congestion, skin rash, anxiety, mental depression, impotence, and hesitancy of urination. It can also produce severe depression in susceptible individuals, and there is some concern over the increased risk of cancer associated with its use. Studies with laboratory animals have produced a link to cancer, and the International Agency for Research on Cancer believes the existing epidemiologic studies "give considerable support to the proposition that long-term use of reserpine increases risk for breast cancer by some 50 to 100 percent." The National Cancer Institute and the National Heart, Lung and Blood Institute both feel (at present) that the risk to life from untreated hypertension far exceeds the potential risk of breast cancer. In many instances, however, alternatives to reserpine are available which have fewer side effects.

PRECAUTIONS

It is essential that reserpine be prescribed in carefully monitored dosages. This drug is best prescribed by itself, rather than in a combination drug product. Hypertension is not a static problem, and treatment and medication should be reevaluated as conditions change.

> WARNING

The safe use of this drug during pregnancy has not been established.

BRAND NAMES: Rau-Sed, Serpasil. Drugs containing reserpine: Rautrax, Rautrax-N, Rautrax-N Modified, Regroton, Salutensin, SerAp-Es, Butiserpazide.

RID. See *Kwell Shampoo and Cream.*

RIDE-ON TOYS. See *Toys, General.*

RIDES. *See Amusement Park Rides.*

RITALIN. *See Sleeping Aids, Nonprescription.*

ROBINHOOD MOTOR HOMES

1972, 1973, 1974, 1975 MODELS
The shower curtains installed in these motorhomes failed to meet minimum flammability standards set by the government.

ROBITUSSIN. *See Cough Medications.*

ROCKING CHAIRS. *See Chairs.*

ROLAIDS. *See Antacid Medications.*

ROLLS-ROYCE BENTLEY

1977 MODEL
Screws in steering may have not been sufficiently tightened, possibly causing full or partial steering loss. Automatic cruise control may not shut off.

ROLLS-ROYCE CAMARGUE

1977, 1978 MODELS
Automatic cruise control may not shut off. Heat from catalytic converter may degrade brake hoses.

1979, 11980 MODELS
Heat from catalytic converter may degrade brake hoses.

ROLLS-ROYCE CORNICHE

1977–1980 MODELS
   Heat from catalytic converter may degrade brake hoses.

ROLLS-ROYCE SILVER SHADOW

1977, 1978 MODELS
   Automatic cruise control may not shut off. Heat from catalytic converter may degrade brake hoses.

1979, 1980 MODELS
   Heat from catalytic converter may degrade brake hoses.

ROLLS-ROYCE SILVER WRAITH

1977 MODEL
   Screws in steering may not have been sufficiently tightened, possibly causing full or partial steering loss. Automatic cruise control may not shut off. Heat from catalytic converter may degrade brake hoses.

1978 MODEL
   Automatic cruise control may not shut off. Heat from catalytic converter may degrade brake hoses.

1979, 1980 MODELS
   Heat from catalytic converter may degrade brake hoses.

ROMILAR CF. *See Cough Medications.*

ROOFING, SHINGLES AND SIDING *(See also Asbestos)*

HAZARDS
   Some roofing shingles, siding shingles, and roofing sheets have been manufactured with asbestos. When worn or damaged, they may release asbestos fibers. Inhaling asbestos fibers can cause cancer or other illness.

PRECAUTIONS
These materials should be left intact and in place whenever possible. If repair or replacement is necessary, follow the general guidelines for handling asbestos products (*see* Asbestos). Damaged siding may be spray-painted to seal in asbestos fibers before working with them.

ROOM FRESHENERS. *See Germicides and Disinfectants.*

ROTARY STRIPPERS *(See also Tools, Power)*

HAZARDOUS MODELS
In June 1979, Consumers Union reported that the following rotary strippers were hazardous because their wires can break off and fly away at high speeds. At five pounds pressure, even the heaviest-gauge model threw some wires.

- Ali Roto Wire Stripper

- Coastal Paint Stripper

- CVI Coarse Rotary Stripper

- CVI Fine Rotary Stripper

- Lomart Coarse Rotary Stripper 19–24

- Lomart Fine Rotary Stripper 19–142

- Nylo Rotary Stripper 3–30

- Roto Tool 3–42

- Super Stripper

- Thompson Roto Stripper

- Thompson 3-Way Interchangeable Roto Stripper

ROTISSERIES. *See Cooking Appliances, Small Electric.*

ROVER 5100 and 5101

1980 MODEL
Brake master cylinder may deteriorate, causing decrease in efficiency of rear brakes.

RUFEN. *See Ibuprophen.*

RUGS. *See Floors.*

RUST REMOVERS. *See Solvents.*

SAAB GL

1977, 1978 MODELS
Fuel-tank vent tube may chafe, causing fuel leakage and fire hazard.

SAAB 99

1977 MODEL
Fuel line may rupture, causing fuel leakage and fire hazard.

1978 MODEL
Center rear belt may be defective. Ice buildup may prevent throttle from returning to idle position.

1979 MODEL
Ice buildup may prevent throttle from returning to idle position.

1980 MODEL
Fuel-pump mounting collar may detach from tank, causing fuel leakage and fire hazard.

SAAB 99 GLE

1978 MODEL
Fuel-tank vent tube may chafe, causing fuel leakage and fire hazard. Handling is clumsy during emergency maneuvers. Driver's view is restricted. Controls are confusing.

SAAB 900

1978, 1979 MODELS
Ice buildup may prevent throttle from returning to idle position.

1980 MODEL
Fuel-pump mounting collar may detach from tank, causing fuel leakage and fire hazard.

1981 model
Open trunk lid is hazardous. Rear view is obstructed by head restraints and wide rear roof pillars.

1982 MODEL
The occupant protection of the 4-door model in the U.S. Department of Transportation 35-mph crash test was rated as poor.

SACCHARIN *(See also Salt; Sweeteners, Artificial)*

It is estimated that 50 to 70 million Americans are regular users of saccharin, including one-third of children under 10 years of age. About 6 million pounds of saccharin are consumed annually. Three-fourths of this amount is consumed in soft drinks. The second largest use is as a tabletop sweetener.

HAZARDS
The FDA proposed banning most uses of saccharin in 1977 because studies determined that the chemical causes cancer in laboratory animals, but Congress postponed this action. However, there is a requirement that foods containing saccharin have warning labels.
The reason saccharin was on the market for so many years without any attempts to ban it can be traced to 1958 federal legislation that placed the burden of proof of establishing the safety of a new additive on industry. This proof had to be established before an additive could be marketed. In addition, no new additives could be called safe if tests showed it was a cancer-causing substance. This rule

did not apply to saccharin because it had been on the market for many years.

PRECAUTIONS
Because laboratory tests link saccharin to cancer, its use should be avoided.

SAFEWAY BRAND DECAFFEINATED COFFEE. *See Decaffeinated Coffee.*

SAF-T-COIL. *See Intrauterine Devices.*

SALAD DRESSING. *See Food Colors, Artificial.*

SAL HEPATICA. *See Laxatives.*

SALT

Many Americans are attempting to reduce the amount of salt in their diets. Studies show a link between sodium and high blood pressure that may lead to heart attack, stroke, or kidney failure. Table salt is composed of two mineral elements: approximately 40 percent sodium and 60 percent chloride. It is the sodium component that is a health concern.

Sodium is necessary for proper functioning of the body, but most Americans consume much more than needed. A healthy body needs, and can use, no more than 200 milligrams of sodium daily. One teaspoon contains about 10 times this amount. The average daily consumption of salt is one to three teaspoons.

Most people can consume large amounts of sodium with no adverse effects. Consumption of one-half to one and one-half teaspoons daily is considered safe for those who do not have high blood pressure. Any excess sodium in the body is excreted by the kidneys in order to keep balance.

HAZARDS
For persons with hypertension, too much sodium is harmful, al-

though the reasons for this are as yet unknown. A problem in kidney functioning may be at fault, and the problem appears to be inherited. Hypertension also is prevalent by race. Blacks are twice as likely to have high blood pressure as whites. Only 20 percent to 40 percent of the population will develop hypertension, no matter how much salt is used.

Over one-third of those persons who have high blood pressure are not aware of it. This is the reason some medical experts feel everyone should consume only low amounts of sodium. Blood pressure should also be checked regularly.

If high blood pressure is present, a low-sodium diet and weight loss, if necessary, will often reduce blood pressure to acceptable levels without the use of antihypertensive drugs. If drugs are taken, a low-sodium diet makes them more effective since the main goal of these drugs is to eliminate as much sodium from the body as possible.

PRECAUTIONS

High sodium levels in foods cannot always be detected by taste. A person wishing to reduce sodium intake must do more than give up pickles, pretzels, potato chips, anchovies, or the salt shaker. Most people would be surprised to learn that a serving of instant chocolate pudding has more sodium than a small bag of potato chips and a scoop of cottage cheese three times the sodium content of a handful of peanuts.

Household staples like baking powder and baking soda are sodium compounds, and are used widely in baked goods. Dairy products should be limited for people on low-sodium diets since sodium is a natural component of dairy products. Preservatives such as sodium nitrite and sodium benzoate are found in many foods. Flavorings such as MSG, soy sauce, catsup, and Worcestershire sauce have high levels of sodium. Salt is often added in large amounts to canned vegetables, and many processed foods contain added sodium. Sodium saccharin is used widely to replace sugar. Even vitamin C is often added to foods in the form of sodium ascorbate.

In addition to foods, some over-the-counter drugs, particularly antacids, contain significant amounts of sodium. Some water supplies are high in sodium, which may need to be considered in the total daily sodium intake.

The best way to avoid foods high in sodium is to read labels carefully. The items listed first on a label are present in the largest amount. Supermarkets carry a variety of foods labels "low-sodium" or "sodium-free." However, these products are usually more expensive.

SANKA BRAND DECAFFEINATED COFFEE. See *Coffee, Decaffeinated.*

SANITARY NAPKINS, DEODORANT. See *Tampons, Deodorant.*

SARDINES. See *Drug and Food Interactions.*

SASSAFRAS TEA. See *Health Foods.*

SAUSAGE. See *Food Colors, Artificial.*

SAUSAGE, IMITATION. See *Casein.*

SAWS, CHAIN. See *Chain Saws.*

SAWS, POWER

INJURIES
In 1980, 73,000 involved home workshop power saws.

HAZARDS
Most injuries result from contact with the blade because of the following.

• The blade guard is not part of the saw, has been removed, or is malfunctioning. The blade guard on portable circular saws can malfunction by staying in a retracted position after the cut is completed.

• The blade jams or binds in the wood and throws the saw toward the operator with portable circular saws, or the wood toward the operator with stationary equipment. Binding can be caused by a dull blade, warped or knotted wood, or forcing the cut.

- The blade continues rotating after the power is turned off.

- Slippery floors lead to a fall onto the blade.
Other injuries are caused by electric shocks.

PRECAUTIONS

Saws should have the following features: a blade guard; anti-kickback features; double-insulation or a three-prong grounded plug to protect against electric shock; dynamic braking, or at least a blade that stops shortly after power is turned off.

HAZARDOUS MODELS

In 1980, the CPSC announced that approximately 55,000 Craftsman Motorized Miter Saws (models 315.23730 and 315.23731) may pose a laceration hazard. There is a danger a user will improperly fasten the carbide blade to the motor shaft, with the possibility that the blade will spin off during use. Sears, Roebuck & Company sold the saws and is conducting a program to repair them.

In 1981, the Rockwell International Corporation voluntarily recalled 70,000 motorized saws that may have a defective switch.

SCOURING POWDERS. *See Cleaning Agents.*

SCUBA REGULATORS

HAZARDOUS MODELS

In October 1979, Under Sea Industries recalled second-stage scuba regulators. An integral exhaust valve may dislodge from its proper position if the purge is depressed and the diver's tongue is blocking the mouthpiece, causing the regulator to flood. The recall applied to the SCUBAPRO model 11-108-000 second-stage regulator and to model 12-103-000 and 12-010-000 regulator systems.

SCULPTURE. *See Hobbies and Crafts.*

SEAFOOD

HAZARDS

Federal inspection of seafood is voluntary in the U.S., and according to the Department of Commerce, less than one-third of the fish consumed here is inspected for chemical residues, parasites, and bacterial contamination. Fish-processing plants are inspected only intermittently for sanitation, but no tests are conducted for parasites or chemical residues in the fish. Chemical residues often build up in offshore coastal water, lakes, and rivers where fish are caught. In addition, though most states try to control fishing in contaminated waters, too often bootleggers succeed in selling illegal fish caught in polluted rivers.

Many processed seafood products such as fish fillets, fish sticks, fish cakes, and breaded shrimp also contain a variety of chemicals including preservatives and bleaches to lighten dark flesh.

SECONAL. *See Sleep Medications, Prescription.*

SEDACAPS. *See Sleeping Aids, Nonprescription.*

SEEDATE CAPSULES. *See Sleeping Aids, Nonprescription.*

SEESAWS. *See Playground Equipment.*

SENOKOT. *See Laxatives.*

SERPASIL. *See Reserpine.*

SER-AP-ES. *See Reserpine.*

SERAX. *See Benzodiazepines.*

SHAMPOOS *(See also Shampoos, Baby; Shampoos, Dandruff)*
HAZARDS

Shampoos contain ingredients that can produce eye and skin irritation; can be poisonous to children who are attracted by the fragrant, colorful contents of the shampoo bottles; or can increase the risk of cancer.

Eye and skin irritation are the most common side effects of shampoo products. But while nearly all shampoo products can irritate if they get into the eyes, certain ingredients are more likely to cause irritation or serious damage than others. Abnormally irritating shampoos can cause painful eye inflammation, conjunctivitis, and sometimes chemical burns, clouding of the cornea, and temporary impairment of vision. Lauryl or laureth sulfates are the most irritating ingredients to the eye, whereas nonionic and amphoteric detergents are much less irritating.

Formaldehyde, a preservative found in some shampoos, can be irritating to both the eyes and the skin. Quaternium-15, which releases formaldehyde, is another preservative that may cause an allergic skin reaction. Natural conditioning agents such as balsam, vitamin E, coconut oil, and cocoa butter can also produce skin irritation.

Boric acid is occasionally added to shampoo products as a pH balance, but it is absorbed rapidly through damaged skin and can be hazardous. Swallowing or absorbing boric acid through damaged skin can cause nausea, vomiting, circulatory system collapse, liver damage, convulsions, and coma. Although there are no reported incidents of boric acid poisoning from shampoo products, caution should be used.

Another source of concern with shampoo products is the presence of nitrosamines that have been proven to be very carcinogenic in animals. Nitrosamines are formed when an amine, such as triethanolamine (TEA) or diethanolamine (DEA) reacts chemically with a nitrosating agent, such as sodium nitrite or 2-bromo-2-nitroprone-1,3-diol (BNPD). Although nitrosamines are not put into shampoos, they can form when the TEA or DEA, which are found in hundreds of shampoo formulations, come in contact with a nitrosating agent. This often occurs on a random basis—one bottle of a shampoo may be contaminated with nitrosamines, whereas another bottle of the same brand may not. Nitrosamines are absorbed through the skin, and may expose a user to far higher levels of the cancer-causing agent than eating nitrite-cured bacon. BNPD is a nitrosating agent that is still found in some cosmetic products. Avoid all cosmetic products containing this chemical. In shampoos containing TEA or DEA as well as BNPD, cancer-causing nitrosamines can be formed. In addition, BNPD can combine with the amines in the skin or in the body to form nitrosamines.

PRECAUTIONS

There are many different shampoo formulations on the market. If formaldehyde irritates your skin, select a shampoo that does not contain this ingredient. If irritation is a problem for you, it may be best to avoid the natural conditioning agents as well and also products containing quaternium-15. Because of their potential for hazard, it may also be wise to avoid shampoos containing boric acid and DEA and TEA. Never use products containing BNPD.

All cosmetic products and medications should be kept out of the reach of small children. Some shampoo detergents—such as the lauryl and laureth sulfates, potassium cocohydrolyzed animal protein, sarcosines and sarcosinates, the sulfosuccinates, and sodium methyl oleoyl sulfate and sodium lauryl isoethionate—can be toxic if swallowed. Quaternary ammonium compounds in shampoos are internal poisons as well.

SHAMPOOS, BABY *(See also Shampoos)*

HAZARDS

Certain chemical ingredients in no-sting shampoos can anesthetize the eyeball. While this is not a dangerous occurrence, it can cause people to overlook other serious irritations or injuries to the eye, since these products can numb the eyes for up to seven hours.

Some baby shampoos also contain formaldehyde, which is a strong skin sensitizer.

SHAMPOOS, DANDRUFF *(See also Shampoos)*

HAZARDS

Antidandruff shampoos usually contain toxic ingredients and should be handled with care and kept out of the reach of children. The antidandruff chemical ingredient selenium sulfide is highly toxic, acting very much like arsenic. It can cause liver, kidney, heart, spleen, stomach, bowel, or lung damage and may be fatal even in small swallowed amounts. Zinc pyritione and salicylic acid are less toxic. Colloidal sulfur is probably the safest ingredient, though it is still moderately toxic if swallowed.

Perhaps the most dangerous ingredient in antidandruff shampoos is resorcinol. Although it is not as toxic as selenium sulfide, if swallowed, it is absorbed through the skin very quickly while selenium sulfide is not absorbed in any significant amount.

PRECAUTIONS

While there are no reported poisonings from ingesting antidandruff shampoos or from absorbing them through the skin, care should be exercised in using these products.

SHASTA CAMPING TRAILERS

1980, 1981 130F, 130S, 160F, 160S, 165S MODELS
These trailers have a swing-away lift arm that allows access to the unit in the closed position. The arm was poorly designed and may break without notice. If this should happen, the lift arm could extend rapidly and cause severe injury.

SHELBY GT350 AND GT500

1967, 1969 MODELS
The aluminum center wheels on some vehicles were installed with inadequate bolt-hole chambers. This will cause lugs to loosen and the wheel to fall off.

1969 MODEL
Because of the design of the fuel filler cap, certain conditions can allow fuel vapors to escape and be ignited by the exhaust.

SHINGLES. *See Roofing, Shingles and Siding.*

SHOPPING CARTS

INJURIES

In 1980, 15,000 involved shopping carts, dollies, or luggage carriers.

HAZARDS

Most injuries involving shopping carts occur to children who suffer lacerations, contusions, fractures, concussions, or similar injuries when the cart overturns, they fall or jump from the cart, or they fall against or run into the cart.

SHOWERS. *See Bathtubs.*

SHRIMP. *See Seafood, Sulfites.*

SHRIMP, BREADED. *See Seafood.*

SIDING. *See Roofing, Shingles and Siding.*

SILVEX. *See Dioxin.*

SINAREST. *See Decongestants, Oral.*

SINE-AID. *See Decongestants, Oral.*

SINE-OFF AND SINUTABS. *See Decongestants, Oral.*

SINUTAB-II. *See Decongestants, Oral.*

SK-APAP. *See Acetaminophen.*

SK-65. *See Propoxyphene.*

SKATEBOARDS

INJURIES
In 1980, 35,000 cases, including fractures, the most common type, and deaths due to collisions with cars and from falls also were reported. Almost half the injuries involved youngsters between the ages of 10 and 14.

HAZARDS
Injuries were caused by accidents that involved lack of protective equipment, poor board maintenance, poor riding surface, defective boards, and/or not enough practice.

PRECAUTIONS
Before using skateboards, riders should check them for hazards such as loose, broken, or cracked parts; sharp edges on metal boards, slippery top surfaces, and wheels with nicks and cracks. Protective equipment such as closed, slip-resistant shoes, helmets, and specially designed padding should be used.

SKATES

INJURIES
In 1978, 125,000 involved roller skates or ice skates. Roller skates accounted for approximately three-quarters of these injuries.

HAZARDS
The main causes of accidents are skating too close; poor skating on uneven surfaces; product structural problems, such as an axle loosening or a wheel falling off; roller skating in traffic.

PRECAUTIONS
In selecting skates, carefully run your hand over metal parts to check for sharp edges and points. Also, inspect roller skates before using them to make certain the wheels are firmly attached.

Many injuries could be avoided if skaters wore protective padding on elbows and knees, tried to fall in a relaxed rather than stiffened posture, fell on flesh or muscle rather than bones or joints, and skated only on smooth surfaces.

SK DIGOXIN TABLETS. *See Digoxin.*

SKIING EQUIPMENT

INJURIES
In 1978, 104,000 involved skiing and skiing equipment.

HAZARDS
Most injuries are suffered by beginners who lack experience, but many are caused by equipment that is not properly fitted, adjusted, or maintained or that is defective.

PRECAUTIONS
If boots are too large the feet can slip forward and back, reducing the skier's ability to control the skis. If they are too tight, they can restrict circulation and cause frostbite. Beginning skiers should use a soft, low boot, rather than the high stiff boot often preferred by experts, because the former can prevent severe leg injuries in a fall.

Bindings must release skiers from their skis in a fall before serious injury, but not too easily or unnecessary falls will occur. Generally, the more ways a binding releases, the better. Also, the use of antifriction devices offers added protection.

Boots and bindings must be compatible with each other or the binding may not operate properly. Bindings should be purchased to fit boots.

The binding release mechanism should be adjusted by a professional each year to ensure that the release tension is correct for your weight and skiing proficiency.

SKILLETS, ELECTRIC. *See Cooking Appliances, Small Electric; Fry Pans, Electric.*

SKIN CREAM. *See Skin Moisturizers and Creams.*

SKIN MOISTURIZERS AND CREAMS

HAZARDS/PRECAUTIONS
Skin moisturizers and creams are used by millions of women every day and every night. Although the majority of users experience few adverse reactions, some women develop skin irritation or an allergic skin reaction, in part because the products are used so fre-

quently and left on the skin for such a prolonged period. Fragrances and preservatives are the most common source of irritation in these products.

When buying a skin cream with a preservative, avoid formaldehyde or quaternium-15, if you have any problem with skin irritation. These are the two most irritating preservatives. Also avoid lanolin in moisturizers if irritation is a problem. Although lanolin is an excellent long-term skin lubricant, some people are allergic to it. Derivative compounds of lanolin, such as acetylated lanolin, are less irritating. Some products also contain urea, which can also irritate the skin.

Other products which should be avoided are those containing the combination of 2-bromo-2-nitropropane-1,3-diol (BNPD), and TEA and DEA compounds. TEA and DEA are amines that can combine with a nitrosating agent such as BNPD to form cancer-causing nitrosamines. Products containing BNPD should always be avoided because the chemical can combine with the naturally occurring amines on the skin, or when absorbed through the skin, with amines in the body, to form nitrosamines as well. The nitrosamines formed in cosmetics are more hazardous than those in foods, such as bacon or hot dogs.

SKYLINE TRAVEL TRAILER

SPECIAL "20" TRAVEL TRAILER

The original tire rims may not be adequate for normal usage. As a result, the tires could blow out under loaded conditions.

1974 NOMAD, LAYTON, GOLDEN FALCON, ALJO MODELS

The spring hangers were not properly welded on some models. This will result in the springs becoming disconnected from the trailer.

1975–1980 LINDY, JAMEE MODELS

Some of the passenger seats were not properly attached to the chassis. These seats do not meet minimum federal standards and may pull loose in an accident. The manufacturer failed to use the correct washers, or any washers in some cases, when attaching the seats to the vehicle.

SLEDS

INJURIES

In 1978, 44,369 cases were reported.

HAZARDS

The following conditions created injuries in the use of sleds.

- Mechanical and structural problems including splintering or breaking while in use; flimsy materials used in construction; and poor steering capability.

- Poor riding conditions including bumps, ruts, rocks, tree stumps and branches, ice, soft snow, and bare patches that result in loss of control.

- Collision with a moving car, another slider, or a stationary object.

PRECAUTIONS

In selecting sleds, avoid equipment with sharp, jagged edges and protruding rivets; look for an energy-absorbing pad for the seat of toboggans; check sleds for easy steering without jamming; and avoid sleds with runners that end in sharp-edged hooks.

SLEEP-EZE TABLETS. *(See also Sleeping Aids, Nonprescription)*

SLEEPING AIDS, NONPRESCRIPTION *(See also Sleep Medications, Prescription)*

Over-the-counter (OTC) sleeping aids are usually formulated with antihistamines, which usually cause drowsiness. All OTC sleeping aids should be avoided. One person in four will experience a troublesome reaction to antihistamines including dry mouth, nausea, vomiting, dizziness, frequent urination, fatigue, or double vision. Antihistamines can also be hazardous for people with asthma, glaucoma, or prostate enlargement. These drugs should not be mixed with certain other drugs, such as seizure medications, sedatives, or depressants. Avoid alcohol if you are taking an antihistamine.

Ingredients used in the past in over-the-counter sleeping aids, but now banned, include scopolamine, methapyrilene, and bromides. Check your medicine cabinet for drugs that contain these ingredients and discard them.

If you are experiencing sleeplessness, it may be a side effect of your diet or other medications you are taking. Caffeine disturbs sleep, as can alcohol. Caffeine is an ingredient in many over-the-counter drugs, so check drug labels if sleeplessness is a problem. Prescription drugs that cause sleeplessness include dextroamphetamine (Dexedrine), methylphenidate (Ritalin, used to combat depression and hyperactivity in children), deithylpropion (Tenuate), phenmatrazine (Preludin), and most appetite suppressants.

SLEEP MEDICATIONS, PRESCRIPTION. *See also Pregnancy and Drugs, Sleeping Aids, Nonprescription)*

While prescription sleep medications may be of assistance for the small percentage of people who suffer from a serious sleep disorder, most problems with sleeplessness are a result of anxiety, overstimulation, worry, or lack of exercise, and should not be treated with a prescription drug. Doctors often recommend a combination treatment for people suffering from sleeplessness which includes relaxation during the evening, taking a long walk before going to bed, drinking a glass of warm milk or herbal tea, sleeping in a cool, quiet, and dark room, or retiring an hour earlier than usual.

HAZARDS

Generally, the use of sleeping aids is not recommended. Many contain alcohol, barbiturates (Nembutal, Seconal), or sedatives (Doriden, Placidyl, Quaalude, Noludar). These drugs may cause dependence. Nonmedical use (often with alcohol) may cause overdosage and death. This is also true of the benzodiazepines which are often prescribed for sleeplessness (Librium and Valium). Benzodiazepines (minor tranquilizers) should never be taken by pregnant women because of the risk of birth defects or by nursing mothers.

Dalmane, a commonly prescribed sleeping aid, contains flurazepaim, which lingers in your system and may cause recurrent drowsiness. It should not be used if you drive or operate machinery.

Barbiturates, commonly used to combat sleeplessness as well, cause hangover effects when first used, and also interfere with blood-thinning medication.

If you do take a prescription sleeping medication you should avoid all alcohol intake and medications prescribed for hay fever, allergy, and colds, as well as tranquilizers, antidepressants, and pain and seizure medications. Make sure you know how your medication affects you before driving or using machinery which requires you to be alert.

Sleep medications are usually not prescribed for repeated, prolonged use, but if you have been taking them for some time, do NOT stop taking them without talking to your doctor first so he can gradually take you off the drugs.

> **WARNING**

If you are pregnant or plan to become pregnant, do not use sleeping medications.

SLEEPWEAR. *See Children's Sleepwear; Clothing.*

SLICERS. *See Kitchen Appliances, Small.*

SLIDES. *See Playground Equipment.*

SLIDING BOARDS. *See Playground Equipment.*

SLINGSHOTS. *See Toy Projectiles; Toys, General.*

SLOW COOKERS. *See Cooking Appliances, Small Electric.*

SMALLPOX VACCINATION

The FDA no longer recommends smallpox vaccinations, and the World Health Organization no longer requires the shot for international travelers. According to the U.S. Public Health Service, the vaccine is recommended only for personnel directly involved in work on smallpox or related viruses.

Occasionally, smallpox vaccine is used to treat herpes simplex infection, warts, and other diseases. The FDA has warned against such uses, which are not only ineffective but may cause death in immunodeficient patients. The USPHS warns that smallpox vaccine should never be used in the treatment of any disease.

SMOKE DETECTORS

Smoke detectors are important for early detection of fire. Because there is usually detectable smoke before there is detectable heat, smoke detectors nearly always give a faster warning than heat detectors. There are two types of smoke detectors on the market: ion chamber detectors, which detect both visible and invisible products of combustion, and photoelectric detectors, which detect only visible products of combustion.

HAZARDS

Ionization-type detectors that use radioactive materials—as do all battery-powered detectors—are used in millions of homes. These radiation materials are similar to those produced in nuclear plants, and can last thousands of years. The radioactive materials are confined in metal containers to minimize exposure levels, and the containers are supposed to withstand high temperatures and other conditions, but only time will tell how safe they really are.

PRECAUTIONS

In purchasing smoke detectors, you may prefer battery-operated detectors because house electricity is occasionally cut off in a fire. However, if you buy a battery-operated detector, look for one that warns you when the battery needs replacing. If you buy a photoelectric-operated detector, it should sound a warning when the bulb burns out.

In installing smoke detectors, put them on or near the ceiling in places where smoke is likely to pass as it rises, such as the tops of stairs. Avoid placing units near air conditioning or heat registers that could blow fresh air past them to keep smoke away.

As few as one or two detectors can provide protection as long as there is one near each sleeping area. It is also advisable, however, to put a smoke detector at the top of the basement stairs.

To maintain the units, replace batteries at least once a year even if the warning device for weak batteries has not sounded.

Test the detector monthly and when returning from vacation or any other absence of seven or more days.

SMOKING DETERRENTS

The FDA has been unable to determine the effect of any of the over-the-counter smoking deterrent drugs on helping smokers quit. However, two ingredients used in smoking deterrents warrant further study as to their possible effectiveness: lobeline, a plant derivative performing an action similar to nicotine; and silver acetate, a salt that is supposed to give tobacco smoke an unpleasant, metallic taste.

The FDA found no evidence that other ingredients, especially flavor extracts, are effective in ending the urge to smoke.

SNACK FOODS. See *Food Colors, Artificial, Food Flavoring Additives; Salt.*

SNOWBLOWERS

INJURIES
In 1980, 18,000 cases of mainly fractures, lacerations, or amputations.

HAZARDS
Most injuries are caused by accidental contact with a moving blade, usually when the hand is in the discharge chute removing clogged snow.

SNOW DISKS. See *Sleds.*

SNOWMOBILES

INJURIES
In 1980, 18,000 cases were reported.

HAZARDS
Injuries occur in accidents with the following kinds of causes:

- Collisions with fixed or moving objects, especially when driving on or beside public roads. Because snowmobiles are so loud, their drivers have difficulty hearing other vehicles.

- Braking suddenly on snow or ice-covered roads.

- Excessive speed, unfamiliarity with the machine, and riding on unfamiliar terrain or near bodies of water.

- Driving while intoxicated, after dark, or too close together. Lighting is often inadequate on snowmobiles.

- Product failure, such as a throttle that sticks open, brakes that fail, or skis that fall off.

PRECAUTIONS

In purchasing snowmobiles, look for the following features.

- Guards for the drive chain and all other moving parts.

- Strong and easy-to-reach passenger handgrips.

- Adequate padding on the dash, steering bar, and back end of the seat.

- A snowflap in back to keep snow off the tail light.

- A windshield that does not have a sharp stiff edge that can injure the driver in a collision.

HAZARDOUS MODELS

Kawasaki Motors undertook a voluntary repair program to correct approximately 16,500 snowmobiles, 1978 and 1979 Invaders and Intruders. When the MGB (molded grouser bar) type of tracks become partially or completely detached from the rubber belts and when the snowmobile is lifted or turned on its side exposing the rotating track, bars can strike the hands, legs, or feet of a person who is lifting the snowmobile or standing next to the rotating track.

SNOWTHROWERS. *See Snowblowers.*

SOAPS *(See also Germicides and Disinfectants)*

INJURIES

In 1980, 8,000 involved dishwasher detergents, laundry soaps, or dishwashing liquids, but excluding hand soaps.

HAZARDS

Detergents have caused more poisonings than any other household product. People think that ordinary soap is relatively harmless so they often leave synthetic soaps, with their brightly colored boxes, within easy reach of young children. The most extensively used surfactant is LAS (linear alkylate sulfonate), a toxic substance. Buildup of LAS has been shown to be fatal to oysters, and has caused liver ailments in mice when absorbed through the skin. It is suspected that prolonged exposure to LAS may present some danger to human beings.

The controversy surrounding phosphate pollution of waterways in the late 1960s led to the development of nonphosphate substitutes, which are 100 to 1,000 times more caustic. The high alkalinity of these new products makes the detergents an indoor problem rather than an outdoor one.

Eyes can receive severe damage. Ingestion of liquid products is particularly hazardous and can severely damage the upper digestive tract through chemical burns. In terms of human health, it is better to use phosphate detergents.

PRECAUTIONS

Keep dishwasher detergents away from the eyes and do not allow them to stay on the skin because they are strong irritants. They also should be kept away from children, especially those with candy-like scents, because they are harmful if swallowed.

SODA. *See Caffeine; Food Colors, Artificial.*

SODA, CITRUS-FLAVORED. *See Brominated Vegetable Oil (BVO).*

SODA, DIET. *See Aspartame; Saccharin.*

SODA MINT. *See Antacid Medications.*

SOFAS. *See Chairs; Pressed-Wood Products.*

SOLAR POOL COVERS. *See Swimming Pools.*

SOLVENTS

INJURIES

In 1980, 20,000 involved paints, lubricants, and solvents including methyl alcohol, turpentine, and rust removers.

HAZARDS/PRECAUTIONS

Petroleum solvents in oil-based finishes pose special hazards: fire, inhalation, skin irritation, poisoning if ingested.

Powdered paint removers carry hazards that are easier to cope with than those of solvent paint removers, yet they can burn eyes and skin and are harmful or lethal if swallowed. While they are safer than organic solvents to use indoors, they should be used with goggles, gloves, and a dust mask.

Dry-cleaning fluids are toxic chlorinated solvents, although they are generally noncombustible. A solvent commonly used for coin-operated dry cleaning is perchloroethylene (or tetrachloroethylene). It can be fatal if inhaled in large doses, and can also cause depression of the nervous system, including lightheadedness, dizziness, sleepiness, nausea, tremor, loss of appetite, disorientation, as well as liver damage. Take precautions about inhaling the evaporating solvent, although once garments have dried, they are safe to wear.

SOMINEX CAPSULES AND TABLETS. *See Sleeping Aids, Nonprescription.*

SOMNICAPS. *See Sleeping Aids, Nonprescription.*

SONIC TIRES. *See Uniroyal Tires.*

SORE THROAT MEDICATIONS. *See Throat Medications.*

SOUND EQUIPMENT

INJURIES
In 1980, 28,000 involved sound equipment including telephones, two-way radios, stereos and accessories, antennas, radios, tape recorders, and record players.

HAZARDS
Many injuries represent ear problems resulting from loud noise. Consumers Union reports that, at high volume, the sound through stereo headphones can damage ears. Extended listening sessions with the volume set at a high level also entail a distinct risk of hearing damage.

HAZARDOUS MODELS
In August 1980, Philips High Fidelity Laboratories, Ltd., recalled approximately 5,600 stereo turntables. The turntables were wired improperly so that "safety fuses," which serve as circuit breakers, do not operate. In the event of a short circuit, consumers could receive a severe electrical shock by touching any metal part on the turntable or any metal components connected to the turntable.

SOUP. *See Casein; Food Poisoning.*

SOY SAUCE. *See Salt.*

SPACE HEATERS *(See also Air Pollution, Indoor; Kerosene Heaters)*

INJURIES
In 1977, 5,800 cases involved mainly burns and carbon monoxide poisoning.

HAZARDS

• Poisoning from carbon monoxide and other pollutants including carbon dioxide, nitrogen dioxide, and formaldehyde from unvented or improperly vented gas space heaters. The levels that these pollutants can reach varies depending on the temperature, air exchange rates with the outside, heater flame adjustment, and ambient air-quality levels.

• Carbon monoxide poisoning from unvented or improperly vented oil or kerosene space heaters, particularly ones which are poorly adjusted and dirty.

• Contact with the flame, heating elements, or hot surface area can ignite clothing, draperies, and other combustibles, or burn skin that is in direct contact.

• Explosion of accumulated gas while attempting to light or relight the burner. Older models lack the safety features, such as a safety pilot valve, that help prevent this.

• Electrical shocks, often because the victim was wet and touched the heater.

FEDERAL STANDARDS

A new CPSC regulation requires the unvented gas-fired space heaters to have an oxygen depletion sensor, which detects a reduced level of oxygen in the area where the heater is operating and shuts off the heater. Heaters with this device came on the market in 1982. They have labels warning of the hazards of carbon monoxide.

PRECAUTIONS

In purchasing space heaters, make sure that:

• Unvented gas space heaters have a label stating that the heater has a federally required pilot-light safety system;

• There is a guard around the flames or the heating coil to keep children, pets, and clothing away from the heat source; and

• Electric space heaters have an automatic switch that cuts off electric power if the heater is tipped over.

When using gas, oil, or kerosene space heaters:

• Light the match before you turn on the gas to the pilot.

• If there is a strong gas smell, turn off all controls and open a window or door, then call a service person.

- Keep a window partially open and the room well-ventilated if you are using an unvented, fuel-burning space heater.

- Never use an unvented heater overnight in the room where you are sleeping.

- Use the proper fuel for oil and kerosene heaters. Gas should never be used in a kerosene heater.

- Never use flammable liquids around a space heater.

- Never completely fill a heater with oil or kerosene because, as the fuel warms, it expands and could spill and flare.

- Heaters used in mobile homes should be of the sealed combustion type (air for burning coming directly from the outside).

When using electric space heaters:

- Do not use an extension cord unless it is a heavy-duty cord rated as high as the current rating listed on the heater.

- Avoid use anywhere in a bathroom, if at all possible, to prevent electrical shock. Never place near a bathtub, shower, or sink. Never touch an electric heater if you are wet.

HAZARDOUS MODELS

In November 1980, Consumers Union reported that Thermador DRA161 and Superlectric brands of electric space heaters pose fire hazards. Consumers Union judged old and new versions of the Boekamp 101P brand not acceptable. In the older one, when the heater was tipped over gently, a chunk of molten wire was thrown out and a live wire and sharp quartz shards were exposed. In the newer version, the redesigned wire guard could not keep a cloth sufficiently far from the heating element.

In October 1982, Consumers Union judged 17 of 18 kerosene heaters it tested as posing a potential burn hazard. Moreover, because it also rated the Koehring Deluxe KR D93 and Sears catalog number 40204 a serious fire hazard, it deemed these two models not acceptable.

SPAS. *See Bathtubs; Hot Tubs.*

SPEAR GUNS. See *Guns, Spear.*

SPEC-T LOZENGES. See *Throat Medications.*

SPECTRACIDE PROFESSIONAL HOME PEST CONTROL PRESSURIZED. See *Insecticides, Household.*

SPORTSCOACH MOTOR HOME

1971, 1972, 1973 (WITH 402 AND 454 cu.-in. engines) 25-FOOT MODELS
On vehicles with cruise control, the throttle sticks partially open when the cruise control is turned off.

SPIRONOLACTONE

This is a prescription diuretic drug used to control high blood pressure and to rid the body of extra fluids due to heart, liver, or kidney disease. A patient should continue to drink normal amounts of fluids while taking this drug, even though urination is more frequent. Taking the medication early in the day will reduce chances of sleep disturbance. Occasionally, use of a diuretic will lower the body's potassium level. If you experience vomiting or diarrhea, call your physician immediately. Eating bananas and oranges is a good source of potassium. The most common side effect, especially for elderly people, is dizziness or confusion when standing up or lying down. To avoid this effect, move slowly when standing or lying down.

HAZARDS

It is important to inform your doctor if you have ever had diabetes, kidney or liver disease, or have been allergic to similar medications. If you are taking any other diuretic, high-blood-pressure pills heart medicine, lithium carbonate, potassium or salt substitutes, alcohol, or medicine for diabetes, inform your doctor so he can adjust the level of your medication.

An allergic reaction to spironolactone will cause a rash, hives, and increased sensitivity to light. Other possible side effects are thirst, indigestion, stomach cramps, and headaches. Breast enlargement and tenderness, especially noticeable in men, will stop when the drug is discontinued.

Spironolactone has caused tumors in rats, but no definite relationship has been established in humans.

> **WARNING**

Call your doctor if you have diarrhea or vomiting or symptoms of high blood pressure such as shortness of breath or swelling of hands or feet.

BRAND NAME: Aldactone.

SPIRONOLACTONE WITH HYDROCHLOROTHIAZIDE *(See also Spironolactone)*

HAZARDS

This drug combines two diuretics, a thiazide and spironolactone, which prevents the loss of potassium. It is prescribed to control high blood pressure and to rid the body of excess fluids and salt, but it has been shown to cause tumors in laboratory animals. In addition, such combination drug products are not as effective as individually prescribed medications. Patients may not need all the ingredients in this product, or they may need them in different doses.

PRECAUTIONS

You should avoid exposure to excessive heat while on this medication, because your body will lose too much salt and water through sweating. Before your physician prescribes this drug, give any history of allergic reaction to thiazides or spironolactone, and of diabetes, kidney or liver problems, gout, or lupus erythematosus. If you are currently taking another high-blood-pressure medication, aspirin or narcotic pain medicine, heart medicine, Indocin or any cortisonelike steroid drug, lithium carbonate, phenobarbital, diabetic medication, or alcohol, inform your doctor so your dosage can be adjusted.

> **WARNING**

This product has been shown to cause tumors in laboratory animals, although no relationship has been established in humans. Notify your doctor immediately if you have diarrhea, vomiting, shortness of breath, or swelling of hands or feet.

BRAND NAME: Aldactazide.

SPRAY STARCHES

PRECAUTIONS
Since the propellants in almost all spray starches are ignitable, it is important to use them away from open flames, a gas stove, for example.

HAZARDOUS MODELS
In February 1982, Consumers Union reported that Easy-On Lemon Fresh and Sta-Flo are lemon-scented, with pictures of lemons on the label, which may tempt children to eat them.

STAIRS

INJURIES
In 1980, 683,000 involved stairs, ramps, or landings.

HAZARDS
Most injuries are caused by falls to which the following often contributed.

- Ice and snow on exterior stairs.

- Obscured vision, often while carrying packages or laundry.

- Poor lighting obscuring vision.

- Tripping on obstacles such as boxes, toys, and other objects.

- Loose carpeting, polished hardwood, and slippery footwear.

- Broken steps, unstable staircases, loose concrete, loose handrails, and other poor conditions on the stairs.

PRECAUTIONS
To be safe, stairs should have:

- Proper dimensions with a run width no less than 10 inches, riser heights no more than 7 1/2 inches, tread width no less than 11 1/4 inches, and stairway slope between 30 and 35 degrees.

- Handrails on both sides with spindles, when present, that are separated by no more than the size of a child's head or body, about 5 inches.

- Proper lighting with self-illuminating switches at the top and bottom of each flight of stairs.

Flights of stairs with landings may be safer than unbroken flights because the landings may break a fall and also make it easier for elderly persons to climb stairs.

STARCRAFT MOTOR HOMES AND TRAILERS

1971, 1972, 1973 MOTOR HOME MODELS
The metal straps used to hold the gasoline tanks on the vehicle were not designed to withstand normal vibration and corrosion over a long period. As a result, in transit they may break and drop the tanks to the ground.

1971, 1972, 1973 STARCRUISER 22-, 24-, 28-FOOT MODELS
In some instances no fuses were placed in the 12-volt electrical system. If an overload were to result, damage to the motorhome from fire and heat could result. The terminals on the circuit breaker, which is located under the kitchen sink, are exposed. As a result, these terminals can easily contact items stored under the sink and cause a short circuit that could cause a fire.

1970–1973 STARCRUISER 22-, 24-, 28-FOOT MODELS
There are two clamp bolts on the steering system that the manufacturer may not have properly tightened. If they come loose, loss of steering will result.

1974 GALAXY, GALAXY SWINGER, STARDUST, STARMASTER TRAILER MODELS
The axle was not properly welded to the trailer. If the welds weaken, the axle will loosen from the frame, and the frame will drop to the ground without warning.

1974 STARMASTER 6 and 8, VENTURE 1060 AND 1080 MODELS
On many models, the grease seal on the axle hub is the wrong

size. As a result, the grease will leak out and cause the axle to lock to the bearing. This could cause a serious accident.

1970–1975 Tent Camping Trailer models
The main lifter cable that holds up the roof could break and allow the roof to fall in on occupants. The roof is relatively heavy and could cause serious injury to the occupants.

STEAM PIPES. *See Asbestos; Pipe Insulation.*

STEREOS. *See Sound Equipment.*

STEW. *See Casein; Food Poisoning.*

STILLMAN DIET, THE *(See also Diets)*

The Stillman Diet is found in the book *The Doctor's Quick Weight Loss Diet*. It claims that the high-protein diet (with virtually no carbohydrates) will cause the body's system to burn more calories daily than other diets that include foods other than proteins. In actuality, most of the initial weight lost consists of water, not body fat. Many dieters find that much of the weight loss from this type of diet is regained soon after regular eating habits are resumed.

HAZARDS
Many physicians feel there is serious harm in this diet. Because it is high in protein, it is also high in fats and cholesterol. High cholesterol intake contributes to the risk of high blood pressure and heart attack or stroke.

In addition, many people do not adhere to the plan's requirement for eight glasses of water a day. Without this fluid intake, excessive strain is put on the kidneys. The brain usually lives on carbohydrates and in their absence, extra strain is put on the liver to break down the protein into glucose, which the brain can use.

Some dieters on the Stillman plan develop ketosis, which gives the mouth a strange taste and causes headaches and sluggishness.

STIMULANTS *(See also Caffeine)*

HAZARDS

Most over-the-counter drugs advertised as "stay-awake" medications or stimulants have caffeine as their main ingredient. The side effects of these products include nervousness, irritability, and inability to fall asleep. Be aware that although you may be kept awake by these drugs, your alertness is diminished. Care should be taken when driving or operating machinery while using these products.

If you are an ulcer patient or pregnant, caffeine products and drugs should be avoided. Use of stimulant drug products should be avoided at all times.

STOOLS

INJURIES

In 1980, 18,000 involved stools, footstools, ottomans, or hassocks. In 1976, 10,675 involved step stools, 6,430 bar stools, and 2,672 hassocks.

HAZARDS

Step-stool injuries are caused mainly by the following conditions:

» Structural failure in which a leg breaks, or the whole stool collapses.

- Loss of balance while standing or kneeling.

- Fall from sitting position (usually a very young or very old person).

- Fall into or over a stool.

- Child climbing on a stool.

- Failure of stool to lock into position.

STOVES. *See Camping Cooking and Heating Equipment.*

STRESSTABS 600 PLUS IRON. *See Iron and Iron Supplements.*

SUBARU

1977 MODEL
In wagons, defect may exist in latch that allows tailgate to open when car is in motion. Ice may build up in carburetor and secondary shaft in cold weather, causing engine stalling. DL ran very wide during hard cornering. Safety belts ride up. Rear view is restricted. In wagon, hairline cracks may develop in fuel tank, causing tank to crack.

1978 MODEL
In Brat, fuel tank may leak, creating fire hazard. Ice may build up in carburetor and secondary shaft in cold weather, causing engine stalling. In wagon, hairline cracks may develop in fuel tank, causing tank to crack.

1979 MODEL
In wagon, hairline cracks may develop in fuel tank, causing tank to crack.

1980 MODEL
Wiper system may fail if wipers are turned on when frozen to windshield. In sedan, door pillar obstructs side view. Open trunk lid is hazardous. The occupant protection of the 4-door GLF model was rated as poor in the U.S. Department of Transportation's 35-mph crash test.

1981 MODEL
Accelerator pedal may bind on mounting bracket and not return the throttle to idle position. In MY, loose wheel nut could cause separation of steering wheel from shaft. Handling is poor in accident avoidance. Open hatch is hazardous to tall persons. On certain manual transmission vehicles, chafing of the front main-wiring harness against threads of the rear-battery hold-down rod may cause electrical short and fire.

1982 MODEL
In MY, loose wheel nut could cause separation of steering wheel from shaft. Handling is unsteady in emergency maneuvers. On certain manual transmission vehicles, chafing of the front main-wiring harness against threads of the rear-battery hold-down rod may cause electrical short and fire.

1983 MODEL
Handling is unsteady in emergency maneuvers.

SUCARYL. See Saccharin.

SUCRETS THROAT LOZENGES. See Throat Medications.

SUDAFED. See Decongestants, Oral.

SUGAR

HAZARDS

The major health hazard from eating too much sugar is tooth decay. But the risk of tooth decay is associated not just with the amount of sugar consumed, but also the frequency of consumption. Frequent between-meal snacks of sticky candy or cookies or day-long use of soft drinks may be more harmful than adding sugar to your morning coffee. Particularly harmful are sugar foods that stick to your teeth and often remain there for many hours.

Sugar contains empty calories and contributes to weight gain, but contrary to popular belief, it does not seem to cause diabetes. The most common form of diabetes is found in obese people, and simply avoiding sugar without weight loss will not correct the problem. There is also little convincing scientific evidence that sugar causes heart attacks or blood vessel diseases.

PRECAUTIONS

Americans are estimated to consume an average of 130 pounds of sugar and sweeteners per person per year. Much of our sugar intake comes not directly from food but comes as an additive in jams, jellies, soft drinks, cookies, cereals, catsup, soup, ice cream, etc. Read labels carefully on all foods to avoid excessive sugar intake—sucrose, glucose, maltose, dextrose, lactose, fructose, and syrups are all forms of sugar, and if they appear first on an ingredient label they are present in high quantities in that food. Practice good dental hygiene, particularly after eating a sugary food, and cut down on betweenmeal sweets and sodas.

SUGAR BEETS. *See Monosodium Glutamate.*

SULFITES

Sulfites such as sodium bisulfite and potassium metabisulfite are preservatives used to prevent discoloration of and bacterial growth on food. Sulfites are widely used in wine, restaurant salads, processed foods, dried fruit, and other products.

HAZARDS
Some people experience an allergic reaction to sulfites. For those hypersensitive to sulfites, exposure is extremely dangerous and can result in severe wheezing, extreme shortness of breath, and coma. Sensitive asthmatics experience the most severe reactions, although in some cases severe reactions have occurred in people with no prior history of asthma.

PRECAUTIONS
Until more is learned about the possible risk of sulfites, anyone with a history of asthma should avoid their use. Below is a partial list of products, which includes sulfites on their ingredient labeling. Sulfites are also often found in restaurant foods that do not list ingredients.

PARTIAL LIST OF FOODS CONTAINING SULFITING AGENTS

Weight Watchers Fruit Snacks
Good Seasons Salad Dressing Mix (different varieties)
Wines (most)
Sunsweet Selected Sun-Dried Apricots
Bonner Golden Raisins
ReaLemon Lemon Juice from concentrate
Paisley Farm Dilled Cauliflower
Old El Paso Pickled Hot Jalapeno Peppers
Sun Maid California Selected Dried Fruits and Raisins Fruit Bits
Trappey's Dulcito Peperoncini Salad Peppers
Liberty Colored Pineapple Wedges
Bell Fruit Cake Mix
Betty Crocker Hamburger Helper
French's Idaho Mashed Potatoes
Pillsbury Apricot Nut Quick Bread Mix
Uncle Ben's Brown & Wild Rice with Mushrooms (and other varieties)

Pillsbury Plus Carrot 'n Spice Cake Mix
Shrimp (some)
Betty Crocker Snackin' Cake Carrot Nut Cake Mix
Betty Crocker Hickory Smoke Cheese Flavored Potatoes
Prescription drugs, including Bronkosol, Decadron, metoclopramide hydrochloride (Reglan Injectable), microNEFRIN

SUNLAMPS *(See also Black Lights)*

INJURIES
In 1980, 7,000 involved sunlamps or heat lamps.

HAZARDS
Most injuries are burns resulting from prolonged exposure.

FEDERAL STANDARDS
In May 1980, the FDA adopted a safety standard requiring that sunlamps be equipped with protective goggles, timers, and other safety features.

SUN MAID CALIFORNIA SELECTED DRIED FRUITS AND RAISINS FRUIT BITS. *See Sulfites.*

SUNSWEET SELECTED SUN-DRIED APRICOTS. *See Sulfites.*

SUPER HIGHWAY II TIRES. *See Firestone Transport Tires.*

SUPERIOR COACH

1973 MVP MOTOR HOME MODEL
The design of the door-locking mechanism is such that it binds and may become jammed. As a result, it could be difficult to exit from the vehicle in an emergency.

SURGERY AND DRUGS

If surgery is planned in the near future, be sure to discuss with your physician, at least a month before the operation, if there is a need to eliminate or change your drug treatment.

Many drugs, even aspirin, can affect the body's response to anesthetics and surgical procedures. Therefore, it is important that your anesthesiologist and surgeon be made aware of any medication you are taking. If emergency surgery is necessary, it is important to inform the anesthesiologist and surgeon of any drug you are presently using. Keep a medical alert card in your wallet or purse.

SUZUKI LJ80, LJ80V, and LJ81

1980 MODEL

Alternator V-belt pulleys may be defective, which could cause broken pulleys to be thrown and engine to be severely damaged.

SUZUKI MOTORCYCLES

1972 GT–550J MODELS

Under certain conditions normal throttle usage will cause undue wear on the throttle valve housing and restrict throttle control.

1978 GS1000C MODELS

In some cases the battery mounting bracket was made too long. As a result it may contact rear master brake cylinder reserve hose and put a hole in the hose. This would cause loss of brake fluid.

1978 GS1000C, GS1000EC MODELS

The fuel tank vent system may not operate properly. By failing to vent the tank the faulty vent system can create a vacuum which could prohibit fuel from entering the carburetion system and cause engine stalling. In addition, this could cause fuel tank expansion due to internal pressure from heat such as direct sunlight.

1979, 1980 GS850GN, GT MODELS

On certain vehicles the wheel joint bolts were improperly tightened and may break off 3 mm from the base of the bolt. If this were to happen the threaded portion of the bolt with the nut could lodge in the rear wheel system and cause lockup at low speeds.

1980 GS850GT, GLT MODELS

In some vehicles the clutch cable can become dislodged from its retainer. This could cause the cable to interfere with the throttle linkage and prevent the throttle from returning to idle.

1980 LJ80, LJ80V, LJ81 MODELS

On some vehicles flawed alternator V-belt pulleys were installed. These pulleys can break, causing damage to other parts of the engine and causing overheating and severe engine damage. Also, part of the pulley could fly off and cause severe injury to a bystander.

SWEET'N LOW. *See Saccharin; Sweeteners, Artificial.*

SWEETENERS, ARTIFICIAL *(See also Aspartame; Cyclamate; Saccharin)*

Much attention has been given to artificial sweeteners during the past decade. The diet-conscious public has spent millions of dollars trying to satisfy its sweet tooth without having to worry about calories. Industry has spent a fortune in marketing hoping to convince consumers that they can satisfy their cravings. There are health risks associated, however, with all artificial sweeteners.

Saccharin is the oldest of the artificial sweeteners. It dominated the artificial sweetener market for more than 60 years, but was overtaken by cyclamate in the 1950s and 1960s. In 1970, cyclamate was banned by the FDA because of questions concerning its safety. Saccharin again dominated the market, although it was later linked to cancer in animals. Aspartame, the newest artificial sweetener, was approved for use in 1981 and can now be found on store shelves.

SWIMMING POOL ALGICIDES. *See Water Contaminants.*

SWIMMING POOLS

INJURIES
In 1976, 54,000 occurred.

HAZARDS
Injuries are frequently caused by the following.

- Falling on slippery walkways, decks, diving boards, or ladders.

- Striking the bottom or sides of the pool because of insufficient depth, or striking protruding water pipes, ladders, or other objects in the pool.

- Drowning when swimming alone or when children swim without adult supervision.

- Being shocked or electrocuted by faulty electrical wiring, improperly used extension cords, and appliances.

- Explosions from excess pressure in the filter tank.

- Swimming under part of a solar pool cover, then being unable to surface for air.

PRECAUTIONS

Accidents can be prevented by the following precautions.

- Install skid-resistant materials or finish on the deck surrounding the pool and on diving boards.

- Avoid sudden drops in depth.

- Indicate safe diving areas with a different color on the pool bottom.

- Paint numbers on the pool edge showing the water depth.

- Use a recommended safety grate over the drain outlet to prevent entrapment on the suction holes.

- Make certain there is sufficient lighting for swimming at night.

- Install ladders with handrails on both sides small enough for a child's firm grip.

- Install a fence around all sides of the pool to prevent unauthorized use by children.

- Round all pool edges to prevent lacerations.

SWINGS. *See Playground Equipment.*

SYNTHETIC VITAMINS. *See Vitamins; Vitamins, Organic/Natural*

T

TABLEWARE

INJURIES

In 1980, 60,000 involved tableware or flatware.

HAZARDOUS MODELS

Cribmates, Inc., voluntarily recalled nearly 29,000 training fork-and-spoon sets imported from Taiwan and sold for use by babies. Metal containing high levels of cadmium may flake off these utensils, posing a moderate to severe health hazard.

TAGAMET. *See Cimetidine.*

TALCUM POWDER

HAZARDS

A study published in August 1982 in the journal *Cancer* links the use of talcum powder to ovarian cancer. The study found that women who dusted their genitals and sanitary napkins with talcum powder were three times more likely to develop cancer than women who did not.

Dr. Daniel W. Cramer, the principal author of the study, suggested that contamination of the talc might cause cancer. It is unclear, however, if the contamination derives from the asbestos content of talc or from a tendency of the ovary to make it more susceptible to carcinogens from both talc and contaminants.

In the 1970s talc was often found to be contaminated with asbestos, a known cause of cancer. In recent years, however, the talc industry is believed to have changed its method of mining to ensure the removal of asbestos from the talc.

PRECAUTIONS

Doctors feel more results from laboratory tests are needed before they can recommend women avoid using talc on their genitals. Caution is advised.

TAMPONS. *See Tampons, Deodorant; Toxic Shock Syndrome.*

TAMPONS, DEODORANT

Deodorant tampons and pads cause skin and vaginal irritation in many women, and their long-term use should be avoided.

TAPE RECORDERS. *See Sound Equipment.*

TAP WATER. *See Salt; Water Contaminants.*

TAT ANT TRAPS. *See Insecticides, Household.*

TEA. *See Caffeine.*

TEA, DECAFFEINATED. *See Coffee, Decaffeinated.*

TEETER BOARDS. See *Playground Equipment.*

TELDRIN. See *Allergy Medications.*

TELEPHONES. See *Sound Equipment.*

TELEVISION ANTENNAS. See *Antennas; Home Electrical System.*

TELEVISION SETS *(See also Black Lights)*

INJURIES
 In 1980, 23,000 cases were reported.

HAZARDS
 Electrical problems resulted in many fires involving pre-1976 portable color televisions with plastic cabinets. Since the late 1970s, most manufacturers have complied with a more stringent voluntary industry standard that strengthened requirements for circuitry, components, and flame resistance of plastic material to reduce the likelihood of fire.
 Covering the ventilation openings by putting sets too close to the wall, radiator, or furniture can cause overheating which can cause a malfunction inside the set and start a fire. Older sets with vacuum tubes tend to produce more internal heat than solid-state models. Moreover, the heat may cause the picture tube to collapse inward and rebound, propelling sharp pieces of glass.
 Electrical shock could result from contact with TV parts carrying hazardous voltages or from simultaneous contact with the TV and a wet surface.
 Spilling liquids into the TV cabinet may cause a short circuit that could start a fire.
 Television sets, especially those manufactured before 1970, give off radiation. Exposure to this radiation increases with the time one watches and distance one sits from the set. Doctors are most concerned about the health impact on children, who not only tend to watch a lot of television, but also are more susceptible to radiation-

related problems than are older persons. Accordingly, medical authorities are especially concerned that young persons who play video games on old televisions will receive excessive radiation exposure. The National Council for Radiation Protection and Measurement estimates that a child who sits 16 inches from the set and uses it two hours a day receives 890 millirems of radiation in the eyes each year. By comparison, a chest x-ray produces only 20 to 30 millirems.

PRECAUTIONS

To avoid hazards from television sets, the following precautions should be taken.

• Always turn off the set when not using it.

• Unplug the set and the antenna when leaving the house for several days.

• Do not cover the ventilation openings with cloth or papers, or place the set too close to a wall or piece of furniture.

• Do not touch the TV controls or antenna with wet hands or when touching a wet surface, any plumbing fixture, stove, or other electrical appliance. Never operate a TV in the bathroom or in the kitchen within reach of the kitchen sink.

• Do not put containers of water or other liquids on the TV cabinet.

• Never expose the set to rain or water.

• If fire begins, try to unplug the set unless there is danger of being burned or hit by flying pieces of glass. Never use water to extinguish the fire unless the set is unplugged.

• To reduce radiation exposure, reduce the time spent watching TV and sit farther away from the set.

HAZARDOUS MODELS

In 1977, Consumers Union reported that Sears catalog number 4423 color TV console posed a potential shock hazard to children and, therefore, judged it not acceptable.

In January 1981, Consumers Union judged the GE 19EC1756K conditionally acceptable because the metal strip behind the top row of ventilation slots may be electrically alive. It is possible to poke something through the slots, touch the live strip, and receive a severe shock. CU considers this model acceptable only if a buyer puts electrical tape over those slots.

TEMPRA. *See Acetaminophen.*

TENTS

HAZARDS

Each year, many people are burned, and some die, in fires involving tents. The most frequently involved ignition sources are candles, fuel-fired cooking and heating stoves, lanterns, and sparks from a campfire. Many tents are extremely flammable. Children's cotton tents will ignite and burn completely within a few minutes. The paraffin treatment used to make some tents waterproof actually may increase flammability.

STANDARDS

Some tent manufacturers have begun to produce flame-resistant tents, and some states are establishing standards for tent flammability.

PRECAUTIONS

Consumers should purchase flame-resistant tents whenever possible. They should never use an open flame in or near a tent.

TENUATE. *See Sleeping Aids, Nonprescription.*

TERMITE TREATMENTS. *See Chlordane.*

TERRO ANT KILLER. *See Insecticides, Household.*

TETRACYCLINE *(See also Drug and Food Interactions)*

This prescription drug is used to treat bacterial infections. It should not be used by pregnant women or by children under 12 years of age because the drug becomes deposited in growing teeth and may cause permanent discoloration and increases the risk of tooth decay.

THIAZIDES

By eliminating extra salts and water from the body, this group of prescription drugs helps control high blood pressure caused by heart, liver, or kidney disease.

HAZARDS/PRECAUTIONS

It is important to monitor the body's potassium level while taking these drugs. A potassium supplement may be necessary, although eating oranges, bananas, and avocados is a good way to maintain the necessary potassium level. Patients who are allergic to other drugs, particularly sulfa drugs, or who have asthma, are most likely to be allergic to this group of drugs. Kidney and liver disease, diabetes, gout, and lupus erythematosus may all be adversely affected by thiazide treatment as well.

Patients should avoid excessive heat while taking thiazides because of the excess loss of salts and water through sweating. Notify your physician if you work in a heated place or plan to travel to a hot climate. Cortisone, digitalis, lithium carbonate, and antidiabetic drugs can all interact negatively with thiazides, so tell your doctor if you are currently taking any of these medications.

Potassium loss should also be reported to the physician. Watch for symptoms of excess thirst, tiredness, drowsiness, restlessness, muscle pain or cramps, nausea or vomiting, diarrhea, or increased heart rate or pulse. Also watch for symptoms of high blood pressure, including shortness of breath and swelling of hands or feet.

IDENTICAL DRUGS: Hydrochlorothiazide (*brand names:* Hydrodiuril, Esidrix); Chlorothiazide (*brand name:* Diuril); Chlorthalidone (*brand name:* Hygroton).

THROAT MEDICATIONS

Medicated lozenges and antiseptic sprays and gargles are over-the-counter medications that promise relief for a sore throat. Sore throats, however, are caused by postnasal drip, dry air in the home, or by viral or bacterial infection, and these medications can do little to cure the cause of a sore throat. The action of gargling may provide some temporary relief of a sore throat, though gargling with warm salt water is perhaps more therapeutic than gargling with a commercial medication. Some lozenges and sprays have a mild anesthetic quality that helps numb the pain, but aspirin is a better pain killer. Chewable aspirin is of little or no aid.

HAZARDS/PRECAUTIONS

While some temporary relief may be provided by sore throat medications, it is important not to treat a persistent sore throat with over-the-counter aids. Rarely, a sore throat may be an indication of a serious bacterial infection such as strep throat. Although easily treated with penicillin, strep throat can lead to serious heart or kidney damage if left untreated. If a sore throat lasts more than a day or is accompanied by fever, check with a physician.

THYROID HORMONES. *See Drug and Food Interactions; Warfarin Potassium/Sodium.*

TIMOLOL MALETATE

HAZARDS

Timolol maletate is an ophthalmic product prescribed for glaucoma. It has been reported to cause respiratory problems and even death when used by patients with asthma and other pulmonary and cardiac problems.

> WARNING

Timolol maletate should not be used by patients with bronchospasm, including bronchial asthma, or severe chronic obstructive pulmonary disease, or by patients who have experienced cardiac failure.

BRAND NAME: Timoptic.

TILLERS, POWER. *See Garden Equipment, Power.*

TIMOPTIC. *See Timolol Maletate.*

TIRES

Every year thousands of tires are recalled because of safety defects. When you buy a tire the seller is required to fill out a tire registration card that includes your name and address and the model of tire you purchased. In the event of a recall the manufacturer is required to notify those people who have purchased the tires involved in the recall using the tire registration forms. Generally, the customer has only 60 to 90 days after receipt of the notice to have the tire replaced. Only the major tire recalls, 2,000 or more tires, which have occurred since 1980 are listed in this book. To find out if your tires have been recalled you may call the Auto Safety Hotline (800) 424-9393 (in Washington, D.C., call 426-0123). Before you call have the brand name of your tires, model, exact size, and DOT serial number. You can find all of this information on the sidewall of your tire.

TOASTER OVENS. *See Cooking Appliances, Small Electric; Toasters.*

TOASTERS *(See also Cooking Appliances, Small Electric)*

HAZARDS
Most injuries are burns caused by the following: fires resulting from the failure of the toaster's release carriage or from electrical failures of the appliance, and contact with the interior or exterior of hot toasters.

HAZARDOUS MODELS
In 1979, Consumers Union reported that Toastmaster models B701, B185, D137, and D114 have crumb trays with sharp edges. It also reported that Sears catalog number 6338 and Proctor-Silex 0101B have ovens that stay on when the door is open and that their baking trays have sharp edges.

TOBACCO SMOKE. *See Cigarettes; Germicides and Disinfectants.*

TOBOGGANS. *See Sleds.*

TODAY. *See Contraceptive Sponge.*

TOILET BOWL CLEANERS *(See also Cleaning Agents)*

INJURIES

In 1980, 32,000 involved cleaning agents including toilet bowl cleaners.

HAZARDS

Toilet bowl cleaners contain an acid that is harmful to skin, eyes, or clothing.

PRECAUTIONS

Wear rubber gloves when using the cleaners. And if you have children, purchase a bottle with a child cap and store out of their reach. It is especially important not to combine an in-tank flush cleaner with ammonia or acid in a bowl cleaner because together they release a toxic gas. Some in-tank cleaners contain chlorine bleaches of great strength that may be fatal if swallowed.

TOLINASE. *See Antidiabetic Agents, Oral.*

TOMATOES. *See Drug and Food Interactions; Produce.*

TOMATOES, CANNED. *See Foods, Canned.*

TOMATO PASTE. *See Foods, Canned.*

TOOLS, POWER *(See also Rotary Strippers; Saws, Power)*

INJURIES

In 1980, 25,000 involved home workshop power tools, including sanders, routers, lathes, jointers, shapers, drills, grinders, buffers, polishers, nail guns, and stud drivers, but excluding power saws and chain saws. Drills are associated with more of these injuries than are any other tools.

HAZARDS

Most injuries result from the following.

- Contact with the cutting surface—a blade, bit, or other sharp revolving surface on drills, sanders, routers, lathes, grinders, jointers, planers, and shapers.

- Electrocutions and shocks, which can be caused by a lack of grounding, sometimes aggravated when working in or around water or around a metal ladder.

- Fires, which can break out when sparks from power tools ignite nearby flammable liquids such as paint, varnish, gasoline, and kerosene. Sparks can also ignite a cloth wrapped around a hot tool.

- Flying materials like sawdust, wood blocks, and other materials being cut.

PRECAUTIONS

The blade guard must be maintained on tools like jointers, planers, and automatic lathes. Overhead guards should also be on tools such as jointers even though pushing work underneath can be inconvenient. On portable tools, there should be a "dead-man" switch that shuts off power when hand pressure is released, and dynamic braking to make the blade or bit stop immediately after the power is turned off. To prevent kickback, it is important not to cut too deeply or too quickly or to cut wood with knots, embedded nails, or screws. To prevent blades and bits from shattering, it is important that not too much pressure is exerted on the tool and that attachments used are the right size. Finally, users must turn off and unplug tools before repairing or carrying them.

Buy a tool with a 3-prong grounded plug or one with double insulation to reduce the risk of electrocution and shock. Also, repair faulty or defective wiring, a frayed electrical cord, or damaged plug.

To prevent electrical fires, do not connect a heavy-duty tool using 12 or 13 amperes to an electrical circuit on which another appliance is operating.

To prevent flying materials, the stock should be held with a clamp or vise, and the operator should wear eye shields or goggles.

HAZARDOUS MODELS

In March 1979, Consumers Union reported that the Shopmate T2130–11 and T2100–11 trigger is likely to pinch the finger.

In May 1982, Consumers Union reported that the trigger lock on the Edison T3150, Wen PR82, Edison T3250, and Wen PR53 failed to disengage when the speed-adjustment knob was set fully clockwise, at maximum speed, and thus judged the models not acceptable.

TOXIC SHOCK SYNDROME

HAZARDS

Toxic shock syndrome is a rare and sometimes fatal disease that has been linked to tampon use, although it has not yet been determined how tampons affect this syndrome. Warning labels are now required on all tampon packages, giving information about toxic shock syndrome and recommending use be discontinued if certain symptoms occur.

This disease may have been present for many years, but was unrecognized. An outbreak in 1980 was highly publicized and led to the withdrawal of Rely tampons from the market because the use of this brand of tampons was reported by significantly more victims of toxic shock. Toxic shock syndrome, however, has been associated with all brands of tampons, especially high-absorbency types. Toxic shock syndrome has not disappeared, although there has been a decline in the publicity surrounding it.

Studies undertaken after the 1980 outbreak yielded useful information, but the cause of the syndrome is still unknown. Of all cases of toxic shock, 85 percent were in women stricken during menstruation. Most of the women were under 30 years of age. The other 15 percent of cases were not connected with menstruation and involved both men and women, whites more often than blacks.

It has been learned that staphylococcus bacteria are present in most cases and seem to produce poisons that cause toxic shock syndrome. Some scientists theorize that superabsorbent tampons trap oxygen, spurring bacterial growth. Others hypothesize that extra-absorbent tampons trap too much fluid. Still other researchers think that some women do not change tampons as frequently as they should, and that this situation promotes bacterial growth. In cases not related to menstruation, the bacteria may have entered through a wound or boil. No one knows why the bacteria may cause the disease in some people and not in others.

The symptoms of toxic shock syndrome include a fever of 102° or more, vomiting, and diarrhea. A sunburn-type rash and later peeling is often present, especially on fingers and toes. There is often a rapid drop in blood pressure, which may result in shock. If these symptoms occur, especially while menstruating, consult a physician and discontinue use of tampons immediately.

PRECAUTIONS

Although toxic shock syndrome is not completely understood, present information indicates some preventive measures can be taken. Women who have already had toxic shock syndrome or have recently delivered a baby should not use tampons at all. If they use tampons, they have a greater chance of developing toxic shock syndrome than do other individuals.

Women who choose to continue tampon use can reduce the risk of developing toxic shock syndrome by avoiding superabsorbent brands and by using tampons only intermittently during menstruation. The risk of getting toxic shock syndrome can almost entirely be eliminated by not using tampons at all.

TOY AIRPLANES. See *Toy Vehicles; Toys, General.*

TOY ANIMALS *(See also Toys, General)*

HAZARDOUS MODELS

In November 1979, R. Dakin & Company recalled approximately 422,000 stuffed mobile toys. The elastic cords suspending the toys pose a strangulation hazard. Each toy is covered with plush fabric and contains a musical chime device. There are eight different toys: Humbug Bee, Embo Elephant, Jolly Polly Parrot, Stanley Stork, Jingle Frog, Lucky Ladybug, Duckswoop, and Jingle Lamb.

In August 1980, Albert E. Price, Inc., recalled approximately 2,300 stuffed mobile toys. There are two types of stuffed animal mobiles, a duck (model 9160) and an elephant (model 9161), which are intended to be suspended from ceilings or cribs with an elastic cord that may pose a strangulation hazard.

In December 1980, the Atlanta Novelty Company recalled approximately 53,000 Squeeze Me Bears. Made in Taiwan, the bear contains a potentially hazardous sharp wire in the stuffing. Also, the noses may fall off, posing a choking hazard to young children.

In October 1980, Hudson Brands, Ltd., recalled more than five million "Pot Belly" line children's stuffed animals for two potential hazards. Small wires may protrude from the toy animals, and the walnut shells stuffed into the bottoms of the "bean bag" variety could be swallowed by children if the toy animals come apart at the seams.

In February 1981, Far East International, Inc., recalled approximately 23,000 children's stuffed teddy bears. The noses and eyes of the teddy bears could be pulled off, posing a potential choking hazard.

TOY BOATS. *See Toy Vehicles; Toys, General.*

TOY BOXES *(See also Toys, General)*

INJURIES

In 1978, 4,262 involved toy boxes or toy chests, mainly children under five years of age who suffered lacerations.

HAZARDS

Injuries from toy chests can occur when a child falls against the corner or edge of the box, or a heavy lid falls with great force, or a box or chest traps the child inside.

PRECAUTIONS

In purchasing toy boxes or chests, look for the following.

• If the chest has a hinged lid, be sure that the lid is lightweight, has a flat inner surface, and has a device to hold it open in a raised position so that it will not slam shut of its own weight. There is some evidence that a lid with protrusions or recessed areas on the inner side may make it more difficult for children to get free should the lid close on them. Also, make certain the device to hold the lid open is not able to pinch.

• Avoid rough or sharp edges on all metal components, or splinters or other rough areas on wooden boxes.

• Rounded and padded edges and corners are desirable features.

• The box should provide good ventilation—either holes on the lid and at least on one side or two opposite sides, or a product with a lid that cannot close completely.

• The lid of the box or chest should not be able to be locked.

TOY CARS. *See Toy Vehicles; Toys, General.*

TOY CHESTS. *See Toy Boxes.*

TOY GUNS. *See Toy Projectiles; Toys, General.*

TOYOTA CELICA

1978 MODEL
Open hatch is hazardous to tall persons.

1979 MODEL
The occupant protection of the 2-door hatchback in the U.S. Department of Transportation's 35-mph crash test was rated as poor.

1980 MODEL
Alternator pulley could break and be thrown.

1982 MODEL
Sharp corners and latch on open trunk lid are hazardous.

TOYOTA COROLLA

1977 MODEL
Gear adjuster may loosen, causing steering instability. Front seat belts tend to ride up; shoulder belts slip off. Fuel filler and tank are vulnerable in a crash.

1978, 1979 MODELS
Gear adjuster may loosen, causing steering instability.

1980 MODEL
The occupant protection of the 4-door model was rated poor in the U.S. Department of Transportation's 35-mph crash test.

1981 MODEL
Open trunk lid is hazardous to tall persons. Driver's rear view is obstructed.

1982 MODEL
Center roof pillar and rear-view mirror could restrict driver's view. The occupant protection of the 4-door model was rated poor in the U.S. Department of Transportation's 35-mph crash test.

TOYOTA CORONA

1978 MODEL
Fuel pressure relief valve assembly may be defective, resulting in stalling. Handling is clumsy in emergency maneuvers tests. Seat belts ride up. Center roof pillar restricts visibility.

1980 MODEL
Alternator pulley could break and be thrown.

TOYOTA CRESSIDA

1981 MODEL
Emergency locking retractor of driver's seat belt may not operate properly. The occupant protection of the 4-door model was rated poor in the U.S. Department of Transportation's 35-mph crash test.

1982 MODEL
Handling is sluggish and vague, especially in emergency maneuvers.

1983 MODEL
Handling is sluggish and vague, especially in emergency maneuvers.

TOYOTA STARLET

1981 MODEL
Open hatch is hazardous to tall persons. Safety belts ride up to neck and abdomen. The occupant protection of the 2-door hatchback was rated poor in the U.S. Department of Transportation's 35-mph crash test.

TOYOTA TERCEL

1980 MODEL
Fuel tank and filler are vulnerable in a crash. Driver's rear view is obstructed by head restraints. The occupant protection of the 2-door model was rated poor in the U.S. Department of Transportation's 35-mph crash test.

1981 MODEL
Handling is difficult in emergency maneuvers. Fuel tank and filler are vulnerable in a crash.

1983 MODEL
During inclement weather, road grime collects on rear window.

TOY PROJECTILES *(See also Toys, General)*

INJURIES
In 1980, 28,000 involved toy projectiles including flying toys, toy bows or arrows, slingshots, and toy guns with projectiles.

HAZARDOUS MODELS
In October 1979, Western Publishing Company voluntarily recalled approximately 180,000 Soft Shot Star Launcher blow-gun toys. Children have choked on the toy's mouthpiece after it separated from the plastic tube.

In August 1979, F.J. Strauss Company voluntarily recalled approximately 3,600 toy cork rifles. Children run the risk of serious eye injuries if they remove the gun's muzzle and fire toward their faces, driving two interior metal rods into their eyes. The rifles, sold in boxes labeled Western Double-Barrel Cork Rifle, were sold for about $1.99.

In February 1979, the CPSC issued a warning about 5,844 double-barreled toy cork shotguns (number 97-5-510) sold by Eagle Family Discount Stores during the 1976 and 1977 Christmas seasons. Children run the risk of eye injury if they remove the muzzle end of the gun barrel, exposing the ends of two metal rods, then fire toward their faces, driving the rods into their face or eyes.

TOYS, ELECTRONICALLY OPERATED *(See also Toys, General)*

HAZARDS
Electronically operated toys can be hazardous to young children. The dangers include electric shock, burns, and a variety of mechanical hazards including sharp edges, points, and dangerous moving parts.

FEDERAL STANDARDS
In 1973, the CPSC issued safety regulations for these toys. Products must have:

- Enclosures that are strong and rigid enough to preserve the safety and integrity of electrical components.

- Potentially hazardous moving parts enclosed or guarded.

- Strong handles and knobs that will not crack or break off.

- An automatic pressure-relief valve if they have any pressurized enclosures, such as a steamchamber.

In addition, they should include the following.

- All live electrical components must be securely enclosed.

- Switches, motors, transformers, and the like must be securely mounted to prevent any nonfunctional movement and possible damage.

- Heating elements must be supported and prevented from making contacts that could cause shocks.

- Products must not be designed for use with water unless the electrical components are contained in a sealed chamber completely separate from the water reservoir.

- Products requiring cleaning with a wet cloth must be designed to prevent seepage of water into electrically active areas.

- Electrical plugs must have a finger/thumb grasping area and must have a safety shield to protect small fingers from accidentally contacting energized prongs.

- Products must not exceed maximum surface temperature requirements.

- Containers for holding molten compounds and hot liquids must be designed and constructed to minimize spills. No container should melt or become deformed when heated.

In regard to labeling, the following are required.

- The package of every product must carry a cautionary message and a minimum age recommendation. No item with a heating element may be recommended for children under 8 years of age. Items reaching very high temperatures cannot be recommended for children under 12 years of age.

- Certain areas of the product must also be labeled, including accessible surfaces that exceed specified maximum temperatures and nonreplaceable lights.

- All cautionary statements that appear on the toy or package must also appear in the instructions.

PRECAUTIONS

In selecting an electrical toy, do not buy one for a child that is too young to use it safely. When the toy is used by the child:

- Supervise this use.

- Be sure that the plug fits snugly into wall outlets or extension cord receptacles.

- Have an adult or responsible older child replace a light bulb on an electrical toy.

- Periodically check the toy for broken parts, frayed cords, and other potential hazards.

TOYS, GENERAL *(See also Pacifiers; Rattles; Toy Animals; Toy Boxes; Toy Projectiles; Toy Vehicles; Toys, Electronically Operated; Tricycles)*

INJURIES

In 1979, 135,000 toy-related injuries were reported to the CPSC.

HAZARDS

Falls on or against toys caused many of these injuries. Others resulted from children swallowing or choking on small parts, placing tiny toys in noses and ears, and cutting themselves on sharp edges and points.

FEDERAL STANDARDS

Under the Federal Hazardous Substances Act and the Consumer Product Safety Act, the CPSC has set safety regulations for certain toys and other children's articles that manufacturers must meet. The following are now in effect.

- Sharp points. Regulations in effect since 1978 provide manufacturers with testing methods to eliminate hazards for children under eight years old.

- Sharp edges. Regulations in effect since 1979 provide testing methods to eliminate these related hazards for children under eight years old.

- Small parts. A regulation in effect since 1980 is designed to eliminate small parts from toys intended for children under three years old.

- Electronically operated toys. Regulations in effect since 1973 are designed to prevent electric shock and burn injuries.

- Pacifiers. Regulations specify that pacifiers must be large enough to prevent choking and must not come apart into small pieces.

- Rattles. Regulations specify that they must be large enough to prevent choking and must not come apart into small pieces.

- Lawn darts. These must not be sold in toy stores and must have labels to indicate they are not toys and could cause serious injury if misused.

- Clacker balls. These must be manufactured so that the plastic balls do not shatter or fly off the end of the cord.

- Sound levels of toy caps and guns. Regulations limit the amount of noise these may make.

- Aluminized polyester film kites. These were banned in 1979 because of the danger of electrocution should they become entangled in power lines.

- Toys with hazardous substances. The Federal Hazardous Substances Act prohibits the use of poisonous and otherwise harmful chemicals in toys and other articles intended for use by children.

HAZARDOUS MODELS

In October 1979, CBS Toys voluntarily recalled 4 million Gabriel Giggle Sticks. Young children have choked on the reed housed inside the interior plastic cylinder that is exposed after the red end caps of the toy are removed.

In November 1979, Montgomery Ward recalled approximately 20,000 toy telephone sets. The two-prong plugs at each end of the cord so closely resemble genuine electrical plugs that children may try to force them into household sockets. The name "Mehanotehnika" is printed on the bottom of each phone.

In November 1979, F.A.O. Schwarz Company recalled approximately 1,000 infant crib exercisers. The 17-inch elastic cord poses a potential strangulation hazard to infants. The toy was made in West Germany.

In March 1982, Gabriel Industries, division of CBS, replaced an estimated 137,000 to 239,000 Creative Playthings Indoor Gym House ladders. The space between the upper rung of the ladder and the platform is small enough for a child's head to become entrapped with the possibility of strangulation.

In October 1979, Durham Industries, Inc., recalled the detachable connector cords sold with approximately 97,000 toy telephone sets. The two-prong plugs at each end of the cord so closely resemble genuine electrical plugs that children may try to force them into household sockets. The cords are sold as part of the model 7028 Holly Hobbie dial/intercom toy phone set.

In June 1979, Acme Specialties Corporation voluntarily recalled thousands of Three Stars plastic ring caps. The ring caps, used in toy guns to produce a loud report, may accidentally explode, causing serious burns to the user.

In October 1980, Playskool, Inc., and the CPSC issued a warning about two Bristle Block components. The Bristle heads and wheels-and-axle assemblies may detach in use and be swallowed by small children.

In August 1980, Rainbow Artisans, Inc., voluntarily recalled approximately 8,000 elastic crib decorations known as "Kickers." The elastic cord of the decoration may pose a strangulation hazard.

In May 1980, Play Spaces International recalled approximately 600 infant toys known as "crib exercisers" or "baby chains." The elastic cord in the toy may pose a strangulation hazard.

In March 1980, the Wham-O Manufacturing Company issued a warning about more than 100,000 outdoor Fun Fountain water toys. The toy consists of a clown hat and head that attaches onto the end of a garden hose so that the hat rises in the air when water flows through the clown's head. Children may receive serious eye injuries if they peer into the water outlet.

In November 1982, Electro-Plastics, Inc., recalled approximately 8,500 Happy Mates squeeze toys. These are small enough to lodge in the throat of a child and cause choking and suffocation. The toys are an orange lion's head with bow tie on an orange handle, a yellow cat's head with bow tie on a yellow handle, a green frog's head with bow tie on a white handle, and a pink pig's head with bow tie on a pink handle.

In October 1982, Danara International, Inc., recalled four squeeze toys. The handles are small enough to lodge in the throat and cause choking and suffocation. Two of the toys have Mickey Mouse heads on yellow handles while the others have Donald Duck heads on blue handles. They are sold under the brand name of Safe-Guard and labeled Walt Disney Character Squeek-a-Toy.

TOY TRUCKS. *See Toy Vehicles; Toys, General.*

TOY VEHICLES. *(See also Toys, General)*

INJURIES

In 1980, 11,000 involved toy cars, trucks, boats, nonflying airplanes, and other vehicles.

HAZARDS

Most of these injuries were lacerations caused by finger entrapment, contact with sharp edges or points, or slipping or tripping on a toy.

HAZARDOUS MODELS

In February 1980, Davis-Grabowski, Inc., issued a warning about approximately 35,000 Fun Ride Trolley Ride toys. In several instances, the cable has broken under the weight of children, causing injuries.

TRACTORS. *See Garden Equipment, Power.*

TRAIL BIKES. *See Mopeds.*

TRAILERS. *See Mobile Homes.*

TRAMPOLINES

INJURIES
In 1980, 6,000 down from an estimated 19,000 in 1975.

HAZARDS
Most injuries are caused by falls resulting in lacerations, fractures, abrasions, punctures, or concussions. More serious injuries like paraplegia also occur.

PRECAUTIONS
It is important that a trampoline purchased should be equipped with frame pads made of a firm, yet flexible, resilient material wide enough to cover the frame and outer hooks of all springs. Before use, it is important to check trampolines for the following potential hazards.

- Punctures or holes worn in the bed.
- Deterioration in the stitching of the bed.
- A sagging bed.
- Ruptured springs.
- Missing or insecurely attached frame pads.
- A bent or broken frame.
- Sharp protrusions on the frame or suspension system.

Most important, one should not attempt tricks beyond one's skill.

TRANQUILIZERS. *See Benzodiazepines; Cimetidine.*

TRANSDERM-V

This prescription drug product helps prevent the nausea and vomiting associated with motion sickness by reducing the activity of nerve fibers in the inner ear. The adhesive unit is placed behind the ear to allow the active ingredient, scopolamine, to pass through the skin into the bloodstream. One unit may last up to 72 hours.

HAZARDS

Do not use Transderm-V if you are pregnant or plan to become pregnant. Children should never use this product. They are particularly sensitive to it and its safety for children is in doubt. Also, before accepting the prescription, tell your physician if you have glaucoma; trouble urinating; obstruction of the stomach, intestine, or bladder; or any skin allergy or skin reaction to drugs, chemicals, or foods.

The most common side effect is dry mouth. Less common is drowsiness, but care should be taken in driving or operating machinery.

PRECAUTIONS

Be sure to have clean hands when attaching the patch.

Call your doctor immediately if you experience disorientation, sensory disturbances, restlessness, hallucination, or confusion. Remove the patch if you suspect it is causing an allergic reaction.

TRANS HIWAY TIRES. *See Firestone Transport Tires.*

TRANSMISSIONS. *See Automobile Transmissions.*

TRANXENE. *See Benzodiazepines.*

TRASH BASKETS. *See Waste Containers.*

TRASH CANS. *See Waste Containers.*

TRAV-AREX. *See Nausea Medications.*

TRAVCO FAMILY WAGON AND MINI-MOTOR HOME

1972, 1973 MODELS
In some models, the neutral bar-bonding screw was installed in the 110-volt distribution panelboard. As a result, the entire vehicle becomes electrified when the system is plugged into a 110-volt system.

TRAVELEZE MOTORHOME

25-, 27-, 30-, 32-, 35-FOOT MODELS
On many models, the wheels supplied with the vehicle are inadequate to carry loads rated at 2,000 pounds. This situation could result in blowouts.

TRAVELLER TIRES. See *Uniroyal Tires.*

TREEHOUSES. See *Playground Equipment.*

TRIAMINIC. See *Decongestants, Oral.*

TRICYCLES *(See also Toys, General)*

INJURIES
In 1980, 13,000 were reported.

HAZARDS
The following conditions may cause injuries in the use of tricycles.

• Poor construction or design including breakage while in use; sharp edges or points.

• Instability causing a tricycle to tip over.

• Striking obstacles and colliding with other tricycles.

- Inability to stop the tricycle, usually because it was built without brakes.

- Entanglement in the tricycle's moving parts.

PRECAUTIONS
In purchasing a tricycle, look for the following features:

- Seats close to the ground, which offer more stability.

- Wheels that are widely spaced, to provide more stability.

- Pedals and handgrips with rough surfaces to prevent the child's hands and feet from slipping.

Also, avoid tricycles with sharp edges, especially on or along fenders, or on the underside of the seat.

TRIMMERS. *See Garden Tools, Power.*

TRIND. *See Cough Medications.*

TRIPLE ANTIBIOTIC OINTMENT. *See First-Aid Ointments and Creams; Neomycin.*

TRISOGEL. *See Antacid Medications.*

TRIUMPH MOTORCYCLES

1969, 1970 TR25W 250cc MODELS
The front brake cable may lop and become trapped on the front mudguard bridge stay lug nut. This could cause the brake to lock up.

1979 TRIUMPH T1400 MODEL
The inner beaded edge of the rear fender does not provide enough

tire clearance when rear suspension is depressed. Heavy pressure on rear tire may cause damage to the tire and possible loss of control.

TRIUMPH SPITFIRE

1977 MODEL
Separator fuel hose may kink, possibly causing fuel tank to collapse.

1978 MODEL
Pedal-accelerator rod connection may be defective. Fuel hose may be incorrect, possibly causing fuel leakage and fire. Separator hose may kink, possibly causing fuel tank to collapse.

1979 MODEL
Casting defect may cause caliper to crack, thereby decreasing brake performance. U-shaped connection pipe may be damaged by right handhorn bracket, possibly causing fuel tank tocollapse.

TRIUMPH TR 7

1977, 1978 MODELS
Windshield wiper system may malfunction due to several causes. Corrosion may cause headlamp motor to fail.

1980 MODEL
Rear view is obstructed by wide rear roof pillars. Open trunk lid is hazardous. Front seat belts tend to ride up. Displays are hard to read; controls are confusing.

TROUBLE LIGHTS. *See Work Lights.*

TUMS. *See Antacid Medications.*

TURKEY. *See Meat and Poultry.*

TURNTABLES. *See Sound Equipment.*

TURPENTINE. *See Solvents.*

TUSSAR. *See Cough Medications.*

TYLENOL. *See Acetaminophen.*

UNCLE BEN'S BROWN & WILD RICE WITH MUSHROOMS. *See Sulfites.*

UNIROYAL TIRES

Zeta and TPC models

This recall was one of the largest in recent history and includes a number of tires made by Uniroyal under different brand names. These tires are susceptible to tread separation. Blisters or bumps in the tread area, tearing or splitting near the edge of the tread, are signs that the tire is undergoing tread separation. The recall occurred on March 12, 1980. See TIRES for more information on tire recalls. The following tires were included in the recall:

UNIROYAL ZERA 40 PR5
    HR78-15-AMVY-445-396,
    HR78-15-APVY-225-525,
    LR78-15-APV4-145-526;

UNIROYAL ZETA 40 PR6
    HR78-15-AJVY-387-447,
    LR78-15-ANV4-015-525,
    LR78-15-APV4-055-136;

EXXON
    HR78-15-AP-145-525,
    LR78-15-AP-145-526;

FISK
    HR78-17-AP-445-525,
    LR78-15-AP-355-346;

GILLETTE
    HR78-15-AP-145-525,
    LR78-15-AP-145-526;

UNIROYAL TPC PR6
  BR78-13-AUFW-145-395,
  BR78-13-AMFW-145-395,
  LR78-15-AJV4-225-396,
  LR78-15-AUV4-016-136;

BIG O
  HR78-15-AP-355-525,
  LR78-15-AP-355-526;

CO-OP MARK 74
  LR78-15-AJ-056-396;

CO-OP MARK 4
  HR78-15-AP-315-525,
  LR78-15-AP-225-526;

DELTA
  HR78-15-AP-145-525,
  LR78-15-AP-145-176;

DELTA RADIAL II
  LR78-15-AJ-056-396;

DIPLOMAT
  LR78-15-AJ-016-396,
  LR78-15-AP-016-136;

K-MART 40
  LR78-15-AJ-016-396;

K-MART SSK
  HR78-15-AP-145-395,
  LR78-15-AP-145-435;

PEERLESS
  HR78-15-AP-145-215,
  LR78-15-AP-145-525;

SONIC
  HR78-15-AP-185-345,
  LR78-15-AP-145-305;

TRAVELLER
  HR78-15-AP-185-305,
  LR78-15-AP-185-265;

VICTORIAN
  HR78-15-AP-185-395,
  LR78-15-AP-145-176;

VICTORIAN II
  LR78-15-AJ-026-176.

UNION TIRES. *See Firestone 500 Tires.*

UNLEADED GASOLINE. *See Gasoline.*

UPHOLSTERED FURNITURE. *See Chairs; Clothing.*

UPHOLSTERY CLEANERS

INJURIES

In 1980, 32,000 involved cleaning agents including upholstery cleaners.

HAZARDOUS MODELS

In July 1981, Consumers Union reported that the Turtle Wax Velour upholstery cleaner was a fire hazard, and that the Blue Lustre powder is an irritant with which consumers should use a dust mask, safety goggles, and gloves. The powder also lacked a needed child-resistant closure.

UREA-FORMALDEHYDE FOAM INSULATION *(See also Formaldehyde)*

HAZARDS

Urea-formaldehyde foam insulation (UFFI) was banned by the CPSC in 1982 because of the "unreasonable risk of injury" it posed for consumers. In April 1983 the Fifth Circuit Court overturned the UFFI ban arguing the commission should have undertaken more lengthy studies before issuing the ban. While the court did not give UFFI a clean bill of health, it faulted the CPSC's scientific methods in projecting the scope of the problem. The CPSC, in conjunction with the U.S. Department of Justice is currently considering an appeal of the Fifth Circuit Court's decision to the Supreme Court.

UFFI is a mixture of urea-formaldehyde resin, a foaming agent, and compressed gas, which can be force-pumped into wall and ceiling cavities to harden into an insulation. In the mixing and curing processes, substantial amounts of formaldehyde can be released. In addition, the insulation often continues to "off-gas" once it is in place and may spread the toxic formaldehyde fumes into the home air for several years after installation. The release of formaldehyde is sensitive to environmental conditions, such as heat and humidity, which increase the levels of off-gasing, and hamper proper installation.

Formaldehyde can cause many short-term or acute symptoms such as nausea, headaches, respiratory problems, memory loss, fatigue, nosebleeds, and other flu-like or asthma-like symptoms. Some people become sensitized after exposure to formaldehyde and experience a severe reaction whenever they come in contact with the chemical, which is used in small amounts in thousands of consumer products from cosmetics to paper bags, to felt-tip pens. Exposure to formaldehyde has also produced cancer in laboratory animals and is considered by many scientists to increase the risk of cancer in man.

PRECAUTIONS

To reduce the amount of off-gasing from UFFI, some steps can be taken in your home: fill all holes, cracks, and gaps in walls and ceilings with spackling compound or caulking; seal seams where the wall and floor meet with caulking or adhesive foam strips; insert nonflammable gaskets in all electrical outlets; paint walls twice with a vapor barrier paint and cover walls with high-quality mylar or vinyl wallpaper, using special vinyl wallpaper paste. Increasing ventilation with outside air also helps dissipate the formaldehyde vapors.

For more information, call the CPSC Hotline at (800) 638-CPSC.

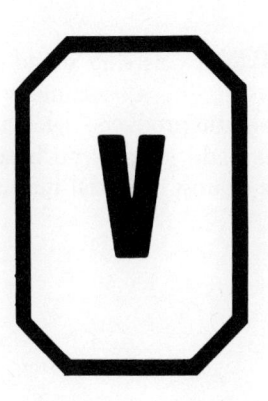

VACUUM CLEANERS

INJURIES

In 1980, 10,000 involved vacuum cleaners and other electric home cleaning equipment.

HAZARDOUS MODELS

In April 1982, Sun Hill Industries, Inc., recalled nearly 1,000 Sun Vacs, a wet vac/dry-cleaning vacuum attachment. An electric shock hazard could result if the product's bucket becomes full of water or accidentally tips over. Water could then be sucked into the vacuum cleaner, soaking the motor and resulting in a potentially severe or fatal electric shock to anyone touching a metallic part of the vacuum cleaner while standing on a wet floor.

In September 1979, Consumers Union reported that Eureka 1289D, Penney's 0463, and Ward's catalog numbers 5000 and 5070 had a potential for shock hazards and, therefore, judged them not acceptable.

VALADOL. *See Acetaminophen.*

VALIUM. *See Benzodiazepines; Sleep Medications, Prescription.*

VAPORIZER MEDICATIONS

Avoid using "aromatic products," such as Vicks Vaporub, in your vaporizer because they add little or no benefit and may even lower your natural defenses against bacterial infections.

VAPORIZERS

PRECAUTIONS
- Unplug the steamer during refills. If there is an overflow while the element is plugged in, the overflow could be electrically live.
- Keep the vaporizer clean. Dirt could breed contaminants that lead to respiratory-tract irritations, allergies, or infections.
- When cleaning, watch out for sharp edges on the underside of the cover.
- Guard against scalding from spillage of hot water.

VEGETABLES. *See Drug and Food Interactions; Food Poisoning; Nitrites and Nitrosamines; Produce.*

VEGETABLES, CANNED. *See Foods, Canned; Lead; Salt.*

VEGETABLES, FRESH. *See Canning, Home; Botulism; Botulism Infant; Produce.*

VELOSELEX 3800 MOPEDS

1969–1973 MODELS
These vehicles do not have the federally required side reflectors.

VERTROL. *See Nausea Medications.*

VESELY CAMPING TRAILER

1973 MODEL
In some models, the wheel bearing and hubs were improperly assembled. This can result in overheating of the bearing and seizing up of the wheel, which can cause the wheel to come off.

1976 MODEL
In some trailers, a small spring was omitted in the assembly of the brakes. As a result, the trailer brakes will fail to function when the towing-vehicle brakes are used.

1977 APACHE MODEL
In many of the vehicles, the electrical system was improperly grounded. The grounding is designed to protect the occupants from electrical shock. As a result of the improper connection, occupants who touch metal surfaces of the trailer could experience an electrical shock, causing injury or death.

VESPA MOTORSCOOTERS

1975 CIAO, MO-PED MODELS
These vehicles did not have the proper certification labels as required by the federal government.

1975, 1976 MODELS
The throttle fails to return to the idle position when released.

1978 P125X, P200E MODELS
On many vehicles there is a 90-degree stamp crease along the curvature of a 3.50-inch by 10-inch wheel rim. As a result of this improper stamping, all stress developed from the vehicle's load is absorbed at the crease, which will create metal fatigue and eventual separation.

VICKS FORMULA 44 AND VICKS FORMULA 44D. *See Cough Medications.*

VICKS VAPORUB. *See Vaporizer Medications.*

VICTORIAN II TIRES. *See Uniroyal Tires.*

VIDEO DISPLAY TERMINALS

HAZARDS
According to a government study, data-display computer units can cause eye strain, blurred vision, color perception difficulties, sore shoulders, numbness, and loss of strength in users' arms. Video display terminal users have higher levels of anxiety, depression, fatigue, and confusion than do control groups.

PRECAUTIONS
To reduce these problems, it may be necessary to reform work schedules and to rethink lighting, window placement, and other elements of office design.

VINEGAR. *See Drug and Food Interactions.*

VINSON ROACH KILLER. *See Insecticides, Household.*

VINYL FLOOR TILES AND VINYL SHEET FLOORING *(See also Asbestos)*

HAZARDS
Asbestos has often been added to both these products to strengthen them. When broken, worn, sanded, cut, or scraped, these products may release asbestos fibers. Inhaling these fibers has been shown to cause cancer in laboratory animals and humans.

PRECAUTIONS
When working with tiles or sheet flooring that may contain asbestos, follow the instruction under general guidelines for handling asbestos products *(see ASBESTOS)*. It is safer to simply cover these products with a new flooring material than to remove them.

VISINE. *See Eye Medications, Nonprescription.*

VITAMIN A *(See also Vitamins)*

Vitamin A is an oil-soluble vitamin stored in the liver. Oil-soluble vitamins are often stored in the body for long periods, whereas water-soluble vitamins are retained for short periods, if at all. Vitamin A is essential for new cell growth and healthy tissues, as well as for vision in dim light.

HAZARDS

A deficiency of Vitamin A can result in night blindness, high sensitivity to light, and other eye problems as well as dry, rough skin that may be more susceptible to infection.

There are also serious side effects associated with large doses of the vitamin. Children and young people who have been given large doses develop an increased pressure in the skull that mimics, very convincingly, symptoms of a brain tumor. However, carotene, a form of Vitamin A found in plants, is practically nontoxic.

VITAMIN C *(See also Vitamins)*

Although Vitamin C has not been proved effective in preventing colds or flu, some studies indicate it may help reduce the length of such symptoms as chill and fever.

HAZARDS

Large doses may cause severe diarrhea, which is particularly dangerous to pregnant women, the elderly, young children, and people with certain illnesses. Large doses also cause the urine to become acidified and, with continuous use, increase the risk of developing kidney stones if you have gout. Doses of 10 grams a day may cause too great an acid load if you have impaired kidney functioning.

Ascorbic acid will also interfere with an accurate reading of some urine sugar testing. Pregnant women who take large doses may cause their newborn babies to develop scurvy because the enzyme system of the fetus has become accustomed to high dosage levels. Vitamin C preparations containing sodium ascorbate should be avoided if you are on a low-sodium diet. There is also some evidence from animal studies that Vitamin C in large doses has a detrimental effect on developing bones.

High doses of Vitamin C can also inactivate Vitamin B_{12} and cause anemia. High doses of the vitamin can also interfere with certain anticoagulant drugs, such as warfarin, to reduce the desired effect of the drug.

PRECAUTIONS

If you are taking an anticoagulant, be sure to check with your physician before taking Vitamin C. Routine aspirin-takers should check with their physicians as well, since ascorbic acid has important interactions with salicylate drugs such as aspirin.

VITAMIN D *(See also Vitamins)*

Vitamin D aids the absorption of calcium and phosphorus in bone formation. Vitamin D deficiency causes rickets, a bone disease that is characterized by skeletal deformation and stunting of growth.

HAZARDS

While excessive intake of Vitamin D provides no benefit, it can be harmful and dangerous.

Too much Vitamin D can cause nausea, weight loss, weakness, excessive urination, and the more serious conditions of hypertension and calcification of soft tissues, including the blood vessels and kidneys. Bone deformities and multiple fractures are also common.

In fact, many symptoms of an excess of Vitamin D mimic those caused by a deficiency of the vitamin. Medical researchers are investigating a link between excess Vitamin D and heart attacks, although definite evidence of such a link has not been found.

People who spend part of their time in the sun with their skin exposed need no other source of Vitamin D, since it is formed in the skin by the ultraviolet rays. Foods fortified with Vitamin D are intended mainly for infants and the elderly who lack exposure to sunlight. The daily requirement of Vitamin D is very small and excess amounts are stored in the body.

VITAMINS *(See also Pregnancy and Drugs; Vitamins, Natural/Organic; specific vitamins by name.)*

Vitamins are organic compounds necessary in small amounts in the diet for normal growth and maintenance of life. Although vitamins are essential, their true role in the body and in nutrition is often misunderstood. Vitamins do not provide energy nor do they construct or build any part of the body. They do, however, help maintain the body and transform food into energy.

For most people, it is not necessary to supplement the diet with additional vitamins. Certain foods and medications, however, do decrease the vitamin levels received through the diet and make a vitamin supplement necessary. The long-term use of barbiturates produces a marked decrease in blood levels of Vitamin D, for example, and adults taking such drugs should receive 10 times the normal daily requirement of Vitamin D. The use of penicillamine to treat Wilson's disease or heavy metal poisoning interferes with Vitamin B_6 metabolism. Isoniazid, a drug used to treat tuberculosis, can produce detrimental effects on the nerves, which can be prevented by increasing the intake of Vitamin B_6.

HAZARDS

Many Americans take vitamins unnecessarily. Except in special circumstances such as pregnancy, infancy, old age, certain genetic or disease conditions, or vegetarian diet, adequate vitamins are consumed through a well-balanced diet. For most people, it is not necessary to supplement the diet with additional vitamins (see table below of U.S. Recommended Daily Allowances [RDAs]). In fact, continued or heavy consumption of the fat-soluble vitamins, such as A and D, may lead to excessive accumulation of the vitamins in the body tissues and result in a toxic overdose. The water-soluble vitamins, such as B-complex and C vitamins, can also cause harmful effects on the body when taken in excessive amounts.

PRECAUTIONS

Taking excessive vitamins is a waste of money and effect. If you think you need extra vitamins, check with your physician. Foods containing an abundance source of one or more vitamins, as well as other important nutrients, are liver, eggs, cheese, fortified margarine, butter, whole or fortified milk, fish, egg yolks, yellow and green leafy vegetables, yellow fruits, nuts, whole-grain foods, lean red meats, shellfish, potatoes, rice, tomatoes, fruit juices, cauliflower, vegetable oils.

UNITED STATES RECOMMENDED DAILY ALLOWANCE

	UNIT*	INFANTS (0–12 MONTHS)	CHILDREN UNDER 4 YEARS OF AGE	ADULTS AND CHILDREN OVER 4 YEARS OF AGE	PREGNANT OR LACTATING WOMEN
Vitamin A	IU	1500	2500	5000	8000
Vitamin D	IU	400	400	400	400
Vitamin E	IU	5	10	30	30
Vitamin C	mg	35	40	60	60
Folacin	mg	0.1	0.2	0.4	0.8
Thiamine (B_1)	mg	0.5	0.7	1.5	1.7
Riboflavin (B_2)	mg	0.6	0.8	1.7	2.0
Niacin	mg	8	9	20	20
Vitamin B_6	mg	0.4	0.7	2	2.5
Vitamin B_{12}	mcg	2	3	6	8
Biotin	mg	0.05	0.15	0.3	0.3
Pantothenic acid	mg	3	5	10	10

Key: IU = International unit; mg = milligram; mcg = microgram

*The U.S. RDA system was developed by FDA for its nutrition labeling and dietary supplement programs.

VITAMINS, ORGANIC/NATURAL *(See also Vitamins)*

Natural vitamins are not superior to synthetic vitamins. In fact, synthetic vitamins, manufactured in the laboratory, are identical to the natural vitamins found in foods, according to the U.S. Public Health Services. They also warn that statements claiming that natural vitamins are superior are false. The human body cannot tell the difference between natural and synthetic vitamins and benefits are derived from either source.

VIVARIN. *See Caffeine; Stimulants.*

VOLKSWAGEN BEETLE

1977 MODEL

In convertible, tail-light lenses may be defective, causing an improper reflection.

VOLKSWAGEN DASHER

1977 MODEL
Open trunk lid is hazardous. Front seat belts ride up.

1978 MODEL
Insufficient tightening of bolts in brakes may cause vibrations when brakes are applied.

1980 MODEL
Brake calipers may have porous spots that allow brake fluid leakage and eventually complete brake failure. Open hatch lid is hazardous.

1981 MODEL
Brake calipers may have porous spots that allow brake fluid leakage and eventually complete brake failure.

VOLKSWAGEN JETTA

1981 MODEL
The occupant protection of the 4-door model was rated poor in the U.S. Department of Transportation's 35-mph crash test.

1982 MODEL
Handles a bit unsteadily in hard turns.

VOLKSWAGEN RABBIT

1977 MODEL
Water leakage could activate starter and move car if in gear. Automatic-transmission accelerator cable could malfunction, causing high engine idle and hesitation. Front seat belts tend to ride up.

1978 MODEL
Improper clamps on pipe leading to brake-booster vacuum pump may cause damage resulting in engine stalling and partial braking loss. Vacuum line may have been improperly installed, preventing return to throttle linkage plate to idle position. Water leakage could activate starter and move car if in gear. Automatic-transmission accelerator cable could malfunction, causing high engine idle and hesitation.

1979 MODEL
Water leakage could activate starter and move car if in gear. Automatic-transmission accelerator cable could malfunction, causing high engine idle and hesitation. Front seat belts ride up. Seat levers are hard to operate. Open hatch is hazardous to tall persons.

1980 MODEL
Automatic-transmission accelerator cable could malfunction, causing high engine idle and hesitation. Fuel could spurt from filler neck if opened rapidly. Rear view is obstructed by head restraints. Open hatch is hazardous. The occupant protection of the 2-door Rabbit convertible was rated poor in the U.S. Department of Transportation 35-mph crash test.

1981 MODEL
Ball-joint lock nuts may not be properly torqued, possibly causing the tie rod to separate from the steering assembly. Fuel could spurt from filler neck if opened rapidly. Rear view is obstructed by wide rear roof pillars and by head restraints.

1982 MODEL
Open hatch lid is hazardous.

VOLKSWAGEN QUANTUM

1982 MODEL
The occupant protection of the 4-door model was rated poor in the U.S. Department of Transportation's 35-mph crash test.

VOLKSWAGEN SCIROCCO

1977 MODEL
Water leakage could activate starter and move car if in gear. Automatic-transmission accelerator cable could malfunction, causing high engine idle and hesitation.

1978 MODEL

Water leakage could activate starter and move car if in gear. Improper clamps on pipe leading to brake-booster vacuum pump may cause damage resulting in engine stalling and partial braking loss. Driver's visibility is restricted. Front seat belts ride up. Open hatch lid is hazardous. Automatictransmission accelerator cable could malfunction, causing high engine idle and hesitation.

1979 model

Water leakage could activate starter and move car if in gear. Automatic-transmission accelerator cable could malfunction, causing high engine idle and hesitation.

1980 MODEL

Automatic-transmission accelerator cable could malfunction, causing high engine idle and hesitation.

1982 MODEL

The occupant protection of the 2-door model was rated poor in the U.S. Department of Transportation's 35-mph crash test.

VOLVO DL

1981 MODEL

Insufficient grounding between the rotor and distributor shaft may cause misfiring or stalling.

1982 MODEL

On certain vehicles with electronic ignition, increased resistance in system wiring connectors may cause ignition misfiring and stalling.

VOLVO 242, 244, and 245

1977 MODEL

Rear-wheel bearings may contain inadequate lubrication, possibly causing shearing of rear axle. Fuel in drain plug area may leak because of improper soldering.

1978 MODEL

Rear-wheel bearings may contain inadequate lubrication, possibly causing shearing of rear axle.

1979 MODEL
The occupant protection of the 4-door model was rated poor in the U.S. Department of Transportation's 35-mph crash test.

VOLVO 262, 264, and 265

1977, 1978 MODELS
Rear-wheel bearings may contain inadequate lubrication, possibly causing shearing of rear axle.

VOMITING DRUGS. *See Nausea Medications.*

WAFFLE IRONS. *See Cooking Appliances, Small Electric.*

WAGONS, TOY. *See Toys, General.*

WALGREEN'S ANT AND ROACH KILLER. *See Insecticides, Household.*

WALKERS. *See Baby Walkers.*

WALL OUTLETS *(See also Home Electrical System)*

HAZARDS/PRECAUTIONS

Most injuries are burns or shocks suffered by consumers who contact wall outlets. Outlets can be especially hazardous to young children since they are installed close to the floor where children can insert metal objects, causing serious burns and severe, possibly fatal, electrical shocks. To reduce this danger, a plastic safety cap should be inserted into unused outlets, or rotary cap outlets, which must be rotated to expose the outlet's slots, should be used.

Other injuries are caused by fires, which often begin when the outlet is short-circuited or overheats. Outlets that are in use should not be covered with draperies, furniture, or other items.

WARD'S GRAPPLER II TIRES. See Firestone 500 Tires.

WARFARIN. See Warfarin Potassium/Sodium.

WARFARIN POTASSIUM/SODIUM *(See also Vitamin C)*

This is a prescription anticoagulant or blood thinner that slows the clotting of blood and prevents harmful blood vessel clots from developing.

HAZARDS

Because the drug reduces natural clotting, it is crucial to avoid internal or external bleeding by closely controlling dosage and be aware of interaction with other drugs and diet. Any symptoms of internal bleeding, including vomiting or spitting blood, black or bloody stools, red or dark urine, new or unusual headache, stomach or backache pain or bruises, should be immediately reported to your physician. You should also contact your physician if you develop nosebleeds, bloody gums, or prolonged bleeding from a cut. Before taking this drug, tell your doctor if you have ever had diabetes, kidney or liver disease, high blood pressure, seizures, or ulcers. A history of these problems would make the use of warfarin potassium/sodium dangerous.

PRECAUTIONS

Your physician should also know if you are currently taking aspirin or arthritis medicine, Atromid-S, antibiotics, antabuse, Dilantin, phenylbutazone, thyroid hormones, or phenobarbital because dosage of warfarin potassium/sodium must be carefully controlled in the presence of any of these drugs. It is also important to have regular blood tests and to review use of this drug frequently. If you miss a dose of warfarin, it should be taken as soon as possible, although two doses should not be taken together. *If you miss two or more days of the drug, call your physician.* Do not take any vitamin products while using this prescription drug, and avoid large amounts of food with Vitamin K (e.g., fish, liver, cauliflower, onions, spinach, kale, and cabbage). Ask your doctor if you may drink alcohol.

> **WARNING**
>
> Before any medical treatment, tell your physician or dentist if you are taking warfarin potassium/sodium. Carry a card in your wallet or purse stating you are taking the drug, in case of accident or emergency. Guard against cuts, as with shaving. *Warfarin potassium/sodium should never be taken by pregnant or breast-feeding women.* It can cause bleeding, which is sometimes fatal in unborn babies and in breast-fed babies. Birth defects are also more common in infants whose mothers use this drug.

BRAND NAMES: Warfarin, Panwarfin.

WARMERS, FOOD. *See Cooking Appliances, Small Electric.*

WASHING MACHINES *(See also Washing Machines, Wringer)*

INJURIES
In 1980, 12,000 involved washers and dryers.

HAZARDS
Most washer-related injuries are caused by the following.

- Putting clothes soaked in a flammable solvent like gasoline through the washing cycle.

- Inserting one's hand into the moving drum.

- Falling over, into, or from a machine.

- A machine being moved.

HAZARDOUS MODELS
In October 1981, Consumers Union reported that the Gibson WA18D3WL allows the operator to open the lid before the tub stops spinning.

WASHING MACHINES, WRINGER *(See also Washing Machines)*

INJURIES
In 1980, 7,000 cases were reported.

HAZARDS
The principal hazard is the power-driven rollers, held together under pressure, that can catch fingers, hair, or clothing and draw them in. The main victims are young children.

PRECAUTIONS
Almost all wringer washers have a safety device that when pushed, releases roller pressure. On older machines, this is often a large button on the side of the washer where the operator normally would stand. Newer models generally have a release bar that runs almost the entire length of the rollers. These devices are more accessible and require less pressure to operate, but they may not be of much help to children. A young child may not be able to reach it, not be strong enough to operate it, or may simply be too frightened to act rationally.

Much more effective is a safety control that stops the rollers when a backward pull is given to an object between them. Once the rollers have stopped, the release bar can be used to remove the pressure. An equally effective safety control on some models is a foot pedal that must be depressed before the wringer will operate. When pressure on the pedal is removed, the wringer stops.

WASTE CONTAINERS

INJURIES
In 1980, 19,000 injuries were reported. In the 1970s, at least 21 children under the age of 10 were killed in accidents in and around unstable refuse bins.

HAZARDS
Most seriously injured children were playing on the bins or handling the slanted side when the heavy metal bins tipped over and crushed them. Most of the unstable bins have a slanted front, but instability can be increased by broken or missing wheels, lids that open toward the slant side and tilt the balance in that direction, trash deposits accumulated along the slant side, and placement on an uneven, slanted, or soft ground surface.

FEDERAL STANDARD
In 1978, the CPSC banned unstable metal refuse bins one cubic

yard or greater in volume. Bins are considered unstable if they tip when tested with a horizontal force of 70 pounds and a vertical downward force of 191 pounds. However, many unstable bins are still in use. These should be modified to increase stability, and children should be warned to stay away from them.

WATCHES. See Batteries, Button.

WATER FILTERS. See Water Contaminants.

WATER HEATERS. See Fireplace Water Heater. Gas Water Heaters.

WATER CONTAMINANTS *(See also Lead; Salt)*

HAZARDS

Bacteria, viruses, runoff materials, organic material, heavy metals, and other dangerous substances lurk in many water systems of American cities, and require special treatment to be removed. Chlorine added to water systems may kill bacteria, but it may not also kill such viruses as polio, infectious hepatitis, and influenza. No viral standards have been developed and viruses are often present. Furthermore, muddy water from construction drainage can protect bacteria from the chlorine.

Hundreds of new chemicals reach market shelves annually and in the process they are added to our water supply. Unfortunately, most of the dangers of using these chemicals will not become apparent for generations.

Organic compounds may actually be added to water systems through the treatments used to get rid of bacteria. Certain organic compounds containing chlorine (chloroform and carbon tetrachloride) cause cancer, yet many water systems use chlorine to kill bacteria.

Most water systems are not tested for heavy metal content such as mercury, selenium, cadmium, arsenic, iron, chromium, barium, and lead. These can often contaminate our water supply, however, through industry discharges. Pipes delivering water to the home have also been found to be part of the problem; lead and cadmium, along with zinc in galvanized pipes, can leak into the water system via these pipes.

Low levels of these heavy metals are needed for health, but can be deadly in heavy concentrations. Lead poisoning is characterized by headache, hyperactivity or unusual lethargy, aggressiveness, loss of appetite, anemia, vomiting, stereotypic repetitive behavior as manifested by excessive grooming, high motor activity, short attention span, low frustration tolerance, hyperexcitability, and impulsiveness. Depending on the degree of poisoning, symptoms may become chronic, lead to mental retardation or severe brain damage, cerebral palsy, blindness, kidney disease, convulsive disorders, and death. Most commonly, it can cause learning disabilities at relatively low levels of exposure.

Initial mercury poisoning symptoms, such as numbness, slurred speech, unusual aggression, and tunnel vision can evolve into deformed limbs, memory loss, and death. Varying amounts of cadmium can induce dyspnea, chest pain, nasal congestion, dry mouth, dizziness, softening of the bones, muscular weakness, weight loss, and death.

Other water pollutants are asbestos, road de-icing salts (sodium and/or calcium chloride), nitrate fertilizers, and other nitrogen-containing compounds (which enter the bloodstream and tie up hemoglobin oxygen-carrying sites causing asphyxiation), and algicides used in swimming pools to kill algae.

Bottled water is not a viable alternative to public water systems. Laws regarding bottled water do not cover certain organic chemicals and pesticides in the water. Some samples have been found to contain bacteria and heavy metals. Water filters and purifiers are also of little help; these can ultimately turn into breeding grounds for bacteria. If water needs purification, boil it before drinking.

For more information on the health hazards associated with water contaminants, see *The Household Pollutants Guide* by the Center for Science in the Public Interest (Garden City, N.Y.: Anchor Books, 1978).

WATER PIPES. *See Lead; Water Contaminants.*

WATER PURIFIERS. *See Water Contaminants.*

WAX REMOVERS. *See Cleaning Agents.*

WEIGHT WATCHERS FRUIT SNACKS. *See Sulfites.*

WELDING EQUIPMENT

INJURIES
There were 19,000 cases involving welding, soldering, and cutting in 1980.

HAZARDS
Many injuries involve damage to the eyes caused by exposure to ultraviolet radiation.

PRECAUTIONS
Protective glasses must always be worn when using welding equipment, as well as gloves and long-sleeved shirts to protect against molten metal and flying debris.

WET CELL BATTERIES. *See Batteries, Wet Cell.*

WHEAT. *See Monosodium Glutamate.*

WHEEL CAMPER TRAILER

1973 MODEL
On some vehicles, the clearance lights do not meet the minimum federal safety standards.

WINNEBAGO MOTOR HOMES

1970 D18, D22, D22C, D24, D24C, D27C MODELS
The door locks and retention components may fail to meet the

minimum federal standards. The screen-door hinge mechanism fails to conform to the minimum safety standards.

1971 CHEVROLET CHASSIS MODEL
The brake line on many models is located too close to the exhaust manifold. This will destroy the brake line, causing loss of brakes.

1972 D18, D22C, D24, D24C, D27C, D28C, D34C MODELS
The door locks do not meet minimum standards (Hartwell brand). Because the striker plate is incorrectly located, the door may inadvertently open.

D18, D20, D22, D27C, D27CL, D28C11, MWRD, MWRG MODELS
The shower curtains may not comply with minimum federal safety standards and be quite flammable.

1976 ITASCA MINNI-WINNI (WITH C BODY ON CHEVROLET CHASSIS) MODEL
On some models, the brake pedal was improperly assembled. As a result, the pedal can become disengaged, causing loss of braking ability.

1975, 1976, 1977 ITASCA 25-FOOT MODEL
In some models, the auxiliary gas tank was installed with brackets that were welded instead of bolted. This can result in premature failure of the brackets with the tank falling off and possibly exploding.

1979, 1980 CHIEFTAIN, SUNFLYER MODELS
The shelf on which the furnace rests is not designed to carry the weight of the furnace and may settle. As a result, the furnace will break away from the flue and release dangerous gases into the occupant compartment.

1979, 1980, 1981, 1982 CHIEFTAIN, SUNFLYER MODELS
The area around the fuel filler is not properly sealed. As a result, vapors can enter the passenger compartment when refueling. If the electricity is on or any LP gas appliances are on, an explosion could result.

WHIRLPOOLS. *See Bathtubs; Hot Tubs.*

WINDOW CLEANERS. *See Cleaning Agents.*

WINDOWS. *See Glass Doors and Windows.*

WINES. *See Casein; Sulfites.*

WIRING. *See Aluminum Wiring; Home Electrical System.*

WOKS, ELECTRIC. *See Cooking Appliances, Small Electric.*

WOODWORK. *See Hobbies and Crafts.*

WOOD- AND COAL-BURNING STOVES *(See also Asbestos)*

INJURIES
In 1980, 9,800 involved wood- or coal-burning stoves and freestanding fireplaces.

HAZARDS
The following conditions created hazards in the use of wood- or coal-burning stoves.

• Stoves and flues becoming extremely hot and starting fires on adjacent walls, floors, and furnishings.

• Contact with the flame or hot surface area that can ignite clothing or burn bare skin.

• Using flammable liquids to start or stoke a fire. Flammable vapors can travel long distances across the floor of a room and ignite if they reach a flame.

• Inhalation of asbestos fibers from cement sheet, millboard, or paper frequently used in the installation of wood-burning stoves. The cement sheet material will probably not release asbestos fibers unless scraped, cut, worn, broken, or sanded. The insulation material, however, may deteriorate in time and begin to crumble.

PRECAUTIONS

In purchasing coal- or wood-burning stoves, look for a stove that has been approved by a nationally recognized testing agency and be aware that an older stove may have cracks that allow carbon monoxide to escape.

In installing these stoves, take the following precautions:

- Keep at least a three-foot clearance on all sides of stoves.

- Place fireproof materials underneath the stove.

- Do not put a stove near drapes, furniture, or other flammable materials or near traffic lanes.

- Do not use a pipe labeled "vent" as a chimney since it can get very hot. Instead, use an all-masonry chimney or one certified as a "residential type" chimney.

In using the stoves:

- Make sure there is adequate fresh air when using stoves and that the flue is cleaned frequently to avoid carbon monoxide poisoning.

- Keep a window slightly open.

- Use the proper fuel.

- Do not store or use gasoline or other flammable liquids in the same room with the stove.

- Never stoke up the fire so hot that it changes the color of the stovepipe.

- Use chimney guards to prevent squirrels and birds from stopping up chimneys.

- Keep the stove door closed or use a metal screen when the fire is burning.

Have these stoves inspected once a year to ensure that all linings in chimneys are intact, the stove is properly adjusted and clean, there is no creosote buildup in the chimney or connector, and there are no cracks or faulty legs or hinges.

If removal of asbestos materials is necessary, see the general guidelines in the Asbestos entry, and consider hiring a trained asbestos contractor to do the work.

HAZARDOUS MODELS

The Jackes Evans Manufacturing Company recalled the glass doors of approximately 1,000 wood-burning heaters. The glass can break, permitting live sparks to escape into the living area. The recall applies to the doors on those model WFL Hearth-Glo wood-burning circulator heaters that contain 11 x 13-inch glass and door frames with an inner diameter of 10 x 12½ inches.

In October 1981, Consumers Union reported that sparks could fly through the air inlets on the Jotul 602B and the Scandia 180 wood-burning stoves unless a piece of fine metal mesh were attached to the back door of the stove. Consumers Union also reported defects in other stoves.

- The Atlanta 60 leaked enough to overheat dangerously; its air inlet tended to fall off when it was adjusted; and its instructions were poor.

- Wards 22035 Heat and Cook Stove was very sloppily made and overheated severely.

- Wards 21021 Franklin Fireplace has a large, thin bottom that could crack under a moderate load; its door handles got hot; and its legs could be dislodged if the stove is pushed.

- Wards catalog number 22037, the only stove rated not acceptable, leaked and overheated.

WORCESTERSHIRE SAUCE. *See Salt.*

WORK LIGHTS

HAZARDS

Extension work lights have caused the following kinds of injuries.

- Electrocution due to faulty insulation or failure to ground the light socket properly.

- Burns resulting from the ignition of gasoline vapors due to a broken bulb.

- Electric shock caused by a faulty cord or exposed female receptacle.

HAZARDOUS MODELS

In 1982, the Mid-State Manufacturing Corporation voluntarily recalled approximately 8,000 metal socket utility clamp lamps. There is a potential shock or electrocution hazard from an electrical short to the metal reflector, lamp base, and handle. The recall covers Mid-State models P60, R208, R68, R205, R65, LX6, and LG9 sold since March 1981 in retail and hardware stores, including Coast-to-Coast, Gamble Skogmo, and some Hardware Hank stores.

In 1974, the CPSC determined that 200,000 household "trouble lights" or "mechanics' lights" sold in the past year posed a danger of electric shock. The flexible plastic handles on these lights bend so easily that they permit you to contact the metal conductors in the female receptacle. The lights were manufactured by A.K. Electric Corporation, but the name of this manufacturer is not on the product.

WRINGER WASHING MACHINES. *See Washing Machines, Wringer.*

WRINKLE REMOVERS *(See also Estrogen)*

HAZARDS

Commercial wrinkle removers are composed of an oil base with estrogen as the primary wrinkle remover. When applied to the skin, some of the estrogen is absorbed through the skin. This is of great concern to many medical doctors because recent studies correlate the intake of the hormone estrogen with cancer in both humans and animals. All use of estrogen as a cosmetic ingredient should be avoided based on these studies.

In addition, these wrinkle removers work by irritating the skin in a "controlled" manner. This can potentially lead to an increase in the skin's aging. It can also lead to substantial and harmful irritation of skin.

PRECAUTIONS

Use of these products should be avoided.

WYGESIC. *See Propoxyphene.*

X

X-RAY, PREGNANCY *(See also Microwave Ovens)*

    The FDA warns against the use of x-rays to evaluate the relative sizes of the fetal head and maternal pelvis in deciding on a cesarean section. The technique, called pelvimetry, can expose the fetus to significant amounts of radiation, and is not usually necessary or helpful in making the decision to perform a cesarean section. Although x-ray examination for purposes other than the measurement of the pelvis is sometimes necessary, according to the FDA's Bureau of Radiological Health, if such an x-ray is not essential, it should be avoided.
    Occasionally, a woman who is pregnant mistakes the early symptoms—nausea, vomiting, breast tenderness, or fatigue—for the symptoms of a disease. In such a case, an x-ray may routinely be ordered. *Be sure to consider the possibility of pregnancy before taking any x-rays.* And if you are pregnant, do not hold a small child while he or she is being x-rayed.

X-TERMINATOR. *See Insecticides, Household.*

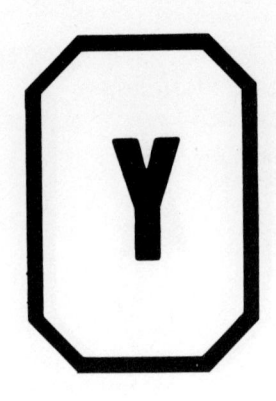

YAMAHA MOTORCYCLES

1976 CHAPPY, LB80-IIAC, LB80-IIHC MODELS
The oil delivery pipe that was one inch too long may have been installed. As a result the pipe may have been kinked during assembly and therefore not allow oil to flow to the oil pump. This could cause the piston to seize and sudden locking of the rear wheel.

1976 RD400C, SX500C MODELS
The improper attachment of the rear brake pedal may cause the pedal to fall off at any time.

1977 XS750D, XS750-2D MODELS
The lock washer that positions the shift cam may come loose and drop into the crankcase. If this occurs the result could be the simultaneous selection of two gears causing the rear wheel to immediately lock up.

1978 XS750E, XS750SE MODELS
The lock washer that positions the shift cam may come loose and drop into the crankcase. If this occurs the result could be the simultaneous selection of two gears causing the rear wheel to lock up.

1978, 1979 XS750SE, XS650SE, XS400E, XS750SF, XS650F, XS650SF, XS650-2F, XS400F, XS400-2F MODELS

The fuel petcock which controls the fuel from the tank to the carburetor may be faulty. As a result a leak may occur and the danger of fire exists.

1980 SR250G MODELS

If the vehicle is subject to severe braking conditions the rear swing arm which supports the rear wheel could bend. This would reduce the operator's ability to effectively control the vehicle.

1980 XT250G MODELS

Because of improper bonding the brake shoes could separate from the brake linings causing loss of braking ability.

YOUTH CHAIRS. *See High Chairs.*

Additional copies of *The Product Safety Book* are available at your local bookstore, or by writing:
> The Consumer Federation of America
> Dept EPD
> 1314 Fourteenth Street, N.W.
> Washington, DC 20005

Make checks payable to the Consumer Federation of America. Please enclose $8.95 plus $1.00 for postage and handling. Allow three or four weeks for delivery.